D1084826

6-11-79

# INFERNAL PARADISE

# INFERNAL PARADISE

*Mexico and the Modern English Novel*

by RONALD G. WALKER

UNIVERSITY OF CALIFORNIA PRESS
Berkeley     Los Angeles     London

University of California Press
Berkeley and Los Angeles, California
University of California Press, Ltd.
London, England

ISBN: 0-520-03197-0
Library of Congress Catalog Card Number: 75-46046
Copyright © 1978 by The Regents of the University of California
Printed in the United States of America

1 2 3 4 5 6 7 8 9 0

To

LESLIE

# Contents

# *Preface*

The predilection for "exotic" locales has long been recognized as a common feature of English fiction from Defoe to Durrell. Yet comparatively little attention has been given to the distinctive role of Mexico in the modern English novel. Despite a pioneering article on the subject by George Woodcock published twenty years ago, and despite the recent efforts of Drewey Wayne Gunn to provide a synoptic view, contemporary criticism has been uncharacteristically dilatory in recognizing and assessing the peculiar fascination that Mexico held for such important figures as D. H. Lawrence, Aldous Huxley, Evelyn Waugh, Graham Greene, and Malcolm Lowry. This book attempts to define the nature of that fascination, to suggest some of the reasons for its emergence, and, above all, to examine its aesthetic consequences in four major novels: *The Plumed Serpent, Eyeless in Gaza, The Power and the Glory,* and *Under the Volcano.*

The first chapter offers an overview of the 1920-40 period which saw European and American artists visiting Mexico by the score, including all five of the English novelists. The effort here is, first of all, to provide a context within which the latter's Mexican writings may be profitably viewed. By looking at those qualities in the Mexican scene that most impressed (and often distressed) writers from various countries—the threat of violence, peculiarities of landscape and customs, the idealistic goals and the practical failures of the Mexican Revolution, the renaissance in the arts, the euhemeristic national myth, and the omnipresent, mysterious Mexican Indian—the chapter outlines the basic elements constituting what I call the Mexican "mystique" in the minds of foreign visitors disposed to mythopoesis. This fertile romantic image, which was exploited (and, inevitably, embellished) in the literary representations of Mexico by so many outsiders, functions as a starting point from which we may proceed to examine the English novelists' particular interest in and response to the Mexican ambience of these years.

The remaining chapters treat two kinds of writing which, viewed in conjunction, shed light on the novelists' understanding of Mexico. In addition to the four major Mexican novels and related shorter fiction, I consider in some detail Lawrence's travel writings, particularly his letters and the pieces collected in *Mornings in Mexico*; Huxley's *Beyond the Mexique Bay*; Greene's *Another Mexico* (published in Great Britain under the title *The Lawless Roads*); Waugh's *Robbery Under Law*; and, for its autobiographical revelations, Lowry's unfinished and posthumously published Mexican novel, *Dark As the Grave Wherein My Friend Is Laid*. Interesting in their own right, the travel books provide illuminating glimpses of the raw material that went into the creative process. They tell us a great deal about the authors' conscious motives for traveling to Mexico, what elements of the country interested them most, and the personal experiences occurring during their trips (some of which reappear in fictionalized form in the novels). With the important exception of Lawrence, who wrote his Mexico-related works while he was still in the country, all the writers produced their travel books after returning home. As a result, the accounts of their Mexican experiences reflect some modification—the first steps toward imaginative amplification and insight—in their outlooks on Mexico. With this in mind, we can see how the travel books serve as a kind of bridge between the writers' highly pejorative, fulminating responses to Mexico at the time of their journeys and the ultimately affirmative (if scarcely less harsh) role played by the Mexican setting in the novels.

Since the Englishmen all experienced in the extreme the attraction/repulsion ambivalence when faced with the putative mystique of Mexico, I have tried to locate relevant factors in their respective careers that may have predisposed them to respond so passionately to the country during their visits. Four of the five novelists in fact came to Mexico with some ulterior interest or concern in mind which they hoped would be further developed or confirmed during their trips for later use in their writing. Such a concern for Lawrence was the dream of Rananim, his utopian colony, as well as his abiding fascination with the primitive mode of being; for Huxley, the chance to reconsider the vitalist doctrines of his one-time mentor Lawrence in the setting which had largely inspired them; for Greene and Waugh, the persecution of the Roman Catholic Church by the socialist state, and other problems related to the policies of the Mexican Revolution in the 1930's. In each case save that of Waugh, their experiences in Mexico involved unexpected developments which not only broadened their original interests but significantly influenced their overall reaction to Mexican existence—thus affecting the novels they were to write about it. Therefore, to aid in understanding more fully the various aspects of the role of Mexico in the novels, I have considered the travel and other pertinent biographical material in full before proceeding with my discussions of the Mexican novels themselves.

With Malcolm Lowry, however, this sequence has been reversed. The two Lowry chapters themselves will, I hope, make clear the necessity for this variance from my usual rhetorical procedure, but a few immediate reasons for it may be mentioned here. For one thing, Lowry is the one writer who seems to have ventured into Mexico with relatively few, if any, outstanding predispositions about the country: his funds were low, he needed a place in which to live inexpensively. (Naturally like any writer he was on the lookout for subject material.) Then too, Lowry's personal contact with Mexico was much more extensive than that of the other English novelists. On his two trips he spent a total of over twenty-five months in the country, while, at the other extreme, Huxley stayed less than one. It is worth mentioning that one result of his greater tenure was that Lowry, alone of all the Englishmen, formed a significant friendship with a native Mexican. Finally, Lowry was the only writer to return to Mexico for any length of time *after* having written his novel set there. This visit of 1945-46, which is recounted in part in *Dark As the Grave*, I have discussed along with the earlier trip in my last chapter.

This book was approaching completion when, quite by accident, I came across a reference to an English novel called *The Fields of Paradise*, by Ralph Bates. By the time I read the novel and looked into the author's background far enough to see his relevance to this study, it was too late to do more than make a few passing references to Bates in my argument. Subsequently I received a letter from Mr. Bates kindly answering my questions about his two visits to Mexico in the late thirties. Because this information rounds out the picture of the English interest in Mexico during the period—Bates being at that time a committed socialist, if no longer the Communist organizer that he had been for fifteen years in Spain—and because *The Fields of Paradise* is a good novel that has not received the attention it deserves, a novel which in fact bears some comparison with the four major English novels in its treatment of the infernal paradise theme, I have added an appendix in which I briefly discuss the novel and Bates's particular response to the Mexican mystique.

In the nearly four years during which I have worked on this study, I have had the good fortune to be assisted and encouraged in various ways by a number of people whose interest in my work and whose consideration for my personal and professional welfare has played a vital part in the completion of the project. It is a pleasure for me to acknowledge my indebtedness, and my sincere gratitude, to the following:

To Graham Greene, Ralph Bates, and Margerie Bonner Lowry, for their generous cooperation in answering my inquiries about personal experiences in Mexico.

To Ross Parmenter, for his hospitality during my stay in

Oaxaca and for sharing with me his extensive knowledge of D. H. Lawrence in Mexico. To Sheryl Sherman Pearson, for allowing me access to her fine study of Lawrence, Greene, and Traven as novelists of the Revolution, and for her interest in my own study.

To Professors Leonard I. Lutwack, John D. Howard, Benedict J. Warren, and J. R. Salamanca, all of the University of Maryland, for their interest and advice early on.

To my colleagues L. Samuel Johnson and Jack A. Haddick of the University of Houston Victoria Campus, who read several of the chapters in rough draft, for their helpful suggestions regarding my use of Hispanic background materials; and D. Leigh Holt, for his perceptive criticisms of some of my more awkward phrasings. To Fran Benham and Bruce Sadjak, librarians at the same institution, for their unselfish and enthusiastic aid in securing hard-to-get materials on short notice.

To Geoffrey Ashton, of the University of California Press, for his sympathetic interest and timely encouragement, and to Carl Mora for the same.

To the Office of Research and Sponsored Activities of the University of Houston, for a summer research grant which enabled me to spend four weeks of study and travel in Mexico after an absence of ten years.

To John D. Russell of the University of Maryland, for suggesting the idea in the beginning; for exceptionally fine advice and incisive criticisms as the study took shape; for his example as a teacher and scholar; and for his infectious enthusiasm.

To my parents, Mr. and Mrs. Ty C. Walker, and my wife's parents, Mr. and Mrs. Donald J. Tucker, for their much-needed and deeply appreciated support. To Linda Wride, for help with the typing.

Finally, and above all, I wish to acknowledge a debt that I can never fully repay, to my wife Leslie, whose emotional and intellectual investment in this project is second only to my own, and whose delight in its completion is, I am sure, second to none. Without her encouragement, her constructive criticism, her much-tried patience and her affection, I would not have been able to undertake, much less complete, this work.

Grateful acknowledgment is made to the following for permission to quote from publications in copyright:

The Macmillan Publishing Co., Inc., Macmillan Co. of London and Basingstoke, A. P. Watt & Son Ltd., M. B. Yeats, and Miss Anne Yeats, for lines from "The Second Coming" and "Easter 1916," from *The Collected Poems of William Butler Yeats*, copyright 1924 by Macmillan Publishing Co., Inc., renewed 1952 by Bertha Georgie Yeats. Harper & Row, Publishers, Inc., Chatto & Windus Ltd., and Mrs. Laura Huxley, for excerpts from *Beyond the Mexique Bay: A Traveller's Journal*, copyright 1934 by Aldous Huxley; *Eyeless in Gaza*, copyright 1936 by Aldous Huxley; and *Letters of Aldous Huxley*, edited by Grover Smith, copyright 1969 by Laura Huxley, copyright 1969 by Grover Smith. Alfred A. Knopf, Inc., and Laurence Pollinger Ltd., for excerpts from *The Plumed Serpent*, by D. H. Lawrence, copyright 1926, 1951 by Alfred A. Knopf, Inc., renewed 1954 by Frieda Lawrence Ravagli; and *Mornings in Mexico*, by D. H. Lawrence, copyright 1927 by Alfred A. Knopf, Inc., renewed 1955 by Frieda Lawrence Ravagli. The Viking Press, Inc., and Laurence Pollinger Ltd., for excerpts from *Phoenix: The Posthumous Papers of D. H. Lawrence*, edited by Edward D. McDonald, copyright 1936 by Frieda Lawrence, © 1964 by the Estate of Frieda Lawrence Ravagli; *The Collected Letters of D. H. Lawrence*, edited by Harry T. Moore, copyright © 1962 by Angelo Ravagli and C. M. Weekley, Executors of The Estate of Frieda Lawrence Ravagli; *Another Mexico* [titled *The Lawless Roads* in the British edition], copyright 1939 by Graham Greene, © renewed 1967 by Graham Greene; *The Power and the Glory*, copyright 1940 by Graham Greene, © renewed 1968 by Graham Greene. J. B. Lippincott Co., Publishers, Jonathan Cape Ltd., and the Executors of the Malcolm Lowry Estate, for excerpts from *Under*

Victoria, Texas                                              R. G. W.
December 1976

Our hermeticism is baffling or even offensive to strangers, and it has created the legend of the Mexican as an inscrutable being. Our suspicions keep us at a distance. Our courtesy may be attractive but our reserve is chilling, and the stranger is always disconcerted by the unforeseen violence that lacerates us, by the solemn or convulsive splendor of our fiestas, by our cult of death. ... The details of the image formed of us often vary with the spectator, but it is always an ambiguous if not contradictory image: we are insecure, and our responses, like our silences, are unexpected and unpredictable. Treachery, loyalty, crime and love hide out in the depths of our glance. We attract and repel.

—Octavio Paz
*The Labyrinth of Solitude*

Oh, beautiful, wonderful land of everlasting springtime, rich with legend, dance and song! You have no equal anywhere on this earth.

—B. Traven
*The Cotton-Pickers*

The camera had seen this unchanged world as a landscape with figures, but figures under a doom imposed by the landscape.... The camera had caught and fixed in moments of violence and senseless excitement, of cruel living and tortured death, the almost ecstatic death-expectancy which is in the air of Mexico. The Mexican may know when the danger is real, or may not care whether the thrill is false or true, but strangers feel the acid of death in their bones whether or not any real danger is near them.

—Katherine Anne Porter
*Hacienda*

# I

# The Fascination of Mexico

## I

"Now when I was a little chap," says Marlow early on in *Heart of Darkness*, "I had a passion for maps. I would look for hours at South America, or Africa, or Australia, and lose myself in all the glories of exploration. At that time there were many blank spaces on the earth, and when I saw one that looked particularly inviting on a map (but they all look that) I would put my finger on it and say, When I grow up I will go there."[1] The age of blank spaces on the earth came to an end, as Marlow well knew, long before the romantic appeal of "going there"—"there" becoming almost anywhere not "here," not at home—had appreciably diminished. In its way, this little reminiscence of the old seaman's childhood captures a feeling about the world, a certain innocence that persisted into the period between the World Wars, even as spaces on the map changed their size and shape with alarming frequency.

In her book *Paris Was Yesterday, 1925-1939*, Janet Flanner recalls one manifestation of this impulse—the destination in this case, a far sight from one of the world's "blank spaces," being of less interest than the ingenuous attitude of the travelers described: "Each June the inexpensive Left Bank hotels began being booked up in advance for the whole summer by new Americans who would settle down for a couple of weeks there as if the quarter were a kind of summer resort and then pass on, full of memories and satisfactions."² For an up-coming generation of writers, predominantly if not exclusively American, Paris was of course to become the modern Mecca; but there were also, for the slightly more adventuresome, Lausanne, Zurich, Rapallo, and Madrid, to name only a few of the well-know expatriate centers. It was a period, perhaps the last, "when the going was good," when the typewriter was an essential piece of one's luggage, when foreign phrases and rates of currency exchange were part of the writer's working vocabulary.

If Paris and the other fashionable cities of mass influx sometimes took on the aspect of the summer resort, there were other parts of the world visited by writers during these years which were less likely to do so: Russia, China, Spain (during the 1930's at any rate) and Mexico. In the summer of 1921 Katherine Anne Porter, then a resident of Mexico City, wrote an article in which she complained of "that choice company of folk who can learn about [foreign] peoples and countries in a couple of weeks. We have had a constant procession of these strange people: they come dashing in, gather endless notes and dash out again and three weeks later their expert, definitive opinions are published. Marvelous!"³ There are many reasons why some writers, including the sententious sort of whom Miss Porter complained, came to a country like Mexico rather than to the more celebrated expatriate centers of Europe. For one thing, if living on the Left Bank was relatively cheap, living in Mexico was cheaper still. For another, "exoticism" was fashionable, and Mexico—with its fabled history, its subtropical volcanic landscape, its millions of Indian peasants, its reputation for sporadic violence, and its cult of death—was a veritable treasure of the exotic. Then too, some of the European and American writers, swayed by Spenglerian prophecies, were convinced that Europe was in decline and that hope for the future might be found in the study and possible emulation of cultures still "unspoiled" by capitalism, science, and technology.

Of course, not a few writers visited Mexico during these

years precisely in order to witness the Revolution (1910-40) and its impact upon Mexican culture; John Dos Passos, Waldo Frank, Archibald MacLeish, Graham Greene, and Ralph Bates come prominently to mind. Miss Porter herself has said that she decided to settle in Mexico "for the express purpose of attending a Revolution, and studying Mayan temple art."[4] Whatever their predetermining motives, writers who came to Mexico for any length of time and came with any real awareness could scarcely have avoided the sense that something momentous was taking place in the country, something first and last profoundly Mexican in character yet with far-reaching implications.

It is beyond the scope of this book to attempt an analysis of the Mexican Revolution (such analyses are not wanting, and the interested reader may find a few of them listed in my bibliography); but any consideration of its interest for foreigners must begin with some sense of the bloodshed that it produced, especially in its first decade. An estimated two million people were killed in the Revolution, among them many of its most prominent figures: Francisco Madero, Emiliano Zapata, Francisco Villa, Venustiano Carranza, Alvaro Obregón, Felipe Ángeles, Francisco Serrano, Arnulfo Gómez and Saturnino Cedillo, all assassinated. There were others more fortunate—Adolfo de la Huerta, Plutarco Elías Calles, Luis Morones, and Tomás Garrido Canábal—who were forced into exile. Then there was the widely publicized execution of Father Miguel Pro, a dissident priest, in 1927. Even in the less turbulent twenties and thirties there were periodic armed rebellions followed by extreme repressive measures, as in the case of the reactionary *Cristeros*; the later *Sinarquistas* were basically nonviolent, but one of their demonstrations against the Revolution resulted in the shooting of over 200 of them by the militia at León. Election years were particularly violent, and not until 1946 was it possible for a president of Mexico to take office without having to face the challenge of armed revolt from his rivals.[5] Even though the period of continuous bloodshed had come to an end by the time that most foreign writers began to make their pilgrimages to "attend a Revolution," social chaos and political strife were still sufficiently in evidence for the outsiders to feel themselves, not altogether unreasonably, in a land of hate, a land suffused with the atmosphere of an "almost ecstatic death-expectancy."

It would be misleading, however, to conclude that violence, actual or incipient, was the sole point of interest for foreigners in Mexico during the Revolution. Just as one of the attractions of the Parisian Latin Quarter was the prospect of associating with the vanguard of modernism in the arts, there was also in Mexico during the 1920's an artistic movement of considerable significance. This movement, considered at the time a renaissance of indigenous culture, was officially sanctioned and supported by President Alvaro Obregón. It reflected the spirit of idealism that prevailed at the conclusion of the militant phase of the Revolution. Such figures as Diego Rivera, David Alfaro Siqueiros, José Vasconcelos, Adolfo Best-Mauguard, and Jean Charlot—many of them having recently returned from extended periods of study in Europe—turned with unprecedented zeal to Mexico's ancient past to discover a racial myth with which to dramatize and ennoble the Revolutionary effort. Public buildings were covered with enormous frescoes depicting in bold colors the overriding themes of Mexican history, culminating in the Revolution; the focal theme, more often than not, was the deracination of the Indian by corrupt and power-mad conquistadors (whether Cortés, the Catholic clergy, the wealthy landowners, the foreign capitalists, or—later on—the fascists) and the "re-conquest" of the homeland by the ragged masses that had become identified with the avowed goals of the Revolution. Unlettered Indian peasants thus were exposed to both art and "history" (more accurately a highly simplified revisionist version of history), neither of which would previously have been accessible to most of them. And what they saw when they looked at these works was the story of paradise lost and regained, with themselves as protagonists.

Several of the foreign writers who visited Mexico in the twenties were influenced, in one way or another, by this spirit of nationalism in the arts. D. H. Lawrence reportedly met Diego Rivera and José Clemente Orozco, the most eminent of the muralists, and while he was contemptuous of their work for the most part, there is much evidence in *The Plumed Serpent* that he had grasped some of the implications of their epic theme. John Dos Passos acknowledged that the Mexican painters had influenced his attempt at "narrative panorama" in the *U.S.A.* trilogy.[6] Katherine Anne Porter was the most deeply involved of all the foreign writers. Early in her tenure in Mexico, which spanned most of the decade, she spoke of the movement as "a veritable rebirth, very conscious, very powerful, of a deeply racial and personal art. . . . I recognized it at once as something very natural and acceptable, a feeling for art consanguine with my own, unfolding in a revolution which returned to find its freedom in profound and honorable sources." Her own stories, she continues, "are fragments, each one touching some phase of a versatile national temperament, which is a complication of simplicities,"[7] a very fitting description of a story such as the fine "María Concepción" (1922). So involved was Miss Porter in what she was later to call "the most exciting period of art in the history of America"[8] that she was for a time hired by the Obregón government to assist in arranging the first exhibition of Pre-Columbian art to be brought into the United States, a project on which she worked for six months gathering materials, writing a monograph and negotiating with American museums. She also became friends with many of the archeologists and artists who were studying indigenous Mexico and wrote several articles concerning Diego Rivera, the spokesman for the short-lived syndicate of Mexican artists.[9] Though many years after her departure from Mexico she was to express scorn for Rivera the man and would-be politician,[10] as late as 1937 she could still offer this testimony to his power in imposing his vision of Mexico upon the world:

No single man in his time has ever had more influence on
the eye and mind of the public who know his work than
Diego Rivera; for he has made them see his Mexico, to
accept his version of it, and often to think it better than
their own. This is no small feat.... For myself, and I believe I speak for great numbers, Mexico does not appear
to me as it did before I saw Rivera's paintings of it. The
mountains, the Indians, the horses, the flowers and children have all subtly changed in outlines and colors. They
are Rivera's Indians and flowers and all now, but I like
looking at them.[11]

The excitement and high hopes of the Obregón years dwin-
dled markedly toward the end of the decade, in large part as
a result of the extremism and the corruption that characterized the regime of Plutarco Elías Calles. The Calles years
(spanning 1924-34, though his term as president ended in
1928) were marked by a radical divisiveness which polarized
Mexican society to such an extent that the earlier spirit of
idealism about Mexico's future began to appear hopelessly
premature. Under Calles the country suffered from a misguided and sometimes brutal attempt, on the part of the government, to harass Catholic clergymen and strip the Church
of all its temporal power. And though the Revolutionary
rhetoric continued to flow, the country in fact moved decid-
edly to the right; land reform and the continuing problems of
the Indian were largely ignored, while foreign investment
flourished, official graft was rampant, and the *jefe máximo*
lived in high style among his henchmen in a posh Cuernavaca
residence. Not until the administration of Lázaro Cárdenas
(1934-40) did the old Revolutionary fervor return, and that
only after drastic steps had been taken. Against the opposition of Calles and his supporters as well as that of the en-
trenched foreign capitalist concerns, Cárdenas implemented
the programs of the Revolution (as expressed in the Constitution of 1917) to the letter. He formed a new and more effective confederation of labor, remodeled the official party of
the Revolution to ensure a popular base so as to obviate the

perennial problem of political succession, achieved a quiet but firm *rapprochement* with the Church after years of bitter conflict, and "distributed more land to peasant villages than all of his predecessors together and more than any president since."[12] Among Cárdenas' boldest and most controversial actions were the seizure of the nation's railways from private concerns and the expropriation of foreign oil companies. Viewed with alarm and outrage abroad, these moves were greeted by an upsurge of patriotic enthusiasm on the part of many Mexicans, who felt themselves free of the modern conquistadors at last.

Yet the Mexican writing by foreigners during these years, in contrast to that of the early and middle twenties, became increasingly skeptical of the Revolution itself and tended to find in its emphasis on material progress an inadequate response to the fundamental needs of the Indian. In the fiction of Katherine Anne Porter the change of outlook could scarcely have been more dramatic. Laura, in "Flowering Judas" (1930), nominally a supporter of the Revolution, is essentially committed to no one and nothing; her disillusionment with the Revolution is imaged in the "gluttonous bulk" of Braggioni, once a slender and dedicated idealist; her life comprised of a series of denials and betrayals, Laura is able to love only what she dreads—violent death—and she finds herself trapped in a state of spiritual paralysis. In *Hacienda* (1934), Miss Porter's disengagement from the Revolution is made overt. The country is controlled by a Calles-type figure who owns several large haciendas and buys up newspapers to ensure that his public image as an "honest revolutionist" is kept intact; meanwhile the government treasury fills with the profits from pay-offs made by wealthy *hacendados* to ensure that the agrarians do not interfere with their lucrative operations. The production of pulque, once a sacred process celebrated in ritual and commemorated in myth, has been reduced to a mere business enterprise and pulque itself to an instrument of repression, dulling the Indians' protest against injustice. The novella ends with the narrator departing in disgust from the hacienda (just as Miss Porter left Mexico one month after her visit to an hacienda on which the tale is based): "I could not wait for tomorrow in this deathly air."[13] Another case in point is B. Traven who, like Miss Porter in her journalistic work of the twenties, began more or less as an apologist for the Revolution. The so-called "jungle novels" constitute a kind of epic concerning the origins and the ultimate outbreak of rebellion on the part of the indentured mahogany workers of provincial Chiapas. Five of the six novels in the series, which began to appear in 1930, evince complete sympathy with the peons, dwelling on their just causes for revolt. However, in *The General from the Jungle* (1939), the final volume, Traven persistently undercuts the presumed value of the revolt by, for instance, demonstrating the utter mindlessness behind the workers' devotion to such slogans as "Land and Liberty!" Early in the novel Traven comments explicitly on the futility of the rebels' aims: "the peons, accustomed for years to masters, tyrants, oppressors, and dictators, were not in truth liberated by the revolution, not even where the feudal estates were divided among the families of peons in little holdings, in *ejidos*. They remained slaves, with the single difference that their masters had changed."[14]

The reference to *ejidos* in the last passage seems almost a direct dig at Cárdenas, for whom the subsidized agricultural collectives were a passionate concern. One of the surprising features of the fiction by foreigners concerning Mexico in the late thirties is, in fact, how comparatively unresponsive it was to the renewed Revolutionary idealism generated by the policies and actions of Cárdenas. With the exception of Malcolm Lowry and Ralph Bates (see Appendix), no foreign novelist I know of was imaginatively engaged by the political ideals identified with Cárdenas—not, at least, in anything approaching the degree to which Traven and Miss Porter shared the Revolutionary optimism of the previous decade. It is of course true that both Graham Greene and Evelyn Waugh came to Mexico in order to investigate the consequences of political actions associated with Cárdenas: Greene's specific concern was with the religious persecution and Waugh's with the oil expropriation. However, when Greene wrote about the Revolution's failure to destroy the priesthood in *The Power and the Glory*, he took pains to set the action in the Calles years, during which the threat was substantial. And Waugh, who clearly did not find Mexico a subject congenial to his imagination during his brief stay, wrote no Mexican fiction at all. That Catholic writers should be less than sympathetic to the struggle of a socialist regime to establish itself once and for all is understandable. But the comparative coolness of writers whose politics, on the face of it, should have elicited such sympathy, is curious. Even the Spanish Republican novelists who fled to Mexico after Franco's victory, and who owed so much to Cárdenas' generosity—writers whose work had previously demonstrated great concern with the same kinds of problems that preoccupied the Mexican President—showed no particular enthusiasm for his ideals in their work. Instead, writers such as Ramón Sender and Max Aub wrote about the difficulties of exile itself or, like Sender, turned from overt treatment of politics to myth and mysticism.

Behind the general reluctance of foreign writers to be fired by the Revolutionary zeal of the Cárdenas years lay the severe change in the world situation by the middle of the thirties. The direction of the times left little room for optimism; in fact, the rise of fascism inevitably made Calles rather than Cárdenas seem the fitting Mexican emblem of the day. (Evelyn Waugh was so preoccupied by the rise of fascism in *Robbery Under Law*—the title tells all—that he insisted upon seeing *both* Calles and Cárdenas virtually as puppets of the Führer.) In any event, those writers who drew upon contemporary Mexico in their work during the 1930's—Traven in *The General from the Jungle*, James M. Cain in *Serenade* (1937), Bates in *The Fields of Paradise* (1940), Greene in *The Power and the Glory* (1940), Lowry in *Under the Volcano* (1947), and Porter in *Ship of Fools* (1962), the last two novels begun in this decade—share a very strong sense of impending crisis, crisis resulting wholly or in part from the failure of humane ideals to prevent recourse to violence. Miss Porter, recalling her ocean voyage from Mexico to Germany in the summer of 1931 which provided her with the subject of *Ship of Fools*, has made an observation that points suggestively to the hollowness at the ethical core of the period:

> In Mexico, and later in Europe, I saw clowns like Hitler ...and I was struck by an idea: What if people like this could take over the world! Of course there were all the good worthy people who didn't believe in the clowns, but these good worthy people still let the clowns commit all the crimes good worthy people would commit if only they had the nerve. How else to account for the collusion in evil that allows creatures like Mussolini, or Hitler, or Huey Long, or [Joseph] McCarthy...[or Calles?] to gain hold of things? Who permits it?...For me as a writer, being on that ship was a godsent experience, and yet I wouldn't have been able to see any of these things in perspective if I hadn't first seen them in Mexico.[15]

Miss Porter's statement concludes on a note profoundly relevant to the four English novels set in Mexico with which this study is primarily concerned: "But in Mexico there was always something good [to counteract the evil]. In Mexico there was always some *chance* of salvation."[16]

## II

Before moving on to a preliminary consideration of the major English novels laid in Mexico during the 1920-40 period, it is necessary to consider the nature of travel-oriented writing generally and the kind of travel writing that we can expect when the country in question is Mexico. Besides works of fiction with foreign settings, travel writing encompasses such diverse forms as letters, diaries and journals, personal and formal essays, and any combination of these collected in full-length travel books. Though they sometimes provide information useful to the tourist or to the social historian, such works should not be confused with either Baedekers or historical studies; good travel writings have an interest all their own. The sojourning writer has left behind the country in whose history, geography and customs he has any claim to expertise. Except in rare cases, he presents himself to us as an outsider and a novice, and his very status as a stranger in a strange land (albeit a professional observer) is both his greatest limitation and his greatest asset as a reporter. For the perceptive foreigner frequently is struck by peculiarities in the unfamiliar scene which the native takes for granted; further, the foreigner's interpretation of whatever oddities he may discover is happily unbound by conventional biases, provincial values, and other factors tending to delimit spontaneous insight. At the same time, however, the imaginative writer may carry with him his own preoccupations of various kinds, and these can influence or even predetermine his reactions to the unfamiliar scene before him. Whether presenting impressions of the native character, landscape or politics; providing an eyewitness account of a particular event (e.g., a street battle, a political convention, a volcanic eruption); or simply describing the author's travel experiences—the best travel writing is generally characterized by subjectivity, by a deliberate focus on the author's state of mind as affected by the strange surroundings.

Throughout her history, Mexico has been blessed with an extraordinary body of literature written by foreign visitors. Madame Calderón's *Life in Mexico* (1843) and Charles Macomb Flandrau's *Viva Mexico!* (1908) are among the most distinguished travel books to have appeared in any literature. As we have seen, during the Revolution, and especially in the 1920's and 1930's, Mexico continued to attract a great many artists from many countries. A fair sampling would include (in addition to those already mentioned) John Steinbeck, Hart Crane, Conrad Aiken, Aldous Huxley, Antonin Artaud,

Benjamin Peret, Gustav Regler, Sergei Eisenstein and Victor
Serge. Some came merely for holiday, some to study or
gather material for their work, some to escape political crises
in their homelands. Whatever their motives for coming, all of
these artists intuited something distinctive, a profound
"otherness" bordering on a national mystique, in Mexico.
Many of them were charmed by this mystique; others found
it distressing; but almost all were fascinated by it one way
and another. Evelyn Waugh correctly identified the source of
this fascination as "the stimulus [Mexico] gives to the imagination. Anything may happen there; almost everything has
happened there.... [But it is] also a distorting mirror in
which objects are reflected in perverse and threatening
forms."[17] More than most lands, more even than other lands
traditionally perceived by Western observers as "exotic,"
Mexico seems almost without fail to have elicited an impassioned response in foreigners. In consequence, the travel
writing about Mexico tends to be doubly subjective.

This inward focus, operating in conjunction with the putative Mexican mystique, lies behind the singular image of
Mexico that has emerged in its travel literature, including fictional works set there. European and American writers, even
those with no particular axe to grind, become preoccupied
with those aspects of Mexican life that lend themselves to
mythopoesis. Interestingly enough, native Mexican artistic
productions have often shared this preoccupation. "Art in
Mexico," according to the novelist Carlos Fuentes, "has always been allied to mythology." Fuentes accounts for this
phenomenon by considering the symbiotic relationship between the landscape and its inhabitants down through the
years:

> [The] physical nature of Mexico—a cruel, devouring,
> sunbaked landscape—is filled with portents of magical
> distraction. Every force of nature seems to have a mythi-
> cal equivalent in Mexico. No other nation is quite so
> totemic.... Whether creating a stone pedestal for the
> worship of the earth goddess Coatlique, a gilded temple

honoring [the Virgin of] Guadalupe, a novel defending the underdog or a mural recalling the heroic past, the Mexican artist has seldom been able to act outside the demands of the all-encompassing myth.[18]

Foreigners such as Lawrence, Lowry, and Porter were receptive to this national myth, though they interpreted it according to the needs and prerogatives of their own art. Ramón Sender, whose work prior to the downfall of the Spanish Republic had been broadly political in emphasis, initiated a new phase of his writing during his three-year exile in Mexico. The change was first evident in *Mexicayotl* (1940), a collection of tales dealing with Pre-Columbian myth and ritual. Sender has said that in Mexico "mythology is still alive in the streets, not merely in folkloric terms but in the folds of the air seen only by poets, children, and an occasional madman."[19] Eisenstein, in Mexico to film the ill-fated epic *Que Viva Mexico!* in 1931, spoke of the influence of a "supernatural consciousness" that dictated the composition of his shots in terms of "primal forms."[20] A more extreme case was Artaud who, "guided by the Invisible," came to Mexico in 1936 to visit the Tarahumara Indians and to participate in their still-surviving peyote rituals. Throughout his four-month stay with this tribe in the northern sierra, Artaud felt himself surrounded by a landscape that literally embodied the ancient myths: "The land of the Tarahumara is full of signs, forms and natural effigies which in no way seem the result of chance—as if the gods themselves, whom one feels everywhere here, had chosen to express their powers by means of these strange signatures in which the figure of a man is hunted down from all sides."[21]

The power of the variegated Mexican landscape to induce a kind of dreamy, visionary state in the observer is a recurring theme in this literature. Steinbeck, for one, was much impressed by this hallucinatory quality. Upon returning from one of at least eight visits he made to the country, he speculated that "the people there live on a mental level about equal in depth to our dream level. The contacts I made there were all dreamlike."[22] When he wrote *The Pearl* (1945), set along the coast of Baja California, Steinbeck returned to the "dream level" and relied on it to give his story the feeling of a folk tale.

> The uncertain air that magnified some things and blotted out others hung over the whole Gulf so that all sights were unreal and vision could not be trusted; so that sea and land had the sharp clarities and the vagueness of a dream. Thus it might be that the people of the Gulf trust things of the spirit and things of the imagination, but they do not trust their eyes . . . or any optical exactness. . . . There was no certainty in seeing, no proof that what you saw was there or was not there.[23]

A striking instance of the theme is found in Traven's "The Night Visitor," in which the protagonist Gales lives alone in a hut somewhere in the tropical bush. Though he is presented in other works as a pragmatist who survives, despite economically hard times, by dint of his shrewdness and adaptability, here Gales willingly succumbs to the lure of the bush:

> I sat down and looked over that greenish-gray sea of jungle. I could think of nothing. My mind came to rest. A wonderful feeling of tranquillity took possession of my soul and body. I forgot earth, and heaven. The eternal singing of the jungle . . . lulled me into slumber, and I did not awaken until I heard the pitiful, harsh shriek of an animal caught by its enemy in the depths of the jungle.[24]

The passage foreshadows Gales's own fate. At the end of the story—after a series of dreamlike visitations by an Indian prince risen from the grave to complain of voracious swine (read deracinating white men) who disturb his rest—Gales leaves his hut and withdraws still deeper into the bush, which looked "in the darkness as though it were stooping slowly though irresistibly upon me where I sat, threatening to suck me into its fangs, intending to swallow me, bone, flesh, heart, soul, everything."[25] In Traven's *montería* novels, not even the natives of Chiapas are immune to the occult powers of the tropical jungle, for (as Traven puts it in the penultimate volume in the series) "in the forest, by night and by day, man is constantly at the mercy of hallucinations, mirages, obsessions."[26]

Traven's restless night visitor is an archetypal figure in the dream-world of Mexico, and his complaint has troubled the sleeping and waking vision of many a foreign traveler to his country. Almost every visiting writer has felt it necessary to comment on the unsettling presence of the Indian, whose way of life, for better and worse, has remained essentially unchanged since the Conquest. Excepting only the fiction of Traven, Miss Porter's work demonstrates the deepest concern for and understanding of the Indian's plight to be found in these works by foreigners. For Miss Porter, the Indians "are the very life of the country, this inert and slow-breathing mass, these lost people who move in the oblivion of sleep-walkers under their incredible burdens; these silent and reproachful figures in rags, bowed face to face with the earth; it is these who bind together all the accumulated and hostile elements of Mexican life."[27] Despite the avowed goal of the Revolution to "uplift" the Indian and restore his ancestral lands after four centuries of virtual bondage, he remains for Miss Porter spiritually inert and materially as poor as ever. To soothe the pain of injustice the Indian relies upon the otherworldly promise of the Catholic faith (and often, as *Hacienda* suggests, upon the "corpse-white liquor," pulque). In "The Fiesta of Guadalupe" (1923), Miss Porter describes the Indians' devotion to the "brown Virgin," the most important religious symbol in Mexico:

> Twenty brown and work-stained hands are stretched up to touch the magic glass [covering the image of Guadalupe at the shrine on the Hill of Tepeyac].... I see the awful hands of faith, the credulous and worn hands of believers; the humble and beseeching hands of millions

and millions who have only the anodyne of credulity. In my dreams I shall see those groping insatiable hands reaching, reaching, reaching, the eyes turned blinded away from the good earth which should fill [them], to the vast and empty sky.[28]

The essay concludes on an apocalyptic note; feeling the wounded heart of the Indian beating "like a great volcano under the earth," Miss Porter voices her hope that "men do not live in a deathly dream forever."[29] A less dire view of the Indian is that of Gustav Regler, who lived in Mexico for over twelve years during a period in which the Indian fared somewhat better than at the time of Miss Porter's residence in the country. At immense remove from Miss Porter, Regler expresses admiration for the Indian's religious devotion, his capacity for belief, which endows his life with a kind of significance that has been lost by modern Europeans. "We [have] to achieve what these Indians had managed to do," writes Regler in *A Land Bewitched* (1955): "to be able to dream of the soul. . . . The Indians had reached a new belief. . . . [Their customs on the Day of the Dead suggest that] among them are dreamers who have mastered death."[30] Notwithstanding his more positive attitude, it is revealing that Regler, like Traven and Steinbeck and Porter—and like D. H. Lawrence—conceives of the Indian as a dreamer. If Regler is less haunted than they by his *own* dreams of the night visitor's complaint, he nonetheless shares with them an awareness of the spiritual lethargy, the fatalism, that has left the Indian unmoved by the Revolution's indigenist efforts: the "old [notion] of the Indians' revolutionary violence is unmasked; to be a rebel a man must be very conscious, while the Indian is still sunk deep in the twilight of his dreams."[31]

Whatever their views of the "somnambulistic" Indian—and of his prospects of regaining paradise by following the path mapped out by Revolutionary ideologues—the foreign writers were unable to indulge in the Mexican dream without its being transformed in their eyes, sooner or later, into nightmare. And at the heart of that nightmare, for the foreigner, lay the specter of violent death. Thus Miss Porter writes of the "very smell of violence...in the air, at once crazed and stupefied. One could easily be murdered for an irrelevant word or gesture...";[32] Artaud of "a theme of death emanat-[ing] from [the rocks]," of reading "everywhere a story of childbirth in war, a story of genesis and chaos, with all these bodies of gods which were carved out like people; and these truncated statues of human forms. Not one shape which was intact, not one body which did not look as if it had emerged from a recent massacre...";[33] and Regler of a land still trembling "beneath the remembered agony of sombre altars laden with human beings, sacrificed by human hands."[34] The latent assumption of such passages (and there are scores of them in this literature) seems to be that the volcanic earth of Mexico, its ancient thirst merely tantalized by the recent carnage of the Revolution, cries out for more blood to compensate the wrongs done its children; that what the Indian "dreams" of is a return to his former eminence, and that one day he will wake up to take his revenge against the modern counterparts of his conquerors.

No doubt such horrific forebodings strain historical probability to the breaking point, or very near it; the Mexican Indian is hardly in a position today to "re-conquer" his homeland even if he were seriously inclined to do so. That very improbability, however, is suggestive of precisely the kind of license travel writers are likely to assume when faced with a mystery all but petrified beneath the hard crust of truism. For the foreigner who feels threatened by violence at the hands of the descendants of the Aztecs—and who thinks of the threat in these terms—is reacting not so much to contemporary historical actuality as to the Mexican mystique. In a land of nightmare, where "optical exactness" is distrusted and there is "no proof that what you saw was there or was not there," where "objects are reflected in perverse and threatening forms," words such as "probability" and "accuracy" begin to lose their usefulness. In such a land even so delicate and

harmless a creature as the butterfly may appear as it does to
Gustav Regler: "Here in Mexico butterflies have Gorgons'
heads upon their wings; their pointed faces and blue-grey vel-
vet bodies are those of rats; yes, they even have thick drops
of blood on their shoulders to inspire terror."[35] There will
always be those who insist that no such butterflies exist, that
the Indian is content to eke out his existence as he has for
over four centuries whether or not the Revolution lives up to
its promises, that Mexico really is a charming, picturesque
country of some interest to the diversion-seeking tourist
whose pocketful of credit cards insures him a ready welcome
from the natives, that Mexico's economic prosperity or (say)
its stance on communism are the essential matters with which
outsiders should concern themselves. There is a place for
views such as these, just as there is a place for Dickens'
School of Hard Facts in which a horse is "defined" as a creature with so many teeth and legs and certain eating habits
and a coat that sheds in the spring and hooves that, for the
common good, must be shod with iron. ("Now, girl number
twenty," says Mr. Gradgrind the schoolmaster in *Hard
Times*, "you know what a horse is.") But imaginative writers,
while not uninterested in "accurate" information, have generally been attracted to Mexico because, perhaps more than
any other country, Mexico assaults the outsider with the
inscrutable, with bewildering contradictions, with the overwhelming sense of a reality beyond the world of Hard Facts.
If these writers deliberately exploit the "mystique" at the
expense of literal verisimilitude (as has been charged), then
Mexico has repeatedly participated as collaborator in the
mythopoeic process. "Mexico," says Graham Greene, and
here he speaks for many, "was something I couldn't shake
off, like a state of mind."[36]

III

D. H. Lawrence, Aldous Huxley, Graham Greene, and Malcolm Lowry are among the most prominent of the writers

who came to Mexico when its imaginative appeal was at its zenith. Their travel writings and novels set in Mexico are of great interest, due in part to the very stature of the four English novelists. *The Plumed Serpent* (1926), *Eyeless in Gaza* (1936), *The Power and the Glory*, and *Under the Volcano* are all major works in their authors' respective canons and among the most significant English novels of this century. The novels individually have received the amount of critical attention that major works deservedly attract. At the same time, however, it is curious that their interrelationships as novels of Mexico have not been fully examined. In this regard travelers, students, and residents of Mexico are a step ahead of the critics, for three of the four novels at least (the exception being *Eyeless in Gaza*, which is only in part set in Mexico) are prominently displayed in English-language bookshops all over the country and are widely read and discussed among the Anglo-American "colony." The fact is that for many these novels, along with their satellite travel writings, seem to epitomize the imaginative response of foreigners to the Mexican mystique.

Though two studies of Anglo-American writers in Mexico have recently appeared,[37] the most suggestive attempt to describe and account for the English novelists' particular fascination with Mexico is still an essay by George Woodcock published in 1956. Professor Woodcock speaks of a "tradition" in the English novel since the First World War, a tradition consisting of works that are "crucial self-revelations" in which the Mexican mystique plays a vital part. After noting the elements of the Mexican scene which especially concerned the four novelists, Woodcock asserts that their basic attitudes toward Mexico were "not mutually incompatible." Lawrence, Huxley, Greene, and Lowry all demonstrate views which "fit into that legend of Mexico as the land of hatred and violence which is encapsuled for Europeans in the story of Maximilian and Carlotta, that tragedy of enlightened good-will destroyed in the maelstrom of political passions."[38] Though he finds "more than one thread of truth" in the legend of Mexico as a land of violence and hatred, Woodcock (who has himself traveled widely in Mexico and has written a travel book, *To the City of the Dead*, published in 1957) finds that the English novelists have left out of account the more gentle and hopeful qualities of Mexican life, that they have distorted Mexico "to an extent beyond the normal scope of fictional license," and that "the curious exaggerations and distortions which appear in [their] accounts of Mexico in fact represent the imposition, over the true map, of [their individual] fears and hopes."[39]

The Woodcock essay offers many useful observations, and I shall be returning to them from time to time later in this book; his point about the violation of the "normal scope" (whatever that is) of fictional license—a violation, if it exists, hardly attributable to the English novelists alone—has already been addressed. At this juncture, however, it is enough to say that Woodcock is being too cautious in calling the Englishmen's views of Mexico "not mutually incompatible." For despite differences in emphasis, there is a remarkable consistency, a deep underlying affinity, not only in their fundamental attitudes toward Mexico but also in the artistic ends which the land is made to serve in their novels. To begin with, as in the works by other foreign writers but even more obsessively here, Mexico is represented as a land saturated with death: the politics, the art, the fiestas and other social customs, the ancient and modern religious rituals, the landscape itself—all are felt to be manifestations of an underlying death-fixation endemic in Mexico. Whereas many of the other foreign visitors were sympathetic toward the ultimate aims of the Revolution and sought to explain or even justify politically motivated violence, the Englishmen (except for Lowry) were highly critical of the movement and saw its violent excesses of a piece with the many sanguinary episodes in Mexico's past. They made no attempt (as Traven, for instance, did in almost every novel) to defend the banditry and brutality of peasants by finding an etiology in the inequities perpetrated by the Díaz dictatorship; no claim that the Revolution was a Holy War fired (as Regler believed) by a "healthy hatred." For the English it was wholesale, gratuitous murder, a manifestation of the essential Mexican character:

> So these men [Lawrence writes in *The Plumed Serpent*],
> unable to overcome the elements, men held down by the
> serpent tangle of sun and electricity and volcanic emis-
> sion, they are subject to an ever-recurring, fathomless
> lust of resentment, a demonish hatred of life itself. Then,
> the instriking thud of a heavy knife, stabbing into a liv-
> ing body, this is the best. No lust of women can equal
> that lust. The clutching throb of gratification as the knife
> strikes in and the blood spurts out!
>
> It is the inevitable supreme gratification of a people
> entangled in the past, and unable to extricate itself.[40]

There are a number of recurring elements in the four English novels besides this preoccupation with death, though
one feels that it is the dominant, controlling factor. One very
obvious feature is a pronounced tendency to rely on highly
charged language and a tone of extreme urgency. It is not
enough simply to say that one is hot and tired and lonely on a
muleback ride through the rugged mountains outside
Oaxaca. When Huxley renders such a scene in *Eyeless in
Gaza* we are told that there "was no sight or sound of life.
Hopelessly empty, the chaos of tumbled mountains seemed
to stretch away endlessly. It was as though they had ridden
across the frontier of the world into nothingness, into an infinite expanse of hot and dusty negation."[41] Or there is Lowry's Consul, withdrawing from a threatening world and
simultaneously glimpsing it through Faustian eyes:

> Night: and once again, the nightly grapple with death,
> the room shaking with daemonic orchestras, the snatches
> of fearful sleep, the voices outside the window, my name
> being continually repeated with scorn by imaginary par-
> ties arriving, the dark's spinets. As if there were not
> enough real noises in these nights the color of grey hair.
> Not like the rending tumult of American cities.... But
> the howling of pariah dogs, the cocks that herald dawn
> all night, the drumming, the moaning...the eternal sor-
> row that never sleeps of great Mexico.[42]

Lawrence, not known for his restraint in other works, writes at a stentorian pitch in his Mexican novel; often the result is merely irritating, but the book contains some of his most engaging mythopoeic passages, such as this description of the volcanic landscape:

> [The] undertone was like the low angry, snarling purring of some jaguar spotted with night. There was a ponderous, down-pressing weight upon the spirit: the great folds of the dragon of the Aztecs...winding around one and weighing down the soul. And on the bright sunshine was a dark stream of angry, impotent blood, and the flowers seemed to have their roots in spilt blood. The spirit of place was cruel, down-dragging, destructive.[43]

Ironically, the sheer force of the apocalyptic rhetoric invokes the force that it is intended to counter, the temporal world, which threatens to smother the consciousness of the protagonists as they fitfully struggle toward (or against) self-knowledge *within* that same nightmarish world of time. The novels are all concerned in part with the necessity of recognizing the inviolability of temporal flux and accepting its primacy; all four employ patterns of cyclical recurrence to dramatize this concern. Huxley's scrambled narrative pattern eventually resolves into a discernible "layering" of time around a recurring series of events involving the fact of mortality. Greene, like Huxley (but in a less elaborate manner) orchestrates the various phases of his protagonist's past until we become aware that the fugitive priest is fleeing from one image of himself across a frontier—psychological as well as geographical—toward another, more innocent self-image, only to return subsequently to accept in full his commitment to "a dying, cooling world." Lawrence has his protagonist undergo a sequence of responses to Mexico (curiosity, repulsion, fear, attraction, submission, withdrawal), a sequence repeated scores of times as the character moves centripetally ever closer to the heart of the dark mystery that is her destiny. In *Under the Volcano* Lowry utilizes a vast network of historical and mythical allusions to establish at once the endless recurrence of the historical cycle of conquest and counter-conquest, and the universality of his protagonists's plight. Cyclicity in these novels is finally both a means for calling attention to the continuous flow of time and also (in another sense) the vehicle by which the human consciousness may, if only for a fleeting moment, transcend time and its attenuations.

Each of the four novels lays emphasis on a profound sense of isolation suffered by the protagonist. This is true even of *The Power and the Glory*, the only novel whose central character is a native Mexican; the "whisky priest's" isolation is in fact doubly severe because of his very proximity to home, for he is a fugitive in his own state of Tabasco where no one (for good reason) wants to harbor him. Engulfed by a vast, inhuman and vacuous landscape, the four protagonists are cut off from reassuring contacts with traditional society and its institutions, from all those bulwarks which civilized man has erected to protect the self from immediate confrontation with elemental, untamed reality. This isolation causes much fear and suffering, as well it might. Yet it is also essential to the kind of experience with which the novels are primarily concerned. The Mexican novels all focus on spiritual struggles that may be called religious: all involve a quest for rebirth, and juxtapose that quest with the political vicissitudes of Mexico during a revolution. Entrapped within a landscape trembling in the throes of revolutionary conflict, the protagonists undergo a process by which the protective layers of the self that had been built up prior to their exposure to the Mexican ambience in its present condition are stripped away. This stripping away amounts to a kind of slow death, portending the swifter and more irrevocable annihilation that the characters fear is imminent. Before that final blow falls, however—sometimes only just before—the process culminates in an expansion of awareness, which comes simultaneously with the stripping away of the final layer of the self: egoistic willfulness, one's innermost conception of oneself as a special case. Like Emily Dickinson's notion of the "Death-blow" that is "a Life-blow to Some/ Who till they died, did not alive become," the moment of ultimate surrender prefigures salvation. I say "prefigures" because in one case—Lowry's *Volcano*—the revelation comes too late to save the protagonist from his headlong descent into the *barranca*, that "general Tartarus and gigantic jakes." And in the other three novels the experience of salvation is made to appear tentative or is in some way qualified so that the process may continue and the cycle begin anew.

While it would of course be idle to claim too much in the way of parallelism between, say, Lawrence's religion and that of Greene, this much can be said: in their Mexican novels both of them insist, as do Lowry and Huxley in theirs, that on this earth there can be no experience of salvation—however it is defined—without an awareness of what loss of salvation means, no rebirth without first a descent into the underworld of spiritual death, no heaven entirely divorced from hell. This is ultimately how the Mexican setting functions in these novels, as an infernal paradise, a dualistic image which conflates all of the horrors and hopes that constitute the spiritual lives of the four protagonists. In each case the character experiences a kind of paralysis, directly the result of a protracted series of vacillations. The character wavers between, on the one hand, the all too human impulse to escape from the terrors of elemental reality embodied by Mexico (or by a particular locality within Mexico, such as Tabasco or the Farolito cantina in Parián); and on the other, the unremitting necessity of accepting that reality and all it involves. After prolonged and anguished indecision, the latter (much more painful) alternative is always, in the end, embraced. Whatever kind of "reward" awaits the character in consequence of his final involvement in the world of nightmare—whether Kate Leslie's translation into a fertility goddess in the neo-Aztec pantheon, Anthony Beavis' nascent mysticism, or indeed the martyrdom of both the whisky priest and the Consul—the growth of consciousness, the death and rebirth of the self, depends on that involvement. As it is rendered in these novels, Mexico is a land where time and again

The blood-dimmed tide is loosed, and everywhere
The ceremony of innocence is drowned....

This is a Mexico more tangibly infernal than paradisal. And yet, as events run their course, Mexico emerges pre-eminently as a land where (again to adapt the words of W. B. Yeats) "A terrible beauty is born."

In addition to this general symbolism of the Mexican setting as the infernal paradise, there are important images in each work that tend to localize the quest for rebirth and give it a clearer focus. My discussions of the novels trace the use of three such images—blood, border, and *barranca*—which gradually become identified with the most compelling forces at the heart of Mexican existence as seen by the English novelists. Since all four writers were simultaneously attracted and repelled by their own contact with Mexican reality, these emblems fittingly represent both the positive and negative sides of their responses. By using such images the novelists are able to bring together the contrarieties in their experience of Mexico and to present them as interdependent. Though blood figures as a notable motif in *Eyeless in Gaza* and *Under the Volcano*, where it is associated with man's guilt and the horror of violence, for Lawrence the image has a special significance. He often uses the trope "dark blood" to identify the "primitive" mode of consciousness which he both feared and venerated in the Mexican Indian. The figure is invoked repeatedly in *The Plumed Serpent* as his heroine proceeds reluctantly toward her fulfillment through immersion in the "sea of living blood" in Mexico. For Greene's hunted priest, a geographical border is the literal and symbolic locus of escape to freedom, while numerous other descriptions imaging the harrowing sense of "life on a border" adumbrate the dominant mode of perception, and the emotional atmosphere, of *The Power and the Glory*. Although the psychological border is employed in the richest variety of ways by Greene (indeed, it is his forte), analogous imagery appears in the other Mexican novels, usually in relation to the quest theme and the literally ambivalent experience of "crossing over" into a new phase of consciousness. In their descriptions of the undomesticated Mexican landscape all four novelists note (often with a sense of disquiet) the abundance of *barrancas*, the deep gaping ravines cutting into the mountainous terrain. For Malcolm Lowry the ubiquitous *barranca* winding through the Dantesque terrain of *Under the Volcano* is—rather like Greene's mountain border—the literal and symbolic destination of his protagonist, who simultaneously fears and longs for descent into it.

The deeply ambivalent Mexico depicted in these novels is thus essentially a symbolic locale in which an inner drama is played out. At the same time, however, the four Englishmen share a penchant for seeing Mexico as a world in microcosm, and they present the political conflicts of Revolutionary Mexico in a manner obviously intended to suggest the corresponding forces in motion elsewhere during the period 1920-40. The novels may be, and have been, read on both levels. But if in the final analysis all the English novels are concerned with a dimension of human experience transcending the particular conflicts embodied in Mexico during this tenebrous period, they are all nonetheless imbued by its distinctive atmosphere.

IV

A final note on the fascination with Mexico as manifested in modern literature. The role played by Lawrence in the creation and popularization of the literary image of Mexico remains singular. For Lawrence was the first major figure to experience Mexico personally and to write about it for the English-speaking public. (Katherine Anne Porter of course preceded Lawrence in Mexico, but her reputation had not yet been established in the 1920's and her journalism and few Mexican stories of that decade could not have had a very wide readership.) Though he was by no means a universally read and admired writer even in his native country, the various adventures of his "wander years" after the First World War were followed by many literate people on both sides of the Atlantic. Through his capacity for outrage against what he considered a dead civilization, his daring to risk failure and humiliation in the ongoing effort to discover and make known the source of true vitality in man ("the touch, the spark of contact...which is most elusive, still the only treasure")—in short, through his very sensibility—Lawrence performed for our times, as Francis Fergusson puts it, "the root function of the poet or seer, at a level where the two functions are hardly distinguishable. One might say that 'the conscience of a blackened street impatient to assume the world' could never quite assume the world while Lawrence was in it."[44]

It is impossible to say just how many Englishmen had reckoned with his horrific Mexican vision while Lawrence was still in the world. What we do know is that, among many other writers mentioned in the preceding pages, Huxley, Greene, Waugh, and Lowry all read Lawrence's Mexican books.[45] However much they were charmed by *Mornings in Mexico* and repelled (or else bewildered) by *The Plumed Serpent*, they could not help being influenced or affected in some way by his daemonic/paradisal rendering of Mexico, so that later when they visited Mexico themselves, they were prepared to look for what Lawrence said was there. Their own Mexican writings demonstrate this, even as they build upon Lawrence's basic dualistic image and refine it according to their own purposes. It is fitting then that we begin with the precursor.

# II

# The "Dark Blood" of America

D. H. Lawrence's American experience began well before he actually arrived on this continent in 1922. One speaks of the "American" experience because that is the term Lawrence habitually used to identify his contact with both Mexico and the southwestern part of the United States. The element of this "America" which interested him the most, its aboriginal religion—whether found in the present-day ceremonials of the Pueblo Indians of New Mexico and Arizona or in the recorded history of the Aztecs and their rituals—seemed to Lawrence an indivisible, monolithic reality that had survived more or less intact since antediluvian times. His predisposition to view America in this way results in a serious confusion in his writings of this period, in particular when he blurs the very important distinction between his own deepest feelings toward Mexico and those toward New Mexico and his mountain ranch there.

Close attention to the comments made by Lawrence in his letters and by friends who were with him during the years 1922-25 reveals that on the whole New Mexico *was* a very pleasant place for him—not quite the utopian "new navel of the world" which Lawrence sought perhaps, but still a most pleasant place in which to live, a kind of sanctuary from the complicated muddle of the ordinary world. Even at its worst New Mexico seemed to him merely too empty, too fixed in the outer life with its aimless movement over a landscape of inhumanly vast proportions. But in Old Mexico Lawrence was always preternaturally aware of the specter of death. There the heavy coils and sharp fangs of the old bloodthirsty gods were all too perceptible everywhere he went—in the stark landscape, the Indian people, the art, the politics.

One of his major thematic concerns in the writings of this period was the store of untapped vitality to be found by the recognition of and partial identification with what he sometimes called the "dark blood-consciousness" of the Indian peoples. This chapter will attempt to demonstrate how, in his search for—and flight from—the pulsating flow of blood which he felt to be the essence of the American spirit of place, Lawrence as it were came to associate Mexico with the systolic and New Mexico with the diastolic functions.

## I

> [The Pilgrim Fathers] came largely to get *away*—that most simple of motives. To get away. Away from what? In the long run, away from themselves. Away from everything. That's why most people have come to America, and still do come. To get away from everything they are and have been.
>
> —*Studies in Classic American Literature*[1]

Even if there were no such continent as America, Lawrence would have invented one: which, in a sense, is what he did anyway. In his letters written during the war we find evidence that Lawrence was developing a cyclical theory of history according to which Europe was entering a death phase while America was approaching an era of rebirth. The theory, which was to receive its fullest treatment later in his *Movements in European History* (published in 1921 but begun in 1918), was formulated at a time when Lawrence decided to disengage himself from the sterile mechanism of Europe and to seek out the vital potential associated in his mind with America.[2] On October 26, 1915, just before the suppression of *The Rainbow*, he wrote to Harriet Monroe:

Probably I am coming to America. Probably, in a
month's time, I shall be in New York.... I must see
America: here the autumn of all life has set in, the fall:
we are hardly more than the ghosts in the haze, we who
stand apart from the flux of death. I must see America. I
think one can feel hope there. I think that there the life
comes up from the roots, crude but vital. Here the whole
tree of life is dying. It is like being dead: the underworld.
I must see America. I believe it is beginning, not ending.[3]

Lawrence did not come to America in a month's time;
though he frequently flirted with the notion of emigrating
there, not for seven years did he actually make the trip. During the interval he began to consider the prospect of seeking
an ideal "centre," a kind of Blessed Isle which he called Rananim, where a community of enlightened souls might settle
and live in hope for the future. He continued to develop his
symbolic interpretation of America, however, and before
long it became the locus of his dream of Rananim.[4] In 1916,
frustrated by his failure to communicate to the hostile English
reading public, Lawrence turned his attention to the study of
American literature. *Studies in Classic American Literature*
(1923), even in its final revised form completed in New
Mexico, expresses a vision of America that is characteristic of
Lawrence before his "savage pilgrimage." Particularly in the
writings of Cooper, Melville, and Whitman, Lawrence saw a
profound expression of the white American psyche cutting
beneath the superficial concerns of democracy and religious
orthodoxy, and responding to the primordial and as yet un-
fulfilled spirit of place.

In much the same spirit, Lawrence exhorts white Americans (in an essay published in the *New Republic* in 1920) to
"take up life where the Red Indian, the Aztec, the Maya, the
Incas left it off. [Americans] must pick up the life-thread
where the mysterious Red race let it fall. They must catch the
pulse of the life which Cortés and Columbus murdered.
There lies the real continuity: not between Europe and the
new States, but between the murdered Red America and the

seething White America."[5] As David Cavitch has aptly put it,
in these pre-Taos essays Lawrence invested America "with
much of his deepest intuition about the self, particularly
about himself. In doing so, he made his imagination dependent, to a large degree, upon the continuing inspiration of the
American continent. He strove thereafter to realize consciously the meaning of the place that he had encoded with
personal significance.... In a very intimate sense, it is *his*
country."[6] Reading Lawrence's letters concerning his plans to
come to this continent after the war, one cannot avoid the
impression that Lawrence is almost looking for excuses to
postpone the journey. When he finally did leave England in
1919 he headed east to Italy (where he stopped off for over
two years), before sailing for Ceylon and Australia. This
period of mental vacillation is perhaps best accounted for by
Cavitch:

> The extremes of anticipation and of aversion which
> mark his long-deliberated approach to the United States
> indicate how much of his inner life with its intense dia-
> lectics of negation and hope he had invested in the image
> of America. The difficulty in acting upon his resolution
> to go there was partly the difficulty of facing the most
> personal and troubling issues that lay behind its sym-
> bolic attraction for him.[7]

Just two days after the Lawrences arrived in Taos, in September of 1922, they were whisked off on a five-day automo-
bile trip to visit the Jicarilla Apache Reservation in northern
New Mexico.[8] Lawrence recorded this experience in "Indians
and an Englishman," a very important sketch because it presents his first impressions of actual "Red Indians." The
encounter was a crucial test of his ideals, as he well knew. In
the sketch he admits his position as a newcomer in this land,
a novice "born in England and kindled with Fenimore
Cooper" (*Phoenix*, p. 94). The reader wonders if the Indians
will live up to his abstract preconception of them. Will he be
let down, repelled? Or will he be perhaps so taken with them

that he will want to join or emulate them in some way? Lawrence also wonders: "What is the feeling that passes from an Indian to me, when we meet? We are both men, but how do we feel together?" (p. 95). His initial answers to these questions express a sense not of disappointment so much as bewilderment and disorientation: "It was not what I had thought it would be. It was something of a shock. . . . [Something] in my soul broke down, letting in a bitterer dark, a pungent awakening to the lost past, old darkness, new terror, new root-griefs, old root-richnesses" (p. 95). Among the variegated crowd of tourists he feels alien, "a lone lorn Englishman, tumbled out of the known world of the British Empire onto this stage: for it persists in seeming like a stage to me, and not like the proper world" (p. 92). He even senses a kind of "unconscious animosity" beneath the sportiveness and spectacle of the Indian dances and chants.

But that first night there occurred a scene which Lawrence would recall a half-dozen years later in "New Mexico," the valedictory essay on his American experience, as a crucial one in inducing his basic intuitive response to the Pueblos and their religion. Wrapped in a red sarape from the cold, Lawrence wanders alone toward a clearing where there is a large campfire near the entrance of an Indian tent. A group of young Indians have gathered around the entrance, and inside an old man chants to a drum-beat.

> His close-shutting Indian lips were drawn open, his eyes were as if half-veiled, as he went on and on, on and on, in a distinct, plangent, recitative voice, male and yet strangely far-off and plaintive, reciting, reciting, reciting like a somnambulist, telling, no doubt, the history of the tribe interwoven with the gods. Other Apaches sat round the fire. . . . I stood wrapped in my blanket in the cold night, at some little distance from the entrance, looking on. (p. 97)

At this point Lawrence has reached the outer perimeter, both in physical location and in emotional attitude, of a circle within which lies a mystery that is at once intimidating and compelling. He is hovering on a kind of frontier—to turn back would mean rejecting what the mystery offers; to go further into the circle would amount to a submission to its unknown dangers. But remaining for the time being on that border, Lawrence is able to observe the profound otherness of the Indians, and partially to identify with it, without relinquishing either his individuality or his "civilized consciousness."⁹ Thus he has attained an ideal vantage point from which he may perceive that the younger Apaches are actually paying no attention to the old man, that the whole scene has "a very perfunctory appearance"; yet even as he remains detached, Lawrence may partake of "a deep pathos...in the old, mask-like, virile figure, with its metallic courage of persistence, old memory..." (p. 98). In this sketch Lawrence elects to remain on the frontier. He decides that perhaps after all it is the best place for him to be with regard to the Indians:

As for me, standing outside, beyond the open entrance, I was no enemy of theirs; far from it. The voice out of the far-off time was not for my ears. Its language was unknown to me. And I did not wish to know. It was enough to hear the sound issuing plangent from the bristling darkness of the far past, to see the bronze mask of the face lifted.... It was not for me, and I knew it. Nor had I any curiosity to understand. The soul is as old as the oldest day, and has its own hushed echoes, its own far-off tribal understandings sunk and incorporated. We do not need to live the past over again. Our darkest tissues are twisted in this old tribal experience, our warmest blood came out of the old tribal fire. And they vibrate still in answer, our blood, our tissue. But me, the conscious me, I have gone a long road since then.... I don't want to go back to them, ah, never. I never want to deny them or break with them. But there is no going back. Always onward, still further. The great devious onward-flowing stream of conscious human blood. From them to me, and from me on.

...I stand on the far edge of their firelight, and am neither denied nor accepted. My way is my own, old red feather; I can't cluster at the drum any more. (pp. 98-99)

It is interesting to note that in the latter part of this remarkable passage the borderline vantage point suddenly yields access to the temporal dimension as well as the spatial and the psychological: "From them to me, and from me on." Lawrence becomes the modern everyman, his frontier vision as it were bridging the gulf between the primordial and the imminent experience of the racial archetype. And this is precisely what he is after, this kind of vision and the expanded consciousness that it offers.[10]

The first stay in New Mexico lasted just over six months, the first ten weeks of which were spent in lodging provided by Mabel Dodge Luhan in Taos. Right after his return from the jaunt to the Apache reservation, Lawrence expressed an appreciation of one quality of the Southwestern locale in particular: "it has a bigness, a sense of space, and a certain sense of rough freedom, which I like. I dread the petty-foggying narrowness of England."[11] But just eleven days after his arrival in Taos he wrote to Earl Brewster of his growing aversion to the Americans' obsession with "freedom." It seemed to him that their supposed freedom was in fact a rationalization for a life-style centered around trivial diversions which insulated the Americans from the source of true vitality, the "spirit" of the continent: "Well, here we are in the Home of the Brave and the Land of the Free. It's free enough out here, if freedom means that there isn't anything in life except moving *ad lib* on foot, horse, or motor-car, across deserts and through canyons. It is just the life outside, and the outside of life. Not *really* life, in my opinion" (*Letters*, II, 717). Then there were the conflicts between Frieda Lawrence and Mrs. Luhan and between Lawrence and his hostess' small colony of artist friends. The combative atmosphere was not conducive to writing: "Everything in American goes by *will*. A great negative *will* seems to be turned against all spontaneous life—there seems to be no *feeling* at all—no genuine bowels of compassion and sympathy.... How can one write about [the United States], save analytically?" (*Letters*, II, 721).

On December 1 the Lawrences moved up in the mountains to the Del Monte Ranch, where they rented a cabin for the duration of that winter. The ranch was seventeen miles outside Taos, with "a vast landscape below, vast, desert, and then more mountains west, far off in Arizona, a skyline. Very beautiful.... Altogether it is ideal, according to one's ideas. But *innerlich*, there is nothing. It seems to me, in America, for the inside life, there is just blank nothing. All this outside life—and marvellous country—and it all means so little to one. I don't quite know what it is one wants..." (*Letters*, II, 732-733). This last sentence seems to sum up Lawrence's general state of mind during his first stay in New Mexico. He was feeling his way along tentatively in a strange country which did not—could not—correspond to his predetermined vision of it. The landscape impressed him, but with the exception of a few close neighbors on the Del Monte Ranch, the people did not.[12] The one truly memorable experience, at the Apache reservation, had occurred at the very beginning of his stay, and nothing since then had transpired to reinforce its significance in Lawrence's mind. He planned a trip to Mexico, where he hoped to find material for his "American novel," and a place in which to write. Probably it was at about this time that Mexico began to assume a larger role in his cyclical theory of history and of consciousness. A few weeks before boarding the train for Mexico City, Lawrence answered an inquisitive correspondent that he was "not disappointed" with America. He continues,

But I feel about U.S.A., as I vaguely felt a long time ago: that there is a vast unreal, intermediary thing intervening between the real thing which was Europe and the next real thing, which will probably be in America, but

which isn't yet, at all. Seems to me a vast death-happen-
ing must come first. But probably it is here, in America
(I don't say just U.S.A.), that the quick will keep alive
and come through. (*Letters*, II, 740)

The extremes mentioned almost lightly here, the "vast death-
happening" and the vital "quick" which will survive the cata-
clysm, would become more severe and threatening after his
exposure to Mexico, where the "vast unreal, intermediary
thing" seemed less substantial than in the United States.

One of the most interesting essays of Lawrence's American
period is "Au Revoir, U.S.A.," which describes his impressions during the journey by train to Mexico City in March of
1923. This is one of the few places where Lawrence explicitly
contrasts the feelings evoked in him by the United States with
those evoked by Mexico. Though he continues to view the
entire continent as sharing the same fundamental spirit of
place, he points out that in the United States the aboriginal
outlook which acknowledged the presence of the "dark gods"
has been stifled by the dominant white "mental-spiritual"
consciousness. As a result, in the States Lawrence feels subdued by a nervous tautness. When he crosses the border,
however, his emotional state changes "from tension to exas-
peration." He sees Mexico as a sort of "solar plexus of North
America," where the atmosphere of violence and general
malevolence characteristic of the continent's inherent nature
is overt and pervasive. "[You cross] the Rio Grande into
desert and chaos, and you sigh, if you have time before a
curse chokes you." You find yourself "in an unkempt Pullman trailing through endless deserts...and at the will of a
rather shoddy smallpox-marked Mexican Pullman-boy who
knows there's been a revolution and that his end is up." Before long you "feel like hitting the impudent Pullman waiter
with a beer-bottle. In the U.S.A. you don't even think of such
a thing" (*Phoenix*, p. 104). But Lawrence prefers this surfac-
ing of hostility to the feeling of being pulled taut by the more
subtle and insidious influences of the North. The trip to

Mexico represents a welcome return to the inner life which was submerged during his initial stay in New Mexico.

Lawrence proceeds to reveal his views of the aspects of Mexico which have an abiding interest for him, and here we come upon an immediate difference between the concerns of Lawrence and those of two later English visitors, Evelyn Waugh and Graham Greene—who, as Roman Catholics, had a much greater interest in and regard for the Hispanic elements of Mexican history and culture. For his part, Lawrence believes that while in the United States white culture is currently dominant, in Mexico the "great paleface overlay hasn't gone into the soil half an inch. The Spanish churches and palaces stagger . . . always just on the point of falling down. And the peon still grins his peon grin behind the Cross. . . . He knows his gods" (p. 105). Though the average tourist usually notes the contrast between the opulence of the Spanish cathedrals and shrines and the stark ruin of the Indian temples and pyramids, for Lawrence the relationship is reversed. The churches are vacuous and inert while the old Aztec carvings at San Juan Teotihuacán "all twist and bite." The great stone heads in the temples "snarl at you from the wall, trying to bite you: and one great dark, green blob of an obsidian eye, you never saw anything so blindly malevolent: and then white fangs." The quintessential pre-Columbian god of Mexico, after all, was Quetzalcoatl, "just a sort of feathered snake. Who needed the smoke of a little heart's-blood now and then, even he" (p. 105).[13] Admitting that he feels "bewildered" by his first exposure to all these emblems of violence, Lawrence sums up the difference he intuits between Mexico and the United States as follows:

. . .Mexico exasperates, whereas the U.S.A. puts an unbearable tension on one. Because here in Mexico the fangs are still obvious. Everybody knows the gods are going to bite within the next five minutes. While in the United States, the gods have had their teeth pulled, and their claws cut, and their tails docked, till they seem real

mild lambs. Yet all the time, inside, it's the same old
dragon's blood. The same old American dragon's blood.

And that discrepancy of course is a strain on the
human psyche. (p. 106)

"Au Revoir, U.S.A." dramatizes a literal passage across the
border, but as the last sentence suggests, Lawrence also sees
the experience as a descent into an alien dimension of consciousness. The vantage point provided by the frontier is
relinquished here, and the strain of transition is evident.

The first trip to Mexico lasted just under four months, during which Lawrence wrote the essay "Pan in America" and
most of the first draft of a novel then called "Quetzalcoatl,"
which would later become *The Plumed Serpent.* In mid-July
the Lawrences went to New York, with plans to sail for
Europe. Frieda was anxious to see her children again after a
four-year absence, but as the time approached for departure
Lawrence became more and more reluctant to leave. "I find
my soul doesn't want to come to Europe," he wrote to his
mother-in-law at the time (*Letters,* II, 750). Some of the mem-
oirs and biographies of Lawrence suggest that he and Frieda
quarrelled violently about his last-minute refusal to go with
her, but there is no general agreement on this point. In any
event, Frieda sailed on August 18 and Lawrence took the
train to Los Angeles. "I ought to have gone to England," he
wrote to Amy Lowell. "I wanted to go. But my inside self
wouldn't let me. At the moment I just can't face my own
country again."[14] From Los Angeles, in the company of Kai
Gótzsche, Lawrence headed back to Mexico, traveling down
the west coast ostensibly in search of a site for his Rananim.
But Lawrence was miserable without Frieda, and after less
than two months he sailed from Veracruz for England.

Coming in the middle of his American sojourn, the return
to Europe that winter of 1923-24 was an important turning
point. The three-month stay was one of the most dismal,
funereal episodes Lawrence had ever known. In a letter to
Witter Bynner he wrote: "Here I am. London—gloom—yel-

low air—bad cold—bed—old house—Morris wallpaper—
visitors—English voices—tea in old cups—poor D. H. L. perfectly miserable, as if he was in his tomb" (*Letters*, II, 765).
Europe seemed to him a "dreadful mummy sarcophagus,"
and he began to long for America:

> Horse, be as hobby as you like, but let me get on your
> back and ride away again to New Mexico. I don't care
> how frozen it is, how grey the desert, how cold the air,
> in Taos, in Lobo, in Santa Fe. It isn't choky, it is bright
> day at daytime, and bright dark night at night. And one
> isn't wrapped like a mummy in winding-sheet after
> winding-sheet of yellow, damp, unclean, cloyed, an-
> cient, breathed-to-death so-called air. (*Letters*, II, 768)

In a ranting, impressionistic essay of this time called "On
Coming Home," Lawrence muses on the English landscape:
"The place feels tight: one would like to smash something.
Outside [the train window], a tight little landscape goes by,
just unbelievable, with sunshine like thin water, a horizon
half a mile away, and everything crowded forward into one's
face till one gasps for space and breath.... Too horribly
close!"[15] In addition to inclement weather and a bad cold
Lawrence had to contend with various unpleasant complications with some of his oldest friends. He made rather a fool of
himself, at the Cafe Royal and elsewhere, imploring acquaintances to come off with him to his Rananim in America, receiving evasive, embarrassed responses. He clashed with
John Middleton Murry over the *Adelphi*, and perhaps over
Frieda, whom Lawrence may have suspected of having a liaison with Murry while he was apart from her in Mexico. In
short, as Graham Hough put it, "his whole connection with
his own country seems to have been violently dislocated."[16]

The Lawrences returned, along with Dorothy Brett, to
New Mexico in March of 1924. In May Frieda acquired a
small ranch from Mrs. Luhan in the mountains above Taos.
The next few months were a time of quiescence and renewal

after the turmoil of the last six months. Lawrence wrote to
Harriet Monroe that he was relieved to be away from the
"depressing swirl of Europe." "I must say [he wrote] I am
glad to be out here in the Southwest of America—there is the
pristine something, unbroken, unbreakable, and not to be
got under even by us awful whites with our machines—for
which I thank whatever gods there be" (*Letters*, II, 786). He
spent his time doing simple tasks—repairing the cabins at
their ranch, baking bread, making furniture, riding, tending
to "Black-eyed Susan," their cow. For the time being he was
content to savor his solitude and absorb the invigorating
spirit of the mountain landscape:

> At present I don't write—don't want to—don't care.
> Things are all far away. I haven't seen a newspaper for
> two months, and can't bear to think of one. The world is
> as it is. I am as I am. We don't fit very well.
>     ...One doesn't talk any more about being happy—
> that is child's talk. But I do like having the big, unbroken
> spaces round me. There is something savage, unbreak-
> able in the spirit of peace out here—the Indians drum-
> ming and yelling at our camp-fire at evening. (*Letters*, II,
> 790)

In the letters of this period one does not often find Lawrence
complaining of the vacuity and tension of American life as he
had during his first stay. Lobo ranch (later renamed Kiowa)
provided him with the sense of home otherwise missing from
his life since the war.

One of the chief results of Lawrence's European interlude
seems to have been an intensified determination on his part
to seek a basis of new life and hope in America. In his essay
"New Mexico" (1928) Lawrence recalled that the Indians, the
ranch, and the mountain landscape amounted to "the greatest experience from the outside world that I have ever had. It
certainly changed me for ever.... [It] was New Mexico that
liberated me from the present era of civilization, the great era
of civilization, the great era of material and mechanical

development" (*Phoenix*, p. 142). That summer and fall on the
ranch, when he began once again to write, Lawrence drew
heavily upon the Pueblo religion, speaking of it much more
authoritatively—and with a stronger sense of identification—
than before. He made several visits to the Apache, Hopi, and
Navajo reservations to observe the dances and feasts, and
wrote vivid sketches of the ceremonials which were collected,
along with four pieces written later at Oaxaca, in *Mornings
in Mexico* (1927). "Dance of the Sprouting Corn" is a highly
subjective, incantatory description of the Indian rites of
spring. As the Indians celebrate the flow of life in their dance,
with man "the caller" connecting the invisible life-influences
from the sky and from the ground, so the essay celebrates
this ritual by which man partakes in the processes of nature,
the germination of the corn. "The Hopi Snake Dance" is a
description and analysis of the Pueblos' animistic religion
and of the rites by which, in "conquering" the living poten-
cies of the natural world (represented by the snakes), man
becomes a "god" in his own vital cosmos. Conquering the
"dragon" cosmos by submitting to it, man is both creator and
creation. In "Indians and Entertainment" Lawrence contrasts
the "day consciousness" of whites, which is mental and verbal, with the pulsating "dark blood-consciousness" of the
Indians. Most whites, Lawrence says, counter the inscrutable
"otherness" of Indians either by detesting them, which is at
least an honest reaction, or by performing "the mental trick"
and fooling themselves into believing that "the befeathered
and bedaubed darling is nearer to the true ideal gods than we
are. This last is just bunk and a lie."[17] In a major statement of
his interpretation of the relationship between the two races,
Lawrence continues:

> The Indian way of consciousness is different from and
> fatal to our way of consciousness. Our way of con-
> sciousness is different from and fatal to the Indian. The
> two ways, the two streams are never to be united. They
> are not even to be reconciled. There is no bridge, no

canal of connexion.

The sooner we realise, and accept this, the better, and leave off trying, with fulsome sentimentalism, to render the Indian in our own terms.

The acceptance of the great paradox of human consciousness is the first step to a new accomplishment.

The consciousness of one branch of humanity is the annihilation of the consciousness of another branch.... And we can understand the consciousness of the Indian only in terms of the death of our consciousness.

...To pretend that all is one stream is to cause chaos and nullity.... The only thing you can do is to have a little Ghost inside you which sees both ways, or even many ways. But a man cannot *belong* to both ways, or to many ways. One man can belong to one great way of consciousness only. He may even change from one way to another. But he cannot go both ways at once. Can't be done. (*Mornings*, pp. 45-46)

The essay goes on to analyze Indian ceremonials in animistic terms: "In everything, the shimmer of creation, and never the finality of the created" (p. 51).

In addition to these essays Lawrence also wrote three tales during this second stay in New Mexico. He must have had his novel-in-progress in the back of his mind all this time, for the letters indicate his desire to return to Mexico and resume his work on it. "The Woman Who Rode Away," *St. Mawr*, and "The Princess"—like the novel—all center on female protagonists caught up in the conflict between the urge to submit to dark malevolent forces and the willful rejection of them in favor of the white "mental-spiritual consciousness." The conflict is typically treated in sexual terms, in the battle between repression and release of the woman's libidinal impulses; the men who provoke these responses in two of the tales are of Indian blood. The conflict is least forceful in "The Woman Who Rode Away" (1925), because the protagonist makes no effort at resistance. The nameless woman seeks out her own annihilation at the hands of the Chilchui Indians. The tale, nominally set in northern Mexico, lacks not only the tension but also the profoundly divided view of Mexico which would characterize *The Plumed Serpent*. In its headlong progress to the sacrificial altar, the story seems almost designed to illustrate Lawrence's contention that "we can understand the consciousness of the Indian only in terms of the death of our consciousness." Dollie Urquhart, the heroine of "The Princess" (1925), remains permanently repressed, though the reader is made aware of her inner longings to be ravished by the Indian guide Romero. When the latter is killed at the end of the tale, Dolly desperately retreats into a shallow respectability, "not a little mad."

Only in *St. Mawr* (1925) is willfulness paradoxically *allied* to submission, as the American woman Lou Witt rejects all men but gives herself triumphantly to the dark spirit of place on her ranch in New Mexico. This novella may be read as a treatment in imaginative terms of the recently intensified negation of modern Europe which Lawrence had experienced on his return to England the previous winter.[18] Like Lawrence, Lou Witt rejects the "cardboard let's-be-happy world" of the hedonistic twenties, a world in which people's wills "were fixed like machines." The indomitable spirit of the wild stallion St. Mawr stimulates in Lou a desire to recover an "ancient understanding" that is lost forever in the likes of Rico Carrington, her emasculated husband. This she finds in the god Pan, who resides in the American landscape:

> "There's something else for me [Lou tells her mother]. There's something else even that loves me and wants me. I can't tell you what it is. It's a spirit. And it's here, on this ranch. It's here, in this landscape. It's something more real to me than men are, and it soothes me, and it holds me up. . . . It's something wild, that will hurt me sometimes, . . . I know it. But it's something big, bigger than men, bigger than people, bigger than religion. It's something to do with wild America. And it's something to do with me. It's a mission, if you like. . . . [It's] my mission to keep myself for the spirit that is wild, and has

waited so long here: even waited for such as me. Now
I've come! Now I'm here. Now I am where I want to be:
with the spirit that wants me."[19]

This malevolent "wild spirit"—which Lawrence could only
vaguely intuit in the Southwest—would assume a more palpable (if not a more comprehensible) form for him in Mexico.
He knew that sooner or later he would have to confront it
there.

## II

Between March 1923 and March 1925 Lawrence went three
times to Mexico. Altogether he spent about ten months in
that republic, as compared to over a year and a half spent in
New Mexico. Though he visited Mexico City several times,
stopping at an inexpensive hotel there a total of about nine
weeks on his various stays, Lawrence loathed the capital. For
him, as for his protagonist in *The Plumed Serpent*, Mexico
City "had an underlying ugliness, a sort of squalid evil" that
made one dread any contact with the inhabitants. Besides, it
did not seem to offer what both Lawrence and Kate Leslie
were seeking in Mexico: "Mexico meant the dark-faced men
in cotton clothes, big hats: the peasants, peons, pelados,
Indians, call them what you will. . . . Those pale-faced Mexicans of the Capital, politicians, artists, professionals, and
business people, they did not interest her."[20] Lawrence spent
most of his time in Mexico in the western and southeastern
provinces: Chapala on the first trip, the villages along the
northern part of the west coast on the second, and Oaxaca on
the third.

The first journey was undertaken between March 18 and
mid-July of 1923. Lawrence and his wife Frieda were joined
by the American poet Witter Bynner and Bynner's friend Wil-
lard Johnson. Bynner's memoir, *Journey With Genius* (1951),
is a primary source of information (though sometimes inac-

curate) and vivid first-hand impressions concerning Lawrence's initial encounter with Mexico. The book has undeniable shortcomings, chiefly deriving from Bynner's ulterior view of Lawrence as man and thinker and from the fact that it was largely written almost two decades after the fact (though Bynner does include letters and diary entries from 1923). Still, even though Bynner's picture of Lawrence verges at times on caricature, there is enough truth in it to make it worth considering in some detail, more particularly since many of Lawrence's basic impressions of Mexico took shape during his first visit.

Bynner and Johnson followed the Lawrences to Mexico City in March 1923 to find that Lawrence had secured lodging for them in the Hotel Monte Carlo. They were shocked to discover that by strange coincidence their room had previously been tenanted by a friend of the foursome, an Englishman named Wilfred Ewart; shocked, because it was on that same balcony to which the bellboy pointed with the pride of an eyewitness, that Ewart had been killed by a stray bullet during a wild fiesta in the street below. News of Ewart's fortuitous death a few months before had, in fact, elicited from Lawrence—before he had set foot in Mexico—the conviction that " 'it's an evil country down there.' "[21] In the weeks that followed their arrival, Lawrence read up on Mexican history and concluded peremptorily that it was " 'all of one piece . . . what the Aztecs did, what Cortes did, what [Porfirio] Diaz did—the wholesale, endless cruelty. The land itself does it to whoever lives here. . . . It's a land of death' " (Bynner, p. 40). Yet at this time Lawrence was writing to his old friend S. S. Koteliansky that he "liked" Mexico, appreciated its scarcity of "pretenses of any sort."[22]

Depending on when he is there and for how long, the non-Latin traveler visiting Mexico City for the first time encounters certain phenomena which defy immediate comprehension, so apparently alien are they to his own culture: the bullfights; the pyramids at nearby San Juan Teotihuacán, with their memorials to ritual human sacrifice; the peasant families crawling on bloodied knees to reach the shrine of the Virgin of Guadalupe, patron saint of Mexico; and that peculiar fiesta known as the Day of the Dead. Lawrence was not in the capital to see the celebration of the latter holiday, but he had heard about the gay pastries shaped like little human skulls hawked on streetcorners by the local children. Bynner recalls Lawrence telling him that in mocking death like this, the Mexicans are trying to " 'fight off the darkness with ridicule. There's no hope or happiness in it, no real gaiety, only a black, crude cynicism. They need a new religion; it's the only thing that can help them. Your Indians of Santa Fe have a live religion.... They are different'" (Bynner, p. 42). Thus, Lawrence was already beginning to sense another major distinction—which was to grow even more important later on—between Old and New Mexico. Bynner reports that Lawrence was also distressed by the sight of the ragged peasants lying abject before the Basilica of Guadalupe during Holy Week:

> "All this is unreal," he complained. "It's all done for the show.... One minute they're groveling in the churches. ...The next moment they're gadding in the streets, full of gaiety and pulque, as though they had never heard of Jesus.... They're not thinking of Christ at all," he grimaced, "except for a morbid pleasure in the fact that he was tortured and murdered. You know how they smear his image with blood. They're out for blood.... The Church is foreign here. They need their own [i.e., Indian] religion, which used to let them kill *ad lib*. That was it." (Bynner, pp. 46-47)

Such incredibly uncharitable remarks stemmed, in part, from the fact that Lawrence had not expected the Indians to be Christians at all, much less such demonstrative ones. Christianity was after all one of the mouldering pillars of the dying Old World that Lawrence thought he had left behind when he set out for America. He had counted on these Indians to "grin [their] peon grin behind the Cross," knowing the potency of their own gods. But all this groveling and gadding by turns did not fit into the picture. Things were not going as planned.

During those weeks in the capital the party visited the old Biblioteca Nacional, the "floating gardens" at Xochimilco, the dilapidated monasteries at San Agustín Acolman and El Desierto de los Leones, and the pre-Aztec pyramids at San Juan Teotihuacán. In the quadrangle of Quetzalcoatl at Teotihuacán, Lawrence stood for some time "looking and brooding," according to Bynner: "The colored stone heads of the feathered snakes in one of the temples were a match for him. The stone serpents and owls held something that he obviously feared" (Bynner, p. 24). Frieda Lawrence's account of the same incident, however, stresses her *own* fear at the "huge stone snake, coiling green with great turquoise eyes," rather than any fear apparent in her husband.[23] Bynner's recounting of the bullfight they attended on April 1, 1923 resembles the version which appears in the opening chapter of *The Plumed Serpent*. Both versions take note of the bloodlust of the "mob" in attendance; the merciless and "cowardly" taunting of the bull; the beast's successful leaps over the wooden barrier surrounding the bullring; the picador's decrepit horse disembowelled by the slashing horns; and the sudden rain. Reacting as much against the crowd as against the fight itself, Lawrence could not tolerate such a spectacle. Like Kate Leslie he left before the end of the first *corrida*, dutifully followed by Frieda. Though Bynner and Johnson were also "revolted," they stayed for the entire show, perceiving before the end some of the grace and precision in the technique of the better matadors. Bynner felt, not unjustly, that Lawrence had failed to give the event sufficient chance to demonstrate its worth, that he had reacted prematurely. In any case, this episode at the bullfight seemed to Bynner to have aggravated Lawrence's revulsion against Mexico.

In the following weeks they continued to travel about the provinces bordering east on the capital. During one nine-day jaunt they visited Cholula, Puebla, Atlixco, Tehuacán, and Orizaba. But Lawrence was dissatisfied. He was looking for a spot in which to settle and begin writing again, and wanted a place near water. Meanwhile Lawrence occupied himself reading up on Mexico and its past. He read, among others, such standards as Madame Calderón de la Barca, Prescott, Bernal Díaz, and some less obvious works such as Lewis Spence's *Gods of Mexico* (1923) and Zelia Nuttall's *Fundamental Principles of Old and New World Religions* (1901). Lawrence also sought out some leading Mexican artists and intellectuals.

His anticipated meeting with the educator-philosopher-politician José Vasconcelos misfired and resulted in a Lawrencian tirade against modern bureaucracy and socialism;[24] however, he did manage to make contact with Miguel Covarrubias and according to Bynner also met José Clemente Orozco and Diego Rivera. For Revolutionary art Lawrence had no great regard. Though the muralists were at least as concerned in their own way as was Lawrence in his with the oppressiveness of European values and the plight of the Indian, Lawrence found their work propagandistic and lacking in sympathy with the Indians as people rather than symbols. (Ironically enough, most of the Mexican painters were of Spanish or mixed blood, and many had gone to Europe to practice their craft during the most violent phase of the Revolution, returning to Mexico in the more hopeful 1920's. Their interest in the Revolution as epic myth with the Indian as chief protagonist, political dogma aside, was thus closer to Lawrence's than he could have realized.)

By early May, Lawrence had found the place "with water" that he was seeking. Leaving Frieda behind in the capital with Bynner and Johnson, he took the train west through the mountains to Guadalajara, and then proceeded by motorboat to the lakeside village of Chapala. This was the first spot in Mexico to which Lawrence took an immediate and intense liking. When the others joined him there he told them that they would " 'really like Chapala. Chapala is really Mexico. It is the place we have been waiting for' " (Bynner, p. 85). For the first time in the more than seven months since his arrival in America, Lawrence had found a location which enabled him to suspend his wanderlust long enough to do substantial writing—in less than eight weeks he wrote most of the first draft of a novel he called "Quetzalcoatl."

However, the time spent in Chapala was not entirely peaceful. Perhaps the very fact that to Lawrence Chapala seemed "really Mexico" precluded peacefulness. In any event it was here that Lawrence received his first extended exposure to Mexican village life, and more importantly, to the life of the Mexican Indian. Bynner contends that what "awed and fascinated and frightened Lawrence most of all in Mexico was the Indians' deep-rootedness in the reality of death" (p. 31). The sporadic threat of violence during those years of the Revolution did little to dispel Lawrence's fear. Luis Quintanilla, a Mexican diplomat and poet and an acquaintance of Lawrence in Mexico, was himself a supporter of the Revolution and particularly alert to the Englishman's hostile feelings toward his country's present situation. Quintanilla writes that Lawrence

> was fascinated by Mexico's colorful personality and, at the same time, frightened by the dramatic events of the Mexican Revolution. He simply could not stand violence, noise, and least of all death. And there was plenty of that during the Revolution that shook the social structure of Mexico. So, Mexico's beauty enchanted Lawrence, but the Mexican political situation horrified him to the point that he saw nothing but tragedy even in the Mexican landscape: its high mountains and snow-capped volcanoes.[25]

The growing aversions to certain elements of Mexican life—to its politics, its radical art, its dark-skinned inhabitants, and its landscape—were beginning to establish a pattern in Lawrence's mind. Though there are important differences among the kind and degree of the aversions involved—Lawrence was, for example, of two minds about the Indian—the link connecting the elements in the pattern is clearly fear of death and violence: the very qualities that Lawrence identified with the "spirit of place" in America. This fear, which became exacerbated because it was not fully acknowledged, colored all his responses to Mexico. He felt that it was useless, for instance, to try to be friends with the Indians because "'[they'll] never understand. You can see it in their eyes.

These people are volcanoes. The volcanoes all over the land are symbols of the people, who will erupt again as they have erupted before. What seems laughter in their eyes...isn't laughter. It's heat turning back into lava'" (Bynner, p. 95).

Now Lawrence had frequently experienced aversions before in his life. The class system, the war, the bodiless spiritualism and moral rigidity of Christianity, and the sterile incursions of modern science and technology had all prompted his vituperation at various times, but he was usually able to make artistic use of these aversions through the iconoclastic modes of satire and prophecy. Here, however, he was apparently so caught up in concocting a new faith and a new ritual based in part on Aztec lore that he was unable to give free reign to his profound intuitive hostilities toward Mexico. The visionary Mexico taking shape in his imagination and the real thing simply refused to be compatible. Lawrence's mistake was in thinking that they should be; I suspect that if he had been more honest with himself concerning his feelings and his motives he would not have been so unnerved by his disappointment that the objective Mexico did not live up to expectation. (There is something of a parallel here between Lawrence's disappointment and the letdown experienced by Malcolm Lowry when he returned to Mexico for his second visit, after having completed *Under the Volcano*. Lowry found that the country was neither as beautiful nor as terrifying as the locale rendered in his novel. Like Lawrence he was unwilling, in *Dark As the Grave Wherein My Friend Is Laid*, to reconcile himself to the disparity between the fictive and the quotidian.)

This conflict between Lawrence's abstract vision—formulated in part before his arrival in Mexico—and the inchoate fears provoked by his presence there helps to account for a series of outbursts and tirades which occurred in Chapala while Lawrence was at work on his Mexican novel. On several occasions Lawrence berated his uncomprehending Indian servants for combing their hair for lice in his presence. He criticized Bynner and Johnson for mixing with common bootblacks at the beach; later, when these young "orphans," as Bynner calls them, attempted to drum up some business in a cafe where Lawrence happened to be dining, he had them all arrested and thrown into jail as public nuisances. According to Bynner, Lawrence viewed all such examples of distasteful behavior on the part of the Indian peons as covert acts of defiance, as attempts to compensate for their longstanding servitude to the whites. Lawrence is even quoted by Bynner as suggesting that the Indians " 'need a Diaz and they know it. . . . [That] was the only kind of government they could ever understand or respect. . . . There must be command; there must be obedience. . . . These people are devils and always will be' " (Bynner, p. 102). This is one aspect of Lawrence's impatience with historical Mexico which finds its way into the visionary Mexico of *The Plumed Serpent*—the elitist, authoritarian emphasis of the Quetzalcoatl cult, so much at variance with the egalitarian rhetoric of the popular Revolution.[26]

Bynner reports that Lawrence was "haunted" by tales of violence circulating in Chapala during their stay: "A local butcher had recently suspected his wife of too much interest in a customer. When she entered the shop one morning she had found her husband absent but his rival's bloody severed head on the counter. Six months later the husband was back, suffering no harsher sentence than an order that he change his occupation. D. H. did not find this order amusing" (p. 181). Other rumors told of nocturnal raids by gangs of local bandits. One night Lawrence was awakened by what sounded like the breaking of glass and saw—or thought that he saw, for Bynner treats the whole incident as a whimsical projection of Lawrence's "neurotic" imagination—a dark hand reaching in to unlock the door. Thereafter an armed guard was posted outside to protect the house at night.[27]

These are chief among the many incidents Bynner uses as exhibits in his case against Lawrence and the latter's subsequent claim that in Mexico he had discovered "the lost trail" of a still vital, if latent, civilization capable of resurgence.

Whatever Lawrence might say about his abstract heroic Indians being the key to the future, Bynner, observing the
Englishman's withdrawal from contact with actual Indians,
accused Lawrence of "fitting [the Indians] into a prearranged
edifice" (p. 69). Admittedly there is good reason for finding
Bynner's depiction of Lawrence suspect. The two writers
were ideological antagonists who spent much of the time (in
L. D. Clark's apt phrase) "observing the universe through
[each] other's faults."[28] Since Bynner dwells on Lawrence's
tantrums and takes every opportunity to belittle his ideas,
the commentary is hardly objective. Moreover, the entire
picture is further complicated by Bynner's grudging admiration of Lawrence's genius. For in spite of the ideological
antagonism, Bynner could not help responding to Lawrence's
personal magnetism. Like so many others who spent any significant amount of time with Lawrence, Bynner admits to
finding him "too overpowering." "I was becoming aware," he
writes, "of a subtler influence [than Lawrence's fits of tem-
per].... Occasionally, in my writing, even in my speech, I
found...echoes of Lawrence's way of seeing and saying
things" (p. 148). Later he adds, "Something in me...resisted
Lawrence; I fell back on doctrinal statements...to support
that resistance. Something deeper in me, though, was being
drawn to him" (p. 179).

Nevertheless, despite Bynner's limitations as an observer
of Lawrence, his basic view of Lawrence's ambivalent response to Mexico, especially the sublimated dread of violence
and death, holds up. Others who knew Lawrence while he
was in Mexico—including the poet-diplomat Luis Quintanilla, quoted earlier—have testified to his essential fear of
the country. The American photographer Edward Weston,
for whom Lawrence sat for a series of portraits in Mexico
City, has written that Lawrence seemed to be in a "highly
neurotic state." To Weston it seemed that Lawrence had
formed "a wrong or one-sided impression of Mexico. Lawrence was bewildered, he was frightened, but he over-drama-
tized his fear [in The Plumed Serpent]." Weston recalls that

in Mexico City in 1926 the "artists and writers" were highly
amused by Lawrence's novel, which had appeared in that
year. Miguel Covarrubias drew a cartoon of Lawrence "at his
desk, writing, triple outlines around him to indicate shaking
with fear!"[29] The widely known specialist on Mexico, Carleton Beals, who saw Lawrence frequently during the first
Mexican trip and who was present at the Vasconcelos fiasco,
remembered Lawrence as follows:

> As for Mexico, Lawrence never understood it. At bot-
> tom he was terribly afraid of the country, always saw
> some secret menace in it. He was ever too frightened and
> neurotic really to examine the things that built up such a
> great fear in him; he could only . . . write a big, insoluble,
> mysterious "X," in a super-tourist fashion, over the
> Mexican Indian. The novelist is forever rushing past
> closed doors and conjuring up all sorts of horrible mys-
> tery and despair and danger lurking behind them. His
> neurotic character made it impossible for him to knock
> and perchance to discover. . . . What Lawrence did was
> to shoot the skyrockets of his morbid fancy over Mex-
> ico, and in the long glimmer of showering sparks he
> caught remarkable glimpses of the land, glimpses so
> strange, so fantastic and distorted, yet sometimes so
> grandiosely true as to make one wonder. . . .[30]

By the first week of July 1923 Lawrence set aside the rough
draft of his Mexican novel for a boat trip on Lake Chapala
followed by a visit to Guadalajara. On the ninth or tenth of
that month Lawrence left Bynner and Johnson behind as he
and Frieda made their way north to New York. Their original
plan to return together to Europe soon dissolved and in late
August they separated. Lawrence's second trip to Mexico,
which lasted just under two months (September 25 to
November 22, 1923), was on the whole the least eventful of
the three. The journey by train, car and horseback down the
west coast was arduous, slow, hot, dirty. Though he did
work, in his long-distance collaborative capacity, on the revi-

sion of Molly Skinner's *The Boy in the Bush*, he did not really
come to write this time; he had left the manuscript of his
Mexican novel behind in New York with his agent. His stated
purpose was to secure a site for the Rananim colony, but
actually he seemed less than eager to settle in Mexico, even
when he had the opportunity:

> On the whole, the west coast is a little *too* wild [he wrote
> to Knud Merrild from Navojóa, Sonora, in October]—
> nothing but wildness.... One wants a bit of hopeful-
> ness. These wild lost places seem so hopeless. But a man
> said he'd *give* me six or eight acres of land near Guay-
> mas, near the sea, in a very wild, very strange and beau-
> tiful country, if I'd only build a house on the place....
> But one feels so out of the world: like living on Mars. As
> if the human race wasn't real. —I don't know what effect
> it would have on one in the end. (*Letters*, II, 754)

That same day he wrote to Bynner that the northwest coastal
region was "much wilder, emptier, more hopeless than
Chapala. It makes one feel the door is shut on one." He went
on to describe the countryside—this is the locale of the opening scenes of "The Woman Who Rode Away"—in a manner
strikingly similar to some of Lowry's renderings of the serpentine path leading to the infernal *barranca* under the
volcano:

> There is a blazing sun, a vast hot sky, big lonely in-
> human green hills and mountains, a flat blazing *littoral*
> with a few palms, sometimes a dark blue sea which is
> not quite of this earth—then little towns that seem to be
> slipping down an abyss—and the door of life shut on it
> all, only the sun burning, the clouds of birds passing, the
> *zopilotes* [vultures] like flies, the lost lonely palm-trees,
> the deep dust of the roads, the donkeys moving in a
> gold-dust-cloud. In the mountains, lost, motionless
> silver-mines. Alamos, a once lovely little town, lost, and
> slipping down the gulf in the mountains.... —There
> seems a sentence of extinction written over it all. (*Let-
> ters*, II, 755-756)

From such a description it is clear that the pattern of associations formed during the initial trip, the pattern clustered around the ubiquitous fact of mortality, was still operative in Lawrence's mind. But he had by no means given free rein yet to his fear of Mexico. Near Tepic Lawrence dared attend another bullfight. He and his traveling companion, the Danish painter Kai Gótzsche, stayed until the end this time, watching as two of the bulls were killed.[31] Lawrence still clung to his original abstract position on Mexico, as is indicated by his letter to Middleton Murry from Guadalajara on October 25, 1923:

> . . . though England may lead the world again, as you say, she's got to find a way first. She's got to pick up a lost trail. And the end of the lost trail is here in Mexico. *Auqi* [sic] *está. Yo lo digo.*
>
> The Englishman, *per se,* is not enough. . . . He has to balance with something that is not himself. *Con esto que aquí está.*
>
> . . . You have to tie both ends together. England is only one end of the broken rope. *Hay otro.* . . . One hand in space is not enough. It needs the other hand from the opposite end of space, to clasp and form the bridge. The dark hand and the white.
>
> *Pero todavía no.* . . . *Todavía no alcanzan. No tocan. Se debe esperar.*
>
> "Learn to labour and to wait." (*Letters,* II, 759)

Despite these assertions in his letters, it seems apparent that Lawrence's mind was not really on Mexico during this second trip: he was too preoccupied by the absence of his wife. By the time he had reached Guadalajara, Lawrence was distraught. Gotzsche wrote to Knud Merrild that Lawrence was impossible to be with, that at such times he was "really insane." Though Lawrence repeatedly insisted that Frieda was miserable without him and would return to join him soon, it seemed to Gótzsche that Lawrence worried that Frieda was only too content to be with her children in Europe. "'I have sometimes the feeling [Gótzsche wrote on October 25, 1923] that he is afraid she will run away from him now, and he cannot bear to be alone.'"[32] Significantly, Lawrence and Gótzsche visited Chapala but stayed only one day this time. Gótzsche saw that Lawrence was "deeply moved" by the spot, for Lawrence "'had *willed himself into belief* that this was the place he loved, and the place to live'" (my emphasis); but Lawrence, feeling that Chapala had "'changed so much'" in the three and a half months since he and Frieda had departed from it together, could not bring himself to remain: "'Somehow it becomes unreal to me now,'" Lawrence told him. "'The life has changed somehow, has gone dead.'"[33] There can be little doubt that it was his personal troubles, which amounted to a potential marital crisis, that blunted Lawrence's responses to Mexico to the point that the whole trip seemed an anticlimax: "There, now I've tried Mexico again [Lawrence wrote to S. S. Koteliansky on October 22]. I was at Chapala for a day yesterday. The lake lovelier than before —very lovely: but somehow alien to me." But the feeling of anticlimax was false, and even Lawrence seemed to realize it. He goes on in the same letter to speak of "a sense of suspense, of waiting for something to happen—which something I want to avoid."[34] At this point, then, Lawrence was not seeking but avoiding the dark passage that lay ahead of him in Mexico. On November 22 he sailed from Veracruz for England to rejoin his wife.

Thus far Lawrence's contact with America had done little to ease the inner tensions which had driven him from England in the first place. But this fact was quickly obscured during his calamitous return to Europe that winter, obscured by the heavy clouds of turmoil and humiliation he found there which left him feeling more homeless than ever, so that America once again seemed to offer the answer. And back he came, along with Frieda and Dorothy Brett, the one friend to comply with his plea to come settle in America. Lawrence thought of going at once down to Mexico to resume work on his novel. But by this time they had acquired the ranch from Mrs. Luhan, and it was here they passed the summer and fall of 1924. As we have seen, he began to look at New Mexico and its vestiges of aboriginal religion with renewed enthusiasm. It was only a matter of time, however, before Mexico began to exert its influence on him once again.

Bynner feels that Lawrence's attitude toward Mexico had changed by this time: "He had by no means forgiven Mexico; but it had obviously become a magnet to his spirit. At least now it attracted him more than it repelled" (Bynner, p. 251). There is no evidence in the letters that Lawrence's basic feelings toward the country had shifted, but if he *was* drawn to Mexico it was a desperate attraction fated to final devastation during his decisive third voyage.

In late October the threesome took the train south to Mexico City, where they stayed again in the Hotel Monte Carlo for two weeks. And once again there was disturbing news of violence in Mexico involving a foreigner. This time the Lawrences learned from Mrs. Zelia Nuttall, an English anthropologist and acquaintance from their first trip, that her friend Rosalie Evans had been killed a few months earlier. (In fact Mrs. Evans, who had for six years defied Mexican law by defending her haciendas against repartition by the government, was something of a cause célèbre among the reactionary foreign element in Mexico both before and after her murder in ambush. Katherine Anne Porter, in a vivid sketch of her character, refers to Mrs. Evans as a "female conquistador."[35]) Whether this incident influenced Lawrence's views of the agrarian ideals professed by Revolutionary politicians of the time is not clear. However, in a letter in which he mentions the killing of Rosalie Evans, he speaks disparagingly of officialdom in the capital: ". . .they're all a bit of a fraud, with their self-seeking bolshevism. . . . I *really* feel cynical about these 'patriots' and 'socialists' down here. It's a mess" (*Letters*, II, 816). The terminology employed suggests that Lawrence associated Mexican Revolutionary politics with European political ideology—another reason for his antipathy toward it.

As on his first trip, Lawrence needed to find a place to

settle for a while so that he could work. This time he decided against Chapala in favor of Oaxaca, a smallish city in the southeastern region of the country. It was the year of a turbulent presidential succession marked by rebellions and reprisals, and the journey by train down to this remote area must have been rather harrowing. Dorothy Brett later recalled that ragged soldiers, heavily armed, rode on their train down from Mexico City. At each stop they could see more troops on the station platforms "grind[ing] long knives." "All the stations are pock-marked with bullets and there are ruined villages and houses everywhere. At every station, rows of silent men in clean white clothes sit along bits of broken walls, their faces in pools of dark shadow from their big hats. But the glinting eyes watch us unceasingly."[36]

Oaxaca today is a very pleasant city, sprawling in a kind of crescent shape around a little hill dominated by the gesticulating statue of Benito Juárez, the favorite son. It lies in a broad valley surrounded by squat brush-covered foothills, with tiers of bluish mountains receding into the distance. There are many fascinating archeological sites nearby (more turn up each year, it seems), the buried cities of the old Zapotecas and Mixtecas—and several good museums in town for less adventuresome visitors. The city of Oaxaca itself is attractive without being cloyingly picturesque: a city of tree-canopied little parks, with the inevitable monuments and oversize bandstands; gangs of children everywhere playing *fútbol*, even up on the hilltop; a sizable open market which is the hub of activity on Saturdays, with Indians from the surrounding villages trekking in with their loads of wares (of astonishing variety); many thick-walled, pale green-stoned, bubble-domed churches. On the whole it is a city with considerable character and charm—more, I should say, than Chapala, which has comparatively little interest apart from the marvelous lake. Oaxaca seems a quiet, rather low-keyed place which, after the frenetic pace and noise and excitement of the capital, induces a welcome indolence in many travelers.

But in 1924 Oaxaca was scarcely so benign. The rebellion

of Adolfo de la Huerta had sent shock-waves as far as Oaxaca, and Manuel García Vigil, the state governor and an opponent of then President Obregón, had been killed the year before. The foreign colony in town had been trapped there all during the trouble—anticipated more of the same— and were full of tales of woe to share with the newly arrived Lawrence party.[37] One can imagine the effect of such tales on Lawrence. Witter Bynner, for his part, believed that Lawrence made a mistake in electing to go to Oaxaca and thereby forgoing "the temperateness and relaxation he could have found in Chapala" (Bynner, p. 254). And Lawrence himself later regretted his decision. In June of 1925 he wrote to Idella Purnell, an old friend from Guadalajara days, "No more Oaxacas for me. I loved Chapala, Guadalajara, Jalisco, much the best: and I do wish we had come there again" (Bynner, p. 254). But at the time Lawrence was not looking for the "temperateness and relaxation" of Chapala. He told Dorothy Brett that he would have to rewrite his Mexican novel in order to make use of the more primitive and alien qualities of Oaxaca: " 'Chapala has not really the spirit of Mexico; it is too tamed, too touristy. This place is more untouched.' "[38] In a letter to Luis Quintanilla early that November he wrote that

> Oaxaca is a very quiet little town, with small but proud Indians—Zapotecas. The climate is perfect.... There are two rivers . . . with naked Indians soaping their heads in mid-stream.
> . . .The advantages of Chapala are, of course, the Lake, bathing and the short journey [from Mexico City]. But [Oaxaca] isn't touristy at all—quite, quite real, and lovely country around, where we can ride.
> . . .Chapala is much more a proper holiday resort.
> (*Letters*, II, 817)

For the purposes of his novel Lawrence had needed Chapala —with its frequent fiestas, its abandoned villas and hotels, its quaint church (Iglesia de la Parróquia) and especially the lake —as a symbolic setting.[39] Now he needed the foreboding

Indian presence and the sense of isolation which he found in Oaxaca. In mid-November the Lawrences secured a house from a local priest and Lawrence immediately began to work on the rewriting of his novel, still called "Quetzalcoatl."

Before long the old terrors, goaded by the stories heard from his new acquaintances, began to assert themselves in Oaxaca. Miss Brett describes a visit to the ruins at Mitla in terms which suggest how much she had already been influenced by Lawrence's attitudes toward Mexico and its indigenous past: "The guide takes us down to the sacrificial stone. ...[The] smell of blood...somehow permeates the whole ruin. It seems lifeless yet full of a dark, fierce life.... We are tired and a bit depressed. An excellent lunch in the little hotel cheers us up, but it is hard to shake off the feeling of blood and fierceness that the ruins give out."[40] Even if we make allowances for Miss Brett's characteristically hyperbolic manner, there can be no doubt as to the basis of such forebodings. This was clearly not the place, nor the time, that would permit the edgy, suspicious foreigner much ease. One day when she was alone in the market Miss Brett was struck violently in the side by a drunken Indian, for no apparent reason. Earlier someone had robbed her of her "precious Toby," her ear-trumpet; weeks later she walked in on another burglar in her hotel room.[41] She also reports that their strolls around the countryside were restricted and that for some time their mail was opened. When local officials learned that a famous foreigner was in their midst they made sure he was "taken care of." Thus Lawrence was wined and dined, taken on tours of government projects, permitted an interview with the state governor. But this kind of treatment scarcely abated the sense of isolation and oppression which had begun already to creep into their minds:

A strange feeling is coming over us [writes Miss Brett]: a dual feeling. One of imprisonment, and then another of a fierce desire to sally forth armed to the teeth and to shoot—to assert ourselves noisily in this noiseless unease. We can find no freedom, for ourselves or in anyone else. Everybody is virtually a prisoner. The Indians are afraid of the Mexicans [i.e., mestizos], the Mexicans are afraid of the Indians, and the [North] Americans are afraid of both.[42]

The same note of oppression, along with the fear of impending violence, is evident in Lawrence's letter of November 14 to William Hawk, a friend back in New Mexico:

> ...everywhere the government is very Labour—and somehow one doesn't feel [that it is] very solid. There are so many wild Indians who don't know anything about anything, except that they are told that every "rich" man is an enemy.—There may be a bad bust-up in Mexico City: and again, everything may go off quietly. But I don't like the feeling. If only it wasn't winter, we'd come back to the ranch tomorrow.
> ...Frieda of course pines for her ranch, and the freedom. So really do I. (*Letters*, II, 818-819)

To Murry, at about the same time, Lawrence wrote of Oaxaca that "everything is so shaky and really so confused. The Indians are queer little savages, and awful agitators pump bits of socialism over them and make everything just a mess. It's really a sort of chaos" (*Letters*, II, 819-820). Peace and freedom on the one hand, and on the other chaos, oppression, isolation, and bloodlust: the pattern was by now complete, the polarities which New Mexico and Mexico represented were immovably fixed in Lawrence's mind. The writings undertaken in Oaxaca would be his last attempt to hold the polarities together in a unified image of the New World of the soul.


III


By the year's end Lawrence began work on four travel pieces (later collected with four other pieces in *Mornings in Mexico* [1927]) in which by various means he tried to mollify his antipathy toward the Indian and his sense of being alienated from Mexico. The four essays are all set in Oaxaca and its environs during the week before Christmas. Their tone—and this is at first surprising when one considers Lawrence's frame of mind in Oaxaca and the fact that he was engrossed in the rewriting of his horrific Mexican novel during this same period—is generally idyllic.

In the first piece, "Corasmin and the Parrots," we find the author seated on a Friday morning at his writing desk in the garden patio of his "crumbly adobe house," observing the fresh sky, the budding flowers, the racket of the parrots in the trees overhead, the weary passivity of the dog Corasmin, and the domestic skills of his Indian *mozo*, Rosalino. All this seems to be mere backdrop as Lawrence launches into a fanciful analysis of the Aztec cosmogonic myth. The Aztecs, we are told, postulated that the earth developed in five stages called "Suns" during which successive orders of animal life emerged and dominated the land until their Sun "convulsed" and was superseded by the next phase. A few creatures of each dying Sun survived into the next Sun, which was dominated by a higher and more intelligent form of life. Thus the plants and insects of the First Sun were succeeded by the fish and reptiles of the Second, the fowls of the Third, the land animals of the Fourth, and by man of the Fifth. The Sixth Sun will bring a yet higher and more complex order of life, though some of the human races will survive.[43] Lawrence prefers this myth over the theory of evolution (which is "like a long string hooked on to a First Cause") because the former allows him a way to account for the great difference between the various orders of life, including the different races of man. Lawrence next proceeds to apply this myth to the creatures around him in the garden. There is a "dimensional gulf" between the dog and the parrots because they are of different Suns. The parrots cannot actually speak, but they reproduce sounds that are like the sounds they are imitating, only "a little more so." That "little more so" is what makes them so disturbing. They mock and caricature the sounds of a man calling the dog and of the dog yapping in response. This mimicry is the parrot's form of revenge for having lost earth-dominance to the dog and later to the creatures of the succeeding Suns. The dog Corasmin's only response to the racket of the parrots is a tired resignation. To Lawrence the dog's yellow eyes seem to say, " 'It's the other dimension. There's no help for it' " (*Mornings*, p. 8).

But Lawrence makes a far more telling application of the Sun myth to the dimensional gulf between himself and his Zapotec servant Rosalino. (Though Lawrence does not say so, presumably he feels there was a kind of "lesser Sun" which distinguished the human races hierarchically.) The black-eyed *mozo* is analogous to the parrots, Lawrence himself to the dog.

> Between us also is the gulf of the other dimension, and [Rosalino] wants to bridge it.... He knows it can't be done. So do I. Each of us knows the other knows.
>
> But he can imitate me, even more than life-like. As the parrot can him. And I have to laugh at his *me*.... With a grin, with a laugh we pay tribute to the other dimension. But Corasmin is wiser. In his clear, yellow eyes is the self-possession of full admission [of separateness]. (*Mornings*, p. 8)

In this opening sketch Lawrence has deftly introduced the central themes of the collection—the immense differentness between the Indian and white consciousnesses, the potential danger of a misguided attempt to compensate for the "gulf," and the possible ways to a kind of mutual recognition if not final communion between the different races. Though in this piece Lawrence has hardly begun to explore the full complexity of these problems, he does suggest that we may cope with the threatening gulf between ourselves and others and between the different aspects of our own consciousness by accepting the fact of differentness without trying simultaneously to exert our will over the other orders. By thus opening ourselves to the plenitude and continuous flux of all life we may transcend our narrow, fragmented consciousness and be in a position to move forward with the flow toward the next phase.

Probably the most provocative and useful analysis to date of *Mornings in Mexico* is that of Thomas R. Whitaker. Whitaker sees the book not as a loosely connected handful of essays but as a unified work which proceeds by dramatic rather than expository method: "[The] book's action appears in the gradually deepening insight of the [speaker] who is ostensibly the writer but who is really the main character."[44] As in Lawrence's best novels, *Mornings in Mexico*, and each sketch therein, proceeds by fits and starts, containing "a vacillating progression of attitudes" which circumvents the linear development of a logical sequence. Whitaker goes on to say that the ego of the "tourist-persona" "must descend to merge and accept what seems darkly inferior and destructive but is really its own unconscious life-source—projected upon a man, an animal, a people, or a landscape. If that acceptance occurs, if the marriage with the 'other' or the 'unconscious' is consummated, the closed and defensive ego may be transcended [and a] new self may step free...."[45]

The next two sketches, as Whitaker points out, are concerned with the "difficulty of abandoning the view that [the Indian] is but an inferior version of [the speaker], of admitting the Indian's valid 'otherness.'"[46] The persona gradually moves from a jeering resistance to a mood of sympathetic acceptance. In the first sketch the Lawrences, along with Rosalino, take a Sunday "Walk to Huayapa." The speaker is put out at the *mozo's* all-purpose answer to each of his questions ("*Como no, Señor*"), and he abruptly dismisses Rosalino as a "dumb-bell." As they approach the village, Lawrence is also estranged from the Mexican landscape. The sense of openness, hugeness, and human nothingness is overpowering. In the vast wilderness the village seems a mere spot, so "alone and, as it were, detached from the world in which it lies." He continues, "Nowhere more than in Mexico does human life become isolated, external to its surroundings, and cut off tinily from the environment. Even as you come across the plain to a big city . . . your heart gives a clutch, feeling the pathos, the isolated tininess of human effort . . . in this wilderness world" (*Mornings*, p. 11). In Huayapa (San Andrés Huayapan) at first no people are to be seen: "Everything hidden, secret, silent. A sense of darkness among the silent mango trees, a sense of lurking, of unwillingness. . . . The sense of nowhere is intense . . ." (*Mornings*, p. 15). When a group of men are finally discovered in the plaza, they "stir like white-clad insects" (p. 16). This group turns out to be a political gathering, with two men canvassing for votes for the upcoming election. Lawrence's separateness continues as he seizes upon this as an opportunity to jeer at what he considers to be a farcical example of local democracy in action:

> My dear fellow, this is when democracy becomes real fun. You vote for one red ring inside another red ring [a political emblem designed to assist the illiterate Indians in distinguishing one party from another] and you get a Julio Echegaray. You vote for a blue dot inside a blue ring, and you get a Socrate Ezequiel Tos. Heaven knows what you get for two little red circles on top of one another. . . . Suppose we vote, and try. There's all sorts in the lucky bag. (p. 17)

But as they walk on, looking for some fruit for lunch along the way, the tone gradually changes. Stopping to rest in the shade by an aqueduct, they spy a half-naked woman washing her clothes in Indian fashion upon a flat stone. Upstream two Indian men sit naked to the waist, "their brown-orange giving off a glow in the shadow . . . [their wet hair seeming] to steam blue-blackness" (p. 21). A congenial old woman stops to barter with them, and bestows some of her folk wisdom. Farther up the road Lawrence encounters another scantily-clad young Indian, and he muses upon "what beautiful, suave, rich skins these people have; a sort of richness of the flesh. It goes, perhaps, with the complete absence of what we call 'spirit'" (p. 22). The walk home is long and dusty and hot, but the speaker enjoys himself, for he is by now in sympathetic relation with the landscape and even with the Mexican concept of time (*"mañana es otro dia"*).

In "The Mozo" the speaker takes a closer look at Rosalino. In a larger sense, however, Lawrence is examining the mentality of the Mexican Indians in general, most of whom are *"mozos"* (servants) in one way or another to the whites. At the outset the speaker points out that Rosalino is in some ways an exception to the generic Indian mentality, and in other ways a fitting example of it. Abruptly he shifts away from Rosalino to this generic Indian, whom he viciously mocks. The Indian mentality finds its origin in the character of the gods and goddesses of the Aztec myths:

> The Aztec gods and goddesses are...an unlovely and unlovable lot. In their myths there is no grace or charm, no poetry. Only this perpetual grudge...one god grudging another, the gods grudging men their existence, and men grudging the animals. The goddess of love is a goddess of dirt and prostitution, a dirt-eater, a horror, without a touch of tenderness. If the god wants to make love to her, she has to sprawl down in front of him, blatant and accessible.
>
> And then, after all, when she conceives and brings forth, what is it she produces? What is the infant-god she tenderly bears?
>
> *          *          *          *
>
> ...It is the sacrificial knife with which the priest makes a gash in his victim's breast, before he tears out the heart, to hold it smoking to the sun. And the Sun, the Sun behind the sun, is supposed to suck the smoking heart greedily with insatiable appetite.
>
> *          *          *          *
>
> *Tarumm-tarah! Tarumm-tarah!* blow the trumpets. The child is born. Unto us a son is given. Bring him forth, lay him on a tender cushion.... Ah, *qué bonito!* Oh, what a nice, blackish, smooth, keen stone knife!
>
> And to this day, most of the Mexican Indian women

seem to bring forth stone knives. Look at them, these
sons of incomprehensible mothers, with their black eyes
like flints, and their stiff little bodies as taut and as keen
as knives of obsidian. Take care they don't rip you up.
(pp. 23-24)

This passage stands out in *Mornings* as an unparalleled example of Lawrence venting his mind of some of the anger, fear,
and downright perplexity which had been accumulating ever
since he had come to Mexico, and particularly during his
third trip. In its unqualified severity, its shrill mock-enthusi-
asm and its explicit repudiation of an entire culture, the passage exceeds everything else Lawrence wrote about Mexico,
even in *The Plumed Serpent*. He concludes this section of the
essay by admitting that usually "these people have no correspondence with one at all. To them a white man or white
woman is a sort of phenomenon; just as a monkey is a sort of
phenomenon; something to watch, and wonder at, and laugh
at, but not to be taken on one's own plane" (p. 24). Thus the
persona has conceded the fact of separateness and has given
some account for it.

The sense of release provided by the candid virulence of
the long passage quoted above proves to have been at least
partially ameliorative, for, as if to equalize matters, the
speaker next turns his attention toward the shortcomings of
the white mentality. To the Indian several of the "white monkey's" concerns are also utterly alien—the obsession with
time down to the minute (as opposed to *'mañana'*); with
space down to the exact number of kilometers (as opposed to
near, far and very far); and with money. In contrast the
Indian lives always in the present, the "eternal now," and by
the instincts and the "soul." The Indian isn't concerned about
abstract thought, but prefers to live each moment with an
immediacy which all but precludes reflection. He is uncon-
cerned with the past and the future as concepts to be
pondered. The "obsidian knife" in the Indian heart strips
from life all these peripheral concerns to "leave the moment,

stark and sharp and without consciousness.... The instant moment is for ever keen with a razor-edge of oblivion, like the knife of sacrifice" (p. 26). The persona, by thus juxtaposing the "two ways," is able to see the best and the worst of both, which is the first step toward transcending the two extremes and moving toward an implied ideal beyond "both the limited awareness here attributed to the Indian and the insane possessiveness of the white man."⁴⁷

The last part of this sketch shifts back to Rosalino, whose history is traced. He is an Indian by heritage, but of necessity he has had to learn the "white monkey's tricks." Eventually the speaker discloses that the *mozo's* extreme moodiness is the result of more than his resentment of his white masters. It seems that in the last revolution he had been conscripted by the army in the city and had refused to comply. He was badly beaten by the soldiers and left to die. But he had escaped to the hills, and ever since he had had a great fear of politicos and of revolutionary soldiers of whatever faction. The persona has finally discovered a real correspondence between himself and his *mozo*: "He is one of those, like myself, who have a horror of serving in a mass of men..." (p. 33). The sketch ends with the speaker openly sympathizing with Indians such as Rosalino: "Not to be *caught!* It must have been the prevailing motive of Indian-Mexico life since long before Montezuma marched his prisoners to sacrifice" (p. 35). Thus, as Whitaker says, "the emotional meaning of the sacrificial knife [has] been completely reversed. The tourist has brooded upon all that is most violent and repulsive in the alien culture, gradually finding common ground."⁴⁸

"Market Day," the fourth sketch, is a paean to the new mode of consciousness which the persona (if not Lawrence himself) has experienced by "seeing both ways." It is above all a religious piece, but unlike his rendering of Pueblo ceremonials in the New Mexican half of *Mornings*, the religion here is strictly inferential, excogitated. Lawrence's theme is the "centripetal flow" of life—in nature and in natural man, the Mexican Indian. The speaker's vehicle for dramatizing this theme is the ebbing and flowing of the masses of Indians from distant villages to Oaxaca on market day. Such people, we are told, are in tune with the elemental principle of life; they are living embodiments of the vitalist ideal, though of course it is the tourist-persona and not themselves who ascribes these values to their activities. The people do not come to town merely to barter their wares, but rather "to commingle." Market day is made up of moments of "contact, with a stranger, a perfect stranger. An intermingling of voices, a threading together of different wills. It is life. The centavos are an excuse" (p. 39). The speaker realizes that a fundamental problem of modern civilized man is that he resists the flow with his goal-oriented values and his linear patterns of thought and expression. But around Oaxaca

> Everything seems slowly to circle and hover towards a central point, the clouds, the mountains round the valley, the dust that rises, the big, beautiful, white-barred hawks...and even the snow-white flakes of flowers upon the dim *palo-blanco* tree....
> Strange that we should think in straight lines, when there are none, and talk of straight courses, when every course, sooner or later, is seen to be making the swoop round, swooping upon the centre.... If I have a way to go, it will be round the swoop of a bend impinging centripetal towards the centre. The straight course is hacked out in wounds, against the will of the world. (p. 36)

Himself at the market, the speaker also begins to respond to the flow of life. And as he partakes of the contact with these "perfect strangers" his former isolation seems to have been dispelled. Not even the disclosure that the *huaraches* for which he barters smell so strange because they have been tanned in human excrement—not even this repels him now: "Everything has its own smell, and the natural smell of huaraches is what it is. You might as well quarrel with an onion for smelling like an onion" (p. 41). There is in the following description a perceptible sense of reverential awe, for this has been an exquisite, a rare experience of true human communion:

It is fulfilled, what they came to market for. They have sold and bought. But more than that, they have had their moment of contact and centripetal flow. They have been part of a great stream of men flowing to a centre, to the vortex of the market-place....

There is no goal, and no abiding-place, and nothing is fixed....

Nothing but the touch, the spark of contact. That, no more. That, which is most elusive, still the only treasure. Come, and gone, and yet the clue itself.

*     *     *     *

Only that which is utterly intangible, matters. The contact, the spark of exchange. That which can never be fastened upon, for ever gone, for ever coming, never to be detained: the spark of contact. (p. 42)

This most elusive of mysteries is compared at the end of the piece with that of the evening star, which partakes of both night and day, moon and sun, yet remains itself. With this symbol, as with much of the thought contained in "Market Day" and the other sketches, Lawrence anticipates his far more ambitious attempt to convey this new mode of consciousness in *The Plumed Serpent*. Though they have considerable intrinsic interest, the four Mexican sketches may be viewed as a type of calisthenics which warmed Lawrence to the subject of his novel. In them he was working out an artistic strategy through which he could begin to come to terms with certain of his deepest fears. But with the exception of a single passage from "The Mozo," he had not yet put his methods—nor himself—to the full test.

It took Lawrence about twelve weeks to finish writing the final version of his Mexican novel. That same day in February when he put down his pen, he "went down, as if shot in the intestines" (*Letters*, II, 833). His illness was diagnosed as tuberculosis, though Lawrence insisted that it was "only" malaria. The combination of his severe illness and the extreme exhaustion attendant upon the completion of a massive creative effort turned him against Oaxaca. In a letter to

Dorothy Brett, who was already back in New Mexico, he voiced his suspicion that the town was infested by malaria-carrying mosquitoes from the nearby river. "I am still in bed," he continued, ". . . [but] hope to be up Sunday, and get away from Oaxaca next week. I hate the place—a let down. . . . But the novel is finished" (*Letters*, II, 831). The Lawrences left Oaxaca on February 24 for Mexico City.

After some difficulty crossing the American border, the Lawrences returned to their ranch in New Mexico by April 5, 1925. He had seen his last of Mexico, but this was not a fact he regretted. To a friend back in Mexico he confided, "I had, and have, a bad feeling about this Mexico of just now. Thank the Lord I am out of it." Later in the same letter of June 10 he continues, "But after all, I'd rather hunt the cow through the timber [at the ranch], though I swear myself black in the face, than try to 'push the business on' in Mexico. . . . [I] shall never forgive Mexico, especially Oaxaca, for having done me in. . . . —Yet my Quetzalcoatl novel lies nearer my heart than any other work of mine" (*Letters*, II, 843-844).

Those last five months on the ranch were comparatively quiet. During his convalescence Lawrence did some writing (*Reflections on the Death of a Porcupine* and *David*, a play), saw few people, traveled hardly at all. He saw it as a time in which "I am just gathering myself together, the last bits of me, as it were, straggling in from the long journey" (*Letters*, II, 835). As winter approached he began to think of returning again to Europe, but in the meantime he languished in the "quiet life" on the ranch: "I've never been down to Taos since we arrived: don't want to go. Am not very keen on seeing people: prefer to be alone on the ranch. That's the best of it, one can really be alone" (*Letters*, II, 847). Just as Mexico had played its turbulent part in Lawrence's inner drama, so now was New Mexico fulfilling its role as sedative. "I wish," he wrote to Amy Lowell, "I could eat all the lotus that ever budded, and drink up Lethe to the source. Talk about dull opiates—one wants something that'll go into the very soul." His publishers clamored for him to correct proofs for his

"Quetzalcoatl" novel, but "I daren't even look at the outside of the MS. It cost one so much . . ." (*Letters*, II, 833). And as for Mexico, he remembered it now with a kind of nausea: "It gave me a turn that time [in Oaxaca]: doubt if I shall ever come again. . . . I feel I never want to see an Indian or an 'aboriginee' or anything in the savage line again."[49]


## IV

Before we turn our attention in the next chapter to *The Plumed Serpent* (the title finally insisted upon by Lawrence's publishers) and to what it has to tell us about the ultimate meaning of Mexico for Lawrence, it is necessary to inquire: why Mexico? For one so abundantly endowed with penetrating vision, it had taken Lawrence a rather long time to prove, to his own satisfaction, what he had known from the beginning—that so far as he was concerned, "it's an evil country down there." Why, one wonders, did he continually return to a land which imperiled his health, his marriage, his state of mind; and why, moreover, did he feel he must set his "American novel" there?

In fact, his original intention in coming to America was to give New Mexico a try, and if he felt it suitable, to found a "new centre" there and proceed to write from that center. Mabel Dodge Luhan more than encouraged him in this plan, providing him with train fare and lodging, as well as her constant "guidance." As he wrote to S. S. Koteliansky soon after his arrival, she "wants me to *write* this country up. God knows if I shall" (*Letters*, II, 715). His hesitation is understandable, for Mrs. Luhan obviously had hopes that he would write *her* up also. At first Lawrence was willing. He and Mrs. Luhan met a few times so that he could gather information about her previous marriages, her supposed rejection of white culture and her relationship with Tony Luhan, a Pueblo Indian whom she eventually married. But Frieda, who never got on well with Mrs. Luhan, objected strongly and the plan was aborted.[50] A case can be made that Lawrence went ahead and used aspects of Mrs. Luhan and her experience in his subsequent fiction of the American period (though surely she could not have approved of the way he made use of her). But during the initial stay in New Mexico, the complications arising from the proximity of Mrs. Luhan and her coterie, the American "shove or be shoved" willfulness that Lawrence loathed, the spaciousness and vacuity of the landscape, the overemphasis on the outer life—all of these made it next to impossible for Lawrence to do any sustained writing. Subsequent to abandoning his projected novel based on Mrs. Luhan's life, he made no serious attempt at working on his "American novel" until he arrived at Chapala seven months later. At Chapala, despite the extreme moodiness already mentioned, Lawrence's creative urge returned with a vengeance. In just eight weeks he produced a nearly complete draft, some 400 pages in typescript, of his novel. Thereafter he continued to work on "Quetzalcoatl," his most ambitious project of the American period by far, only when he was in Mexico.

Lawrence intended to write about a religious upheaval which would result in a renewed awareness of the "spirit of place" of the American continent. There can be little doubt that he saw more evidence of a living religion in the ceremonials of the Pueblos than he ever found during his sojourns in Mexico. But other considerations made Mexico a more plausible locale for the kind of novel Lawrence was contemplating. For one, Mexico was at that time a land where upheavals were not only possible but almost commonplace. Furthermore, despite his almost total lack of sympathy for contemporary Mexican politics and for Revolutionary art, Lawrence perceived elements in the emerging mythos of the Revolution which suited his purposes: the resurgence of indigenism, the "re-conquest" of the land after four centuries of European dominance, and the attempt to cast the Church of Rome as the arch-villain in Mexican history. In contrast, in the United States, no conceivable leap of faith could bring one to believe

that the Pueblo Indians were in a position to stage a successful revolution. Lawrence recognized this as early as September of 1922, just weeks after his arrival in Taos. To his sister-
in-law Else Jaffe he wrote that "these Indians are up against a
dead wall, even more than we [whites] are: but a different
wall" (Letters, II, 721). Lawrence realized that Pueblo society
in America was "doomed" by education and eventual assimi-
lation into the majority culture.[51]

Another important reason behind Lawrence's decision to
transfer his American novel to Mexico was that the Pueblo
religious ceremonies, in themselves, did not encompass the
whole of what Lawrence felt to be America's "spirit of place."
In the words of L. D. Clark, Lawrence "had to get to the
Aztecs before he could shape his [final] understanding of
America, to their land and what was left of their spirit."[52]
Lawrence wrote to Mrs. Luhan during his second journey
that Mexico "is really a land of Indians: not merely a pueblo."
And again, "This is the Indian source: this Aztec and Maya"
(Letters, II, 761, 764). The Pueblos had a vitalistic religion
which made a deep impression on him. But they did not have
—as the Aztecs and other Mexican Indian cultures did—a
written history, which included a tradition involving "dark
gods" and ritual human sacrifice. As E. W. Tedlock, Jr., has
said of Lawrence's attraction to Aztec symbols and rituals,
"Here was a way to give his philosophy of the blood consciousness, once only intuited, a history and a sanction, a
hierarchy and a pantheon...."[53] The god Quetzalcoatl in
particular (though actually a pre-Aztec god) suited Lawrence's mythic design of the "dying and reviving gods," an
archetype underscored by his reading of The Golden Bough.
In Mexico furthermore "there was an abundance of astro-
nomically based symbolism of cosmic and human vitalistic
unity—evening star, morning star, the moon.... Besides
this there [were] the...handicrafts in the markets; the landscape's contrast of fecundity with arid waste; the mixture of
privilege and poverty; the emphasis on male pride; and the
omnipresent awareness of death...."[54]

Though Lawrence had to go almost 1,500 miles south of Taos to find the spot he was looking for at Chapala, and another 500 to arrive at Oaxaca, he did not travel light. He carried with him a weighty cargo of lore from the Pueblos. Mabel Dodge Luhan, for reasons of her own, was the first to charge Lawrence with "[having] to go to Mexico to write down what he [had absorbed] of Taos...."[55] Frank Waters, a novelist who specializes in fiction concerning the Southwest, finds the Pueblo of Taos "transported in its entirety" to the Sierra Madre home of an apocryphal tribe called the "Chilchuis" in "The Woman Who Rode Away." When we read *The Plumed Serpent*, says Waters, its evocation of prehistoric belief is so plausible that we "almost forget that all the Indian values come directly from New Mexico, from Taos, like everything Lawrence wrote of Mesoamerica. The dark, somber, serape-clad *Indios* have the magic of the Red Indians of the North. The drumbeats echo the rhythm of the Pueblo drums. And the dances are always the Round Dance or Friendship Dance, as danced by both whites and Indians in mixed gatherings in Taos."[56] One senior Lawrence scholar, Lawrence Clark Powell, goes so far as to call *The Plumed Serpent* a "Southwest classic."[57]

Those critics who are aware of Lawrence's attempt in *The Plumed Serpent* to blend his religious intuitions from New Mexico with his symbolic design located in Mexico have generally found that much was lost in the transmutation. Of these perhaps the most important and suggestive case is presented by Graham Hough in his study of Lawrence, *The Dark Sun*. Hough contends that serious artistic deficiencies result from Lawrence's persistence in seeing "the revelation of life received in New Mexico and the revelation of death in Old Mexico" as one.[58] Lawrence had always interpreted the various indigenous American cultures to be descendants of a monolithic antediluvian race, sharing the same religion which expressed their common understanding of their relation to America's "spirit of place." But on a deeper, more intuitive level, Lawrence's feelings toward the Pueblos were, as we have seen, quite different from his feelings toward Mexican Indians. The problem lies in the fact that Lawrence was apparently only half aware of his divided response to these two groups and the psychic terrains they inhabited; or, if he was consciously aware of it, he scarcely ever gave overt emphasis to the distinction in his writing. Hough suggests that Lawrence elected to graft his New Mexican onto his Old Mexican experience as a defensive measure, a distancing device. For Lawrence's confrontation with America was "perhaps the central revelation of his life," as Hough says. His intuitive response to the Pueblo religion was finally so positive that Hough is led to conclude that Lawrence may have felt in danger of being drawn across the dimensional gulf, of attempting to "return to the tribe," an enterprise he knew intellectually to be futile. So in order to avoid this disaster,

> Lawrence transfers the whole experience that had moved him so profoundly to Old Mexico, where in fact he had periodically been obliged to flee.... He lost a good deal by the transference. The beautiful immediacy of the New Mexico sketches is gone. He has to place his actual religious experience in a partly excogitated setting, to present it as a revival of a defunct Aztec religion whose pantheon is not particularly sympathetic to him and whose ritual he has to invent. But this is necessary.[59]

Up to a point, Hough's argument is sound. Lawrence's conscious, intellectual interest in the Aztecs was largely antiquarian, based on his readings in Indian history and mythology. The real Mexican Indians with whom he came into contact (with the exception of the *mozo*, Rosalino, in *Mornings in Mexico,* and even he was attractive chiefly as a symbol) he could not abide. And it is true that the vitalist religion which seemed so spontaneous and intuitive in the Southwest became, when superimposed onto the Mexico of *The Plumed Serpent,* forced and ultimately mechanical. And yet the transmutation *was* necessary: even crucial. Hough sees Lawrence's unconscious motivation to be his fear of accepting the ultimate consequences of his religion of the dark blood, his need to find a pretext for repudiating a people and a locale which he actually wished to embrace. What Hough does not seem to recognize, though, is that beneath Lawrence's abstract interest in the Aztecs lay a subliminal imperative which, emanating from his horror of violence and death, far transcended his attraction to the Pueblos. In short, Mexico was much more compelling as a symbol of psychic revolution.

In the last analysis, however—and only after the important distinctions have been recognized—one returns with new awareness to the fact that Lawrence's period of inner crisis involved the entirety of his American experience, in both Old and New Mexico. The complex of anxiety and dread which three times compelled him to come to Mexico also drove him back desperately to seek the balm of New Mexico. New Mexico may have been, as Lawrence later determined, the greatest experience from the outside world that he ever had. Perhaps, after all, New Mexico really was a place of fulfillment for Lawrence—or at least as close as he could ever come to finding a locale that embodied his religious ideals. However, the willed transference to Mexico was irrevocable, because only a part of Lawrence actually *wanted* to find anything like paradise. As a writer he required the stimulus of negations as well as ideals. A character in *Kangaroo*, for instance, justly accuses Somers/Lawrence of "[going] round the world looking for things you're not going to give in to."[60]

An essential part of Lawrence's aesthetic and of his approach to human behavior ever since the writing of *Women in Love* was his concentration upon the continuous flow of primal energy between opposite poles. Lawrence's imagination demanded a tension between hope and despair, affirmation and negation, thought and impulse, separateness and conciliation. The exploration of such opposites is precisely what enabled him to maintain that state of keen awareness from which he could penetrate the surface appearances of a place or of his characters in a particular place. (The dependence upon these oppositions as a creative stimulus and as a mode of perception dictated his use of the frontier experience and associated imagery in "Indians and an Englishman," "Au Revoir, U.S.A.," *The Plumed Serpent,* and "The Flying Fish.") Since New Mexico and Mexico offered him such a polarity—were indeed the sum and climax of all the polarities —Lawrence needed them both. Mexico, with its infernal and blood-soaked "dragon," was the galvanizing "centre" toward which he progressed, as he said, centripetally. However, this circuitous movement *toward* was too painful and exhaustive to be sustained for very long at a time. Lawrence had to resort to a compensatory centrifugal movement, to flight back to the ranch in New Mexico which, in the end, became a sanctuary, a locus of psychic regress, a return to the Garden. Without this refuge to turn to, Lawrence would sooner or later have been destroyed on the altar of his own apocalyptic imaginings. But without the stimulus provided him by that "evil country down there," prolonged existence on the mountain ranch would have amounted to an unending feast on lotus blossoms: a total submersion in the sweet scented waters of oblivion. In *The Plumed Serpent* Lawrence created out of his inner divisions a dualistic image, the infernal paradise, and identified it with Mexico. Such was the potency of that image, and the collaborative magnetism of the land itself, that it would be difficult for the novelists who followed him there (whatever they might think of Lawrence and his work) to escape its influence.

# III

# The Plumed Serpent:
# *Lawrence's Mexican Nightmare*

## I

The essential function of art is moral. Not aesthetic,
not decorative, not pastime and recreation. But moral.
The essential function of art is moral.
But a passionate, implicit morality, not didactic. A
morality which changes the blood, rather than the mind.
Changes the blood first. The mind follows later, in the
wake.

—*Studies in Classic American Literature*

"Oh no!" said Kate in front of the caricatures [de-
picted in the frescoes at the National University in Mexico City]. "They are too ugly. They defeat their own
ends."

"But they are meant to be ugly," said [the young Mexican painter] Garcia. "They must be ugly, no? Because
capitalism is ugly, and Mammon is ugly, and the priest
holding his hand to get the money from the poor Indians
is ugly. No?" . . .

"But," said Kate, "these caricatures are too intentional. They are like vulgar abuse, not art at all."

—*The Plumed Serpent*[1]

Lawrence's protagonist Kate Leslie wakes up on the morning
of her fortieth birthday with a profound sense of *volta*. Staring out at Popocatepetl and Ixtaccihuatl, the portentous twin
volcanoes, Kate wonders, *Why have I come to this high*

*plateau of death?* This question, in one form or another, becomes the novel's refrain, though as time passes a corollary question concerning Kate's future takes over: Will she leave Mexico and abandon all it represents or will she remain and submit?

One should always be wary of the easy and often misleading assumption that a character in a work of fiction "speaks for" or "represents" the author, not least when the character is female and the author male. It is reasonable enough to say that various elements in Kate's character were suggested by the two women whom Lawrence knew best while in America, Frieda Lawrence and Mabel Dodge Luhan. Kate is certainly not Lawrence himself, although on occasion her experiences and impressions of Mexico resemble his own. Nevertheless, in *The Plumed Serpent* Kate may be seen in large part to be acting out the role of a *potential* Lawrence, not unlike the tourist-persona of *Mornings in Mexico*—the Lawrence who might irrevocably have delivered himself over to the "dragon" of Mexico, which the man himself finally would not and could not do. By tracing to their end the elaborate modulations of that central strain, "To Stay or Not to Stay" (the title of Chapter IV), we should arrive at an understanding of the last and most important meaning of Lawrence's encounter with Mexico. "It was no good Kate's wondering why she had come [to Mexico]. Over in England, in Ireland, in Europe, she had heard the *consummatum est* of her own spirit. It was finished, in a kind of death agony. But still this heavy continent of dark-souled death was more than she could bear" (*The Plumed Serpent*, pp. 45-46).

So it seems to Kate on the morning of her birthday as she looks out upon the awesome landscape with its effect of "a ponderous, down-pressing weight upon the spirit: the great folds of the dragon of the Aztecs...winding around one and weighing down the soul. And on the bright sunshine was a dark stream of an angry, impotent blood, and the flowers seemed to have their roots in spilt blood. The spirit of place was cruel, down-dragging, destructive" (p. 45). Death lay behind her in Europe and before her in Mexico. Graham Hough has observed that it is characteristic of Kate to be "driven back and forth between two repulsions rather than drawn by contrary attractions."[2] Yet there is a difference, as Kate realizes later this same day, between the life-denying mechanism of modern Europe and the kind of death embodied for her in Mexico. This latter, or so at least Lawrence would have us believe, amounts to an annihilation of the European consciousness, the goal of which annihilation is the release of new life through the realization of a greater consciousness. Lawrence's own ambivalence toward Mexico keeps the tale of Kate's descent into darkness and subsequent rebirth from being as schematic as this description suggests,[3] but that thorny ambivalence is the essence of the vision of infernal paradise. Not long after Kate's reflections upon the stark and threatening landscape she reads a news article concerning the return of the old Aztec gods in the western village of Sayula (the fictional name for Chapala). Should she flee from the "cruel, down-dragging, destructive" spirit of Mexico, or should she remain and seek it out? After considering her dilemma Kate decides she wants to go to Sayula:

> She wanted to see the big lake where the gods had once lived, and whence they were due to emerge. Amid all the bitterness that Mexico produced in her spirit, there was still a strange beam of wonder and mystery....
>
> *     *     *     *
>
> Quetzalcoatl! Who knows what he meant to the dead Aztecs, and to the older Indians, who knew him before the Aztecs raised their deity to heights of horror and vindictiveness?
>
> All a confusion of contradictory gleams of meaning, Quetzalcoatl. But why not? Her Irish spirit was weary to death of definite meanings, and a God of one fixed purport. Gods should be iridescent, like the rainbow in the storm. Man creates a God in his own image, and the gods grow old along with the men that made them.... Gods die with men who have conceived them. But the

god-stuff roars eternally, like the sea, with too vast a
sound to be heard. . . . Ye must be born again. Even the
gods must be born again. We must be born again. (pp.
53-54)

The stages of Kate's reactions in these scenes from Chapter III
are similar to those of the persona toward the Mexican ambience in the sketches of *Mornings in Mexico*. From isolation
Kate moves to the sense of oppressiveness, the dread of violence, and then to a lingering curiosity, partial identification
and tentative acceptance. The only stage absent here is the
initial jeering at the "otherness" of the order of life existing
across the "dimensional gulf," of which Lawrence spoke in
"Corasmin and the Parrots."

In his full-length study of *The Plumed Serpent*, L. D. Clark
has observed that throughout the novel whenever Kate is on
the verge of self-awareness, she tends to retreat from further
contact with the source of mystery; she retreats either into a
state of willfulness or a state of fear and consequent isolation.
In both states her withdrawal from contact is temporary,
serving actually as a preparation for further exposure to the
source of new discovery. Kate's quest is presented as a recurring sequence of encounters with the mysterious *otherness* of
Mexico. Each cycle of confrontation and withdrawal brings
her closer to self-realization through submission. Lawrence
here anticipates the reliance upon cyclicity as a narrative
device and as a theme found in *Eyeless in Gaza*, *The Power
and the Glory*, and *Under the Volcano*. Like the other novelists his concern is with the permutations of consciousness and
of spirit. But Huxley, Greene, and Lowry all use cyclicity in a
manner that places greater emphasis on the role of the past
(near and remote, personal and societal) in shaping the
future. Lawrence, in trying to dramatize through Kate's vicissitudes the new mode of consciousness toward which she is
moving, focuses primarily on the "now" as a distinct departure from her pre-Mexico past. Clark points out that "Kate's
vacillation can take odd forms; it divides her response even

when she is close to identifying herself with the Indians and their country, or with Ramón and his mission, now and then leading her into opposition to a belief she otherwise professes." Clark also observes that Lawrence typically embodies both sides of her consciousness—her attraction and her repulsion toward Mexico—in the motif of heaviness or weight on the spirit, as in the descriptions of the dragon's folds beneath the landscape on the morning of Kate's birthday.[4]

Kate's progression toward acceptance of mystery is obviously intended to be taken as a paradigm of religious rebirth, expressed primarily in sexual terms. But the scenes in *The Plumed Serpent* which make the most powerful and lasting impression almost without exception treat of violence, with the unfortunate result that Kate's gradual embracing of the dark mystery of Quetzalcoatl degenerates in the reader's mind to an acceptance of bloodshed and cruelty. One understands, of course, that Lawrence's myth calls for a submission to the forces of darkness represented in the novel by violent acts, sexual and otherwise—the "annihilation" spoken of earlier—before rebirth may occur. However, the incidents of overt brutality are for the most part vividly imagined, while the purported rebirth at the end is merely asserted, by sundry means, tentatively and unconvincingly.

In the first chapter Kate, along with her American cousin Owen Rhys and his friend Bud Villiers, attends a bullfight in Mexico City on the Sunday after Easter. With the modern "will-to-happiness" they are prepared to enjoy a "gallant show," but before long Kate, who "really hates common people," is disgusted by the "degenerate mob" in attendance. The *corrida* itself is still more disturbing to Kate. The wounded bull at first puts up a valiant fight against the taunting, "cowardly" *picadores*, and the frenzied crowd cries out for spilt blood. The worst sight of all for Kate is the bull goring, time and again, a blindfolded horse (they wore no padding in those days) between the hind legs: "The shock almost overpowered her . . . . This she had paid to see. Human cowardice and beastliness, a smell of blood, a nauseous whiff of bursten

bowels!" (p. 10). Kate can stand no more. She runs out into
the exit tunnel, but it has begun to rain so she must wait
there: "She could not get out of her eyes the last picture of the
horse lying twisted on its neck with its hind-quarters hitched
up and the horn of the bull goring slowly and rhythmically in
its vitals. The horse so utterly passive and grotesque" (p. 14).
It is a ghastly episode, the psycho-sexual implications of
which for Kate are all too clear. Yet an immediate consequence of this event is that Kate meets for the first time, while
waiting for the rain to stop, General Cipriano Viedma, who
will play an important role in her religio-sexual transformation. They exchange cordial invitations for visits, but Kate is
relieved to escape the bullring and even "that nice man" with
"that heavy, black Mexican fatality about him, that put a
burden on her" (p. 18). Should she flee from this ominous
Mexican fatality, or should she submit to it? In this first volu-
tion of the cycle Kate decides to withdraw from further contact. But even as she retreats toward Sanborn's to drink her
tea, to eat a bit of strawberry shortcake, and to try to forget,
she cannot avoid "[feeling] again . . . that Mexico lay in her
destiny almost as a doom. Something so heavy, so oppres-
sive, like the folds of some huge serpent that seemed as if it
could hardly raise itself" (p. 18-19).

Here we have the initial instance of Lawrence's essential
ambivalence in *The Plumed Serpent*. It would seem clear that
through Kate, Lawrence is expressing his conscious revulsion
against the bullfight and other such secular purgations of the
traditional Mexican bloodlust. As he has his narrator remark
in Chapter III, once Mexico "had had an elaborate ritual of
death. Now it has death ragged, squalid, vulgar, without
even the passion of its own mystery" (p. 45). The loss of
meaningful ritual may be linked with the sterility of modern
social contact and politics evidenced at the tea party in Tlaco-
lula which Kate attends in Chapter II, and with the flatulence
of contemporary art that she witnesses when she goes to see
the frescoes at the University in Chapter III. All of these signs
of the stagnation of modern life are identified by Kate, on the

morning of her birthday, with the emptiness of her own past, which she intends to leave behind her when she moves to Sayula. Yet despite Kate's (and Lawrence's) conscious repudiation of the bullfight, the remainder of the novel has Kate moving, by fits and starts, toward an acceptance of the most disturbing implications of that bullfight.[5]

"To Stay or Not to Stay"—the question is like a great flashing neon sign towering above the path of Kate's vicissitudes in the succeeding chapters. Her cousin Owen is returning to the States in Chapter IV and asks her if she will go along. Kate is tempted, for she fears the "down-pulling" force of Mexico, but she decides to stay on in hopes of discovering a new source of life. In Chapter V she experiences a powerful response to the sight of Lake Sayula, of the bronze swimmer who announces that the lake belongs to the old gods, and of the fragment of an icon given her from the talismanic waters by her Indian boatman. But soon her negative reaction to the intimidating landscape around her hotel in Sayula is almost as strong: "already the silence was of vacuity, arrest, and cruelty: the uncanny empty unbearableness of many Mexican mornings. Already she was uneasy, suffering from the malaise which tortures one inwardly in that country of cactuses" (p. 93). In the next chapter the German hotelkeeper dismisses the cult of Quetzalcoatl—which she has stayed in Mexico to see—as a fraud, as a mere "front" for a national socialist party. Kate mulls this over but refuses to accept his estimate, for she is desperate to discover a source of "magic" in her life. She rents a house in the village of Sayula. Though the house itself is well protected (being enclosed, in the old Spanish style), and though she has a whole family of Indian servants there with her, Kate withdraws from all contact with the outside world when she learns of the nightly attacks by gangs of thieves (Chapter VIII). A few days later, however, we find Kate visiting at Jamiltepec, the villa of Don Ramón Carrasco, leader of the neo-Quetzalcoatl movement. The Indian general, Cipriano, is also there and that evening he suddenly proposes marriage to Kate. She is moved by the sense of yearning which emanates "from his physical heart," but she refuses. She then tells Don Ramón that although she enjoys looking at brown-skinned people, she is glad that she herself is white. Yet even as she says this, "she knew he [Ramón] was more beautiful to her than any blond white man, and that, in a remote, far-off way, the contact with him was more precious than any contact she had known" (p. 187). These subterranean currents of feeling for the two men are the "First Waters" which provide the title of this chapter (XII). In Chapter XIV Kate returns to her home in the village, depressed and contrary. The house seems empty and squalid, her servants disgust her. She feels a "terrible longing" for her home in Ireland: "She . . . smelt the smell of Mexico, come out in the hot sun after the rains: excrement, human and animal dried in the sun on a dry, dry earth. . . . [She] felt she could bear it no more: the vacuity, and the pressure: the horrible uncreate elementality, so uncouth, even sun and rain uncouth, uncouth" (pp. 217-218).

Even though Kate has not yet given her assent to Don Ramón's vitalist religion, her mind is already in constant flux between these extremes of acceptance and denial, staying or leaving. Geoffrey Firmin of *Under the Volcano* finds himself in similar straits, but Lowry uses his protagonist's dilemma to emphasize an essential isolation, an isolation that is permanent because it is willed. Thus the Consul is "always more or less" in his "sanctuary," the bathroom, walled off from basic contact with the world by an almost endless and convoluted solipsism. Kate's mind, no matter where she might be physically, is always in transit; it is the elemental quality of Mexican existence which heightens her varying states by seeming palpably to embody them. But her introspection, unlike the Consul's, invariably results in a further openness and vulnerability to outside influence. Like the tourist-persona of "Market Day," she mentally whirls "round the swoop of a bend impinging centripetal towards the centre."[6] Each revolution of the cycle impels her closer to the "centre" of true contact with the mystery of the other dimension.

Certain scenes dramatize Kate's sense of being in a kind of frontier or neutral zone between opposite poles. A good example is in Chapter VII where Kate goes to the village plaza and sees a group of Quetzalcoatl-worshipers forming a circle around a drum, chanting. "Kate was at once attracted and repelled. She was attracted, almost fascinated by the strange *nuclear* power of the men in the circle. It was like a darkly glowing, vivid nucleus of new life. Repellent the strange heaviness, the sinking of the spirit into the earth, like dark water" (p. 119). Though her initial response is a divided one, Kate somehow knows that "here and here alone...life burned with a deep new fire.... [Surely] this was a new kindling of mankind." Deep within herself Kate senses the kindling of the same "new fire," yet "she preferred to be *on the fringe*, sufficiently out of contact" (p. 119, my emphasis). In a scene which brings to mind Lawrence's own reactions to a circle of chanting Apaches in "Indians and an Englishman," Kate is momentarily situated on a frontier between the white and Indian consciousnesses. But for Kate even the border experience is a fleeting one; so concerned is Lawrence here with the flow of all life that he cannot be overly concerned with the benefits (or limitations) of "life on a border," a primary motif in the writing of Graham Greene. When the crowd in the plaza begins to join in the singing of Quetzalcoatl hymns, Kate responds inwardly but does not sing. However, "almost mesmerized," she does participate in the circle dance, choosing a dark-skinned stranger for her partner. For the time being she has crossed over the border and arrived in the polar region where she submits to the "living mystery," a step which Lawrence could not permit himself to take. Here Kate feels her personal desires subsumed "in the ocean of the one great desire," knowing for the first time the "clue" of contact with the greater self, "the quiet spark, like the dawn-star" (p. 128). But the moment the dance ends Kate hurries back to her home clinging to "her new secret, the strange secret of her greater womanhood..." (p. 129). Though this scene is perhaps the best pure example in *The*

*Plumed Serpent* of the experience of passage across a frontier (and back), there may be some justification for seeing all of the myriad instances of Kate's vacillation between accepting or rejecting Mexico collectively as a recurring frontier pattern.

Chapter XIX, "The Attack on Jamiltepec," is decisive for Kate. At the villa for a visit, Kate is present during the attempted assassination of Ramón generated by the Knights of Cortés, a Catholic organization (curiously prophetic of the so-called *cristeros,* who terrorized the countryside a few years after Lawrence's last stay in Mexico). Indeed, not only is she present, she actually participates in this veritable bloodbath. When Ramón is wounded Kate picks up a revolver and shoots one of the assassins. She watches, "spellbound," as Ramón recovers his strength sufficiently to dispatch an assailant "with short stabs in the throat, one, two, while blood shot out like a red projectile" (p. 293). When it is finally over, the toll is seven men killed. Thanks in part to Kate's efforts Ramón's life is saved, though his knife wound is serious and it takes him several days to recover. Alone back in her house in Sayula in Chapter XX Kate is "numbed"; her bonds with humanity have been broken; she longs only for peace, solitude, oblivion. But at her "very centre" she realizes that the flame of her "inmost soul" has been rekindled by Ramón—not least, one suspects, by his facility with a knife (recalling the Eros/Thanatos epiphany at the bullfight). When Cipriano calls on her one day and asks her to go with him back to Jamiltepec, she agrees. Riding with the general in a boat on the lake she suddenly notices his "undying Pan face" and recognizes in him the "bygone mystery of the twilit, primitive world." She feels herself succumbing to his "old dominant male" power, until she has "swooned prone beneath...the ancient phallic mystery" (p. 309). When Cipriano again asks her to marry him and become a goddess in the Quetzalcoatl pantheon, she finally accepts and they are married by the rites of the nascent religion.

L. D. Clark sees these two chapters as climactic so far as

Kate's quest is concerned. "Of all the estrangements and reconciliations that Kate undergoes in Mexico," says Clark, "this one is critical. Hereafter she is committed, whatever lingering doubts may remain with her." Though Kate refuses at first to agree to a civil ceremony, Clark points out that this is only because she is still "fond of her vestige of resistance."[7] When she is invited to attend the opening of the church of Quetzalcoatl, she goes to sit at Cipriano's feet during the ceremony. During "Huitzilopochtli's Night" (Chapter XXIII) she witnesses the ritual execution of the surviving assassins, coldly performed by Cipriano. Kate is "shocked and depressed" by the executions, and again she withdraws temporarily to the solitude of her house in the village. But when Cipriano appears a while later and asks her to return with him to the church, dressed in the green robes of the fertility goddess Malintzi, she again submits. That night, in the newly consecrated temple of Quetzalcoatl, they consummate their marriage. Afterwards Kate ponders the day's events:

> . . . when she remembered his stabbing the three helpless peons, she thought: Why should I judge him? He is of the gods. And when he comes to me he lays his pure, quick flame to mine, and every time I am a young girl again, and every time he takes the flower of my virginity, and I his. It leaves me insouciant like a young girl. What do I care if he kills people? His flame is young and clean. He is Huitzilopochtli, and I am Malintzi. (pp. 392-393)

The identification of Eros and Thanatos here becomes explicit and, what makes it harder to accept ethically, conscious.

Kate finally agrees to be legally married to Cipriano, but on the condition that he permit her to return home to Ireland for a while. She has decided that her life is changing too quickly, that she is not yet ready for the total submission of her individual will both to Cipriano and to the "greater will" of the gods. But Kate's reluctancies at the novel's end are mere spurious gestures toward her former contrary self. The question is no longer "To Stay or Not to Stay" but rather "To Stay or Not to Go." Yet her final acquiescence to remaining "Here!" (the title of the final chapter) is equivocal. Along with the purported benefits of her religio-sexual transfiguration, part of her reason for not returning to Ireland is surely negative, involving her horror at the prospect of becoming a middle-aged, lonely "grey-ribbed grimalkin" in Europe. But for some reason she needs to preserve the illusion that she is *compelled* to stay in Mexico. Thus, when Cipriano declares his love for her at the end she chooses to interpret his words as a kind of imperative: " 'You won't let me go!' " she says (p. 445).

Most critics are agreed that beginning with Chapter XIX ("Attack on Jamiltepec"), *The Plumed Serpent* begins to stretch the reader's credibility far beyond the bounds of fictional license. Kate's facility in reconciling herself to Cipriano after he performs the ritual murders is the nadir of the book, as Graham Hough has stated. The last third of the novel, Hough continues, amounts to "the degradation of the character of Kate—evident, inconsistent, yet unrecognized by Lawrence as a degradation. Kate, who was disgusted, horrified to the roots of her being by the bull-fight, is merely made 'gloomy and uneasy,' 'shocked and depressed' by the killings she has witnessed. She begins to see them as part of the will of God."[8] Despite the rhapsodic descriptions of sexual transport it seems clear that Kate's sensibilities have been dulled. In the last chapter there appears a brief aside which offers more evidence of the change that has taken place in her: "Kate could hardly remember now the dry rigid pallor of the heat, when the whole earth seemed to crepitate viciously with dry malevolence...." (p. 426); if Kate has nearly forgotten that almost palpable malevolence the reader has not, thanks to Lawrence's powerful evocations of the Mexican landscape earlier in the novel. Ultimately it is Kate's active involvement in the Quetzalcoatl movement which renders her incredible. To Hough the "excogitated ceremonial diverges farther and farther from...anything that Kate could reasonably be expected to participate in. . . . Kate as an interested observer of the Quetzalcoatl movement is probable and consistent. Kate as an active participant is simply not the same figure as we have learnt to know in the earlier part of the book."⁹

Kate's determination at the end "not to go" away from Mexico would be less questionable if the two men whom she believes to be responsible for her remaining were more sympathetic. The characterization of Cipriano is one index of Lawrence's inability to fathom the Mexican Indian. So uncomfortable is Lawrence with the alleged Indian-ness of Cipriano that he must give the general the polite social manners of the drawing room whenever Cipriano mingles with the elite set, as in the tea-party scene of Chapter II. For all his alleged dedication to the ideals of Don Ramón, and despite Lawrence's attempts to present him as an embodiment of the "undying Pan," Cipriano impresses one as the stereotypic Latin American *caudillo*, waiting impatiently for any opportunity to seize power by force. He remains a repulsive figure, a caricature as "strident" and "vulgar" as any of those in the Revolutionary frescoes scorned by both Lawrence and Kate.

The failure of Don Ramón is considerably more complex, and more engaging. For one thing, it is indeed ironic that Lawrence chose as his leader of the Indian revival, his "living Quetzalcoatl," a man of pure Spanish blood. Not only is Ramón of European heritage, he is a wealthy aristocrat and an intellectual educated in the North (at Columbia University). All of this, combined with the fact that Ramón bestows upon Kate the name of the supposed "fertility goddess" Malintzi, links the Quetzalcoatl movement of *The Plumed Serpent* with the Conquest of the Aztecs by the armies of Cortés rather than with the re-conquest that is the putative historical myth of both the novel and modern Mexico itself. Malintzi was the Nahuatl equivalent of the Spanish name Marina, and the Indian word was hispanicized later to Malinche. This woman was anything but an Aztec goddess: it was Malinche, a Nahua princess given as concubine and translator to Cortés, who conspired with the Spaniards in the overthrow of the indigenous Indian empires. In Mexican lore she is wryly termed the mother of the "new" Mexican race of mixed blood, her descendants known as *hijos de la chingada* (sons of the violated one).[10]

Like Kate, Ramón goes through a process of change whereby he gradually compromises his ideals—in his case compromise with political imperatives which involve the use of force and the spilling of blood. It is strange that such an important character as Ramón is developed so little in the first third of the novel. He appears briefly in a few early scenes, but for the most part he is a kind of *presence* vaguely associated with the mystery toward which Kate gravitates until she settles in Sayula and begins to make regular visits to the villa at Jamiltepec. Perhaps this is fitting, however, since the mystery is more compelling, for the reader at any rate, when it is not concentrated in the actions and words of a specific person, least of all a demagogue. It is not until Chapter XI, "Lords of the Day and Night," that we are allowed an extensive view of Ramón. Here Lawrence abruptly shifts his narrative viewpoint from Kate to Ramón. This unorthodox step is probably designed to establish the sincerity of a man whose pretensions would otherwise seem immediately suspect. Ramón is presented alone in his room at the villa, in the attitude of prayer and meditation, "[breaking] the cords of the world" in order to be "free in the other strength" (p. 168). After an hour he emerges to take a walk around his hacienda, benignly overseeing his laborers and artisans. Then, after changing into his Quetzalcoatl garb, he beats on a drum to announce an assembly of worshipers. Seven men, stripped to the waist, gather round him and enter a trance-like state, chanting and singing in unison. Ramón delivers a sermon full of recondite symbolism on the theme of the eternal "Now" of the snake. After the Song of the Morning and Evening Star is sung, Ramón exhorts his "lords of the day and night" to be masters not of men but *among* men. He tells them of the sacrament of oneness, of the true contact; and of the importance of neither taking nor receiving, of never assuming possession of any worldly thing, but only saying "it is with me." Thus, in this first direct glimpse at the leader of the nascent religion we find Ramón advocating that man is a steward, not a master, of this world.

On three different occasions Ramón disclaims any interest in politics or personal power. Always it is his general, Cipriano, who urges him to consider various plans by which, backed by Cipriano's army, Ramón might assume control of Mexico. In Chapter XII Ramón insists that he has no intention of becoming another Porfirio Díaz. Rather, Ramón is concerned with "the inside of the egg," with the soul and its rebirth, not with man's outer "shell." Cipriano, on the other hand, has dreams of world conquest: "'wouldn't it be good [he asks] to be a serpent, and be big enough to wrap one's folds round the globe of the world, and crush it like that egg?'" (p. 191). But Ramón knows that all such schemes are betrayed in the end. He feels that his people would betray him—that even his friend Cipriano, sooner or later, would betray him. In Chapter XXII Cipriano implores Ramón to grant him the authority to utilize military force so that the new religion may be spread, until it becomes established as the state religion of Mexico. Again Ramón resists, preferring to "wait awhile" and let Quetzalcoatlism "spread of itself" (p. 358). Meanwhile tension is building between the new cult and the Catholic Church. Though Ramón is determined to remain free of the "taint of politics," already he is being denounced in the churches as an antichrist. He fears that such resistance will force him to ally with the socialists, who are at present in control of the government (a clear allusion to Plutarco Elías Calles). Cipriano openly favors the alliance and endorses their undertaking a "Holy War" which would ultimately seek to make theirs the dominant religion in the world. But again (in Chapter XVII) Ramón disavows any concern with such a scheme. Though there is but one "God-Mystery," each nation, he feels, must have its own savior, its own myths, its own church.

Ramón believes that " 'God must come to Mexico in a blanket and in huaraches, else He is no God of the Mexicans, they cannot know Him' " (p. 359). He declares that he is "the living Quetzalcoatl," but the pronouncement is not to be understood as the delusion of a megalomaniac. For Ramón, it is rather a symbolic gesture. He tells Kate that

"Quetzalcoatl is to me only the symbol of the best a man may be, in the next days. The universe is a nest of dragons, with a perfectly unfathomable life-mystery at the centre of it. . . . I call the mystery the Morning Star. . . . [Man] is a creature who wins his own creation inch by inch from the nest of the cosmic dragons. Or else he loses it little by little, and goes to pieces." (p. 271)

One of the things which saves Ramon from the one-dimensionality and stridency of a character such as Cipriano is the fact that he has moments of personal weakness—of apprehension, fatigue, and disillusionment with his fellow cultists. I would concur with the judgment of John B. Vickery, who has found that Ramon "is no messiah with a mystique of his own perfection, slickly programming the next move and imperturbably grinding up the opposition. . . . [He] is constantly tempted to deny his people. . . . Preoccupied with his own quest and indifferent to their happiness and well-being, he confesses at times to detesting and despising the masses."[11]

But after the "Attack on Jamiltepec" the tenor of the novel rapidly changes, for Ramón no less than for Kate. The concocted ceremonials, the "written hymns of Quetzalcoatl," and the labored sermons appear with greater frequency. In the "Marriage by Quetzalcoatl" (Chapter XX), the ritual worship in the transformed church (Chapter XXI), and the deification of Cipriano in "The Living Huitzilopochtli" (Chapter XXII) the symbolism is increasingly garish and redundant. The nadir of Ramón's career as Mexico's savior and as a man is reached in the ritual executions of Chapter XXIII. Two prisoners, a man and a woman, are led out onto a platform above the chanting throng of worshipers. These two, former servants of Ramón who had conspired with the would-be assassins, are called "grey dogs" and traitors. Their necks are broken at Cipriano's command, their unblessed bodies cast into lime. Four more prisoners, the only survivors of the band of assailants, are "convicted" of being cowards (because of their surprise attack and because they outnumbered the forces protecting Jamiltepec). One of the four draws the green-tipped twig of Malintzi and is spared. The other three draw black twigs. Declaring that the "Lords of Life are the Masters of Death," Cipriano quickly "stabbed the blind-folded men to the heart, with three swift, heavy stabs" (p. 379). In his role as high priest, Rámon/Quetzalcoatl blesses the souls of the three victims for eventual renewal. In the church their spilt blood is ceremonially expiated.[12]

Several critics have mentioned the fact that these executions are not the mere barbarous excesses they appear to be; assassins are after all executed in most societies even today. But this is not really the point. So far as Ramón's original ideals are concerned, their purity and otherworldliness have been permanently lost. No amount of pseudo-ritualistic tom-foolery can compensate for *his* giving sanction—and "religious" sanction at that—to these brutal acts designed, in part, to reinforce his own power. Stewards among men have suddenly been transformed into the "Lords of Life" and the "Masters of Death." From here it is but a short step to the ascendancy of Cipriano's schemes for seizing power:

> ...a kind of war began. The Knights of Cortes brought out their famous hidden stores of arms...and a clerical mob headed by a fanatical priest surged into the Zócalo [in the capital]. Montes [the socialist president of Mexico] had the guns turned on them.... [It] looked like the beginnings of a religious war. In the streets the white and blue serapes of Quetzalcoatl and the scarlet and black serapes of Huitzilopochtli were seen in bands, marching to the sound of tom-toms....
>
> \*    \*    \*    \*
>
> Then Montes declared the old Church illegal in Mex-

ico, and caused a law to be passed, making the religion
of Quetzalcoatl the national religion of the Republic. All
the churches were closed. All the priests were compelled
to take an oath of allegiance to the Republic, or condemned to exile. The armies of Huitzilopochtli and the
white and blue serapes of Quetzalcoatl appeared in all
the towns and villages of the Republic. Ramón laboured
ceaselessly....
The whole country was thrilling with a new thing,
with a release of new energy. But there was a sense of
violence and crudity in it all, a touch of horror. (pp. 420-
421)

In the novel's last chapter Ramón is again relegated to the
periphery of our attention. The focus is on Kate's circuitous
movement toward the "decision" not to leave Mexico. The
relative absence of Ramón suggests that Lawrence could not
quite bring himself to explore the ultimate human consequences of the kind of compromise which Ramón has been
forced to make in order to establish the primacy of his "vitalist" religion. L. D. Clark has attempted to defend Lawrence's
religious design in *The Plumed Serpent* in part by interpreting
the absence of Ramón himself at the end as evidence of Quetzalcoatl's spiritual regeneration made manifest in nature and
man. Clark makes much of the fact that in the final chapter
the November rains fall, the dry earth comes to life, an ass
foals, and men are observed loading a cow and a bull onto a
boat: "The bond of sympathy between man and beast...
stands in contrast to the violating rites of the bull fight: the
Mithraic splendour has returned."[13] The meteorological and
zoological observations here are accurate, but it is difficult to
dispel the conviction that, despite his presumed conscious
intention, Lawrence has used elaborate means to *embrace* the
terrible revelation of the bullfight.

A number of readers have been quite impressed by the involved system of symbols interwoven throughout the book:
Lake Sayula, the Morning and Evening Star, the bird (*quetzal*) and the serpent (*coatl*), the sky and the earth, female and

male, the dark blood, the circular dances and the bullring, the dying and reborn gods, and many others. In his laudatory introduction to the Knopf edition of the novel William York Tindall has termed *The Plumed Serpent* "a great metaphor for a feeling about reality" (p. xiv). The novel must be judged, says Tindall, less on the merits of its characters than for its intricate pattern of symbols and images which embody the theme of rebirth on the sexual, religious, and political levels. "More like a tapestry or a painted window than like the novels we are used to, it triumphs by arrangements of shape and color. Not people but functions, the characters exist like figures in the carpet only by relationship with other parts of the great design" (p. ix). Kenneth Rexroth has described the novel as "a book of ritual, of the possible that would never be, of potentialities that would never emerge. It is a book of ceremonial prophecy, but prophecy uttered in the foreknowledge it would never be fulfilled." The presentation of the religion of Quetzalcoatl, Rexroth continues, is meaningful primarily for Lawrence himself, as an expression of his personal religion.[14] Katherine Anne Porter, whose extensive knowledge of Mexico lends additional weight to her views, sees the novel from a similar perspective, but she is somewhat more severe in her assessment: "Mexico, the Indians, the cult of the Aztec god Quetzalcoatl...all these are pretexts, symbols made to the measure of [Lawrence's] preoccupations."[15] Most incisive of all perhaps is Harry T. Moore, whose mixed reaction to the book does not prevent his discerning the fallacy of looking for pattern alone. Calling the book a "tremendous volcano of a failure," Moore sees it as "somewhat like an opera with magnificent music and a ridiculous libretto."[16]

Of course, whether Lawrence's religion strikes us as "ridiculous" is not a question of first importance. Like Dante or Milton or Yeats or any other artist he has the right to discover or to formulate whatever system of beliefs he chooses, as well as the right to make use of that system in his art. What matters is how convincingly he conveys his vision in producing a meaningful imaginative experience. In Lawrence's case we know that in his novels he was primarily concerned with the spontaneous and unlimited release of the lifeflow, rather than with static systems that identified or analyzed or categorized that flow. But in *The Plumed Serpent*, as Graham Hough has said, Lawrence "falls into just the sort of conscious systematising that he condemns. This is one of the cases where something that is not yet clear and articulate, perhaps could never be, is forced to explicitness by Lawrence, regardless of the cost."[17] This is an extremely perceptive remark, and it goes right to the core of the problem. *Why* did Lawrence force his intuitive apprehension of mystery into explicitness? He certainly knew better. In *Kangaroo*, for example, R. L. Somers disdains in the Australians a quality he calls "the visual travesty," that is, the need to verify the existence of inchoate phenomena (such as the "dark gods of the bush") by empirical means. Accused by a native of being a negativist, Somers replies:

> "But I'll give in to the Lord Almighty, which is more than you'll do—"
> "Oh, well, now—we'd give in to Him if we saw Him," said Jaz....
> "All right. Well, I prefer not to see, and yet to give in," said [Somers].[18]

This is the perspective which gets buried in the grandiose rhetoric of the last third of *The Plumed Serpent*. Not that *Kangaroo* is the better novel; but in it Lawrence is more successful in making the "dark gods" an engaging, *felt* presence both in the landscape and the consciousness of the protagonist.

Lawrence resorted to a stultifying metaphysic in *The Plumed Serpent* for the same fundamental reason that he grafted his intuitive impressions of the Pueblo religion onto his abstract and horrific interpretation of that "evil country," Mexico. In combining the two into an elaborate system Law-

rence compelled a personal resolution of the tensions that
had provided his imaginative stimulus—and his private
nightmare—since about 1915. This resolution does not fully
make its way into the novel itself; the infernal paradise
remains as ambivalent as ever—the paradisal elements irrevocably askew, like a remake of *Fantasia* directed by Federico
Fellini—a primary symbol, to be refined by Lawrence's suc-
cessors in Mexico. But the arduous process of writing *The
Plumed Serpent* was psychologically a critical experience,
one which proved to be a kind of purgation of Lawrence's
inner demons. Lawrence seems to have gained a partial recognition of this in later years. In an often-quoted letter to
Witter Bynner from Italy in 1928, he wrote:

> ...about *The Plumed Serpent* and the "hero." On the
> whole, I think you're right. The hero is obsolete, and the
> leader of men is a back number. After all, at the back of
> the hero is the militant ideal: and the militant ideal, or
> the ideal militant, seems to me also a cold egg. We're
> sort of sick of all forms of militarism and militantism.
> ...On the whole I agree with you, the leader-cum-fol-
> lower relationship is a bore. And the new relationship
> will be some sort of tenderness, sensitive, between men
> and men and men and women, and not the one up one
> down, lead on I follow, *ich dien* sort of business.[19]

Ramón's accommodation of violence and Kate's final determination not to leave Mexico may have resulted in their degradation as fictional characters and in the artistic ruination of
*The Plumed Serpent*. But precisely because of their self-
effacement in favor of the dark blood, Lawrence was able to
free himself from the strangle-hold which "his" America had
assumed over his own consciousness. A brief account of
some of Lawrence's post-Mexico writings—most notably
"The Flying Fish"—offers further evidence that in willing into
existence the Mexican nightmare that was *The Plumed Serpent*, Lawrence had exorcised his deepest fears associated
with the malevolent spirit of place in America.

II

Just as in *St. Mawr* Lawrence re-created in imaginative terms his intensified loathing for Europe and his hopeful return to America after the catastrophic winter visit of 1923-24, so in the fragment called "The Flying Fish" we find him presenting his renewed hopes for Europe after his American crisis. The fragment was begun during Lawrence's illness in Oaxaca. He dictated it to his wife as they made their way north to the Mexican border. Lawrence had planned to deal eventually with "regenerate man, [living] a real life in this Garden of Eden"—a statement which leads one to believe that Lawrence, with the nightmare of Mexico and *The Plumed Serpent* behind him, was prepared to envision a more beatific paradise in this work. But as he later commented to curious friends, the fragment was written " 'so near the borderline of death' " that he could never quite " 'carry it through in the cold light of day.' "[20] One can only regret that Lawrence was not able to return to this intriguing piece. Even as he left it, however, "The Flying Fish" is a work which is worth consideration here for its illuminating portrayal of a man emerging from the "cruel, down-dragging, destructive" atmosphere of Mexico.

Gethin Day, a forty-year-old Englishman visiting southern Mexico to study its peculiar vegetation, returns to his hotel one hot October evening to find a cablegram summoning him back to England: " 'Come home else no Day in Daybrook.' "[21] Daybrook is his family's Tudor home situated in the Midlands. It had been built by Sir Gilbert Day, who had also written the mystical *Book of Days*, a beautifully bound volume treasured by the family. While Gethin Day has been wandering around the world, his older sister Lydia has been the sole "Day in Daybrook." The arrival of the summons indicates that Lydia is either dead or dying. For the moment, however, Gethin is unable to think of returning to England, for he is feverish from malaria and must take to his bed.

Gethin's travels had been rather aimless until he arrived in

Mexico. Here he had discovered "something in the hard, fierce, finite sun of Mexico, in the dry terrible land, and in the black staring eyes of the suspicious natives"—something which had transformed his life (*Phoenix*, p. 782). In this Mexican ambience Day had perceived the unreality of the "common day" (the mundane outlook of the white consciousness) and the fierce vitality of the "Greater Day" (the Indian "dark blood-consciousness"). And this broadened viewpoint had enriched his life, had made him aware of the "dark Sun" pulsating behind and through the ordinary sun. But now Gethin Day is weary of Mexico, depressed by the expressionless black eyes of its Indians and the "lethargy, the ennui, the pathos . . . of an exhausted race" (p. 780). In fact, summons or no, Day is ready mentally if not physically to return to England:

> He wanted to go home. He didn't care now whether England was tight and little and over-crowded and far too full of furniture. He no longer minded the curious quiet atmosphere of Daybrook in which he had felt he would stifle as a young man. He no longer resented the weight of family tradition. . . . Now [that] . . . the uncommon day [had shown] him its immensity, he felt that home was the place. . . . He wanted to go home, away from these big wild countries where men were dying back to the Greater Day, home where [now] he dare face the sun behind the sun, and come into his own in the Greater Day. (p. 783)

At the end of November he is finally well enough to ride the train east to Veracruz for his voyage home. Veracruz seems to Gethin Day a vacant neutral zone, a "point where the wild primeval day of this continent met the busy white man's day, and the two annulled one another. The result was a port of nullity, nihilism concrete and actual, calling itself the city of the True Cross" (p. 790). This is one of Lawrence's most effective and revealing uses of the "border" image, conveying the sense of arrest and mutual annihilation at the "cross" between the dark consciousness and the white. The "port of nullity" is correlative to Gethin Day's mental state during the brief hiatus between his experience of Mexico and his return home to Europe, and between his near-death and his recovery.

He boards the ship and the next morning sails "away from the hot shores" into the Gulf of Mexico. During the passage through the Gulf to the Atlantic, Day spends most of his time alone staring off from the bowsprit at the sun, the clouds, the water, the dolphins and flying fish. In all of these he observes the "jewel-pure eternity" of the Greater Day. (The kind of rebirth suggested by such a phrase and by the objects that Day ponders on the sea voyage was bound to have been a less disquietingly ambivalent one than that induced by ritual violence and the cult of Quetzalcoatl.) There is a period of stormy weather, seasickness, and much sleep when the ship enters the rough gray Atlantic. But on the third evening a refreshing rain begins to fall and they start to pass out of the turbulence. On this hopeful note the story abruptly breaks off. With its depiction of a man turning away from the inimical atmosphere of tropical Mexico toward the incipient calm and the "common day" of home, "The Flying Fish" offers a pivotal expression of Lawrence's liberation from the psychic tensions of the American period. The fragment "reveals a surprising surge of joy in Lawrence, in spite of his illness," as David Cavitch puts it. By the "end" of the tale Lawrence "appears relieved of bitterness, liberated from dread, happily independent of the outer world, and pleased with his own soul. . . . A sense of relief and a spirit of celebration characterize the whole tone of the fragment. . . . [It] is the outpouring of lyricism during . . . [a rare] moment of self-acceptance —achieved, perhaps tragically, at whatever cost."[22]

Like Gethin Day, Lawrence was ready to leave America and give "home" another try. "It's a pity, really, to leave the peaceful ranch, and the horses, and the sun," he wrote to a neighbor back in New Mexico. "But there, one's native land has a sort of hopeless attraction, when one is away" (*Letters*,

II, 857-858). The Lawrences sailed for England on October 22, 1925 after almost three years spent on the American continent. Though after "The Flying Fish" Lawrence turned again to using England as the locale of his fiction, he could not bear to remain there himself. Winter was coming, and after a week of visiting his sisters in the Midlands, two weeks in London, and about two weeks in Germany with Frieda's family, the Lawrences followed the sun south. "There is something I like very much about the Mediterranean," he wrote to Dorothy Brett from Spotorno; "it relaxes one, after the tension of America" (*Letters*, II, 868). To S. S. Koteliansky, a partner in the original formulation of the paradisal dream back in 1915, he wrote the next January: "I think on the whole I like the Mediterranean countries best to live in. The ranch still doesn't attract me, though sometimes in my sleep I hear the Indians drumming and singing. I still wish my old wish . . . [but that] Rananim of ours, it has sunk out of sight" (*Letters*, II, 876).

In "Europe *v.* America," a short essay written in early 1926, Lawrence says that he has decided the chief difference between the people of the two continents is that the Western civilization existing in America is much more tense than that in Europe. The Americans take themselves and their role in the world more seriously, to the point that they are unable to slacken their grip on themselves for fear that the world would collapse as a result. With the Europeans, on the other hand, "there is still, at the bottom, the old, young insouciance. It isn't that [they] *don't care:* it is merely that, at the bottom of them there *isn't* care. Instead there is a sort of bubbling-in of life" (*Phoenix*, pp. 117-118).[23] Having discovered the virtues of "insouciance" and of "tenderness" in the relations between men and women, Lawrence was prepared to turn away from the burdensome problem of finding mankind's spiritual salvation through probing the "dark blood-consciousness" of primitive peoples. The writings of the period 1922-25 may be seen as a kind of collective apotheosis of Lawrence's dependence upon place to embody his own "quests." By the time he wrote *Lady Chatterly's Lover*—a novel which reads as though its author had never set foot in America—the function of place had changed and become less central to his thematic concerns. As for his own restless wanderings about the world, Lawrence was now able to see them for what, in large part, they were—an illusion. "I've been a fool myself, saying: Europe is finished for me. It wasn't Europe at all, it was myself, keeping a strangle-hold on myself. And that stranglehold I carried over to America..." (*Phoenix*, p. 118). But even if there were no such continent as America, Lawrence would have invented one: which, in a sense, is what he did anyway.

# IV

# Mexico as Scapegoat: Huxley, Lawrence, and Beyond the Mexique Bay

The prose of the advertising folder describing a Caribbean winter cruise was staggeringly banal, but its message was somehow portentous: "'follow the old *conquistadores* into the glamorous romance of the Spanish Main...[and] feel your Nordic Personality melt and expand....'"[1] When Aldous Huxley and his wife Maria set off aboard H.M.S. *Britannic* in January of 1933, bound for the West Indies, Central America, and Mexico, he was sufficiently armed with the intellectual's weaponry of irony and skepticism to scoff at this warning in disguise. He had for some time been aware, like D. H. Lawrence before him, that for the Northern European, direct, prolonged exposure to a tropical environment could be a disquieting experience. In his essay "Wordsworth in the Tropics" (1929), Huxley had observed that the romantic "who exports [his] pantheistic worship of Nature to the tropics is liable to have his religious convictions somewhat rudely disturbed. Nature, under a vertical sun, and nourished by the equatorial rains, is not at all like that chaste, mild deity who presides over...the cozy sublimities of the Lake District."[2] Huxley's own earlier travels to India, Burma, and Malaya demonstrated to him that though the tropical ambience is fantastically beautiful, "it is also terrifying, it is also profoundly sinister. There is something in...great forests...

105

which is foreign, appalling, fundamentally and utterly inimical to intruding man. The life of those vast masses of swarming vegetation is alien to the human spirit and hostile to it."[3] But while Huxley was intellectually prepared to disbelieve the advertising brochure's hyperbolic claims about the "glamorous romance of the Spanish Main," he was demonstrably ill-equipped at this time to accept or understand the spiritual travail he would begin to experience during his journey through Central America, and especially Mexico.

I

Huxley's account of this trip appears in *Beyond the Mexique Bay: A Traveller's Journal* (1934). Since this book consists primarily of its author's reflections—sometimes presented in full-scale essays—inspired by the scenes observed on his trip, it will be convenient to approach it thematically rather than as a sequential narrative of events. In order better to determine what Mexico meant to Huxley during his visit we may begin by observing the differences between his impressions of that country and those of the other places described in *Mexique Bay*. The first forty pages sketch his brief visits to Barbados, Trinidad, Venezuela, Panama, Jamaica, and British Honduras. These pages consist in the main of effusions of high spirits, gentle ironies, harmless amusements, and generally innocuous musings on local dress, entertainment, and economics. There is one brief scene in which the sight of two native women performing domestic tasks disturbs him with a "quality of extraordinary alienness and unfamiliarity, of being immeasurably remote" (p. 13), but this temporary sense of estrangement—an adumbration of more serious and troubling such moments to come—is no more at this point than a single dissonant note in a chorus of approbation.

By far the most sizable portion of the book is devoted to Huxley's impressions of Guatemala. This section is much more carefully written, more serious and thoughtful, than the chapters preceding it and the section on Mexico with which the book concludes. An encounter with an Indian border guard who makes a special point of examining and reexamining the Huxleys' papers elicits a tolerant and compassionate reflection on the unfortunate necessity of overcompensation among underdeveloped nations and oppressed peoples. A visit to the Mayan ruins at Quirigua prompts, as one might expect, a realization of "man's triumph over time and matter and the triumph of time and matter over man" (p. 42). The characteristically "antiphallic" art of the Mayas provides Huxley with an opportunity to state an hypothesis concerning the extreme limits on artistic freedom in primitive cultures ruled by an omnipotent "local Pavlov."

Then there is a long, rambling essay on contemporary politics in which Huxley compares the proliferation of nationalism, militarism, and mass violence in contemporary Europe with not dissimilar conditions in the various Central American states. Again and again he sets the Hispanic nations, with their history of tribal unity at a primitive level, side by side with the European fascist powers, whose recent imposition of nationalistic homogeneity and racial mythology he sees as a regression toward the primitive. In a revealing—if somewhat facile—statement Huxley asserts that "Central America, being just Europe in miniature and with the lid off, is the ideal laboratory in which to study the behavior of the Great Powers" (p. 74).[4]

One aspect of Guatemala—indeed of Hispanic America as a whole—which held considerable interest for Huxley was its blending of different cultures. Other observers, among them D. H. Lawrence, had questioned the degree to which this *mestizaje* has been successful, but Huxley does not, at least not at first. There are many passages in *Beyond the Mexique Bay* describing strange ceremonies in Indian villages which seem to hold equal reverence for the canonized saints and sacred images, and for the tribal shaman with his collection of talismans. But for Huxley, the fact that the Indian "primitives" have been for two centuries in contact with European civilization, the fact that their very primitiveness "expresses itself, to a great extent, in terms of our culture"—these are the reasons that he initially finds the Indians of Central America "uniquely interesting" (p. 163).

Huxley's response to Guatemala, for the most part, seems just and favorable. "[We] have been engaged . . . strenuously in exploring this country," he wrote to his father in late March of 1933, "one of the most delightful and most interesting I have ever seen." He goes on to sum up his feelings as follows: "It is a country where one [would] like to spend a long time, studying the endlessly queer interactions of paganism and Catholicism, looking at the dances, attending the really amazingly picturesque markets, and looking for antiquities—to say nothing of enjoying the amazing beauty of the mountain landscape." (*Letters*, p. 368)[5]

Yet near the end of Huxley's stay in Guatemala, as the time for heading north toward Mexico approaches, there is a gradual but perceptible shift in emphasis. Particularly in the descriptions of indigenous scenes, his intellectual fascination with cultural hybridism begins to give way to a deepening concern and subtle disquiet over the inscrutable "alienness" of Indian people. With increasing frequency passages appear which exemplify an antipathy born of incomprehension. The most memorable of these scenes occurs during a day-long tour of Ciudad Vieja and its church and convent. Entering the church, Huxley takes note of a devout Indian squatting in the dust, beating on a drum and playing a five-note tune on a crude whistle. The sight would not ordinarily be cause for alarm, except that the Indian retains this posture—staring off blankly into space, his eyes "black like boot-buttons and no less perfectly inexpressive"—and repeats the same simple tune over and over, for twelve hours nonstop (p. 123). This spectacle of inscrutable "nothings [the dark Indian eyes] focused upon nothing" clearly annoys Huxley: "Frankly, try how I may, I cannot very much like primitive people. They make me feel uncomfortable" (p. 124).

Now this is one of the most significant truths that Huxley

discovered about himself on the entire trip. Perhaps even more remarkable than the realization itself is the fact that, unlike D. H. Lawrence, Huxley is able openly to accept his instinctive dislike of the Indians he encountered. Having made this admission, however, he fails to follow up with a consideration of the reasons behind his antipathy. The failure to explore more deeply into his growing aversions is a primary weakness of *Beyond the Mexique Bay* as a personal record. As the critic George Woodcock has pointed out in his recent study of Huxley, the travel book is "curiously mask-like. . . . [One] always feels that the writer is not revealing fully what goes on in his thoughts, that the long passages of generalized reflections on sights and experiences really conceal deep and inarticulate movements of the mind, which one glimpses [only] occasionally. . . ."[6] Ironically, in a discussion of the societal restrictions suffered by Mayan artists, Huxley makes an important observation which applies equally to himself:

> . . .sooner or later even the most highly civilized and emancipated person comes to a *mental frontier* which he cannot pass—comes to it, of course, unaware, and does not realize his inability to go further; for it is of the essence of these inward barriers that they never reveal their presence, unless, as the result of some fortunate or unfortunate conjunction of cirumstances, we are shaken out of our second nature and transported violently to the other side of what is thenceforward perceived to have been an arbitrary limitation of our freedom. (p. 44, my emphasis)

What Huxley apparently was unable to understand at the time of the trip was that his pilgrimage through Central America and Mexico could have been an inner journey toward precisely this kind of "mental frontier."

What is it that kept Huxley from exploring the inward terrain? In part, no doubt, he is correct in suggesting that one is not consciously aware, at the time one first experiences the sudden emergence of irrational and unfamiliar feelings toward others, that such a reaction represents a confrontation with one's own inward barriers. Yet it cannot be said that Huxley was unaware of his personal limitations. In each of his novels of the 1920's he had satirized characters whose habitual asceticism and intellectual abstraction resembled similar tendencies in himself. He was sufficiently cognizant of these shortcomings to have Phillip Quarles, his alter ego in *Point Counter Point*, concede that "the pursuit of Truth is just a polite name for the intellectual's favourite pastime of substituting simple and therefore false abstractions for the living complexities of reality...."[7] While in the Central American tropics, however, Huxley was no more able to act upon this admonition than was Phillip Quarles in the novel.

The controlling pattern of abstraction evident throughout *Mexique Bay* is that of analogical thinking. Everywhere he goes, whatever he sees, Huxley's first concern seems to be discovering correspondences—or antitheses—between indigenous life and the European experience with which both he and his readers are more familiar. "One wonders," comments George Woodcock, "at the virtually automatic reaction, the mental tic; almost any excuse, no matter how apparently trivial, may set the fertile Huxley mind on its speculating path, relating the remote particularities of Central American villages to the general themes of human existence."[8] Indeed, it was this marked propensity which induced the oversimplified conclusion that Central America is "just Europe in miniature and with the lid off." At times, this method of comparison/contrast produces a striking insight. Perhaps the single best illustration of the illuminating analogy appears in a chapter which begins by contrasting the Indian belief in magic with the European world's disavowal of magic in favor of science and technology. When tribal sorcerers fail to ward off an influenza epidemic by the use of divining apparatus, the Indians interpret the incident not as evidence of the ineffectuality of magic, but as proof positive of the need for more and better sorcerers to combat evil spirits and the death they bring. Huxley has set us up for what seems to be a direct

antithesis between two modes of existence, until he concludes: "The moral of all this is clear. . . . Transferred from
the realm of international politics to that of magic, it is just
the familiar argument of those who clamour for bigger and
better armaments" (p. 190).

But if the analogical method of Huxley is an appropriate
vehicle for the free play of mind on broad subjects open to
speculation, it also has strict limitations. When confronting a
concrete thing or place or person apparently foreign to its
experience or understanding, the analogical mind, this one at
least, flounders. Visiting the mouldering Mayan ruins at the
border village of Copán, Huxley comes upon a species of
architectural design which defies even his considerable inter-
pretive powers. The ruins are felt to be

> profoundly, incommensurably alien. . . . [The] Euro-
> pean visitor to Copan . . . looks at the astonishing works
> around him, but looks at them from across a gulf; they
> exist in a universe of sentiment and discourse that is not
> his universe. . . . It is impossible to know by personal
> experience what the people who made such things felt
> and thought. . . . What were they really up to? *Quien
> sabe?* (pp. 207-209)

This response is symptomatic. More and more, when he is
unable to find a correspondence, he abandons all further
inquiry by simply denying that any meaning is accessible.
Where another writer, such as B. Traven or Malcolm Lowry,
would seize upon these examples of an alien, mysterious reality that seems to deny rational comprehension, would almost
gloat upon their primacy, Huxley only feels threatened.


## II


Once Huxley arrives in Mexico all the mounting tension and
hostility comes to a head, and the tone of *Mexique Bay* dark-
ens violently. At one point, when the Huxleys are staying in

the capital during the dry season, he confesses, "I have never felt so thoroughly bad-tempered as during the weeks . . . in Mexico City" (p. 300). The best he can do by way of explaining his ill temper is to concoct a rather wistful theory about the correlation between "the inward weather of the mind and the physical climate of the external world." He elaborates as follows: "That blood lust of the Aztecs, that still surviving preoccupation with death, those sudden Mexican violences— perhaps, in part at least, these are the products of the local air. Judging by my own state of mind, while I was in Mexico City, I should think it almost probable" (p. 301).

Huxley's impressions of the country are overwhelmingly negative—uncharacteristically so for one whose travel books strive for detachment and objectivity.[9] According to his account, the drive to Taxco is miserable. The town proves to be a dissipated, rather disgusting colony for wayward artists. The celebrated church there is sumptuously ugly; he has never seen a building so meticulously ill-proportioned (p. 309). Of a performance by a troop of cabaret artists in Puebla, the only memorable feature is "the really staggering animality of the female performers. . . . There is a certain mixture of blood and a certain Mexican environment which evidently produces a type of woman more horrifyingly animal, more abysmally whorish in appearance, than any I have seen in any other part of the world" (p. 292). A "domesticated" forest near a coffee *finca* south of Oaxaca may seem like paradise to tourists, "but for the inhabitants, it feels only too painfully like Mexico" (p. 237). (This, by the way, is one of the few instances in which Huxley evinces even a passing awareness of paradisal elements in the Mexican ambience. But unlike the other English novelists, whose pejorative observations were tempered sooner or later by intimations of at least a potential paradise in Mexico, Huxley uses the occasion merely to launch into a discussion of landscape poetry— followed incongruously by a brief consideration of Mexican social problems that prevent the country from resembling even a stylized, literary Eden.) Oaxaca itself is not unimpressive in its architecture, Huxley decides; however, the most remarkable thing about Oaxacan buildings is that they remain intact in spite of "three major earthquakes, in spite of seven sieges . . . in spite, above all, of four centuries of Mexican existence . . ." (p. 262). The Mexican section of *Beyond the Mexique Bay* abounds with this kind of bilious commentary. Taking his cue from Lawrence, and then trying as it were to exceed the older novelist's fear-induced excoriations, Huxley glances at the landscape and the dark-skinned people of Mexico and perceives something unnamable because it is inarticulate, but something repeatedly felt or imagined as wholly malevolent and subhuman—provoking in Huxley what can only be termed a biased, irrationally vituperative response.

Significantly, the few Mexican items singled out by Huxley for any degree of praise—the Zapotecan ruins at Monte Albán, the blue-tiled colonial facades of Puebla, the lurid Revolutionary murals of José Clemente Orozco, the "queer" ecclesiastical architecture at Cholula—are without exception objects, man-made artifacts, which have at least partially succeeded in resisting the attenuations of time. Such items lend themselves with relative ease to detached reflection and intellectual comprehension, especially for someone as well versed in the plastic arts as Huxley.

When Huxley reflects on the elemental Mexican landscape we are once again made aware of the severe limitations of his intellectual posture in coming to terms with a world where (in the words of Wallace Stevens) life is motion. Traveling much of the time by horse or burro through the southern parts of the Sierra Madre range, he was forced to traverse numerous *barrancas*, or deep ravines, "horrible gashes in the earth [which] make a disquieting impression" (p. 136). He observes that it is only possible for a sensible man to worship nature when it is other than he finds it in Mexico, when, in short, it has been subdued by roads and bridges and tunnels as in Europe. "Untamed, nature seems not so much divine as sinister, alarming, and, above all, obstructive" (p. 138).

Though there are not many extended descriptions of "untamed" nature in *Mexique Bay*, the ones that do appear follow a quasi-determinist doctrine quite at odds with the vitalist creed that Huxley professed in *Do What You Will*. Specifically, Huxley expresses a fear of two elements he sees as dominating the Mexican landscape. The first is nullity: "Our road wound across vast hills, bare and utterly dry—the grandiose emblems of a perfect hopelessness. A magnificent landscape; but one looks at it with a sinking of the heart; there is something profoundly horrifying in this immense, indefinite not-thereness of the Mexican scene." Riding in a bus crowded with shawled peasant women, they proceed down and up the *barrancas*, "across unbridged streams . . . [crashing] on over the unmetalled road, through the huge, glaring nonentity of the landscape" (p. 261). Secondly, there is the allied fear of inhuman diabolical power, as witnessed in this brooding sketch of the infernal Mexican ambience:

> The country seemed to grow drier and drier as we advanced. Great bald hills of baked clay rose on either side of the valley, and in the stony dust of the plain a hellish growth of cactuses ferociously flourished. Sometimes, but very rarely, we would pass a man walking, or perched on the rump of his ass; but the emptiness of this parched landscape was so complete, the silence so absolute, that it was as though the man were not there at all. Human life seemed, somehow, too hopelessly irrelevant to be possible. (pp. 287-288)

We have already seen how Huxley's initial interest in the mixture of cultures represented by the Central American Indian gradually gave way to an instinctive dislike of the alien "primitives." But as with all the other newly emergent feelings, once he had crossed over into Mexico—that is, into the frightening region of an unacknowledged "mental frontier"—his unease, his barely recognized hostility toward Indians, soon accelerated into outright revulsion and disgust. Certain episodes in the book which exemplify this development linger in the mind because of their unqualified truculence. When the Huxleys are forced to wait in the hot sun for a ride to Miahuatlán, an hospitable Indian woman invites them to pass the time inside her domicile, which happens to be a one-room reed hut with a thatched roof. One might expect that Huxley would welcome this as an opportunity to learn firsthand about the personal existence of an Indian family. But instead of relating any conversation or any impression of the woman, he focuses on her dwelling, in particular on how meagerly it is furnished. The only items classifiable as luxuries, Huxley tells us, are a rifle and ammunition, an enormous sombrero embroidered with gold and silver thread, and a sewing machine. The woman herself is quite forgotten, as the objects are used for an excuse to expound on the Generic Indian's scale of values:

[The Indian] is without furniture, his house lets in the wind and rain, he has . . . no water supply, no chimney, no change of clothes. Innumerable wants to be supplied. But . . . [what] he laboriously saves up for, centavo by centavo, is, first of all, a gun, so that he can, if the need arises, murder his neighbour; second, a princely hat in which to swagger abroad and excite the general envy; and finally (more, no doubt, to show off than from any humane desire to spare his wife unnecessary labour) a sewing-machine. (p. 245)

On one occasion—the most execrable example of racial denigration in the book—Huxley is not content merely to construct a composite Indian out of the things owned by one Indian family. Instead he must make the Indians themselves into things, reducing them by implication to the level of reptiles or other forms of subhuman life, so that they might be more easily classified, judged, and dismissed:

The scene [at Miahuatlán], as it reveals itself to the wandering spectator, is typical—a standard Southern Mexican back-cloth. At the centre of things lies the great desert of a glaring plaza, with tortoise-eyed Indian women sitting in the dust, each with her three *pimientos*, her nine bananas, her half-dozen of tomatoes, arranged in geometrical patterns on the ground before her. Above the market towers the vast church, hopelessly dilapidated and shored up against irremediable collapse by a precarious structure of poles and beams. Along the streets of half-ruined houses the donkeys come and go, flapping their ears; bare feet move noiselessly through the dust, and under enormous hats, under close-drawn shawls one catches the reptilian glitter of Indian eyes.

The spectacle, I confess, always made my blood run pretty cold.... [These] Mexican places...are appalling not so much because of what is there as because of what isn't there. A Black Country [industrial] town is a fearful sin of commission; Miahuatlan and its kind are sins of omission. Omission of the mental and the spiritual, of all that is not day-to-day animal living.... [An industrial town] embodies the corruption of a higher good than has ever been aimed at, at any rate since the fall of the indigenous empires, by the Indians....

Here, at Miahuatlan, there...was and there still is just the deep-rooted weed of primitive human life. If you happen to be a primitive human being, it must be quite a pleasant place to live in. But if you happen to have come within sniffing distance of the transcendental lilies [of civilization], how unspeakably depressing!... If Miahuatlan were the only possible alternative to Middlesborough, then really one might as well commit suicide at once. (pp. 248-250)

As George Woodcock has justly observed regarding this passage, Huxley demonstrates what amounts to "an active resistance to comprehension.... But such descriptions are useful to observers who find the Indian way of life so alien that they do not wish to enquire deeply into it."[10]

The last important element in Huxley's depiction of Mexico in his travel book concerns violence. It must be remembered that *Mexique Bay* was written at a time when the scars of the First World War were still painfully apparent and the very real prospect of more devastating wounds in a Second was becoming all too clear. The contemporary situation in Europe was much in Huxley's mind throughout his trip in 1933. In his account of his stay in Mexico, Huxley exploits examples of local violence in order to pronounce on the programmatic use of force by European powers.[11] Again his approach to his subject is broadly theoretical. Only occasionally are we permitted a hint of the author's personal reactions. Since Huxley's thesis is that violence has an orgiastic function, he is most interested in the communal rituals by which Mexicans both express and purge their collective lust for violence. At a bullfight in Etla, Huxley—like so many other foreign witnesses of this particular spectacle—registers disgust at the crowd's unanimous desire to see blood spilled. In Mexico City the celebration of Judas' Day on Easter Saturday involves a pale-faced, top-hatted, big-bellied image which is paraded through the streets, hanged, set afire, and blown to bits by fireworks contained inside the figure. Huxley compares this ceremony to the burning of the effigy of Guy Fawkes in England. In both cases the original event being commemorated is largely ignored. The Mexicans, for their part, are taking symbolic revenge upon the exploitative *gringo* capitalists. But Huxley believes the ritual goes far deeper than this, for lingering in the Mexican psyche are the vestiges of ceremonial human sacrifice:

> Victims are no longer gutted and eaten in honour of Huitzilopochtli or Tezcatlipoca, no longer drowned for the Tlalocs, flayed for Xipé, burnt for the god of fire and decapitated for the goddess of fertility. The modern Mexicans have to be content with the mere emblems of human sacrifice. But even a symbolical sacrifice is better than no sacrifice at all.... [And the] pleasure is heightened when...[the immolation] can be made to destroy the life-sized image of a man. (p. 303)[12]

A close reading of *Mexique Bay* suggests Huxley felt that despite these purgative rituals the violence latent in the Mexican landscape and its indigenous people amounted to an

almost tangible presence: "[The] monuments of murder," he
recalls, ". . . one came upon them at every second turn of the
road" (p. 246). The monuments referred to here are graves
and flowers. But on one occasion, descending the mountain
road into Miahuatlán, Huxley actually did pass a human
corpse lying along the roadside. His reaction to this sight is
evasive in the self-protective manner that has been used
throughout the book whenever the author feels confused
and/or threatened by his subject. He reflects on the "domestic" nature of Mexican killings, the pattern of private rivalries
and vendettas, and the unfortunate association of guns with
manhood. A similar confrontation along a Mexican roadside
became the germ from which Malcolm Lowry was to produce
his elaborately subjective meditation on death (among other
things), *Under the Volcano*. Where Lowry's characters are by
implication accounted culpable for merely talking while a
man lies dying before them, Huxley, for all his intellectual
acuteness, seems unaware of his own relation to the moral
questions posed by the encounter. But the comparison is un-
just. For like Lowry, who was eight years writing his novel,
Huxley required time to brood upon his experiences in Mexico—more time than the six months he spent on *Beyond the
Mexique Bay*.

In the midst of his circumlocutory musings about death
and violence along the road to Miahuatlan, Huxley interjects
a note that is evidently intended to amuse and reassure the
reader, and perhaps himself as well: "And yet the country is
not unsafe for travellers. . . . All that strangers need fear is
meeting with a drunkard. . . . But happily all the few Indians
we met were as sober as judges . . ." (p. 246). Anthony Beavis, the protagonist of *Eyeless in Gaza* (1936), is not so fortunate in his encounters as Huxley professes to have been. During his journey to Mexico, Beavis not only crosses paths with
a pistol-waving drunken Mexican (who does not strike Beavis as amusing at all),[13] but also with many of the other hostile forces which Huxley was unable to come to terms with in
*Mexique Bay*. In the interval between the travel book and the

novel, Huxley went through a period of personal crisis that changed the direction of his life and career as a writer. During his prolonged struggle to complete *Eyeless in Gaza*, he ultimately succeeded in retracing his path through the "mental frontier," this time with all his faculties fully engaged. The novel provides a much more economical account of the Mexican experience than the travel book does; Central America is all but dropped. But at the same time the novel gives more coherence and meaning to the trip as an *inner* journey by integrating it into a complex thematic pattern that develops over the course of a man's lifetime. However, before we proceed to an examination of what is perhaps Huxley's most important novel, we must first consider the underlying motives behind his decision to come to Mexico in the first place.

## III

Like the other inveterate travelers with whom we are concerned in this study, Huxley took pause, from time to time, to ponder the basis of his peripatetic existence. In his first travel book, *Along the Road* (1925), Huxley distinguishes between the mere tourist, who travels because he has been led to believe that this is what the "best" people do, and the true traveler, who is genuinely interested in the "real things" located in foreign parts, unfamiliar things to which he may be exposed only through travel. The true traveler is "insatiably curious, he loves what is unfamiliar for the sake of its unfamiliarity, he takes pleasure in every manifestation of beauty."[14] This line is not atypical. Indeed, in *Along the Road*, Huxley projects an image of himself as the carefree dilettante of the 1920's for whom travel is, along with reading, "the most delightful substitute for thought." When such a figure heads for parts unknown, he "pleasantly forgets" that his mind exists at all.[15] Escapism, in fact, is seen as one of the chief delights of travel. Since he can be no more than an

interested stranger in foreign lands, the traveler should glory
in the pleasant diversion to be had from his detached perspective. Properly seen, travel is a kind of game, and, so long as it
is "not treated as the serious business of life, [it] is a very
good one."[16]

This rather cavalier approach to travel seems to have been
shaken by Huxley's round-the-world trip of 1925-26, described in *Jesting Pilate: The Diary of a Journey* (1926). In
India, Burma, and Malaya he was confronted for the first
time with the intimidating atmosphere of the tropics. His self-
appointed traveler's role as detached observer was found to
be deficient—indeed impossible to maintain. The European
traveler's customary vantage-point in the tram or the sidewalk cafe was out of the question here. And more was at
stake in the tropics than "occasional diversion." In the tropical jungle the traveler was unable to dismiss the depression
brought on by "too much company . . . [by] the uneasy feeling that he [was] an alien in the midst of an innumerable
throng of hostile forces."[17] From the evidence of *Jesting Pilate*
it seems clear that travel no longer functioned as a "substitute
for thought"; rather, the exposure to foreign places furnished
the necessary stimulus for fresh thought. "A sensitive man
can't go round the world and come back with the same philosophy of life as the one he started with," says Kingham, a
character in a Huxley novella of this period.[18] Back in London, Huxley testifies to the broadened outlook he had gained
from his trip:

> I set out on my travels knowing, or thinking that I
> knew, how men should live, how be governed, how edu-
> cated, what they should believe. . . . I had my views on
> every activity of human life. . . . Now, on my return, I
> find myself without any of these pleasing certainties. . . .
> But . . . I acquired two important new convictions:
> that it takes all sorts to make a world, and that the estab-
> lished spiritual values are fundamentally correct and
> should be maintained. . . .
>            *           *           *           *

But if travel brings a conviction of human diversity, it brings an equally strong conviction of human unity. It inculcates tolerance.... [One realizes that] a oneness underlies...diversity. All men, whatever their beliefs, their habits, their way of life, have a sense of values. And the values are everywhere and in all kinds of society the same....[19]

Relativism, open-mindedness, advocacy of unity in diversity—scrutinizing this passage, one cannot but wonder what happened to these beliefs by the time Huxley stepped into the plaza at Miahuatlán, Mexico. Of course part of the trouble was that they *were*, in fact, beliefs rather than personal feelings. And the emotional turbulence he experienced in Mexico was itself, as we have seen, masked by an overcompensating intellectualism. It is particularly ironic that this manifestation of a divided sensibility appeared during a period when Huxley had been espousing the virtues of human wholeness, a doctrine he had come to believe in while under the influence of D. H. Lawrence. Nor was the forfeiture of "wholeness" his only heretical gesture made during the journey to Mexico. One of the basic reasons (however unconscious) for going there and a major result of the trip, was Huxley's final shedding of what Woodcock has aptly called "the gospel according to Lawrence."[20]

The complex relationship between Huxley and Lawrence may be described as one that depended upon a series of paradoxes: mutual respect and envy, warmth and antagonism, temporary intellectual accord and abiding instinctual disparity. It was an attraction between opposites who often clashed, but such collisions seemed for a time to set off sparks which illuminated a ground of common concern.[21] Their first encounter took place during the war, in December of 1915, when Lawrence invited Huxley to join in an ill-fated plan to found a utopian colony in Florida. Though they saw each other only once or twice at this time, Lawrence's personal magnetism captivated the normally cautious and skeptical

Huxley, who agreed to join the venture at a subsequent date. Having had the chance to give the unlikely scheme more thought, Huxley was relieved when it eventually fell through.[22] Years later Huxley recalled that Lawrence's

> Village of the Dark God would doubtless have disintegrated like all the rest. It was better that it should have remained, as it was always to remain, a project and a hope. And I knew this even as I said I would join the colony. But there was something about Lawrence which made such knowledge, *when one was in his presence*, curiously irrelevant.... What mattered was always Lawrence himself, was the fire that burned within him, that glowed with so strange and marvelous a radiance in almost all he wrote.[23]

The two men met again briefly in early 1924, when Lawrence made one of those brief revisits to postwar England he had come to dread. They did not become intimate friends, however, until their reunion in Florence in October 1926, after the Huxleys had returned from their trip around the world. From that time until Lawrence's death at Vence, in March of 1930, they spent much time together.

Before Huxley got to be close friends with Lawrence in 1926, there appeared in his fiction several characters who are often taken to be satirical portraits of Lawrence. The most interesting of these is J. G. Kingham, a man of working-class background who is regarded as a writer of great talent though deplored as a "barbarian" by the elitist literary set in "Two or Three Graces" (1926). In conversation and in his writing Kingham has acquired the "trick" of getting hold of a word such as "passional" (cited as one of his "too favourite words"), and, "if he liked the sound of it, [he would] work it to death."[24] As a thinker Kingham espouses ideas resembling some of Lawrence's. Kingham is fond of executing wild verbal "dissections" upon his friend Dick Wilkes, the narrator of the story, because of the latter's detachment and narrow rationalism. Kingham believes in the primacy of the emotions and the intuitions as conduits to the full, intense life. In one of his books Kingham has written that " 'Nothing that intensifies and quickens life is futile.' "[25]

But Kingham is also rather a hypocrite, an egotist, an absolutist, an exploiter of other people's timidities. It becomes apparent that Kingham's greatest strengths—the qualities which make him an engaging personality—also account for his considerable weaknesses:

> Kingham liked scenes. He loved to flounder in emotion—his own and other people's. He was exhilarated by these baths of passion; he felt that he really lived, that he was more than a man, while he splashed about in them. And the intoxication was so delicious that he indulged in it without considering the consequences. . . .
>
> [Once] emotionally committed, Kingham would never admit a mistake—unless, of course, his passion for self-humiliation happened at the moment to be stronger than his passion for self-assertion. . . . A single powerful impression would be allowed to dominate all other [subsequent] impressions. His intellect was put into blinders, the most manifest facts were ignored.[26]

Many of these points anticipate judgments, both critical and laudatory, which Huxley was later to express concerning Lawrence after the formation of their close friendship. The rationalist narrator of "Two or Three Graces" wonders why he should "put up with [Kingham], in spite of everything." Again, the answer is prophetic: "He was somehow important for me, deeply significant and necessary. In his presence I felt that my being expanded . . . [and] along the dry, sand-silted, desolate channels of my being life strongly, sparklingly flowed."[27]

By the time he returned to his home in Florence from his trip through the Orient, Huxley found himself in a state of intellectual uncertainty which made him vulnerable to new philosophical influences. He was now deliberately seeking "a positive philosophy to replace his unwilling nihilism," as

Woodcock puts it. At the time "Lawrence's vitalism seemed
. . .to fill the moral vacuum."[28] Lawrence himself seemed to
provide the living embodiment of human wholeness which
Huxley required as he became progressively more aware of
the imbalances in his own mental constitution. Although he
admitted that Lawrence was at times "difficult to get on with,
passionate, queer, violent" (*Letters*, p. 288), Huxley's esteem
was sufficiently great that he could record in his diary for
December of 1927 that Lawrence was "'one of the few people
I feel real respect and admiration for. Of most other eminent
people I have met I feel at any rate that I belong to the same
species as they do. But this man has something different and
superior in kind, not degree.'"[29]

The first fruits of Lawrence's direct influence in Huxley's
writing appear in *Point Counter Point* (1928) and its nonfiction companion piece, *Do What You Will* (1929). In these
two works Huxley attempts to come to terms with the doctrine of vitalism by pitting "life-worshippers" against figures
who represent some form of psychic or philosophical fragmentation which militates against the fullness and intensity
of life. The method used in *Do What You Will* involves a sustained attack upon a group of writers and thinkers (including
Wordsworth, Swift, Shelley, St. Francis, Baudelaire and Pascal) carefully selected as examples of the various means of
life-denial, against which Huxley juxtaposes long editorial
explanations of the vitalist creed as he understands it.[30] If, as
we are told, the guiding principle of the vitalist is to live
intensely and to be heedless of inconsistencies, the best way
in which this may be accomplished is functionally to internal-
ize what Huxley calls the creed of balanced excesses:

> The aim of the life-worshipper is to combine the ad-
> vantages of balanced moderation and excess. The mod-
> erate Aristotelian partially realizes all his potentialities;
> the man of excess fully realizes part of his potentialities;
> the life-worshipper aims at fully realizing all—at living,
> fully and excessively living, with every one of his colony

of souls. He aspires to balance excess of self-consciousness and intelligence by excess of intuition, of instinctive
and visceral living; to remedy the ill-effects of too much
contemplation by those of too much action, too much
solitude by too much sociability, too much enjoyment
by too much asceticism. He will be by turns excessively
passionate and excessively chaste.... He will be at
times a positivist and at times a mystic; derisively scepti-
cal and full of faith.... In a word, he will accept each of
his selves, as it appears in his consciousness, as his momentarily true self. Each and all he will accept—even the
bad, even the mean and suffering, even the death-wor-
shipping.... He will accept, he will live the life of each,
excessively.[31]

More interesting than the creed itself, however, is Huxley's
self-revelatory criticism of certain of the "orthodox perverts," especially in the essays on Swift and Pascal, with
whom he has much in common. In the long piece on Pascal,
Huxley first praises the French philosopher for rejecting the
illusions of the rationalist academic philosophers. But though
Pascal was acute enough to perceive that "the basis of reason
is unreasonable," and that the first principles of reality come
not from the mind but from the heart, he unfortunately un-
covered this truth with the wrong organ: "instead of discovering the heart with the heart, he discovered it with the head.
It was abstractly that he rejected abstractions, and with reason that he discovered unreason. His [antirationalist] realism
was only theoretical; he never lived it."[32] From here it was
but a short step to Pascal's choice of "an irrational abstraction to believe in—the God of Christianity," and thus to the
suppression of part of his human vitality.[33] One wonders
whether, in fulminating against Pascal like this, Huxley is
really striking out deviously against his own rational and
abstract endorsement of an irrational doctrine. Jerome Meckier's comment on this question is apropos. Meckier has
pointed out that Huxley was probably already struggling
against a half-conscious suspicion that "he was not by any

means a congenital or potential worshipper of the phallic consciousness, that his intellect and his erudition would always take precedence over his emotions and intuitions. . . ." The same conflict would emerge again a decade later, when Huxley demonstrated that he was bound to "approach even a subject as enigmatic as mysticism with as much rationality as possible."[34]

Huxley's other full-scale attempt to put his newly acquired Lawrencian beliefs to the test, *Point Counter Point*, suffers from similar handicaps but in a more compelling way. In an otherwise devastating panoramic vision of the utter baseness and futility of modern life, Huxley's portrayal of Mark Rampion is a conspicuous failure. Thematically, Rampion's role in the novel is crucial, since amidst the gallery of "modern perverts" such as the satanist Spandrell, the hypocritical spiritualist scholar Burlap, and the detached intellectual novelist Quarles, Rampion is the one basically affirmative character.[35] Rampion's proclamations against intellectual abstraction and distorted sexuality, his impassioned defense of "phallism" and the vitalist ideal of balance or wholeness are obviously intended to be taken seriously as potential antidotes to the malaise of postwar civilization as presented in the novel. Rampion is eloquent enough in his exposition of Lawrencian values. One does not quibble with his definition of true civilization as harmony and completeness, or of barbarism as lop-sidedness and fragmentation. His description of the ideal man is in many ways admirable:

> A man's a creature on a tightrope, walking delicately, equilibrated, with mind and consciousness and spirit at one end of his balancing pole and body and instinct and all that's unconscious and earthy and mysterious at the other. Balanced. Which is damnably difficult. And the only absolute he can ever really know is the absolute of perfect balance. The absoluteness of perfect relativity.[36]

The problem with Rampion is not in the ideas he advocates, but in the character himself. As Lawrence wrote to

Huxley, "your Rampion is the most boring character in the book—a gas-bag."[37] Huxley himself later admitted that Rampion is "just some of Lawrence's notions on legs. The actual character of the man was incomparably queerer and more complex than that" (*Letters*, p. 340). Rampion is not an active participant in any of the major plot developments in the novel. With the single exception of his wife's recollection of their courtship and early married years (Chapter IX), the only activity in which Rampion overtly engages throughout *Point Counter Point* is talk. Furthermore, like the fragmented "perverts" who inhabit the world of the novel, Rampion is a static character; he is no more perceptibly altered or affected by the horrors which occur in the story than is Denis Burlap, who in the final scene is romping with his Beatrice in a bathtub like a child. In his writer's notebook, Phillip Quarles states admiringly of Rampion that he "lives in a more satisfactory way than anyone I know. . . . [His] opinions are lived and mine, in the main, only thought."[38] The major irony in this novel—though it is almost certainly unintended—is the fact that the individual who is supposed to embody as well as verbalize the doctrines of vitalism and human wholeness is himself so abstract, lifeless, and inert.

   *Point Counter Point* and *Do What You Will* represent the closest approach to Lawrencian values Huxley was able to manage in his writings. In the works that follow, the influence of Lawrence the man and the ideologue is still felt. But whereas in *Point Counter Point* and *Do What You Will* Huxley seems to be struggling toward an acceptance and partial emulation of Lawrence, in works such as "After the Fireworks" and *Brave New World* there is a sense that the author is moving *against* certain elements in Lawrence of which he increasingly disapproves. In fact, close examination of their thinking during the period of 1926-29 indicates that there were basic though unacknowledged differences between Lawrence's ideas and Huxley's interpretation of them. These differences help to account for Huxley's gradual shift in direction after 1929, when it appears that he began to see Lawrence more and more as he had caricatured him in Kingham of "Two or Three Graces." Huxley's brand of vitalism, in retrospect, seems in many ways less vital than Lawrence's. For the ideals mouthed by Rampion concerning civilized "completeness" and "equilibrated" man are really an extension of the predilection for compromise or balance between body and mind, a major theme in Huxley's novels as early as *Crome Yellow* (1922). Lawrence, on the other hand, was generally less interested in balancing than in transcending the body-mind dualism through a kind of fusion that would engender the discovery of a "new centre of consciousness."[39] What Huxley came to fear was that in later works like *Kangaroo* and *The Plumed Serpent*, Lawrence's attempts to create fusion were not genuine because the role of the mind was down-played. In the words of Jerome Meckier, "Lawrence was against one form of imbalance: the mentalization of one's instincts and feelings. Huxley comes to feel that Lawrence's alternatives increasingly tend toward another form of imbalance: the emotionalization of the mind." With this realization, as Meckier goes on to point out, Huxley begins to re-evaluate the whole notion of balance or completeness as an ideal.[40]

Though there are many ironic allusions to Lawrence in the collection entitled *Brief Candles* (1930), the story which contains the most substantial and suggestive reinterpretation of Lawrence is "After the Fireworks." Here the Lawrencian persona is represented sympathetically but not uncritically in the character of Miles Fanning. Fanning is a well-known middle-aged English novelist staying in Rome. He has made his reputation by writing romantic novels which usually deal with the sensual liberation of young women. Though Fanning is wary of young "spiritual adventuresses" who read his books and then, either through correspondence or by personal contact, try to "attach themselves like lice" to a famous author, he allows himself to be approached by Pamela Tarn, a beautiful young English girl whose romantic fantasies have been shaped chiefly by Fanning's heroines. At first Fanning dominates their relationship by assuming the role of man of the world, patron and teacher of culture. This frustrates Pamela, who is clearly interested only in an ego-inflating sexual alliance with the celebrated champion of libidinous release. He takes her to see the Etruscan ruins at Villa Giulia. Here he tells her at length of the virtues of "civilized" oneness and harmony, epitomized by the Etruscans and their gods as represented in their art. In particular, an icon of the Etruscan Apollo signifies to Fanning the highest ideal—a complete and integrated god for complete and integrated men and women. Existing before the "great split" between "spirit and matter, heroics and diabolics, virtue and sin, and all the other accursed antitheses" that were ushered in by Plato, Euripides, and the Christians, the Etruscan Apollo does not admit the separate existence of these polarities, but "somehow includes them in his own nature and turns them into something else—like two gases combining to make a liquid."[41] Modern civilization, Fanning tells Pamela, is still being torn apart by its warring antitheses: "These Etruscans were on a better track. If only people had the sense to follow it! Or at least get back to it."[42]

More than just balance or compromise, Fanning's beliefs emphasize the quest for transcendence and the longing to return in sensibility to the pre-scientific past—that is, precisely those notions of Lawrence which Huxley was now finding most difficult to accept. One of the major tasks of the story is convincingly to demonstrate the ultimate futility of Fanning's ideals in modern times. Though he strives to be a "'worshipper and self-appointed priest'" of the Etruscan god, "'it's difficult [he tells Pamela]. . . . Perhaps it's even impossible for us to recapture.'"[43] The pathos which attends the character of Miles Fanning is particularly intense in the last third of the story, when we witness the failure of his determined attempt to live by his beliefs. The sexual relationship which Fanning had tried to discourage finally commences, but as the weeks pass their difference in age (thirty years) proves to be a barrier which cannot effectually be transcended. By the end of the story their roles have shifted. Pamela is now cool, aloof, and self-confident, her mind already preoccupied with plans for new conquests elsewhere. Meanwhile Fanning, after a rather humiliating attack of jaundice, is now the more desperate one. He is in a state of utter confusion: his wholeness and balance are blighted, his passions have suddenly become "heavy, serious, intense," and his sexual desire for Pamela has turned into a kind of "focused rage." The failure of Fanning's ideals is implied when he admits that the Apollo has "abandoned" him to these insufferable cycles of lust and renunciation. In "After the Fireworks," then, Huxley suggests that the Lawrencian persona is ultimately unable to overcome the body-mind polarity. Also, Fanning's decline, although in the story it is not interpreted in overtly philosophical terms, seems almost to be a case history supportive of Huxley's contention that "Lawrence's . . . was not a very good philosophy for old age or failing powers."[44]

The most formidable remaining obstacle in the path of Huxley's retreat from vitalism and primitivism was removed on March 2, 1930. Within a week of Lawrence's death Frieda Lawrence invited Huxley to collect and edit her husband's letters. It was a task that was to occupy Huxley for the next two and a half years. The arduous process of reviewing Lawrence's life, his travels, his diverse friendships, his evolving ideas—surely this accelerated the revaluation of Lawrence that had been underway in Huxley's mind since at least 1929. He must have discovered in the letters flaws in Lawrence's character of which he had not been fully aware; no doubt he came across examples of Lawrence's duplicity, as when Lawrence had offered qualified praise of *Point Counter Point* in a letter to Huxley, while in writing to Dorothy Brett he dismissed the novel as a "bit cheap sensational."[45] In any event, by mid-July of 1931 Huxley was willing to offer a partial criticism of Lawrence in a letter to Victoria Ocampo, editor of the Argentine journal *Sur:* "I enormously admire Lawrence's books and I greatly loved him personally—but in reading him I often suffer from a kind of claustrophobia, I have the impression of having been swallowed up..." (*Letters*, p. 349). Three months later, in a letter to the critic G. Wilson Knight, Huxley's tone is more severe: "...the Life business isn't enough. Too much insistence on it makes Lawrence's books oppressively *visceral*. Reading, one feels like Jonah in the whale's belly. One longs for the open air of intellectual abstraction and pure spirituality—if only for a change of climate" (*Letters*, p. 353).

Huxley wrote *Brave New World* (1932) between May and August of 1931, while he was still at work editing Lawrence's letters. Considering this, one might find it strange that there is no Lawrencian persona in the novel. Some have mistakenly assumed that John "the Savage," born and raised on an Indian reservation in New Mexico, is Huxley's final attempt in fiction to create a portrait of Lawrence. But John bears no perceptible resemblance to Lawrence. A tragic victim of psychological traumas suffered during his childhood, John is the product of his own private pathology. When he was a young boy his mother Linda had made him feel responsible for her miserable lot among the "insane" Indians—if he had not been conceived, Linda might have escaped back to civilization. John's horror of sexuality, his puritanical idealization of undefiled Woman, stem from his having witnessed both Linda's adulterous acts with strange men and the severe punishment she received from the jealous Indian women for those acts. Moreover, John is clearly *not* a genuine "savage" for he has never been accepted as a member of the tribal culture. It is significant that John is not given the title of "Savage" until he arrives in the "Fordian" society of London. Quoting passages from Shakespeare as he wildly rebukes the sexuality of Lenina Crowne ("'There's hell, there's darkness, there is the sulphurous pit, burning, scalding, stench, consumption'"), flagellating himself in *Penitente* fashion for experiencing natural desires, John seems anything but a Lawrencian life-worshiper.[46] Only in the novel's two penultimate chapters, during his confrontation with World Controller

Mustapha Mond, does John even begin to articulate values
that bear any relation to those of Lawrence. Here John rejects
the stable but sterile ways of the Brave New World as "too
easy." In their place he claims "the right to be unhappy,"
which includes acceptance of fear and rage, pain, filth, disease, old age, the mystery of death, and all the other myriad
"inconveniences" that are integral parts of human existence.
Finally, unable to secure a place in either civilized or primitive cultures, John finds that even these beliefs are an intol-
erable burden: he hangs himself.

Without a human embodiment of Lawrence or even an
effective spokesman for his doctrines, Huxley himself—as
narrator—must assume the role of commentator on the relative presence or absence of desirable elements in the two cultures posited by *Brave New World*. Thus, in a very real way,
his depiction of primitive living in this novel is a more direct
and accurate indication of his current attitudes toward vitalism than we have had to date. Huxley had not yet been to
New Mexico, and the chapters set there (VII-IX) are the result
of a combination of extensive research and imaginative
skill.[47] His descriptions of Indian fertility rituals, sexual and
cosmological myths, and initiation ceremonies owe a considerable debt to Lawrence's evocations of Pueblo Indian life in
such pieces as "Indians and an Englishman," "Dance of the
Sprouting Corn," "The Hopi Rain Dance," and "New Mexico." But though some of the incidentals are the same—the
"pulsating" chants and drum beats, the handling of live
snakes, the symbolic sprinkling of corn, the "dusting" feath-
ers, the obsidian-masklike Indian faces—the prevailing tone
is quite different. Lawrence's renderings of Indian life in such
pieces as the above are poetic and reverential. In contrast,
Huxley's descriptions of the ceremonial life at Malpais
(badland) pueblo are prosaic, terse, and emotionally con-
stricted. Whatever religious significance the ceremonies
might have had for the reader is undermined by the inclusion
of mundane details such as flies, dust, piles of rubbish, the
smell of unwashed bodies, the sagging and toothless faces of

decrepit old men. By the time an eighteen-year-old boy is whipped until he collapses, his blood spilt back into the earth, the reader is made to share in the revulsion felt by Bernard Marx and Lenina Crowne—and by their author. Over the course of the novel one feels that Indian culture is seen to be somewhat less loathsome and sterile than Fordian culture, but that is about as far as Huxley goes toward endorsing primitivism in *Brave New World*. The two alternatives, as Huxley was to say years later, merely offer a choice between "insanity on the one hand and lunacy on the other."[48]

It should be kept in mind, however, that the central theme of *Brave New World* is not primitivism but "the advancement of science as it affects human individuals."[49] The three chapters devoted to Bernard and Lenina's impressions of Malpais pueblo are little more than an intermezzo falling between the far more elaborate descriptions of the futuristic society that is the primary focus of attention in the novel. Huxley's artistic strategy, in this case, did not require a particularly profound exploration of Lawrence's Divine Ground and its dark-skinned inhabitants, and so his treatment of them is rather perfunctory. While the imagined response of Bernard and Lenina provides a meaningful clue as to Huxley's shifting allegiances, it should not be taken as a final and unequivocal declaration of independence from Lawrence. Before Huxley permitted himself to go on public record as repudiating those doctrines of Lawrence he now found objectionable, he had to examine firsthand the terrain and people which had inspired them.

"What is needed now, I feel," Huxley wrote just twelve weeks before he sailed for Central America and Mexico, "is an acceptable philosophical system which will permit ordinary human beings to give due value both to Lawrence's aspect of reality and to that other aspect, which he refused to admit the validity of—the scientific, rational aspect" (*Letters*, p. 365). Huxley was entering a period of his life which was dominated by his quest for such a philosophical system. But not a trace of what he was seeking was anywhere evident in Mexico. Indeed, as we have seen, what Huxley discovered while traveling through that country was an intractable and threatening alienness which seemed to negate the claims of both Lawrence's vitalism and the more orthodox notions of European scientific progressivism.

However, there is reason to suppose that one of the factors contributing to Huxley's prejudicial and inordinately negative reaction to Mexico was his need once and for all to shed the influence of Lawrence. For his career as a writer was at a crossroads. He had begun to turn away from "pure" satire and from the kind of novel in which ideas are juxtaposed for their own sake. In *Brave New World* he had taken his first step in the direction of the more didactic novel. During the past six years he had gone as far as his talent and his philosophical understanding could carry him toward making artistic use of Lawrencian doctrine. To continue creating Mark Rampions or even Miles Fannings would inhibit future growth and new discoveries. The trip to Mexico, then, provided Huxley with a convenient opportunity to strike out against Lawrence, and, what is more, to do so at those spots in Lawrence's thought which Huxley now considered most vulnerable.


IV


At two crucial junctures near the end of *Beyond the Mexique Bay* Huxley embellishes his reflections upon the Mexican scene with judgmental allusions to Lawrence. Immediately after his abusive and facile description of the "standard Southern Mexican back-cloth" at Miahuatlán, Huxley remarks that

> Lawrence wrote eloquently of Oaxaca and Lake Chapala, with passion, sometimes over-emphatically, of the merits of that rank weed-life of the natural man. But it is

significant that he spent only a few months in Mexico and that, wherever he lived among primitives, he found it necessary, in spite of the principles he had made his own, to refresh himself by occasional contacts, through books, through civilized men and women, with the lilies of the mind and spirit.[50] The attempt to return to primitiveness is both impractical and, I believe, wrong. For a lily is a lily and we know, by direct intuition and by discursive reasoning, that it is better than a weed. (*Mexique Bay*, pp. 249-250)

Lawrence is further criticized for repudiating science as a whole on the basis of its occasional misapplications. Huxley believes that "the only thing that can prevent science from being misapplied is more science of a higher quality" (*Mexique Bay*, p. 250).[51] Just as Lawrence had come to Mexico initially determined to prove, regardless of any evidence to the contrary, that primitivism offered viable solutions to the problems of modern life, so also came Huxley, equally determined beforehand that the notion of returning to primitivism was impractical and wrong. Almost everything he saw in Mexico was interpreted as supportive of this predetermined notion. Huxley's defense of science, cited above, is another indication of how far he had come since he had had Mark Rampion hold forth against "Newton's and Henry Ford's disease," nurtured and spread by the "horrid little scientists."[52]

In the concluding chapter of *Mexique Bay*, set on board the ship making its way north through the Gulf of Mexico, Huxley combines general reflections on his journey with an extensive critical reassessment of Lawrence's primitivism and of *The Plumed Serpent*, which he was rereading at the time. Huxley objects to the novel's conclusion, which "Lawrence himself has used all his extraordinary powers to make incredible" (p. 311). In the first two-thirds of the novel Lawrence gives us many powerful descriptions of the hopeless squalor of the primitive existence led by a people who have not yet reached the mental and spiritual stage of consciousness, but only that of the "dark blood." As a result of these descriptions, Huxley says, the reader shares the protagonist Kate Leslie's strong revulsion against Indian people. Yet at the novel's end, we are asked to renounce mind and spirit and to immerse ourselves in a sea of living blood. We cannot accept this injunction, and neither, Huxley feels, could Lawrence: "Lawrence's own incomparable descriptions of the horror of unadulterated blood have made [acceptance] impossible. It was impossible even for himself; he could not accept his own invitation. The facts of his life are there to prove it. Kate stayed, immersed in the primitive blood of Mexico; but Lawrence went away" (p. 312). To compensate, or rather overcompensate, for his own growing doubt, Lawrence must prove to Kate, his readers, and himself that "immersion in blood is good." But the more stridently he shouts down his doubts, the less convincing he becomes. For Huxley, the novel's "artistic failure is evidence of some inner uncertainty of conviction" (p. 313).

There is a good deal of truth in Huxley's criticism of *The Plumed Serpent*. But of far greater moment is the fact that Huxley is now able to distance himself from Lawrence, to define himself against Lawrence's example. The former ideal, the complete, integrated, "equilibrated" man, is nowhere invoked; Lawrence himself is recognized as a man who exhibited, at least in the later part of his life, an unfortunate imbalance favoring the body and the "dark blood." Once he has discerned Lawrence's alleged failure, it is easier for Huxley openly to confess that he no longer believes that a synthesis of even the best elements of the primitive and modern worlds is a viable possibility:

> The advance from primitivism to civilization, from mere blood to mind and spirit, is a progress whose price is fixed; there are no discounts even for the most highly talented purchasers. I thought once that the payment could be evaded, or at least very greatly reduced; that it was possible to make very nearly the best of both worlds. But this, I believe, was a delusion. The price that

has to be paid for intellect and spirit is never reduced to any significant extent. To Lawrence it seemed too high, and he proposed that we should return the goods and ask for our money back. When man became an intellectual and spiritual being, he paid for his new privileges with a treasure of intuitions, of emotional spontaneity, of sensuality still innocent of all self-consciousness. Lawrence thought that we should abandon the new privileges in return for the old treasure. . . . In practice, he found that it was psychologically impossible to return the new privileges or be content with the primitivism that had been paid away for them. It was even impossible for him to make a fictitious personage do so, at any rate convincingly.

. . . We must be content to pay, and indefinitely to go on paying, the irreducible price of the goods we have chosen. (pp. 314-315)

Jerome Meckier is probably correct in observing that in this passage Huxley "foists on Lawrence a very narrow and literal primitivism." It may also be true that Huxley finally "retreated from the challenge Lawrence offered . . . [and failed] permanently to come to terms with the revolutionary quality of Lawrence's thought and personality."[53] But for the sake of continued intellectual growth and artistic integrity, the break was a fundamental necessity. So preoccupied with the break was Huxley that he did not realize at the time that the apparent negations associated with Mexico would represent, in the long run, something much more far-reaching and significant to himself than the success or failure of Lawrence's creed. Only by recreating his Mexican experience in the imagined world of *Eyeless in Gaza* did Huxley demonstrate an acute awareness that it had ultimately presented him a more valuable arena for self-discovery and spiritual insight than his affair with Lawrencian ideas ever did.

Still, it is ironic that the only English novelist of Mexico to acknowledge Lawrence's direct influence at all should be the one to diverge the most from Lawrence's example. Of the three major Mexican-set novels considered in the chapters following, *Eyeless in Gaza* represents Mexico in a manner that least resembles the dualistic image created initially in *The Plumed Serpent*. Despite this difference, however, the mythic pattern of Huxley's novel is essentially that of the other novels, with Mexico playing a crucial role in the unfolding of that myth.

# V

# Time and the Healing of Wounds in Huxley's Eyeless in Gaza

Huxley had conceived the idea for *Eyeless in Gaza* by 1932, before his journey to Central America and Mexico. But the writing did not come easily. In a letter of November 9 he informed his American editor that he was "now meditating a novel—feeling rather incapable of getting it underway . . . but hoping that the thing will begin to flow one day. If it does start flowing, it might well be finished by the end of next summer. But this is all very uncertain . . . for I know by bitter experience that I can't force myself to write anything that is not ripe. . . . Meanwhile I am just accumulating notes and writing experimental pages."[1] The trip interrupted his working plans for four months, and upon his return the following June he was occupied primarily with the writing of *Beyond the Mexique Bay*. Still, he found time to resume work on his novel later that summer, and when the travel book was completed in November he was again able to devote his energies to writing the novel. "The theme, fundamentally, is liberty [he wrote to a correspondent on December 22]. What happens to someone who becomes really very free—materially first . . . and then mentally and emotionally. The rather awful vacuum that such freedom turns out to be. But I haven't yet worked out the whole fable—only the first part" (*Letters*, p. 376). However, the novel was apparently not "ripe," the creative "flow" not yet forthcoming, and in March of 1934 Huxley wrote Edward Sackville-West of plans to travel in Italy over Easter: "I feel in need of a change of scene, being stickily engaged in a novel I can't quite find a satisfactory machinery for" (*Letters*, p. 378).

Huxley's letters indicate that his difficulties with *Eyeless in Gaza* occurred contemporaneously with a period of physical and mental distress that lasted until mid-1935. On October 13, 1934 he wrote that a "sort of horror of any kind of personal contact with people...has kept me sealed in for months. A mania really—though having an excuse in a self-preservative husbanding of my small resources of physical and therefore psychological energy.... [It seems to be a] personal, psychological slump.... I work at a difficult novel about the problem of freedom" (*Letters*, p. 385). Huxley made many references in his correspondence of this period to chronic insomnia, anxiety, intestinal problems, fatigue, and acute depression. The crisis seems to have been exacerbated by dread of an impending war in Europe: "I'm hard at work on a novel that won't get finished," he wrote to Robert Nichols in 1935. "Expect to be in England in another month or so—unless of course we're plunged in war by then. In which case we shall probably all be dead. I wish I could see any remedy for the horrors of human beings except religion or could see any religion that we all could believe in" (*Letters*, p. 398).

Following closely upon the Mexican trip and the break with Lawrencian doctrine, the fits of depression Huxley suffered in 1934-35 appear to have been a more prolonged and intense version of his unsettled condition (described in *Jesting Pilate*) after he returned from the Orient in 1926. In both cases the impact of the journey so jolted his philosophical outlook and his accustomed notion of himself that he underwent a kind of psychic withdrawal. George Woodcock speaks of this state as "the sense of disastrous emptiness that often precedes profound spiritual changes."[2] From its inception early in 1935, the prescribed "cure" to Huxley's distress had philosophical and spiritual overtones. F. M. Alexander, the Australian-born physiologist, philosopher, and author of *The Use of the Self* (1932), treated Huxley's physical symptoms much in the manner of Dr. Miller, the guru-figure of *Eyeless in Gaza*. The treatment involved the use of non-toxic drugs, breathing exercises "of the Yoga sort," and mental concentration aimed at a disciplined method of "mind and body control." According to Maria Huxley, by early 1936 Alexander had "made a new and unrecognizable person of Aldous, not physically only but mentally and therefore morally.... [He] has brought out, actively, all we, Aldous's best friends, know never came out either in the novels or with strangers. It [the change] comes in the novel too" (*Letters*, p. 400).

It was at about this time that Huxley also underwent a radical transformation in political and religious beliefs. Always a great reader of mystic writers, Huxley, with some guidance from Alexander and from Gerald Heard, began to give credence to the value of the mystical experience as a possible solution to his—and the world's—problems. On November 19, 1935, he wrote: "I am working at my book and in the interval talking over ways and means, with Gerald [Heard], for getting an adequate pacifist movement onto its feet. The thing finally resolves itself into a religious problem —an uncomfortable fact which one must be prepared to face and which I have come during the last year to find it easier to face" (*Letters*, p. 398). Though Huxley was reluctant to discuss such matters in any great detail in his letters, it seems clear that, in response to an urgent need for some ameliorating politico-religious stance, Huxley experienced (or perhaps willed) a kind of spiritual conversion sometime in mid-1935. Not long after, his health was restored, he became actively engaged in the pacifist movement, his creative powers were replenished in full. In March of 1936 Huxley finally completed *Eyeless in Gaza*, a novel dramatizing a conversion experience. "Oh, how I hate that novel," wrote Maria Huxley. "...Not meaning that it is not very good. When I say I

hate it it is for very different and personal reasons. The
misery it has caused us and so on" (*Letters*, p. 400). Yet, as
Huxley's biographer Sybille Bedford has observed, it was
very likely the writing of this novel which more than anything else "served him as the main discipline towards the
break-through" from his depression.[3]

Not surprisingly, the personal background to the writing
of this novel comes very close to being its central theme.
What might be called the kernel plot or narrative present, the
crucial sequence of events taking place between August of
1933 and February of 1935, concerns a period of intense crisis
in the life of forty-two-year-old Anthony Beavis.[4] We
observe his metamorphosis from a detached and cynical
scholar to a sincere and committed pacifist and mystic, from
an inwardly dead man to one committed to living. Pivotal in
this process of transformation is Beavis' trip to Mexico in
early 1934, the accounts of which occupy relatively few
pages in the novel. In Mexico Beavis is confronted with some
of his deepest fears and hostilities. While still in Mexico he
begins to come to terms with these elemental passions in himself from which his ascetic style of life in England had previously shielded him. And it is in Mexico that he meets Dr.
James Miller, the anthropologist and philosopher who becomes his spiritual model. But though *Eyeless in Gaza* is
obviously semi-autobiographical, it is not "pure" *roman à
clef*. For one thing, the time of Anthony Beavis' ennui, his
self-questioning and disillusionment—the period in which his
imagined freedom becomes a "rather awful vacuum"—has
been shifted, significantly, to the months just *prior* to his
Mexican journey. Immediately upon his return to England,
Anthony embarks upon the hard road of spiritual rebirth.
Between these two states of being lies the dread "mental frontier" mentioned so glibly in *Mexique Bay;* Anthony's painful
but necessary experience of crossing over that psychic boundary occurs during his stay in Mexico.

I use the term "kernel plot" for the sake of convenience,
since the account of Anthony's regeneration in the narrative

present is disjointed by an achronistic structural scheme which meanders through five different periods in Anthony's life. In Chapters One and Three, set on Anthony's forty-second birthday, August 30, 1933, we find him perusing a pile of photographs in which static images representing key moments in his past are preserved in random fashion, as in memory:

> Somewhere in the mind a lunatic shuffled a pack of snapshots and dealt them out at random, shuffled once more and dealt them out in different order, again and again, indefinitely. There was no chronology. The idiot remembered no distinction between before and after. . . . The thirty-five years of his conscious life made themselves immediately known to him as a chaos—a pack of snapshots in the hands of a lunatic.[5]

Anthony has evolved a theory of personality from his reading of Blake, Proust, and Lawrence. According to this theory, man is no more than a succession of separate states. Since there is no such thing as an individual person, a unified being, people cannot be held morally accountable for their actions: "Good and evil can be predicted only of states, not of individuals, who in fact don't exist, except as the places where the states occur. It is the end of personality in the old sense of the word" (*Gaza*, p. 107). This notion, reminiscent in some respects of the life-worshiper's creed outlined in *Do What You Will* (1929),[6] is actually an elaborate rationalization which enables Anthony conveniently to eschew responsibility for events in his past. The scrambled structure of *Eyeless in Gaza* appears at first to embody this theory. The reader is not permitted to trace the unravelling of any single thread of plot to its climax without numerous intrusions. In the first seven chapters we jump from 1933 to 1934 to 1933 to 1904 to 1902 to 1926 back to 1934, and so on throughout the novel.

About two-thirds of the way into *Eyeless in Gaza*, however, one begins to realize that the chaos is only apparent.

The reader discerns the five distinct time-frames, and—necessarily—begins to sort them out and reconstruct their histories. Several early chapters, set between November 6, 1902 and January of 1904, concern Anthony's reaction to his mother's death and his schoolboy experiences. Attending his mother's funeral is the crisis of Anthony's boyhood, his first exposure to the finality of death: "Leaning forward, Anthony looked into the hole [i.e., the grave]. It seemed extraordinarily deep. He shuddered, closed his eyes; and immediately there she was . . . white again in the satin evening-dress when she came to say good-night . . ." (p. 29). But when he opens his eyes there is only that yawning black hole in the ground. In the months following, Anthony tries to adjust to the vague sense of loss and loneliness by forming attachments with his schoolmates, in particular with Brian Foxe. In the second time-frame, June 1912 to July 1914, Brian and Anthony are close friends while at Oxford together, along with Mark Staithes and several other boys from their public school. Already a voracious reader, Anthony begins to engage in discussions of fashionable ideas with intellectual and bohemian types. He becomes involved in a sexual alliance with Mary Amberley, a promiscuous older woman and mother of two young girls. In a reckless attempt to impress Mary, Anthony betrays Brian by seducing Brian's fiancée. One of the most crucial events in Anthony's life—an incident that is not disclosed until near the end of the novel—is Brian's discovery of this betrayal and his resultant suicide. Anthony finds his friend's battered body at the foot of a cliff and is thereafter pursued by guilt, which impels him progressively to withdraw from further human entanglements. In the third time-frame, 1926-28, Anthony becomes involved again, albeit peripherally, in the lives of the Amberley family and their bohemian set, which includes several characters from public school and Oxford days. At social gatherings this group flaunts the life-style of the postwar decade: escapism through drugs, the initial thrill and eventual boredom of sexual promiscuity, frivolous dabbling in financial and political schemes, the soothing smugness of easy cynicism. Conventional values are seen to be dead, and Anthony, who has lost the vestiges of his youthful ideals during the war, luxuriates in his role as amused and detached observer at these affairs. By this time he has lost all affection and regard for Mary Amberley, whom he blames in part for Brian Foxe's suicide. But he becomes acquainted with Mary's daughter Helen. The fourth time-frame, set in 1931, largely concerns Helen's disenchantment with her marriage to a loveless, sexless, and all but mindless husband. The final sequence opens in August of 1933, near the end of the purely sexual relationship that has developed between Anthony and Helen Amberley. After the abrupt termination of their affair, Anthony begins to progress toward the crisis which precedes his conversion. He goes through a period of self-doubt and questioning of his mode of existence, travels with Mark Staithes to Mexico, participates in the pacifist movement back in England, and seems at the novel's end to be on the verge of reuniting with Helen in a more profound and enduring relationship.[7]

To reconstruct Huxley's disjointed narrative like this does not imply that the novel itself fails to achieve coherence and clarity. On the contrary, in discussing the achronistic narration I impose a temporal scheme only to emphasize its underlying order. The preceding outline shows that the recurring elements in each of the five time-frames are death, loss, aging, decay: all manifestations of temporal flux. At the end of each sequence except the last, Anthony, confronted by the relentless force of time, retreats further into self-protective isolation and intellectualism.[8] Thus, Huxley's fragmentary and circuitous presentation creates an initial confusion which compels one to become involved in the process of discovering a principle of continuity or order in Anthony's life, a principle which Anthony himself has rejected in favor of snapshots randomly dealt by a lunatic. In the words of Jerome Meckier, the novel "begins by mimicking but ends by satirizing" Anthony's escapist theories of personality and time.[9] As soon as he begins to scan those snapshots, Anthony's attempt to escape flux and the attendant responsibility for past events is doomed. For although the photographs succeed in freezing the moment, the mind cannot. Again and again in *Eyeless in Gaza* dramatic occurrences intrude upon Anthony's intellectual cocoon, until he is forced to recognize that the past is always alive somewhere in the mind. Only when he acknowledges the essential wholeness and continuity of his experience is he able to find meaning in life for the first time—to find meaning, that is, in actively pursuing it. Thus, though much more elaborate in execution, Huxley's temporal scheme, with its underlying emphasis on cyclicity and continuity, serves very similar thematic ends to those of *Under the Volcano* and *The Power and the Glory*.

Not the least of Huxley's accomplishments in *Eyeless in Gaza* is his ability to induce in the reader a gradual perception of order within chaos at the very time that Anthony moves toward this same awareness. Anthony's defensive theory of static moments is undermined by the uncontrollable flow of mental associations which returns his attention to the past. In the first episode of the kernel plot, on the same August afternoon in which he has examined the snapshots, Anthony is making love to Helen (Amberley) Ledwidge, his mistress, on the flat rooftop of his house near the Mediterranean. Their affair is strictly a casual arrangement based on the physical needs of each, with no bother about genuine human relationship, commitment, or love. Anthony has not permitted himself even to get to know Helen very well:

> Enquiry and exploration would land him in heaven knew what quagmire of emotion, what sense of responsibility. And he had no time, no energy for emotions and responsibilities. His work came first. Suppressing his curiosity, he went on stubbornly playing the part he had long since assigned himself—the part of the detached philosopher, of the preoccupied man of science who doesn't see the things that to everyone else are obvious. (p. 3)

But as they lie there naked in the sun, their passion spent, something happens which abruptly jolts Anthony out of his detachment and complacency into immediate, literal contact with elemental reality. From an airplane passing overhead falls a dog: "With a violent but dull and muddy impact, the thing struck the flat roof a yard or two from where they were lying. The drops of a sharply spurted liquid were warm for an instant on their skin. . . . From head to foot both of them were splashed with blood. In a red pool at their feet lay the almost shapeless carcase . . ." (p. 113). At first Anthony tries to dismiss this freak occurrence with a sarcastic remark, but Helen, who has a long-standing revulsion against anything connected with gore, sobs hysterically. The sight of Helen in this abandoned state evokes in Anthony "an almost violent movement of love for this hurt and suffering woman, this *person*, yes, this person whom he had ignored . . . as though she had no existence except in the context of pleasure" (p. 114). He tries to approach her in the spirit of this new emotion, but Helen shrinks away from any contact with him. She quickly withdraws indoors, showers, dresses, and walks out of Anthony's life.[10] That night Anthony is suddenly awakened from a recurring nightmare he has had since his boyhood. In the dream he is forced to consume a thick, gummy substance which expands and hardens inside him until, near the point of gagging, he wakes up. On this occasion he tries to go back to sleep but the dream and the events of the day have set his mind in motion: "A huge accumulation of neglected memories broke through, as it were, into his awareness. Those snapshots. His mother and Mary Amberley. Brian in the chalk-pit, evoked by that salty smell of [Helen's] sun-warmed flesh, and again dead at the cliff's foot, among the flies—like that dog . . ." (pp. 124-125). In this method of free association Huxley has chosen a most appropriate vehicle for his theme of spiritual awakening. In contrast to the willed abstractions and heavy-handed analogues which cloud matters in *Beyond the Mexique Bay*, the subjective, spontaneous mental associations used here serve to illuminate the essential realities that unify Anthony's entire life into a continuous process—awareness of which amounts to his one hope for recovering his essential humanity.

One event in Anthony's life which plays a most important part in his mental associations has been heretofore overlooked by critics. The reason for this oversight is not difficult to determine, for the event is not overtly emphasized in the novel. No separate narrative sequence is devoted to the years 1914-15. But there are occasional references in other time-frames to that period, during which Anthony had received a serious wound that would have a determining effect upon his later life. The most extensive reference appears in Chapter Eight, set on that same hot August day in 1933. While still engaged in lovemaking on the rooftop with Helen—and just before the precipitous visitation from the heavens in the form of the dog—Anthony discusses a freak accident in which he was involved during the war:

> . . . [Helen] touched the pink crumpled skin of the scar that ran diagonally across his thigh, an inch or two above the knee. "Does it still hurt?" she asked.
>
> "When I'm run down. And sometimes in wet weather." He raised his head a little from the mattress and, at the same time bending his right knee, examined the scar. "A touch of the Renaissance," he said reflectively. "Slashed trunks."
>
> Helen shuddered. "It must have been awful!" Then, with a sudden vehemence, "How I hate pain!" she cried. . . .
>
> She had pushed him back into the past again. That autumn day at Tidworth eighteen years before. Bombing instruction. An imbecile recruit had thrown short. The shouts, his panic, the blow. Oddly remote it seemed now . . . like something seen through the wrong end of a telescope. . . . Physically, it was the worst thing that had ever happened to him . . . and the lunatic in charge of his memory had nearly forgotten it. (p. 66)[11]
>
>                    *        *        *        *
>
> "How long were you in the hospital with that wound?" she asked in another tone.
>
> "Nearly ten months. It was disgustingly infected. They had to operate six times altogether."

"How horrible!"

Anthony shrugged his shoulders. At least it had preserved him from those trenches. But for the grace of God ..."Queer," he added, "what unlikely forms the grace of God assumes sometimes! A half-witted bumpkin with a hand-grenade. But for him I should have been shipped out to France and slaughtered—almost to a certainty. He saved my life." Then, after a pause, "My freedom too," he added. "I'd let myself be fuddled by those beginning-of-war intoxications. 'Honour has come back, as a king, to earth.' But I suppose you're too young ever to have heard of poor Rupert [Brooke]. It seemed to make sense then, in 1914. 'Honour has come back...' But he failed to mention that stupidity had come back too. In hospital, I had all the leisure to think of that other royal progress through the earth. Stupidity has come back, as a king—no; as an emperor, as a divine Führer of all the Aryans. It was a sobering reflection. Sobering and profoundly liberating. And I owed it all to the bumpkin."
(p. 68)

When we recall that Huxley thought of *Eyeless in Gaza* as a novel about "the problem of freedom," the importance of this passage increases still further. Anthony's "liberation" from the past—that is, his withdrawal from the world of time and sentience—had begun during the period of convalescence from his leg wound. In his personal brush with death Anthony's fear of ineffable flux, a fear which had begun with the loss of his mother in 1902 and which was compounded by guilt after the suicide of Brian Foxe twelve years later, must have reached a new intensity. Thus his self-imposed role as "the detached philosopher" and "preoccupied man of science" actually originated in those "sobering reflections" of 1914-15.

If Anthony had been generally successful during the last eighteen years in obscuring reality by looking at it as through the wrong end of a telescope, he is no longer able to do so after being so rudely immersed in materiality by the intrusion of the battered dog. The next episodes in the narrative present all reveal an Anthony Beavis who is increasingly dissatisfied with his sterile existence. One sleepless September night less than a week later, Anthony passes the time by rereading parts of *The Man Who Died*. Though previously Lawrence had been instrumental in the formulation of Anthony's theory of personality as a "succession of states," here Lawrence's apotheosizing of the "vast resoluteness of life" in all forms strikes Anthony as naive at best. Anthony reflects that mere life or primal energy is not worthy of the reverence of intelligent human beings. Lawrence had not bothered to look at raw life under a microscope—nor had he ever been drenched in dog's guts—and so he had not perceived that matter alone was only base and appalling. Beavis concludes that Lawrence's belief in "the animal purpose" amounts to a misguided endorsement of "submental passion" and "violent and impersonal egotism" (p. 272).[12]

The following morning (September 5, 1933) Anthony awakens to find his friend Mark Staithes in his bedroom staring at him. In the ensuing conversation Anthony confesses that he is discontent with himself and his accustomed way of life:

> "I have a feeling...that I'd like to get it over, get things settled. On another basis.... The present one... I'm a bit bored with it.... It won't do.... It's a basis that can't carry more than the weight of a ghost. And in order to use it, I've turned myself into a ghost.... These last few days I've had a queer feeling that I'm not really there, that I haven't been there for years past. Ever since ...well, I don't know when. *Since before the war*, I suppose." (p. 276, my emphasis)

Later Anthony contemplates his "ordinary London life,"

> the lunches with men of learning and affairs, the dinners where women kept the conversation more gossipy and amusing—and the easy, meaningless successes, which his talents and a certain natural charm always allowed

him to score at such gatherings, had made him all but completely forget his dissatisfaction, had masked the pain of it, as a drug will mask neuralgia or a toothache. . . . [The] old quiet life! So quietly squalid, so quietly inhuman and, for all the expense of thought it entailed, so quietly mad. (pp. 357-358)

Anthony realizes that despite his attempts to react against his stuffy and pedantic father's way of life, he too is becoming "a man in a burrow," imprisoned in his ascetic retreat from the real world. He sees himself as a kind of coward, a coward morally and perhaps physically as well—he is not certain of the latter, for unlike Mark Staithes, Anthony is untested, has always avoided any kind of risk.

Staithes proposes a trip to Mexico to participate in a provincial revolution. It would be just what Anthony needs, says Staithes. "'Death. . . . It's the only thing we haven't succeeded in completely vulgarizing.'" "'It's a comfort . . . to think that death remains faithful. . . . If we choose to risk our lives, we can risk them as completely as ever we did'" (pp. 311-312). Mark Staithes assumes the pose of a kind of "code hero" such as those found in the fiction of Hemingway. The difference is that Huxley consciously presents Staithes as a fool, a man who disguises his masochism in these romantic schemes. Mark has no great belief in the Mexican revolution in which he wants to take part. It would not even be revolution for the sake of revolution, but "for mine," he admits. And if it succeeds, will the revolution improve the plight of the oppressed peasants? "'It never [does],'" he says. "'What did the French peons get out of their Revolution? Or our friends, the Russians, for that matter? A few years of pleasant intoxication. Then the same old treadmill. Gilded, perhaps; repainted. But in essentials the old machine'" (p. 354). Although Anthony is aware of the foolishness of this venture, it still attracts him as a chance to test the "basis" of his life in order to find out if he is no more than a "ghost" or if he is "really there": "Mark's enterprise might be stupid and even disgraceful; but, however bad, it was still preferable to that quietude of work and occasional detached sensuality beside the Mediterranean" (p. 358).

The two travelers disembark in Puerto San Felipe in December 1933. They are greeted by "an emaciated woman, prematurely old and tired, beyond the limit of her strength" (p. 374). Their brief stopover in her house is punctuated by the screams of a young girl, the woman's daughter, who writhes in her bed with fever. They travel on by pack-mules to the mountain village of Tapatlán.[13] The hotel there is squalid, and, thanks to the bedbugs, the heat, and an attack of dysentery, sleep is hard to come by. The next day they visit the marketplace in the local plaza, where the slabs of meat in the butchers' stalls are covered with a crust of flies. Indian women squat impassively in the dust by their piles of withering fruit and vegetables. "From under hat-brims, dark eyes regarded the strangers with an inscrutably reptilian glitter that seemed devoid of all curiosity, all interest, any awareness even of their presence" (pp. 376-377). Here in Tapatlán, it is "an immense fatigue even to be living and conscious." "'When I die,'" Anthony remarks, "'this is the part of hell I shall be sent to. I recognize it instantly'" (p. 377).

It would seem that we have returned to that land regarded with so much hostility in *Beyond the Mexique Bay*. And so we have. However, there is a significant difference in the presentation of "inscrutable" Mexico in *Eyeless in Gaza*, for here the traveler's pejorative response to the country and its people is viewed as an inherent part of his personal trials. If Anthony instantly recognizes "hell" in Mexico, this is because he finds himself in a landscape so utterly strange to him that it assumes the function of an external correlative for his unsettled state of mind:

There was no shade, and the vast bald hills were the colour of dust and burnt grass. Nothing stirred, not even a lizard among the stones. There was no sight or sound of life. Hopelessly empty, the chaos of tumbled moun-

tains seemed to stretch away interminably. It was as though they had ridden *across the frontier* of the world out into nothingness, into an infinite expanse of hot and dusty negation.
  . . . Anthony was so tired that he could scarcely think or even see. The landscape seemed to advance and retreat before his eyes, turned black sometimes and faded away altogether. . . . Image succeeded image in a phantasmagoria that it was beyond his power to exorcise. It was as though he were possessed. . . . (pp. 401-402, my emphasis)

Anthony's sense of being "possessed" is due less to any occult powers residing in the Mexican ambience than to the fact that he has crossed the border into the dark underside of his own consciousness. His labyrinthine course through nothingness, emptiness, and interminable chaos can only lead him toward the dreaded confrontation with the specter of death. And because Anthony's capacity for both sublimating and rationalizing painful realities is considerable, he must face death in one form or another no less than three times in the Mexican chapters. On the first occasion, at the seedy hotel in Tapatlán, Anthony unintentionally angers a dapper young Mexican *hacendado* by refusing the latter's invitation to join him for a drink. Anthony's limited facility with Spanish renders him helpless to explain that he means no offense, that the reason he cannot drink is that he is trying to recover from dysentery. His fumbling protestations only further infuriate the drunken Mexican, who suddenly pulls out a revolver. (The scene has an additional irony in that, far from being an "inscrutable" Indian with "reptilian" eyes, the *hacendado* is apparently of Spanish blood, with "comprehensibly expressive" eyes, a man who takes pride in his firm treatment of the peons on his coffee *finca*, but still a Mexican who clearly wants nothing better than to impress this "foreign cavalier" by his largesse. Anthony, in his ignorance, thus doubly offends the man—pricks both his racial and his nationalistic pride—and then reacts as if he were confronted

by a murderous Villista.) Terrified, Anthony leaps for cover
behind a large pillar, where he waits for the man to make his
next move:

> Anthony imagined the revolver suddenly coming round
> the pillar into his face . . . —he would feel the muzzle,
> pressed against his back, would hear the *ghastly explo-
> sion*, and then . . . [ellipsis in original] A fear so intense
> that it was like the most excruciating physical pain pos-
> sessed him entirely; his heart beat more violently than
> ever, he felt as though he were going to be sick.
>
>        *     *     *     *
>
> The noise of the revolver going off—that was what he
> dreaded most. The horrible noise, sudden and annihilat-
> ing *like the noise of that other explosion years before.*
> His eyelids had stiffened and were irrepressibly trem-
> bling, ready to blink, in anticipation of the horrifying
> event. . . . [It] was through a kind of mist that, peeping
> out, he saw the door open and Mark moving swiftly
> across the room, Mark catching the young man by the
> wrist . . . [ellipsis in original] The pistol went off; rever-
> berated from walls and ceiling, the report was cata-
> strophically loud. Anthony uttered a great cry, *as
> though he had been wounded* and, shutting his eyes,
> flattened himself against the pillar. Conscious only of
> nausea and that pain in the genitals, those grippings of
> the bowels, he waited, reduced to a mere quivering em-
> bodiment of fearful anticipation, for the next explosion.
> Waited for what seemed hours. Dim voices parleyed in-
> comprehensibly. Then a touch on his shoulder made him
> start. He shouted, "No, don't," and lifting eyelids that
> still twitched with the desire to blink, saw Mark Staithes,
> demonstrating . . . a smile of friendly amusement.
> "All clear," he said. "You can come out." (pp. 378-
> 379, my emphasis)

Viewed from a different perspective and with perhaps a few
minor directorial alterations, this scene might have provided
the substance for slapstick humor; but instead of Mack Sen-

nett, Huxley gives us vintage Hitchcock. Despite the absurdities of the situation and of the manner in which it was provoked, the encounter is absolutely serious and fraught with horror for Anthony, for he is reliving the experience of his wound, an experience far transcending the mere physical injury. The "ghastly explosion" he awaits tremulously is as much the detonation of that hand grenade "thrown short" as the report of the *hacendado's* pistol. Anthony, one recalls, has reason to fear explosions: Brian Foxe's suicidal leap and the descent of the dog (a *fox* terrier) had resulted in "explosions" which Anthony would as soon forget—had thought, in fact, that he had all but driven from his memory.

The second episode in the Mexican chapters which compels Anthony's mind to return to the psychological traumas associated with his wound occurs on January 10, 1933, along the mountain road toward Oaxaca. Mark's mule stumbles and he is thrown down onto some rocks. His left knee is badly cut and bleeding profusely. Looking at Mark's wound, "Anthony frowned . . . as though the pain were his own" (p. 403). But Mark is contemptuous toward any attempt to take care of the injury, and the next day when Anthony suggests a change of dressing, Mark scornfully rips the old bandage off the raw wound, thus starting the bleeding again. Anthony notices that the gash has begun to fester, and again he winces "as though the pain were his" (p. 406). In his eagerness to arrive on time to take part in the planning phase of the revolution, Mark refuses to rest or seek medical aid. At the end of the day's travel he collapses. The following morning he is delirious with fever, the infection having spread down the leg to his ankle, and Anthony sets out to find a doctor back in the last village. After riding for two hours, "the miracle happened," as he stumbles upon Dr. James Miller and brings him back to Mark. The leg is by now gangrenous and must be amputated. As there is no one else, Anthony must assist in the operation by holding the black and swollen leg. He is by turns apprehensive, tense, and nauseous during the ordeal. But with calm and firm reassurances from Miller, Anthony manages to endure the sight of all the blood and of "those broad flaps of skin turned back, like the peel of a huge banana"; the "stink of mortified flesh"; and the rasping sound of the saw's teeth "biting into bone" (pp. 428-430). These sensations would in themselves be unpleasant enough for most people to witness firsthand. In Anthony's case they are all the more difficult to tolerate because of the memory of his own "disgustingly infected" leg, the six operations, the ten months in the hospital, the scar, the residual pain. Anthony's determination to stay and assist Miller in the amputation is the all-important first step toward overcoming his fear of death.

Acceptance by Anthony of the extent of death's dominion is not complete, however, until a third and decisive encounter three weeks later. This time it is death by proxy which Anthony must contend with, for he is not directly threatened—though he might well have been. Dr. Miller, on a visit to examine his convalescing patient, brings news of the failure of the Oaxacan revolution. The governor's troops have triumphed. The insurgent leaders were captured and executed. Mark's reaction is characteristic; he bemoans the fact that he was not permitted to march proud before that firing squad, sharing in a few last jokes with his brave confederates. Anthony, however, is shaken by the realization that had they arrived in time to participate in the *coup d'état*, they too would have been shot, would be dead at this moment. So overcome with this prospect is Anthony that he takes very little part in the ensuing long debate between Staithes and Dr. Miller concerning the ethical implications of mass violence. In fact, in a novel replete with his talk and musings, Anthony's relative silence in this key scene is most eloquent. While Miller touts enlightened anthropology and Staithes defends the necessity of "facing danger courageously," what is going on in Anthony's mind? We are not told, yet we know. And we know, for once without having to be told, because Huxley has so carefully prepared us for this moment. This scene is the functional climax of the novel, the point at which chaos finally gives way to continuity— and to Huxley's credit, the climax seems quite convincing, for it is articulated not in the usual rhetorical manner, but in the novel's very structure. In sum, the reader shares with Anthony a sense of *déjà vu:* the close brush with death, the fortuitous reprieve, the sigh of relief abbreviated by an after-the-fact paroxym of fear. But in 1915 the fear had overwhelmed the relief, and what stayed with Anthony, despite his elaborate defense mechanisms, was the bald terror of mortality. Now, in 1934, experiencing the entire pattern again, he suddenly remembers there was that sigh of relief too, which implies that life might just be worth living even in the face of such dangers. Millions were bludgeoned in the trenches in 1914-18; the Oaxacan rebels were lined up and shot so they they would all drop right into their graves. Anthony could easily have been one of the faceless victims of mass slaughter, but both times he was spared—first when he was wounded and made "unfit" for the trenches, and now when his companion's freak injury kept them from joining the abortive revolution. This combination of actual and vicarious confrontations with death renders Anthony's nascent awareness of the fact of mortality more balanced and finally healthy. If time wounds, he realizes, it also heals.

Meanwhile, Mark Staithes has reached the conclusion that Miller is a hopeless idealist. Unlike Miller, Mark will not be bothered with so futile a gesture as trying to save the world from its certain course of destruction. All he can do, says Mark, is " 'look on. It won't be for long, anyhow. Just a few years; and then . . . [ellipsis in original]' " (pp. 443-444). Mark caps his argument by cynically quoting a verse from the Earl of Rochester:

> Then old age and experience, hand in hand,
> Lead him to death, and make him understand,
> After a search so painful and so long,
> That all his life he had been in the wrong.
> Huddled in dirt the reasoning engine lies,
> Who was so proud, so witty and so wise.

But when Mark looks conspiratorially at Anthony, expecting him to approve the phrase "huddled in dirt" as an appropriate description of man's true condition before as well as after death, Anthony, having detected a greater personal significance in the earlier lines—"After a search so painful and long,/ . . . all his life he had been in the wrong"—can only declare his decision to "'go and make myself ridiculous with Miller'" (p. 444).

The remaining chapters in the narrative present, set back in England, consist chiefly of entries in Anthony's journal, the recording of which he considers a requisite step toward the self-knowledge that makes self-change possible. The entries demonstrate his continuing re-evaluation of himself in light of Miller's beliefs and his own recent experiences. About six weeks after his return from Mexico, Anthony's process of growth has brought him to the point where he must seek workable answers to the problems posed by his former outlook. "Query: how to combine belief that the world is to a great extent illusory with belief that it is none the less essential to improve the illusion?" (p. 64). By February 23, 1935, when the final chapter takes place, Anthony has effectually undergone his spiritual regeneration, though the process is continuous and open-ended. He has discovered "by some immediate experience," *beyond* intellect alone, that "the point was in the paradox, in the fact that unity was the beginning and unity the end, and that in the meantime the condition of life and all existence was separation, which was equivalent to evil. Yes, the point, he insisted, is that one demands of oneself the achievement of the impossible" (p. 470).

So long as existence is seen only in terms of irremediable negations, as a disjointed series of accidents which doom man to failure and "separation," death looms as the ultimate and inevitable judgment on the human condition and is thus to be feared. But once Anthony is able to view life as "a test, and education—searching, difficult, drawn out through a lifetime, perhaps through long series of lifetimes" (p. 470), his fear of death and all the other manifestations of temporal flux may be transcended.

Sybille Bedford points out that *Eyeless in Gaza* was "the

expression of a stage in a lifetime of development.... One stage, but a crucial stage; a point of no return. Aldous never went back on the convictions he had come to [in the course of writing the novel]."[14] In the alembic of the imagination the journey to Mexico, which had seemed to Huxley such a dead end at the time of his visit, was revealed as an essential station on the path toward transcendence. It is true that he exhibits in the novel little real understanding of (or, what is worse, interest in) contemporary Mexico, sketching the land in oblique and generalized terms. Further, it is true that in comparison with Lawrence, Greene, Lowry—and, on another level, Ralph Bates (see Appendix)—Huxley is markedly less attuned to Mexico's paradisal possibilities. To his sensibility the country is almost unrelievedly infernal. Nevertheless, for Huxley no less than for Anthony Beavis, passage through that region amounted ultimately to a realization of profound inner darkness. And such a realization was requisite before he might behold perennial light.

# VI

# Graham Greene and "Life on a Border"

## I

North to Scandinavia, south to Liberia, Sierra Leone and the Congo, east to Istanbul aboard the Orient Express and to Vietnam, west-southwest to Cuba, Haiti, Paraguay, and Mexico—the list of remote places to which Graham Greene has been drawn at one time or another over an extensive career as a novelist might be that of a veteran diplomat or a foreign correspondent with a special gift for sensing where social unrest or violence is likely to erupt next. Indeed, the frequency and the range of his travels (the above are but a selection of highlights) give weight to the notion that Greene is, after Conrad, the most international of English novelists. Of course, the works of both Conrad and Greene may be seen within the larger tradition of travel-oriented writings by itinerant Englishmen dating back to Childe Harold and beyond. But what seems to set Greene apart from so many of the English writers who have exploited the exotic is his cosmopolitan outlook, most conspicuously witnessed in his treatment of political material throughout his fiction. As Anthony Burgess has noted, "British politics are too small for Graham Greene...." Contrasting Greene's views with those of Evelyn Waugh, another English novelist who traveled widely when the going was good between the world wars, Burgess finds that even while abroad, Waugh consistently identified himself with traditional English upper-class values.

For Greene, on the other hand, social and spiritual isolation constitutes an artistic imperative which precludes strictly parochial concerns, and thus the "furniture of England is a distraction and an irrelevance."[1]

I shall be returning to the Greene-Waugh pairing in another context later in this chapter, but at this point it will be useful to pursue the contrast offered by Burgess a step further. Viewed from a different angle Greene's attraction to particular kinds of settings suggests a narrowness not shared by Waugh. Greene's deep and abiding interest in failure, squalor, and violence has impelled him to seek out those regions which epitomize his personal preoccupations. If Waugh journeyed to the Mediterranean, to Africa, and to Mexico with a considerable freight of attitudes which were only reinforced by his exposure to these places, at least his concerns were broadly identifiable with those of an established social and intellectual element in English life. But Greene's journeys, on the whole—especially as they are presented in his travel writings—have provided him with the opportunity to engage primarily in self-exploration, to pursue his own obsessions as they are bodied forth in strange and remote settings.

"Strangely enough the mental geography of his novels remained unaltered. Wherever he might choose to live now, he had found his mythical region once and forever as a young man. . . ." These words, which describe Doctor Jorge Julio Saavedra, the once-fashionable Argentine novelist in *The Honorary Consul* (1973), apply to Greene as well. The settings of Greene's novels—whether the tropical forests of Mexico, a *léproserie* in the Congo, or the gang-land underground of Brighton—show such a marked similarity in their emphasis on the "seedy" that critics have coined the term "Greeneland" to identify them all. " 'My region,' " confesses Doctor Saavedra, " 'is the region of extremes.' "[2] Since this region of extremes is above all a sector of "mental geography" Greene is quite as capable of finding it in his native England as in remote countries. However, his usual practice has been

to locate it in those lands where the actual squalor and corruption and violence are more pervasive than in the domestic
setting. At the same time, the presence of these lurid elements
in a strange and exotic locale necessarily lends them a certain
romantic appeal and excitement which would not be so
readily generated by viewing them against a more familiar
background.[3] This combination of attractive and repulsive
factors, objectified in a single highly charged landscape,
operates as a vehicle quite appropriate to Greene's particular
metaphysical concerns.

In *Journey Without Maps* (1936) Greene explains his view
of the "deep appeal" of seediness, a notion which must be
grasped before proceeding to Greene's peculiar response to
Mexico. He identifies three levels of human development: the
civilized, the seedy or semi-civilized, and the primitive. The
journey described in this book moves through each of these
phases as Greene proceeds from London to Liverpool (characterized by the seediness found amidst civilization) to Free-
town in Sierra Leone (the semi-civilization found on the edge
of the primitive), to the villages of the Liberian bush, back
again to seediness at Monrovia on the Coast, and thence to
England. The heart of the travel book concerns Greene's confrontation with the primitive, but the whole process of going
back in time to the human origins is instructive for the
explorer:

> ... there are times of impatience [Greene writes], when
> one is less content to rest at the urban stage, when one is
> willing to suffer some discomfort for the chance of find-
> ing—there are a thousand names for it, King Solomon's
> Mines, the "heart of darkness" if one is romantically in-
> clined, or more simply ... one's place in time, based on a
> knowledge not only of one's present but of the past from
> which one has emerged.

The idea is elaborated a few paragraphs later. "It is not, of
course, that one wishes to stay for ever at that level, but
when one sees to what unhappiness, to what peril of extinc-

tion centuries of cerebration have brought us, one sometimes has a curiosity to discover if one can from what we have come, to recall at which point we went astray."[4]

Stemming as they do from Greene's critical view of modern life in the abstract, these passages provide a memorable statement of one motive for his interest in regions which take him back beyond "the urban stage." At the same time, however, such journeys represent fitful attempts at uncovering—or, more accurately, reconstructing—a personal myth located, like Wordsworth's (but *unlike* Lawrence's) in the past, in etiology. One has to read Greene's travel writings on both levels, for they consist of an interweaving of topical observations on the external scene and personal, sometimes confessional, utterances. To begin with, in *Journey Without Maps* we discover that the primitive holds an undeniable attraction for Greene, who finds in it that the "sense of taste [is] finer, the sense of pleasure keener, the sense of terror deeper and purer...[and] the sense of supernatural evil" felt more intensely than is possible in the modern civilized world.[5] Many references to Greene's boyhood fantasies and dreams in conjunction with anecdotes about tribal rituals and "bush devils" make clear the identification between primitive life and the prelapsarian innocence of childhood.[6] However, Greene's interest in locating "at which point we went astray" inevitably leads him to seediness, which is linked in his mind with the trials and traumas of adolescence. The seedy society, like the adolescent, "*is* nearer the beginning.... [It] has begun to build wrong, but at least it has only begun; it hasn't gone so far away as the smart, the new, the chic, the cerebral."[7]

Primitive-childhood on the one hand, modern-adulthood on the other—these, ultimately, are the radical "extremes" between which Greene's mind moves, though it is not essentially engaged by either one. Since the two poles do not exist side by side in time or in space, the tension between them is felt most acutely in the frontier zone where they are joined and, at the same time, separated. Seediness—adolescence—

is the crucial phase of life for Greene. His attitudes toward it, shaped in large part by a crisis suffered during his own adolescence, are profoundly ambivalent. In general terms, this borderline phase of the Greene myth (projected onto external frontiers and seedy locales) is characterized by fear and apprehension, the first awareness of human corruption, divided loyalties associated with betrayal, and a preternatural, almost sublime sense of excitement:

> One was an inhabitant of both countries: on Saturday and Sunday afternoons of one side of the baize door [i.e., at home], the rest of the week of the other [i.e., at public school]. How can life on a border be other than restless? You are pulled by different ties of hate and love. ... In the land of skyscrapers, of stone stairs and cracked bells ringing early, one was aware of fear and hate, a kind of lawlessness—appalling cruelties could be practised without a second thought; one met for the first time characters, adult and adolescent, who bore about them the genuine quality of evil. . . . Hell lay about them in their infancy. [A doubly revealing turn on the Wordsworth line.]
>
> There lay the horror and the fascination. One escaped surreptitiously for an hour at a time: unknown to the frontier guards, one stood on the wrong side of the border looking back. . . . It was an hour of release—and also an hour of prayer. One became aware of God with an intensity—time hung suspended—music lay on the air; anything might happen. . . . [8]

Of all the external "regions of extremes" visited by Graham Greene, Mexico was the first which fully embodied in its landscape, its culture, and its politico-religious conflicts the electric atmosphere of the border so fundamental to Greene's imagination. The psychological-border motif had appeared sporadically in his novels of the early and middle 1930's, before his trip to Mexico in 1938. And in *Journey Without Maps* we find him referring frequently and explicitly to the symbolic nature of borders of various types. But in Africa Greene was impressed foremost by the innocence which he detected in the inhabitants of the villages of the Liberian bush country. As a result his reflections about the inward borders he was crossing on the trip are generally characterized by a minimum of tension or oppression: "...all the time, below the fear and the irritation, one was aware of a curious lightness and freedom...one was happy...one had crossed the boundary into country really strange; one had gone deep this time."[9] Greene's feelings for Africa and for the "primitive" Africans he encountered were largely positive and sympathetic, though there were moments when he experienced an elemental terror for which the only precedent was his childhood dreams of threatening forces, of a nameless power outside that *"has got to come in."* Even these, however, are recollections of the period *before* he trod the border between love and hate, heaven and hell. Although Greene's reflections on borders in his African travel book indicate the direction in which his sensibility was tending at the time, one senses that Greene had not yet fully realized the richest possibilities of the emerging myth, nor how he would articulate it in his subsequent writing. His immediate progress in these regards may be seen in such works as "The Basement Room" (1936, written on the return trip to England) and *Brighton Rock* (1938), the first of the Catholic novels. But the fullest and most explicit (if somewhat quirky) attempt to give expression to the myth is his Mexican travel book. *Another Mexico* (1939) is replete with border symbolism and associated imagery, often accompanied by fragmentary references to Greene's adolescent crisis. At the same time, the book juxtaposes the lost-childhood myth with the adult's spiritual pilgrimage through Mexico, a land which was itself suffering a period of crisis. Greene documents in copious detail the anxiety and outright hostility elicited in him by this predominantly "seedy" republic. The occasion for the trip—to investigate the persecution of the Catholic Church in Revolutionary Mexico—offered Greene an additional benefit he probably had not foreseen. Mexico (and especially the "Godless state" of Tabasco) impressed upon Greene, as Africa could not, the centrality of his own religious faith to the entire experience that he called "life on a border."


## II

> What a relief it is sometimes to find oneself on a material frontier, a frontier visible to the eyes, tangible—even when in Berlin it is a wall. For most of us have all our lives in this unhappy century carried an invisible frontier around with us, political, religious, moral.... Nearly forty years ago I stepped across such a frontier when I became a Catholic, but the frontier did not cease to exist for me because I had crossed it. Often I have returned and looked over it with nostalgia....
>
> —Letter to a West German Friend[10]

Greene's entry into Mexico at Laredo seemed to him momentous. "Every half-hour," he writes in *Another Mexico*, "I walked down to the river bank and looked at Mexico; it looked just the same as where I was.... I could imagine... [that] people like me were waiting on the other side, staring across the Rio Grande at the money-changers and thinking: 'That's the United States.'... It was like looking at yourself in a mirror" (p. 14). Since the passage into Mexico from Laredo involves crossing a long, narrow, heavily-trafficked bridge which prolongs the whole process of entry, one necessarily has time to ponder, if one chooses, the significance of the crossing itself. "The border means more than a customs house, a passport officer, a man with a gun. Over there everything is going to be different; life is never going to be quite the same again..." (p. 13).[11] A frontier—and this one especially—is among other things a vantage point, a dividing-line which visually accentuates a sense of the proximity of change in one's life before the change actually occurs.

> Over there . . . were Chichen Itzá and Mitla and Palen-
> que, the enormous tombstones of history, the archeolo-
> gist's Mexico; serapes and big hats and Spratling silver
> from Taxco to delight the tourist; for the historian the
> relics of Cortes and the [other] Conquistadores; for the
> art critic the Rivera and Orozco frescoes; and for the
> business man there were the oil-fields of Tampico, the
> silver-mines of Pachuca, the coffee-farms in Chiapas,
> and the banana groves of Tabasco. For the priest prison,
> and for the politician a bullet. (pp. 14-15)

Stimulated and shaped by the unique perspective of the frontier, such pre-crossing thoughts, both the hopeful expectation
and the fear of danger, may prove ultimately to be distortions of actuality. But because they heighten the traveler's
awareness of the beginning of something new and important,
they are for Greene as vital—almost as meaningful perhaps—
as the reality he will experience "over there": "The atmosphere of the border—it is like starting over again; there is
something about it like a good confession: poised for a few
happy moments between sin and sin. When people die on the
border they call it 'a happy death'" (p. 13).

*Like starting over again.* The Prologue of *Another Mexico*
makes clear which point in time it was that Greene experienced anew as he stood "poised" in the atmosphere of the
Mexican border. The most critical frontier ever traversed by
Greene, as suggested earlier, was the crisis of his adolescence.
It began when his parents determined (against his wishes)
that he must board at St. John's, the boys' dormitory at Berkhamsted School, where his father was headmaster. Leaving
behind at age thirteen the affection and comfort and security
of an upper-middle-class home, Greene entered a new and
squalid world "smelling of sweat and stale clothes," a world
of "stone stairs, worn by generations of feet, leading to a dormitory divided by pitch-pine partitions that gave inadequate
privacy—no moment of the night was free from noise, a
cough, a snore, a fart."[12] Outwardly shy and bookish at this

age, Greene fell prey to the pranks of more aggressive boys
who quickly saw their advantage over him. Here is his
account of this period from *A Sort of Life:*

> I had left civilization behind and entered a savage coun-
> try of strange customs and inexplicable cruelties: a coun-
> try in which I was a foreigner and a suspect, quite liter-
> ally a hunted creature, known to have dubious associ-
> ates. Was my father not the headmaster? I was like the
> son of a quisling in a country under occupation. My
> elder brother Raymond was a school prefect . . . in other
> words one of Quisling's collaborators. I was surrounded
> by the forces of the resistance, and yet I couldn't join
> them without betraying my father and brother.[13]

We do not know all of the circumstances involved, but it is
clear enough from Greene's account that he felt estranged
from both home and school, the two opposed "worlds" separated by a mere green baize door just beyond his father's
study. What made this division so unbearable, as Philip
Stratford has pointed out, was the "artificiality of the separation." Greene's "sentence of . . . imprisonment in alien territory was imposed and enforced from the friendly side of the
border. . . . [For] Greene there was a constant confusion of
values, a permanent sense of injustice, and betrayal at the
heart."[14] In retaliation Greene became adept at truancy. He
invented any excuse to avoid chapel, boys' games, classes, so
that he might escape to the safety of the woods nearby. The
crisis was finally ameliorated, for the time being, by a dramatic flight from "home" and eventually by six months of
psychoanalysis in London. Thus summarized, this may seem
little more than the familiar tale of the sensitive new boy's
unsettling introduction to the traditional clubbishness and
hazing of the English public school. But it was obviously
much more than that. One has only to read Greene's account
of his subsequent attraction to Russian roulette as a means
for dispelling boredom to see how deep and permanent the
effects of the trauma were. The experience remained so pain-

ful in memory that as late as 1959 Greene found it necessary
to abandon a novel in progress that had its setting in a public
school. He had revisited Berkhamsted and found it frighten-
ingly unchanged. "I couldn't bear mentally living again for
several years in these surroundings [he writes in his autobiog-
raphy]. A leper colony in the Congo was preferable, so I
went to Yonda in search of a burnt-out case."[15]

What makes the adolescent crisis so important as far as
Greene's writing is concerned is the fact that it shaped his
way of looking at experience and gave him the "primary
symbols" to which he would return, after his conversion to
Catholicism, with new understanding:

> And so faith came to one—shapelessly, without dogma,
> a presence above a croquet lawn, something associated
> with violence, cruelty, evil across the way. One began to
> believe in heaven because one believed in hell, but for a
> long while it was only hell one could picture with a cer-
> tain intimacy....
>    ...[Later] one began to have a dim conception of the
> appalling mysteries of love moving through a ravaged
> world.... [But it] remained something one associated
> with misery, violence, evil.... (*Another Mexico*, p. 3)

These were the memories which came to Greene more than
twenty years later as he gazed across the Mexican border,
and which stayed with him after he had crossed over the
bridge and stood gazing back. "The rabbits moved among
the croquet hoops and a clock struck: God was there and
might intervene.... The great brick buildings rose at the end
of the lawn against the sky—like the hotels in the United
States which you can watch from Mexico leaning among the
stars across the international bridge" (p. 12).

The crossing of the border at Laredo was to be just the first
in a complicated series of what may be called generic border
experiences undergone by Greene as he approached the
"other Mexico" in Tabasco and Chiapas, the infernal "region
of extremes" where he was later to set his Mexican novel.

Indeed, the perspective of the border assumes such a crucial importance in the travel book and, in more varied and suggestive ways, in *The Power and the Glory* (1940) as well, that it is essential at this point to discuss Greene's adaptation of the border sensibility to literary purposes. In his autobiography Greene quotes from Browning's "Bishop Blougram's Apology" a passage concerning the ambivalent appeal of "the dangerous edge of things" and says that the passage might serve as an epigraph for all his novels—fittingly, since boundaries and divisions of one kind or another do appear in most of his fiction. This "dangerous edge of things" is frequently employed as the central feature of a novel's setting, as in the mountain border between Tabasco and Chiapas in *The Power and the Glory*, or the little port town along the Paraná River between Argentina and Paraguay in *The Honorary Consul*. In these cases the geographical frontiers figure significantly in plot developments and ultimately acquire symbolic meanings. Sometimes, however, the sense of the border appears merely as a figure of speech in a description of something which may have no relation to a literal boundary, as when a murderer in *This Gun for Hire* (1936) finds that human relationships bring him into contact with his own buried feelings "as if he were passing the customs of a land he had never entered before and would never be able to leave."[16] Borderline associations may operate on a purely symbolic plane and, as such, articulate a novel's central theme. In *Brighton Rock*, for example, Greene emphasizes the difference between the religious values of good and evil and the humanistic values of right and wrong by repeatedly describing the Catholic characters as being in a different "world" from the secular characters. On occasion Greene has applied the border sense as a structural device, as he does in *The Power and the Glory* by counterpointing a series of scenes involving the fleeing priest with scenes depicting the activities of his pursuers. In whatever way it is used, the border pattern is fundamentally a technique of perceiving things in suggestive spatial relationships.

A border, by its mere existence, calls attention to the presence of some manner of duality. As they are perceived spatially, two general types of duality may be distinguished: those which convey primarily a sense of polarity, and those which convey most emphatically a sense of contiguity. In the first of these types of duality the border, whether literal or figurative, operates as a separator or barrier between polarized entities. It divides them from each other, although in a sense it also connects them. The border which stresses contiguity rather than polarity functions so as to join or connect adjacent entities, and yet it also marks a fine line of distinction between them. For instance, when the priest in *The Power and the Glory* finally reveals his identity to the man he knows will betray him, it is "as if they had climbed out of their opposing trenches and met in No Man's Land among the wire to fraternize."[17] The primary stress falls upon their temporary alliance in the neutral zone, but clearly the two men are still enemies. Frequently there is this kind of implicit overlap between the two types of borders.

Borders of both types need not be literally visible in order to effectuate a sense of duality in Greene's fiction. Such forces as sympathy, trust, imagination, and the Church's sacraments can conjoin otherwise disparate characters, just as hatred, revenge, lust, pity (as Greene uses the term), social class, and religious or political faction can serve as impenetrable barriers. Of course it is not at all unusual for a novelist to employ these and other forces as obstructions to human relationships. What distinguishes Greene is his insistence upon perceiving and articulating these dualities primarily in spatial terms. For example, here is how Greene renders the alienation of the whisky priest who, even while performing a clandestine mass at great risk to himself, is awed by the demonstrative mortification he witnesses in the worship of Indian peasants: "He felt humbled by the pain ordinary men bore voluntarily; his pain was forced on him. . . . [An] absurd happiness bobbed up in him again before anxiety returned: it was as if he had been permitted to *look in from the outside* at the population of heaven" (my emphasis).[18] The spatial image here brings into focus a fine irony. The priest feels himself an outsider even as he administers the sacrament of communion. The scene adumbrates the tragic duality of his character and of the role he must play in the novel. At the same time, because of the priest's preoccupation with redemption—available to others but somehow, he feels, denied to himself—the ultimate dualism is involved. Despite all his shortcomings as a priest, so long as he is there Tabasco cannot quite be a "Godless state." Instead it is a battleground (explicitly described as such in the passage cited previously) between the two eternities, the infernal paradise.

There are many such instances in Greene's fiction where the border sensibility is used to dramatize, in spatial terms, his metaphysical concerns. But it can also accommodate less lofty matters. Sometimes the *absence* of essential boundaries produces a special tension or confusion. This is a rather common feature in Greene's entertainments, where an inability to distinguish between the two "sides," between one's friends and enemies, between "ordinary" citizens and pathological murderers, exacerbates the already potent danger of trusting other people. In a few cases Greene's characters look on borderlessness as a desirable condition. For Krogh, the millionaire Swedish industrialist in *The Shipwrecked* (1935), nationality is a thing of the past. " 'Krogh doesn't think in frontiers. He's beaten unless he has the world.' "[19] Two of Greene's communist characters, Dr. Czinner in *Orient Express* (1933) and Father Rivas in *The Honorary Consul*, are obliged by their ideology to strive for a society in which boundaries of class and wealth are abolished.

With its origins in his adolescence, Greene's border sense is very closely related to the treatment of memory in his novels. Though his writing shows a heavy reliance on the faculty of memory, the memory-technique chiefly used is one through which highlights are retained at the expense of nuances. Selective retention, or what may be called the memory formula, as it were compels his protagonists to focus on decisive, formative moments from the past, each moment seen as a border over which the character has crossed and to which he returns in reverie. The pattern is epitomized by the episode of literal border-gazing and border-crossing in the Prologue to *Another Mexico*, where memory operates as a junction or bridge between the fear and restlessness of adolescence and that of the adult confronting an equally unsettling mystery "over there." In this way time itself becomes spatialized in Greene. Those scenes in which the charged atmosphere of the border triggers associations from the past, imparting the sense of "starting over again," are of the utmost importance to Greene's fiction.

An excellent example of Greene's use of selective memory as an integral part of the border experience may be found in his most recent novel, *The Honorary Consul*. The protagonist, Dr. Eduardo Plarr, is himself a border creature. An inhabitant at various times in his life of both Paraguay and Argentina, and of both the provinces and metropolitan Buenos Aires, Plarr is a man of mixed blood—English on his father's side and Latin on his mother's. When he was a boy, Plarr and his mother fled Paraguay because of a violent political upheaval in which his father, a revolutionary, took active part. In middle age Plarr has come to settle in the little unnamed port on the border, where he is kept under a loose surveillance as a Paraguayan refugee and the son of a "dangerous" man. His life in the port is basically peaceful, even dull. But he languishes in the tranquility, for he takes pleasure in staring out over the river at twilight, remembering his past and waiting for news of his father, who is rumored to be incarcerated on the other side. Escaping from Paraguay,

The young Plarr and his mother reached the river port at almost *this hour of the evening* on their way to the great noisy capital of the republic in the south...and *something in the scene*—the old colonial houses, a crumble of stucco in the street behind the waterfront—two lovers embracing on a bench—a moonstruck statue of a naked

woman and the bust of an admiral with a homely Irish
name—the electric light globes like great ripe fruit above
a soft-drink stand—*became lodged in the young Plarr's
mind as a symbol of unaccustomed peace*, so that, at
long last, when he felt the urgent need to escape somewhere from the skyscrapers, the traffic blocks, the sirens
of police cars and ambulances, the heroic statues of lib-
erators on horseback, he chose to come back to this
small northern city to work, with all the prestige of a
qualified doctor from Buenos Aires. Not one of his
friends in the capital . . . came near to understanding his
motive: he would find . . . they assured him . . . a town
where nothing ever happened, not even violence.[20]

This description—with its heavy emphasis upon carefully
selected details from the near and remote past—is crucial to
an understanding of Plarr's later behavior in the novel. The
"unaccustomed peace" associated with the port actually
proves to be an illusion, for it is precisely this scene imprinted
on his mind which represents the severance of his family ties
and the end of his childhood. To redeem those painful losses
and to confront the reality which he has evaded ever since,
Plarr must in some sense cross the border in an effort to
rescue his father, or at least (as it turns out) a father-surro-
gate in the person of the kidnaped honorary consul, Charlie
Fortnum. However unconscious the real basis of Plarr's
attraction to the border town, the fragmentary memories
which the place evokes with ever greater frequency eventually replace the desire to escape with the more urgent need to
"take up the thread of life from very far back, from so far
back as innocence."[21]

Greene has said that "the creative writer perceives his
world once and for all in childhood and adolescence, and his
whole career is an effort to illustrate his private world in
terms of the great public world we all share. . . ."[22] His own
methods for remaining at once faithful to his private vision
and projecting it onto the larger world—the most important
of which are his choice of a "region of extremes" for novelistic

settings, the frontier perspective, and the selective-memory formula—account for both the intensity and the narrowness of his work. To say the least, Greene's imaginative vision is distinctive. It is, in the words of R. W. B. Lewis, "the human situation made scenic."[23]

### III

[It] is the mark of frontiers—the evil of frontiers perhaps —that things look quite different when you pass them.

—Letter to a West German Friend[24]

Considering the quantity of work which resulted—a handful of journalistic pieces, two short stories, a travel book, and a novel, all related to his travel experiences—Greene's sojourn in Mexico in the late winter of 1937-38 was astonishingly brief, just eight weeks. He had been commissioned by a publisher, Longmans, to make the trip in order to study the plight of the Mexican Catholic Church, which had for over a decade been engaged in a running feud with the Revolutionary government. By the time of Greene's visit the persecution had passed its peak and, under the administration of President Lázaro Cárdenas, there was a gradual move toward greater tolerance. In many provincial areas, however, the struggle continued, nowhere more so than in Tabasco, where Greene hoped to spend a good deal of his time. His impressions of the country were naturally influenced by the purpose of the trip—*Another Mexico* is part polemic, part travelogue —and by his choice of areas to visit.

After quick stopovers in Nuevo Laredo and Monterrey, Greene arrived by train in the city of San Luis Potosí, capital of the north-central state bearing the same name. The uniqueness of this state as far as he was concerned lay in the fact that here the churches remained open and priests were allowed freely to perform their official duties. For all practical purposes the state was controlled by General Saturnino

Cedillo who, though not himself a practicing Catholic (according to Greene), recognized the expediency of permitting the locals to worship as they pleased. General Cedillo had at one time been a proponent of the Revolution, but through the years he had become more and more conservative. By 1938 he was a wealthy *caudillo* powerful enough to order, without expecting or receiving much opposition, that the water supply of San Luis be drained away to irrigate Las Palomas, his sizable hacienda in the hills outside the city. The purpose of Greene's stay in San Luis was to interview this man to whom the city owed "so much of its happiness and unhappiness. You couldn't drink enough water," writes Greene, "but you could have your children taught that Christ had risen" (*Another Mexico,* p. 48).

Greene spent a week in San Luis Potosí waiting for the general's subordinates to arrange the interview. In *Another Mexico* Greene tells how he passed the time wandering about the city, which he finds lovely. Visiting the central cathedral for mass, he is quite moved by the physically demonstrative devotion of the Indian peasants—old women shuffling over the stone floor on their knees toward the altar, laborers in dungarees holding out their arms for minutes at a time in the attitude of the crucifixion. This spectacle, the same sort which had so disgusted D. H. Lawrence in Mexico fifteen years earlier, impresses Greene as an indication that the Christian faith here has endured despite the government's campaign against the Church. "A day's long work is behind, but the mortification goes on. This is the atmosphere of the stigmata, and you realize suddenly that perhaps *this* is the population of heaven [anticipating the whisky priest's glimpse of them "from the outside," discussed earlier]—these aged, painful, and ignorant faces: they are human goodness. . . . You would say that life itself for these was mortification enough . . ." (p. 41).

But this early reassurance was not sufficient to keep Greene from being appalled already by other aspects of Mexican life. On Sunday of the first week in March he attended a rodeo at the bullring in San Luis. The main attraction was to be a cockfight. The elaborate and festive preparations for this event puzzle Greene. It is only "death on a small scale," but these people insist on making rules, evidently hoping thereby "to tame death." "Three lines were drawn in the sand: death was like tennis. The cocks crowed and a brass band blared. . . . And suddenly one felt an impatience with all this mummery, all this fake emphasis on what is only a natural function; we die as we evacuate; why wear big hats and tight trousers and have a band play?" (p. 46). The cocks, apparently as unimpressed by all the fanfare as is the foreigner in attendance, at first show no inclination to fight, until the crowd begins to jeer and two attendants press the beaks of the birds together. Soon the onlookers get what they seem to have come for. The defeated bird, its eyes pecked out, is lifted up by its legs until the blood pours from its beak in a thin dark stream onto the sand. "Children stood up on the stone seats and watched it with glee." The rodeo proceeds to other events, but "with death over, it wasn't worth staying for all the rest" (p. 47), and Greene makes his way out. "That, I think, was the day I began to hate the Mexicans," he writes (p. 46). Again one is reminded of Lawrence and his similarly precipitate reaction to the bullfight.

Greene sought relief from the unsettling cockfight by going to late Sunday mass at the Templo del Carmen. "To a stranger like myself it was like going home. . . . [All] along the walls horrifying statues with musty purple robes stood in glass coffins; and yet it was home. One knew what was going on" (p. 47). This is a good early example in *Another Mexico* of the characteristic return to a refuge, the pacifying withdrawal behind the boundary of the familiar. It is significant that Greene is able not only to dismiss the unsettling implications of the sanguinary decor in the Mexican churches—taken by all three of his counterparts as an emblem of the Mexican death-fixation; but also, unlike them, that he is at pains to dissociate the paraphernalia of Mexican Catholicism from the violent excesses of the contemporary Revolution. Repeat-

edly Greene contrasts the holistic spiritual view of life represented for him by the Church with the view posited by the
new secular gospel of the Revolution. The latter he character-
izes as reductive, vacuous, and self-aggrandizing. The opposition is neatly illustrated at one point where Greene considers (or pretends to consider) what life would be like if the
Revolutionary gospel were to find general acceptance: "Even
if it were all untrue and there were no God, surely life was
happier with the enormous supernatural promise than with
the petty social fulfillment, the tiny pension and the machine-
made furniture" (p. 47). While such statements serve Greene's
didactic purposes well enough, they also expose certain basic
inadequacies in his understanding of the Mexican context
from which these questions arose.[25]

Greene's meeting with General Cedillo came at a crucial
time in the latter's career. Though he was an old military ally
and personal friend of President Lázaro Cárdenas, Cedillo's
growing following among conservative elements and his
unwillingness to enforce in San Luis Potosí the federal
government's programs regarding both the Church and land
redistribution made him a threat to the stability of Cárdenas'
regime. Greene had heard the widespread rumors that Cedillo
was planning a rebellion, and there were already signs that
Cárdenas was preparing to act against that eventuality.
(Some months after Greene's visit General Cedillo was in fact
hunted down and shot by federal troops.) In *Another Mexico*
Greene emphasizes Cedillo's human side rather than his role
in Mexican politics. This is rather surprising since Cedillo, as
one of the few remaining leaders powerful enough to pose a
threat to Cárdenas and his leftist policies, would seem to
have been a promising subject for Greene in his case against
the Revolution. But Cedillo was apparently not enough of a
Catholic, or an ideologue of any kind, for Greene to have
been much impressed by him as a sign of hope. The general's
somewhat flashy hospitality, his many possessions, his peasant appearance, and his distaste for political discussion are
fully detailed. Yet along with these benign attributes, Cedillo

is surrounded by signs which indicate his present position—the troupe of hangers-on, the nervous pistoleros along the road, the armed personal bodyguard. Stalling off the interview, General Cedillo takes Greene on a personal tour of his hacienda. "All the time we sat there [in the car] the five hundred [federal] troops were waiting at Las Tribas for orders to move, while the dangerous man padded on his great flat feet round the farm" (p. 56).

Finally that evening the general reluctantly submits to the Englishman's questions. It is clearly not a situation that Cedillo relishes. He sweats and squirms as the words "Fascism" and "Communism" and "parliamentary system" are intoned, responded to, and dismissed. He seems to Greene not so much a dangerous man as a man beyond his depth, an adept soldier and ranchero whose misguided ambition has cast him in an unsympathetic role. Greene concludes that General Cedillo is "caught in a maze of friends and enemies with similar faces. That is how I see him—the young Indian trooper with the round Indian face turned middle-aged, the bitterness of political years souring the innocence" (p. 60). In short, he has been made into a character in Greene's own world.

From San Luis Greene trained south to Mexico City, where he stayed a little over a week. At first the capital seems very pleasant to him, not at all what he had expected to find. It does not seem part of the same land which General Cedillo trods with his great flat feet but rather a pleasant European capital, a luxury town like Luxembourg. Gradually, however, he becomes aware that

Mexico City is older and less Central European than it appears at first—a baby alligator tied to a pail of water; a whole family of Indians eating their lunch on the sidewalk edge; railed off among the drugstores and the tramlines, near the cathedral, a portion of the Aztec temple Cortés destroyed. And always, everywhere, stuck between the shops, hidden behind the new American

hotels, are the old baroque churches and convents, some
of them still open, some converted to the oddest uses. . . .
(p. 69)

such as cinemas, government libraries, warehouses, garages,
newspaper offices, and shops. A minor theme running
throughout *Another Mexico* is Greene's impatience with the
"boyish" high spirits characteristic of Mexican social behavior. "It is this boyishness, this immaturity, which gets most
on the nerves in Mexico," he says. "Grown men cannot meet
in the street without sparring like schoolboys. . . . [They]
have passed childhood and remain for ever in a cruel anar-
chic adolescence" (p. 73). These words, reminiscent of some
of Lawrence's tirades on the same subject, demonstrate again
the link in Greene's mind between Mexico and his own adolescence, especially his isolation and victimization at the
hands of bullies at Berkhamsted School. In general, his comments on the contemporary scene in Mexico City show a tendency, as one might expect, to downplay the importance of
both the indigenous, pre-Hispanic culture and the avowed
achievements of modern Revolutionary culture. He goes to
see the frescoes by José Clemente Orozco, which he admires,
and those by Diego Rivera, which he disparages (again like
Lawrence) as grandiloquent and crudely didactic. Rivera's
figures, in a fresco entitled "Creation," are "all outstretched
arms and noble faces, white robes and haloes. . . . It adapts
Christian emblems to a vague political idea, and they become
unbearably sentimental in the new setting. . . . [The] Son in
Rivera's 'Creation'—what is he but Progress, Human Dignity, great Victorian conceptions that life denies at every
turn?" (p. 75). On the other hand the revered image of the
Virgin of Guadalupe, with its supposedly miraculous origin,
Greene finds deeply impressive—"the dark-skinned Indian
Virgin bending her head with a grace and kindliness you will
find nowhere in mortal Mexico" (p. 96). One day he takes a
Cook's tour to both the Monastery of San Agustín Acolman
and the pyramids of San Juan Teotihuacán. The former,

founded and planned by twelve Augustinian monks in the early sixteenth century, is for Greene a remarkable achievement, its "great tall church" a "building of such beauty" (p. 90). But the much older Indian pyramids only leave him with a sense of flatness and vacancy, their mathematical precision "as inhuman as a problem in algebra" (p. 92). Nor is Greene particularly impressed by the Temple of Quetzalcoatl, which so haunted Lawrence's waking dreams. And as for the "obsidian knife" used by the Aztecs for human sacrifice, it seems "as hygienic as surgeons' instruments" (p. 91).

A far more tangible threat to Greene's peace of mind than the reminder of Aztec violence was the prospect of renewed violence in modern Mexico. Back in the capital he read in the newspapers almost daily accounts of political murders— "'Riddled with bullets' is the stock phrase" (p. 88). Upon seeing the monument in Chapultepec Park to *los niños perdidos*, boy-heroes of the war between Mexico and the United States, Greene decides peremptorily that "All the monuments in Mexico are to violent deaths." "Perhaps," he goes on, "it is the atmosphere of violence—perhaps only the altitude, seven thousand-odd feet—but after a few days no one can escape the depression of Mexico City" (p. 88).

After about ten days in the capital Greene began his "journey downhill" by rail to the east coast. As he left the city he learned of President Cárdenas' expropriation of the foreign oil companies, including a major British interest. "One had been aware, of course . . . that trouble was boiling up; but it had been boiling for nearly a year now—nobody had been expecting this sudden—crazy—action" (p. 103). Greene began to ponder the possibility that violent revolution would again break out in Mexico—not an unreasonable notion at the time, though the response among Mexicans turned out quite the opposite—and his itinerary called for at least six more weeks in the country. (Of course, given his proclivity toward living on the edge of danger, this situation must have held a certain attraction for Greene.) But news travels slowly in the more isolated regions of Mexico, and where he was going the inhabitants had not yet felt the shock-wave of patriotism and the concomitant xenophobia. He was not to see signs of these developments until he reached San Cristó-bal de las Casas a few weeks later.

Against the advice of a consul in Veracruz Greene booked passage down the coast to Tabasco on a small, rickety, flat-bottomed steamboat, the *Ruiz Cano*. A life insurance policy was included in the price of the ticket. At nightfall he boarded the tiny boat on which he was to spend almost two days of unrelieved fear and misery. The following description shows how Greene's perspective was suddenly altered by the sight of the *Ruiz Cano* and the anticipation of the journey which lay ahead of him. The boat was

> a flat barge with a few feet of broken rail, an old funnel you could almost touch with your hand from the shore, a bell hanging on a worn piece of string, an oil-lamp and a bundle of turkeys. One little rotting boat dangled in-adequately from the davits. . . . Forty-two hours or so in the Atlantic, in the Gulf of Mexico—I have never in my life been more frightened. . . . I had the feeling that my journey had only just begun; Laredo wasn't the frontier, and I thought with nostalgia of that first Mexican hotel [in Nuevo Laredo]. . . and the thunder cracking over the skyscraper across in the United States. (pp. 116-117)[26]

This is the first instance of the shifting frontier, a series of which transitions are reserved for the middle part of *Another Mexico*. What fear Greene had experienced before he crossed the bridge at Laredo was countered by hope and expectation. Here the fear is much more extreme and immediate, so that, in retrospect, the border in the north seems almost unreal; it elicits only nostalgia. "It is before you cross a frontier that you experience fear," Greene writes (p. 120). The frontier over which he passes on the way to Tabasco marks the boundary of "another Mexico"—the dangerous crossing seems to anticipate it—the Mexico where there are no priests, where the churches have been reduced to rubble, where few tourists dare venture, where the sovereignty of the socialist police state is virtually unchallenged. Furthermore, from a personal standpoint the journey-within-a-journey to Tabasco means that Greene is surrendering himself to an almost total isolation. Cut off completely are his contacts with the outside world, with correspondence, news, the few acquaintances he had made in the capital: with the Church and its sacraments.

On such a voyage it becomes necessary for the mind to conceive of a goal, some point in time and space at which the nightmare will surely come to an end and relief be found. If the forty-two-hour "crossing" from Veracruz to the Tabascan port of Frontera (which means frontier) amounted to a border of entry into the "Godless state," the boundary between Tabasco and Chiapas assumed the role of a terminal frontier. For beyond that state line lay San Cristóbal de las Casas, which was, Greene had been assured, a "very Catholic town" (p. 93). In Las Casas (as he calls it), formerly the capital of Chiapas, the churches were now open, and though priests were still officially banned from performing their duties openly, mass was held in private homes. Approaching his first contact with Tabasco, Greene "began to regard...Las Casas...as the real object of my journey—and the beginning of going home" (p. 94).

The most severe of all the anti-clerical campaigns of the 1920's and 1930's in Mexico had been waged in Tabasco. Until just a few years before Greene's visit the state had been under the control of Tomás Garrido Canábal, a man grimly puritan by temperament and a fanatical socialist. Garrido had decreed that only married priests could remain in Tabasco. He organized a private army of "Red Shirts" (one of whose leaders distributed business cards identifying himself as the "personal enemy of God"). The job of this band of thugs was to terrorize those who dared disobey Garrido's edicts, which included a 9:30 p.m. curfew in the state capital of Villahermosa and the prohibition of alcohol. Under his direction all of the churches in the state had either been destroyed or else converted to secular functions. Priests who defied his anti-clerical laws were hunted down and killed, often without benefit of a trial. Only when Garrido expanded his operations to Mexico City (after he had been appointed minister of agriculture) and his Red Shirts began to harrass Catholic worshipers in the capital did President Cárdenas finally take action against the dictator from Tabasco. Garrido was exiled to Costa Rica in 1937, but his policies in his home state were still largely enforced.[27] Greene points out that all the priests in the state had fled or been shot "except one, who existed for ten years in the forests and the swamps, venturing out only at night; his few letters, I was told, recorded an awful sense of impotence—to live in constant danger and yet be able to do so little, it hardly seemed worth the horror" (p. 123). Significantly, in *Another Mexico* Greene first mentions this hunted priest—one of the chief sources of his protagonist in *The Power and the Glory*—during his account of the entry into Frontera, even though he did not actually learn about the man until days later when he was in Villahermosa.[28] Whether or not the connection is intentional, in writing his travel book Greene implicitly identifies himself with the fugitive priest. This identification is first made clear when the *Ruiz Cano* docks and the customs officers "came on board, their revolver holsters creaking as they climbed the rotting rail. I remembered a bottle of brandy in my suitcase" (p. 123). Greene was to make brandy the "whisky priest's" favorite drink, and it was for illegal possession of a bottle of brandy that he would be arrested in Book II of the novel.

Though he stayed only briefly in Frontera, the impression it left on him was vivid. On a walk through this little port where the fine opening chapter of *The Power and the Glory* is set, Greene observes that there is "nothing to be seen but one little dusty plaza with fruit-drink stalls and a bust of [General Alvaro] Obregón on a pillar, two dentists' and a hairdresser's. The buzzards squatted on the roofs. It was like a place besieged by scavengers—sharks in the river and vultures in the streets" (p. 124). After a hot night spent on board the docked ship, Greene set off the next morning inland up the Grijalva

River toward Villahermosa. During this ten-hour ride he became acquainted with Doc Winter, an American dentist who had lived with his family in Frontera the last five years. Doc Winter, the model for the character of Mr. Tench in *The Power and the Glory*, is a miserable man whose only tangible emotion is the desire to escape the tropics. He remains in Frontera because of the profits to be made from putting in gold fittings and caps. The living example of what life in the tropics can do to one, Doc Winter offers Greene a portent of things to come: "without a memory and without a hope in the immense heat, he loomed during those days as big as a symbol—I am not sure of what, unless of the aboriginal calamity, 'having no hope, and without God in the world'" (pp. 149-150).[29]

Greene spent almost a week in Villahermosa, "Garrido's capital." Settled into a hot and fetid little hotel, a place literally overrun by tropical insects, he reflects again on the last priest of Tabasco: "as the cockchafers buzzed and beat one felt the excitement of this state where the hunted priest had worked for so many years, hidden in the swamps and forests, with *no leave train or billet behind the lines*. . . . One felt one was *drawing near to the centre* of something—if it was only of darkness and abandonment" (p. 132, my emphasis). The figure of the battlefield, as Greene uses it here, suggests a paradoxical development of the border pattern. He has crossed over a frontier—one that is both geographical and psychic—into a region that is itself a borderland, a terrain fought over by the forces of "darkness and abandonment" on the one hand and the force of light on the other. Only here, in Tabasco, the latter has been driven temporarily underground. An earlier passage treats the same notion more explicitly.

The world is all of a piece, of course; it is engaged everywhere in the same subterranean struggle, lying like a tiny neutral state, with whom no one ever observes his treaties, between the two eternities of pain and—God

knows the opposite of pain, not we. It is a Belgium
fought over by friend and enemy alike: there is no peace
anywhere where there is human life; but there are . . .
quiet and active sectors of the line. Russia, Spain, Mexico—there's no fraternization on Christmas morning in
those parts. (p. 27)

If one keeps in mind the kind of battle Greene is envisioning,
Tabasco becomes, so to speak, the most fiercely disputed
ground within the active sector. Here, despite the apparent
victory of the "Godless state," there is no end to the conflict,
the antagonists are never reconciled. Probably this insight
was never fully conscious when Greene was in Mexico, but in
the travel book one can see already the first stirrings of a
theme that would become a major one in the Mexican novel
published two years later: the belief (painfully arrived at)
that "abandonment" has not finally won out, that, through
the unlikeliest of agents, the militant God continues to wage
battle for the souls of men, and to no small effect. Despite all
appearances to the contrary, Tabasco is not utterly infernal.

While actually "marooned" in Tabasco, however, Greene
found very little evidence to support such a belief. For one
thing, there was the "dreadful lethargy" of the Tabascan
Catholics themselves. Unlike the faithful in Mexico City,
Veracruz, and Chiapas, the Tabascans could not muster the
energy, much less the courage, to hold secret masses and
baptisms. Perhaps, Greene reflects, this lethargy is due to the
extreme heat, the stench of the river and the swamps; or perhaps it is because there are not enough Indians in Tabasco
"with their wild beliefs and their enormous if perverted ven-
eration, to shame the Catholics into *some* action" (p. 145).
Soon Greene becomes depressed by the overwhelming evidence of spiritual vacuity in Villahermosa:

Nothing to do but drink gassy fruit drinks (no miracle in
the Godless state will turn this aerated water into wine)
and watch the horrifying abundance of just life. You

can't open a book without some tiny scrap of life scut-
tling across the page . . . and when the lights come out, so
do the beetles: the pavement by the green sour riverside
is black with them. You kill them on your bedroom
floor, and by morning . . . they have been drained away
by . . . the hordes of ants. (p. 146)

A third element of the population of Villahermosa which
alarmed Greene were the police. Early in his stay in the capital he paid a visit to the chief of police. Kept waiting for over
an hour, he had a chance to absorb the general atmosphere of
the police station.

The dirty whitewashed walls, the greasy hammocks,
and the animal faces of the men—it wasn't like law and
order so much as banditry. The police were the lowest of
the population: you had to look for honesty on the faces
of the men and women waiting to be fined or black-
guarded. You gained an overwhelming sense of brutality
and irresponsibility as they took their rifles down from
the rack and sloped away on patrol or ambled drearily
across the yard in the great heat with their trousers open.
These were the men who a few weeks later [after
Greene's departure] were to fire into a mob of unarmed
peasants attempting to pray in the ruins of a church.
(pp. 136-137)

As he passed a week in Villahermosa waiting for a plane to
take him across the border into Salto de Agua, the Godless
state came more and more to seem like a prison from which
there was no escape. He would be stuck here always, like
Doc Winter. The many whites who had settled in Tabasco
had become "absorbed" all too successfully into the tropical
ambience, into the swarms of "just life." Greene's fears were
not mollified by the discovery that there were many inhabitants of Villahermosa with the names Greene or Graham.
"[There] was something rather horrifying and foreboding in
this—for an unabsorbed Greene. . . . Señorita Greene went

swinging round the plaza on the evening promenade; and one found oneself haunted by fancies, as if fate intended to take in its octopus coils yet another Greene." Then someone points out to him one more Greene avatar, even more haunting—"a seedy Mexican, with a drooping hat and a gun on his hip..." (p. 139). Along with his fear, Greene's hostility toward Mexicans reached a higher pitch in Villahermosa. "No hope anywhere: I have never been in a country where you are more aware all the time of hate. Friendship there is skin deep—a protective gesture. That motion of greeting you see everywhere upon the street, the hands outstretched to press the other's arms, the semi-embrace—what is it but the motion of pinioning to keep the other man from his gun?" (p. 150). This rather wild conjecture about the social habits of Mexicans is directly related in Greene's mind to the severity of the anticlerical campaign of which he saw considerable evidence in Tabasco. Indeed, so outraged is he by the visible signs of the abuses produced by this one Revolutionary plank (seen in its most extreme form in Tabasco) that he dismisses outright the many genuinely humane goals of the entire movement, insisting that it has merely institutionalized hate.

> There has always been hate, I suppose, in Mexico, but now it is the official teaching: it has superseded love in the school curriculum. Cynicism...is the accepted ideology. Look through the windows of the Workers' Syndicate in Villahermosa and there on the wall of the little lecture room are pictures—of hate and cynicism: a crucified woman with a lecherous friar kissing her feet, a priest tippling with the wine of the Eucharist, another receiving money at the altar from a starving couple. (p. 150)

To combat his restiveness, Greene passed the time each evening reading Trollope's *Dr. Thorne* and Cobbett's *Rural Rides*, both "overwhelmingly national" books which offered him a welcome contrast to the inimical atmosphere of Tabasco. In a further effort to allay his boredom and his fear he fantasizes about home.

I have never in my life been so homesick . . . I lay on my back and tried to project myself into home . . . . I built up the familiar in my mind carefully, chair by chair, book by book—the windows just there, and the buses going by, and the squeals of children on the Common. But it wasn't real: *this* was real—the high empty room and the tiled and swarming floor and the heat and the sour river smell. (p. 154)

Thus the forced attempt to fall back on the memory formula typifying "home" is overwhelmed by the greater reality of "here." This mental contest between the two extremes, the "pattern of alternance" in Greene's sensibility, is still another manifestation of frontier experience.

After this miserable week in Villahermosa—where the whisky priest in *The Power and the Glory* would twice be jailed and finally executed—Greene finally managed to secure a seat on a plane which carried him over the border into Chiapas. Looking down from the plane he sees "the Godless state, the landscape of a hunted man's terror and captivity—wood and water, without roads, and on the horizon the mountains of Chiapas like a prison wall" (p. 156). It would seem that Greene's own escape is imminent. But the very location of those imprisoning mountains, it turns out, shows how the lines on a map can deceive the weary explorer. For his destination, the Chiapan village of Salto de Agua, is still on *this* side of the mountains. And when he lands in Salto, Greene realizes that the "goal" of Las Casas and the peace it represents are still beyond reach. "The wooded mountains rose steeply at the back [of the village], shutting out ventilation. It was . . . Chiapas, [but] no one spoke a word of English. . . . I had a sense of being marooned . . . [ellipsis in original] even the dentist would have been welcome. . . . I was overcome by an immense unreality: I couldn't recognize my own legs in riding-boots. Why the hell was I here?" (pp. 156-157). Though it does not even begin to still the unsettling implications of this last question, the literal reason for Greene's presence here was that he had committed himself to making an excursion to the ruins of Palenque, a

day's ride by mule from Salto. He had needed some excuse to
officially justify his presence in the area. The real reason, had
it been discovered, might well have resulted in his being deported from the country as an "undesirable alien" (as Malcolm Lowry, on flimsier contentions, was deported in 1946).
During the next few weeks, with but a single exception until
he returned to Mexico City, Greene's loneliness grew steadily
more acute—even in the Liberian bush he had traveled with
his cousin and a troupe of twenty-five native attendants. "For
the first time I was hopelessly at a loss because of my poverty
of Spanish; always before there had been *someone* who
spoke English. . . . Now I felt a mistake might land me anywhere" (p. 157). Yet, as miserable as he no doubt was, one
more than suspects that this is precisely the kind of situation
which another side of Greene relishes. Lost in a strange and
dangerous land with no assurance of where to go next or how
to behave—this is the quintessential experience for Greene,
and finding it is like "starting over again."

Palenque was fourteen hours off. The long, bumpy ride in
the blazing sun took its toll, and by the time Greene and his
guide arrived the Englishman was utterly fatigued, stiff, and
feverish. Indifferent to the ruins to begin with, Greene's
physical condition only made matters worse. "It seemed to
me that this wasn't a country to live in at all, with the heat
and the desolation; it was a country to die in and leave only
ruins behind" (p. 168). The next day, after a rest and several
bowls of hot corn coffee taken so that the fever could be
sweated out of him, they rode on to a coffee *finca* operated
by Herr R., a middle-aged German, and his sister. The renewed contact with these English-speaking, kindly Europeans
(models for the Lehrs in *The Power and the Glory*) gave
Greene a much-needed lift in spirits. After a day and a half of
relaxation here, Greene and his guide returned to the road for
the rugged trip back to Salto de Agua. From Salto, Greene
flew on to Yajalon, a little village in the foothills. During his
week-long stay in Yajalon he met the people upon whom he
would base the characters of Mrs. Fellows, her daughter

Coral, and the treacherous mestizo of his Mexican novel. Hoping to arrive across the mountains in Las Casas by Holy Week, Greene became desperate to get away from Yajalon. "One got an appalling claustrophobia in this small place wedged in among the mountains round its locked decaying church, and time just going by . . ." (p. 195). But the airplane he had counted on was already days late, so he decided to make the trip by mule with the help of a guide.

The three-day journey up and across the mountains and into Las Casas was the emotional climax of Greene's entire visit to Mexico. Since, as we have seen, he had come to view these mountains as the terminal frontier of the Godless state (despite their being well inside Chiapas on the map), the long climb amounted to a protracted border crossing—one which yielded some crucial discoveries along the way and which ended in a manner he had not anticipated. The mountain path wound steeply up some 7,000 feet, but the many deep *barrancas* made the distance seem even greater. The two travelers spent the cold nights in tiny settlements where the courtesy and genuine good nature of their Indian hosts reminded Greene of the "innocence" he had encountered among the primitive tribes in West Africa. In a book so full of admissions of his "pathological hatred" for the Mexican people and the duplicity of their friendliness, Greene's obvious admiration for the mountain Indians is all the more conspicuous. He notes, for example, that his mestizo guide is wary of meeting up with the Indians, for he "couldn't put up in their presence that Mexican façade of *bonhomie*—the embrace, the spar, the joke—with which they hide from themselves the cruelty and treachery of their life" (p. 203). Free for the time being from both the fear and the severe climate of the tropics, Greene experiences moments of rare peace and joy. Despite the immense difficulty of the climb, the journey affords flashes

not exactly of beauty but of consciousness, consciousness of something simple and strange and uncomplicated, a way of life we have hopelessly lost but can never quite forget. There was a moment at a little brown pebbly river when the guide took a bowl from his saddlebag and filled it with water from the stream and made himself a kind of gruel with a ball of corn—the mules drank and I stood on a stone and washed my face and hands and the shadow played on the stream, and it was like peace and natural happiness. And there was food at a little isolated Mexican farm, the floor strewn with sweet-smelling pine-needles—tortilla and beans and chicken and rice and coffee, the body's needs so easily quieted.

. . . [That evening] we came out of the forest on what seemed to be at last the top of the world nine thousand feet up—a great plateau of yellow grass, across which flocks of sheep and goats came driving together from three quarters of the globe, a few mud huts, some men on mules cantering bareback by, an Indian herd in his pastoral tunic, a horn winding, and the last pale golden light welling across the plain, dropping down over the ridge which ended it as if over the world's edge, so that you thought of the light going on and on through quiet peaceful uninhabited space. It was like a scene from the past before the human race had bred its millions. . . . (pp. 207-208)

If Las Casas had not been on the other side of that ridge Greene might have perceived this place in terms similar to those used by Scobie in *The Heart of the Matter* to describe a moment of exquisite freedom from human complications: ". . . this was the ultimate border he had reached in happiness."[30] But before Greene gets very far from the ridge there is yet another impressive sight which captures his attention, a sight which transforms the whole scene into a religious experience:

. . . there was an even older world beyond the ridge—the ground sloped up again to where a grove of tall black crosses stood at all angles like wind-blown trees against the blackened sky. This was the Indian religion—a dark tormented magic cult. The old ladies might swing back and forth in the rocking-chairs of Villahermosa, the Catholics might be dying out "like dogs" [i.e., without benefit of the last rites], but here, in the mountainous strange world of Father [Bartolomé de] Las Casas, Christianity went on its own frightening way. . . . The great crosses leaned there in their black and windy solitude, safe from the pistoleros and the politicians, and one thought of the spittle mixed with the clay to heal the blind man, the resurrection of the body, the religion of the earth. (p. 208)

This, then, is the boundary which marks the end of the Godless state for Greene. Behind him down the mountains are the ragged police station, Señor Greene with the pistol on his hip, the teeming hordes of "just life." Directly ahead, that "very Catholic town," Las Casas, lay waiting for him.

Lawrence had Oaxaca and its obsidian-eyed Indians; in the same city Malcolm Lowry had his cantina, El Farolito; for Greene there was Holy Week in Las Casas. In each case the paradisal garden, under the blazing sun of Mexico, was charred to a waste of hot cinders. Las Casas itself was a pleasant enough town. There Greene found a decent hotel with a bed and cleaned sheets, cooked meals, cold bottled beer, news over the radio, and many English-speaking people—"luxuries" he had not enjoyed since leaving Mexico City four weeks earlier. Furthermore the town's twenty-two churches were all still standing, and five of them were open to the public, although no priests were permitted entrance. Attending secret mass in a private home, Greene was once again able to partake of the sacraments of his faith, and the sense of returning to the religion of the catacombs could only have excited him. Indeed, the Holy Week festivities were on the whole most impressive, especially when on Holy Thursday the Indians poured down from the mountains "to see the crucified Christ" and to worship in their unorthodox fashion (p. 220). However, for Greene personally the week was an

ordeal. Not only had the news of the oil expropriation
reached Las Casas, but also there was the even more incendi-
ary news that Britain had responded by breaking off diplomatic relations with Mexico. All over the country Mexicans
were rallying round President Cárdenas, applauding his bold
and unprecedented move to free Mexico from the yoke of
foreign capital interests. Greene, apparently the only Englishman in town, provided the local zealots with a convenient
scapegoat. The abuse began one evening when he joined a
large crowd that had gathered in the town plaza to greet a
general who was scheduled to make a public appearance.
When the general failed to arrive the crowd became restive.

> All that happened was that the atmosphere of hostility
> thickened—and directed itself against me. A drunken
> group passed and repassed, throwing out gibes; they had
> revolvers under their waistcoats, so there was nothing to
> be done but sit . . . pretending not to hear. I was suffering
> for the ancient wrongdoing of the oil pioneers, the tire-
> some legal rectitude of the English Government. From
> that evening the hostility never lifted: I couldn't sit in the
> plaza for more than a few minutes without a gibe. It
> preyed on the nerves: it was *like being the one unpopu-
> lar boy at school.* (p. 218, my emphasis)

Crossing over the mountains into Las Casas, the territory of
peace and relative religiosity, by a fluke proves to be the
single most painful experience of "starting over again"—
Greene is once more the quisling's son in an embattled zone.

For this latest "betrayal" Greene could not forgive Mexico.
The remainder of his stay in the country was colored by his
hate and resentment.[31] Yet, reduced to reading an American
women's magazine in Las Casas, he had to admit that at least
in Mexico one could still find traces of a faith that was enduring, perhaps even thriving amidst all the adversity. "I loathed
Mexico," he writes, "but there were times when it seemed as
if there were worse places. . . . Here were idolatry and
oppression, starvation and casual violence, but you lived
under the shadow of religion—of God or the Devil. 'Rating

for Dating'—it wasn't evil, it wasn't anything at all, it was just the drugstore and the Coca-Cola, the hamburger, the graceless, sinless, empty chromium world" (pp. 225-226). On his last evening in Las Casas, Greene fell ill with a bad case of dysentery. He was nevertheless determined the next day to ride the bus down the mountains to Tuxtla Gutiérrez, the capital of Chiapas, where he planned to catch a plane which would take him to Oaxaca. Heading down again toward tropical Mexico, he saw through the bus window a group of Indians on a precipice ahead, hands above their heads in a crude gesture of supplication. But when the bus reached the spot the Indians were nowhere to be seen. "It was like the boundary of a faith—we were leaving behind that wild region of great crooked crosses, of the cave dweller faces bowed before the crucified Christ.... We were going back and down to the picturesque Mexico of the pistolero and the ruined monastery..." (pp. 238-239).

Things did not get any better during Greene's last week in Mexico. Oaxaca, the town so important to both Lawrence and Lowry, Greene finds "lovely in its way, but I was too sick and tired to care for any way.... I was back where sometimes I had longed to be—on the tourist track..." (p. 242). The ruins at Mitla were more impressive than those at Palenque, but no matter how interesting the sights now, "I'd had enough; I wanted to get home, not linger in even the most agreeable Mexican town, and Oaxaca was agreeable" (p. 244). On the train to Puebla, Greene jotted down "the random thoughts of a bored man," the most painful reading in all of *Another Mexico* (and tellingly similar in phrase and image to the most pejorative passages in Lawrence and Huxley):

How one begins to hate these people—the intense slowness of that monolithic black-clothed old woman with the grey straggly hair—removing a tick—blowing her nose—trying to put up a blind or open a lemonade bottle, mooing with her mouth wide, fixing her eyes on people meaninglessly for minutes at a time, slowly revolving her black bulk all of a piece like a mule. . . . The hideous inexpressiveness of brown eyes. People never seem to help each other in small ways, removing a parcel from a seat, making room with their legs. They just sit about. If Spain is like this, I can understand the temptation to massacre. (p. 246)

Yet, almost astonishingly, Puebla seemed to Greene the only town in Mexico in which it would be possible to live with some degree of happiness. "It had more than the usual wounded beauty: it had grace" (p. 248). Again, however, it is the town's colonial flavor which he most appreciates.

From Puebla he took an express bus north to Mexico City, where he arrived on April 21. The much-needed medicine, the rest, the renewed contacts with the "civilized" world— none of these did much to alleviate Greene's depressed state of mind in "a country of disappointment and despair" (p. 256). For in the last five weeks he had come full circle:

> It was like beginning things all over again. I had forgotten in Chiapas the hatefulness of Mexico City: the shops full of junk—bad serapes and bad china and hideous elaborate silver filagree—the taxis hooting all the time. What had exhausted me in Chiapas was simply physical exertion, unfriendliness, boredom; life among the dark groves of leaning crosses was at any rate concerned with eternal values. (p. 256)[32]

After brief junkets to the fashionable resort towns of Taxco and Cuernavaca, Greene took the train down the mountains again to Veracruz. Though on his last brief visit (before the horrible boat trip to Tabasco) he had found Veracruz a rather gay and attractive town, it held no further interest for him now, so he boarded the German liner on which he had booked third-class passage for the trip home. The passengers were largely Germans and pro-Franco Spaniards, but the differences of nationality and ideology were before long subsumed by a general sense of borderlessness: ". . . on a ship the borders drop, the nations mingle—Spanish violence, German stupidity, Anglo-Saxon absurdity—the whole world is exhibited in a kind of crazy montage" (p. 270).

*Another Mexico* ends with a coda set back in England. Needless to say, Greene did not find, in the London of 1938, the "home" which he had fantasized that night in Villahermosa. What he found instead was a London of grit, of noisy trams and ubiquitous Air Raid Precaution posters. Here the "telephone wires were cut, the anti-aircraft guns were set up on the common outside, and the trenches were dug." From this perspective Greene begins to wonder "why I had disliked Mexico so much: *this* was home. One always expects something different" (p. 277). This is one of the important insights offered by the generic border experience recorded in *Another Mexico*. The progressive stages—looking across, crossing, looking back, then recrossing, and finally looking back from the familiar side to the unfamiliar—disclose, in the end, the fundamental cyclicity of experience in *all* regions. All of the boundaries ultimately meet in an inward, mythic region where distinctions blur and polarities merge into a homogeneous world "engaged everywhere in the same subterranean struggle . . . like a tiny neutral state, with whom no one ever observes his treaties. . . ." In London Greene "tried to remember my hatred [of Mexico]. But a bad time over is always tinged with regret. I could even look back on the dark croquet lawn under the red-brick skyscraper of classrooms with regret: it is as if everywhere one loses something one had hoped to keep. . . . Why—on the Gulf—had that seemed bad and this good? I couldn't remember" (p. 278). With Europe edging steadily toward violence, Greene's experience of Mexico began to assume a new shape as part of a larger, unalterable design: "Mexico is a state of mind" (p. 278).

## IV

*Another Mexico* has been too often considered merely as a "trial study" of the materials which Greene put to better use in *The Power and the Glory*. It is quite true that the outlines of several of the characters in the novel may be traced to actual persons described in the travel book, and that many of the places and incidents that constituted a part of Greene's travel experiences reappear in one form or another in *The Power and the Glory*. Naturally it is instructive to compare Greene's treatment of his materials in the two books in order to gain insight into his creative practices. But the point that needs to be stressed is that *Another Mexico* has considerable merit in its own right as a work of creative nonfiction, independent of its relation to the novel. In order to compare Greene with his English counterparts I have found it necessary occasionally to point out those areas in his interpretation of the Mexican scene which reflect his particular bias rather than the objective situation (insofar as the latter can be determined). However, in spite of its polemical element, what gives *Another Mexico* integrity as a travel book is its insistence—voiced in the several ways discussed above—that significance lies in the journey *as a journey* rather than in anything so pretentious as the "real story" about Mexico. We may better appreciate the merits of *Another Mexico* as a testament of self-exploration by comparing and contrasting it briefly with Evelyn Waugh's nonfiction book about Mexico, *Robbery Under Law* (1939).

At first glance the two books seem to have much in common. Waugh visited the country about four months after Greene's departure, and stayed there for the same length of time, two months. As Roman Catholics both men were quite concerned about the effects of the religious persecution on the lives of both the Mexican laity and the clergy. And because of their interest in this problem both writers were inclined to be skeptical about the Mexican Revolution. Furthermore, their Catholic viewpoint tended to make them emphasize the Hispanic culture at the expense of the indigenous, though this predilection is even more extreme in Waugh then in Greene. The fact that Waugh cites Greene's book in *Robbery* no less than half a dozen times, and does so usually in a spirit of accord, contributes still more to the impression that the two writers are kindred spirits who came to Mexico with similar interests and left with similar reactions to the country. But despite these general parallels, there are vast differences between *Robbery Under Law* and *Another Mexico.*

The physical conditions of a journey naturally contribute to the perspective from which one will view the country visited. Waugh came to Mexico to write a book about it, but he combined the work with a holiday. Traveling with his second wife Laura, he arrived at Veracruz on a luxury liner, was met by a Mexican acquaintance (obviously someone of Waugh's political persuasion) who accompanied him as guide and translator wherever he went in the country, and soon checked into the Hotel Ritz in Mexico City, where he spent most of his time. When the Waughs did make an excursion outside the capital it was usually to a spot in the conventional "tourist belt"—Puebla, Taxco, Cuernavaca and Oaxaca. And yet, his comparative insulation to the contrary, Waugh's trip was not entirely pleasant. "It would be idle," he writes "to pretend that a visit to Mexico, at the present moment, can be wholly agreeable; the pervading atmosphere ranges from vexation to despair, and only the most obtuse traveller could escape infection. . . . [There] is at the moment no opportunity for solid happiness in Mexico."[33]

Early in *Robbery Under Law* Waugh admits that the disadvantage of traveling a great deal, as he had done during the last twelve years, is that "one's mind falls into the habit of recognizing similarities rather than differences" (p. 3). One of the chief characteristics of the book is Waugh's tendency to see Mexico—particularly its politics—in purely English terms. He states that he "went to Mexico . . . in order to verify and reconsider impressions formed at a distance" (p. 2). And again, "I was a Conservative when I went to Mexico and . . . everything I saw there strengthened my opinions" (p. 16). He confesses that his knowledge of Mexico was "meagre and purely academic" before his visit (p. 5). His interest in the country was prompted specifically by President Cárdenas' expropriation of the oil companies and the resultant break in diplomatic relations between Mexico and England. In answering the question of why we should be concerned at all about the actions of such an obscure and relatively weak nation, Waugh cites reasons that are political in nature: its dangerous proximity to the United States; its financial status as a debtor to both England and the United States; its vast untapped natural resources, particularly oil; its political instability during a time of fascist expansion throughout the world. The intrinsic interest, not to mention the distinctive nature, of Mexican politics and culture is apparently not worth bothering over. Instead, Waugh contends that an understanding of Mexico can provide an important "object-lesson." If one could understand recent events in Mexican history, he believes, "one would come very near to understanding all the problems that vex us today" (p. 3). Moreover, Mexico's progressive "decline" since its independence from Spain offers us a warning about the dire consequences of unchecked liberalism. "There is no distress of theirs to which we might not be equally subject," he declares. "Every marked step in [Mexico's] decline, in fact, has corresponded with an experiment towards 'the Left'" (pp. 277-278). Given this narrowly proscriptive and hortatory emphasis, the following passage becomes an ironic commentary on the limitations of Waugh's book on Mexico: "The fascination of Mexico lies in the stimulus it gives to the imagination. Anything may happen there; almost everything has happened there. . . . [But it is] also a distorting mirror in which objects are reflected in perverse and threatening forms" (p. 272).

Precisely the problem with *Robbery Under Law* is that Waugh's encounter with Mexico does not engage his imagination, only his opinions. *Robbery* is in no strict sense a travel book at all but a book about issues, a book of political reportage. Thus Waugh charges that during the ten years in which it was controlled by General Plutarco Elías Calles, the Mexican government "made *no pretense* of *any* other motive than the *total* and *immediate* extermination of Christianity"

(p. 239); that the Mexican labor union C.R.O.M. was "the virtual master of each successive President," and that the union was "a *definitely* communist, proletarian revolutionary body under the same international auspices which caused the Leninist revolution in Russia" (p. 237); that during the last century those leaders who "have brought [Mexico] to her present pitiable state, were, *without exception*, enemies of her religion," and that it is "*only* through the Church that Mexico can recover health and unity" (p. 256); that the oil-company confiscation and the agrarian reform policies of the Cárdenas regime amount to "robbery under law," and that President Cárdenas himself is a willful saboteur whose goal is to "ruin the whole nation in order to reduce the disproportionate prosperity of a part of it . . ." (p. 178); that "*every* German settled [in Mexico] constitutes a Nazi unit under the direction of party headquarters" (p. 267).[34] To attempt a point-by-point refutation of these absurd allegations is beyond the scope of this study. In any case such an attempt is not necessary; the tendentious tone and the patently oversimplified reasoning of these passages speak for themselves.

Now *Another Mexico* is also, as we have seen, a book containing its author's outspoken views—some of which are in agreement with those of Waugh in *Robbery Under Law*. But the manner in which Greene presents his opinions, however partisan they may be, is somehow less objectionable. In the first place, because Greene deals much more fully with his journey itself—and because of the generally dire and exasperating nature of that journey—one is inclined to feel that Greene has earned the right, so to speak, to take a dim view of the country in which he was so miserable. This is not to say that one must agree with Greene's characterization of Mexico as a "land of hate," only that this conclusion grew out of personal experiences which, as he renders them, supply the grounds for his disaffection.

The interest of *Another Mexico* transcends the "issues" which, in part, it treats. A few examples from the two books will demonstrate this distinction. Due to their interest in the religious situation both writers make a point of noting evidence that Catholicism endures despite the persecution. For Waugh, the Shrine of Guadalupe was "the most impressive sight in Mexico" (p. 234). To lend weight to this assertion Waugh provides an account of the miraculous appearance of the Indian Virgin and follows with a rather tedious analysis of the "facts" supporting the veracity of the legend. The highlight of Greene's stay in Mexico was his coming upon the grove of crosses in the Chiapan mountains. Seen in the context of his arduous journey out of the Godless state, the Indian crosses emerge as a symbol which requires no analysis to expound or defend its significance as the catalyst of new religious insight. Similarly, where Waugh purports to offer a "factual" commentary on the fraud and corruption of Mexican political leaders and their policies, Greene subordinates political matters to the basic human interest of a figure such as General Cedillo. If the oil confiscation to Waugh was an issue which provoked his ire even before he considered coming to Mexico, to Greene enduring the gibes in the plaza at (San Cristóbal de) Las Casas it was an integral part of an onerous personal experience. Finally, it is significant that of all the writers we are considering in this study, only Waugh elected not to make use of Mexico in a work of fiction. This is probably just as well, however, since unlike Lawrence, Huxley, Lowry, and Greene, he had not perceived Mexico with a novelist's eye.

## V

During the two-year period between his return to England and the appearance of *The Power and the Glory*, Greene continued to re-evaluate the "state of mind" first impressed upon him in Mexico. *The Confidential Agent* (1939), an entertainment written during this interval, sheds light on the changes in Greene's thinking. Though the book is set in England, its protagonist is an agent from a "land of hate" (obviously Spain) caught in the throes of a civil war. Formerly an

eminent classical scholar, the agent D. has had his life
blighted by the war. His wife was murdered "by mistake," his
house has been bombed, and D. himself has been faced
almost daily with the very real prospect of death and treachery for several years. However, an assignment to go to England to secure coal for his side in the war promises him, or
so he believes, a welcome relief. Even before his ship docks at
Dover (that fabled boundary), D. discovers that his mission
is in jeopardy. He approached

> *the barrier*—"First-Class Passengers Only"—and looked
> through. The other man was approaching through the
> fog.... D. saw first the pressed trousers, then the fur
> collar, and last the face. They stared at each other *across
> the low gate*. Taken by surprise, they had nothing to
> say. Besides, they had never spoken to each other; they
> were separated by different initial letters, a great many
> deaths—they had seen each other in a passage years ago,
> once in a railway station, and once on a landing field....
> ...It was a misfortune that they were both traveling
> on *the same boat* and that they should have seen each
> other like that *at the barrier between the two classes,
> two* confidential *agents wanting the same thing.*[35]

Here a series of interrelated borders coalesce to suggest multiple levels of significance inhering in the situation. By means
of a swift accretion of associated details we move from the
literal barrier between first- and second-class passengers, to
the implied barriers of wealth and social class, to the two
rival agents working for different sides in their country's civil
war. Yet at the same time the barrier is a "low gate" which
exposes the two men to each other's view. Suddenly, as
memories emerge from their common past—including the
emblems of conjunction such as the passage, the railroad station, and the landing field—we become aware of a basic contiguity which offsets their political and class opposition.
They are indeed rival agents, no longer quite confidential,
"wanting the same thing."

The major irony of *The Confidential Agent* is that, if any-

thing, existence is even more terrifying and gratuitously destructive in "peacetime" England than in D.'s homeland.
After being beaten, robbed, and implicated in several violent
deaths, he realizes bitterly the frailty of his illusions regarding England.

> . . . [D.] gave it up; this wasn't peace. When he landed in
> England he had felt some envy—there had been a casual-
> ness, even a certain sense of trust at the passport control,
> but there was probably something behind that. He had
> imagined that the suspicion which was the atmosphere
> of his own life was due to civil war, but he began to be-
> lieve that it existed everywhere; it was part of human
> life. . . . It was as if the whole world lay in the shadow of
> abondonment.[36]

This insight informs Greene's treatment of Mexico in *The
Power and the Glory*. Set entirely in the "other" Mexico, the
novel places great stress on the spiritual lethargy and vacuity
of existence in a place seemingly doomed to "darkness and
abandonment." But conspicuously absent—or at least much
muted—in the novel is Greene's hostility toward the land he
had excoriated in *Another Mexico*. The choice of a native
Mexican for his protagonist no doubt provided, from a tech-
nical standpoint, the detachment necessary to deflect
Greene's personal grudge against the country, if not his dis-
agreement with its politics. It seems quite clear that in the
process of writing and reshaping his interpretation of his
Mexican experience Greene broadened the boundaries of his
own sympathy. After all, like the two agents, both Greene
and the fugitive priest of Tabasco wanted the same thing in
the end. For Greene had discovered that hate is, at bottom,
"just a failure of imagination."[37]

# VII

# A Mexico of the Mind:
# The Power and the Glory

I fled Him, down the nights and down the days;
I fled Him, down the arches of the years;
I fled Him, down the labyrinthine ways
Of my own mind. . . .

—"The Hound of Heaven"[1]

I

If the setting in a "region of extremes" is always important in Greene's novels, in *The Power and the Glory* this is particularly so. As Richard Hoggart has observed, the novel's theme "is indivisibly priest-and-land."[2] Throughout the tale Greene plies the whole range of his scenic skills to sustain a remarkable unity of setting, tone, character, and theme. Yet it is interesting to note that in contrast with D. H. Lawrence (in *The Plumed Serpent*), Greene devotes relatively little space to extended descriptions of the Mexican landscape. The difference may be suggested by the following comments on the Mexican landscape in Greene's travel book, comments which —from a writer with a reputation for having created a distinct fictional world—may come as rather a surprise. In this passage Greene is, curiously enough, closer to Huxley than to Lawrence.

Only the big decorative poster-shapes of the maguey broke the monotonous landscape of mountain and parched plain. The scene, I suppose, was beautiful in a way, but I felt in sympathy with [William] Cobbett, whose *Rural Rides* I had just been reading before I looked out of the [train] window. He judged a landscape by its value to human beings—not as the Romantics did, in terms of the picturesque. The Romantics would have enjoyed the Mexican scene, describing it as "sublime" and "awe-inspiring"; they scented God in the most barren regions, as if He were a poet of escape. . . . They preferred the kind of Nature which rejects man.

But Nature appals [sic] me when unemployed or unemployable—I can give only lip service to the beauty of the African bush or the Cornish coast.[3]

The fact is that Greene is not really interested in landscape for its own sake. Yet in his novels he still manages to convey an almost overwhelming sense of the atmosphere of a place. Now both Lawrence and Greene use physical setting as a primary symbolic device, but Greene's setting is chiefly established by the use of scrupulously selected details which tend to cluster together in a way so as to typify or suggest the overall quality of a locale, which may itself be presented as a microcosm.[4] Thus with a minimum of straight description Greene, as it were, synecdochizes Mexico by periodic references to filth, muddy or stagnant water, carious teeth and toothaches, dilapidated huts, vomit and excrement, severe heat, sudden tropical rains, roaches and beetles and mosquitoes, snakes and rats, sharks and alligators, a crippled mongrel bitch, and the ubiquitous, ever-patient vultures. Anyone who has been to Tabasco can verify that such things are there in sufficient abundance. But when one is presented with *only* this kind of detail one is obliged to recognize a common denominator or basis for correspondence: in this case, dissolution. The ambience which permeates *The Power and the Glory*—with the significant exception of the interlude across the border in Book III—is an ambience dominated by the fact of mortality, of loss, of temporal flux tending toward entropy. In short, it is an infernal world, "besieged by scavengers."

The physical setting in a novel is meaningful in the way that it reflects (or indeed affects) the quality of the lives of the inhabitants. In *The Power and the Glory* the dissolution embodied in the setting corresponds to the general attenuation that is prevalent in the lives of the characters. Greene's people, situated in Tabasco, are all in some sense exiles—isolated for the most part from each other, and with no assurance of permanent roots. The state's churches have been reduced to rubble by Garrido Canábal's Red Shirts. And with the destruction of the churches, the force of tradition, which had once provided security and order to many of the inhabitants, has been nullified. The overriding sensation in the lives of these characters is pain. The pain may be psychological, or even metaphysical; it may result from loneliness or fear or guilt as well as from an actual bodily hurt such as a toothache, a menstrual cramp, or a bullet wound. Over a span of time the awareness of pain as a recurring fact of one's life is necessarily registered through the memory, that crucial faculty in Greene's writing. Isolation and spiritual "abandonment," dissolution and loss, and that burdensome memory of the chronic pain which all of these bring—such thematic elements, often expressed at strategic moments through the use of border imagery, may be profitably traced as they develop throughout the novel.

## II

The structure of Greene's Mexican novel rests upon a series of encounters between a variety of secondary characters and the protagonist, an unnamed "whisky priest" who is being hunted down by the Tabascan police.[5] Books II and III present the hunt from the perspective of the priest, while Books I and IV are given over, for the most part, to the secondary characters as they view the fugitive. These secondary characters operate as foils—or, in some cases, as analogues—to the priest. They help to define the origin and nature of pain as it exists for these people at this time and in this singular place.

In addition, these characters illustrate several possible reactions to the presence of pain in their lives by the ways in which they register or fail to register an awareness or memory of pain over a span of time.

The novel opens with a lengthy sketch of Mr. Tench, an expatriated English dentist who makes his living in the squalid port town of Frontera. By virtue of his profession Mr. Tench has daily contact with pain and dissolution, which he combats as best he can with the tools of anesthesia and cheap Japanese drills that last no more than a month. The dentist himself suffers from an obscure and chronic pain which he calls indigestion. But the source of his pain is really his utter isolation.

> Home: it was a phrase one used to mean four walls between which one slept. There had never been a home. [He] moved across the little burnt plaza where the [bust of the] dead general grew green in the damp and the gaseosa stalls stood under the palms. It lay like a picture postcard on a pile of other postcards: shuffle the pack and you had Nottingham, a Metroland birthplace, an interlude in Southend.[6]

In passing, it is worth pointing out how strikingly similar the imagery utilized in this memory-formula is to that of a key passage from *Eyeless in Gaza*: "Somewhere in the mind a lunatic shuffled a pack of snapshots and dealt them out at random, shuffled once more and dealt them out in different order, again and again, indefinitely." These are explicit examples of the concern with cyclicity, both as theme and as narrative device, that is present in varying degrees in all four of the major English novels of Mexico.[7] For his part, Mr. Tench has been estranged from his wife and children for fifteen years. He thinks of his family sporadically and nurses futile hopes of someday leaving Tabasco, where he is not at all happy, and returning to his English "home." Though fragmented images of his wife and children drift in and out of his mind continuously, Mr. Tench can scarcely recall them as human beings. " 'It's funny what a man remembers,' " he says. " 'You know, I can remember that watering-can [in an old family photograph] better than I can remember the kids. It cost three and elevenpence three farthings, green; I could lead you to the shop where I bought it. But as for the kids . . . I can't remember much else but them crying' " (p. 19). Mr. Tench's memory is selective indeed. Unlike Huxley's Anthony Beavis, Mr. Tench is no intellectual; he has no philosophy of personality by which to escape reality. But the basic strategy is much the same nonetheless, for the dentist's obliviousness to essentials is in fact his basic weapon against pain, while his remarkable retention of meaningless details serves to fill the mental cavity and preserve it from being crushed under the weight of sheer boredom: "That was the whole world to Mr. Tench: the heat and the forgetting, the putting-off till tomorrow . . . for what?" (p. 11).

In the opening chapter Mr. Tench walks out "into the blazing Mexican sun and the bleaching dust" (p. 9) to claim an ether cylinder which is to be delivered on this day by the *General Obregon,* the little boat from Veracruz. Before long he forgets his mission, and by the end of the chapter he has lost his train of thought no less than eight times. "Mr. Tench stood in the shade of the customs house and thought: What am I here for? Memory drained out of him in the heat. He gathered his bile together and spat forlornly into the sun. Then he sat down on a case and waited. Nothing to do" (p. 10). But there is at least one memory which even Mr. Tench cannot dislodge; it takes him back to the very origins of his etherized existence:

> Mr. Tench's father had been a dentist too—his first memory was finding a discarded cast in a waste-paper basket—the rough toothless gaping mouth of clay, like something dug up . . . . It had been a favourite toy: . . . fate had struck. There is always one moment in childhood when *the door opens* and lets the future in. The hot wet river-port and the vultures lay in the waste-paper basket, and he picked them out. We should be thankful

we cannot see the horrors and degradations lying around
our childhood, in cupboards and bookshelves, everywhere. (p. 15, my emphasis)

The implication here is that the details of the memory-formula associated with decay—with the grave itself—had
somehow propelled Tench across the border of childhood
toward an awareness of the fact of death, a change which
shaped his future as surely as the dentist shapes the cast to
retard the process of decay. Thus we observe Mr. Tench in
his middle age in Tabasco tossing up a bit of sod to drive
away vultures. So far as he is conscious of anything of significance, it is the irreversible and ubiquitous force of dissolution. When he meets the fugitive priest (of whose identity
he is not yet aware), one of the first things he notes is the
shocking condition of the man's teeth. The stranger's "dark
suit and sloping shoulders reminded [Mr. Tench] uncomfortably of a coffin: and death was in his carious mouth already"
(p. 18).

The two men drink a bottle of brandy together in the
secrecy of Mr. Tench's office (Tabasco being a prohibitionist
state) and share their "memories" of the past. The stranger
nostalgically remembers how happy Tabasco had been in the
days before the Red Shirts. But Mr. Tench has noticed no
particular change. The place was as awful then as now—after
all, as he says, " 'There's no difference in the teeth' " (p. 20).
Mr. Tench's dimly acknowledged pain, unlike the priest's, is
limited to his personal difficulties; it is not the product of a
religious sense, for Mr. Tench has none. The priest is called
away by an Indian child to help a sick woman, thereby missing the boat which would have carried him off to Veracruz
and safety. After his new acquaintance's reluctant departure
Mr. Tench realizes that he has once again missed his ship-
ment of ether. "It didn't matter so much after all," Greene
writes; "a little additional pain was hardly noticeable in the
huge abandonment" (p. 24).[8]

Mr. Tench is part of a group of characters whom Greene

calls (in the British edition of the novel) "bystanders." Some of these characters do possess the religious sense which is absent in the dentist. As a result, a major cause of the pain they suffer is the feeling of spiritual abandonment and vacuity which has descended upon them since the destruction of institutional religion in Tabasco. First, there is a family of five that appears in several brief scenes in which the mother reads aloud from the saccharine story of a dashing young Mexican priest who is martyred by the socialist state. In reading the story to her children, the mother is trying to keep alive the memory of the "old days" before the persecution. Within the confines of her own home, at least, she is able to keep the pain of loss neutralized. Her husband, however, is more sensitive to this metaphysical pain. For him the pious story is "like our own childhood." He would prefer to put the book away and try to forget their loss, for the memory only intensifies and prolongs the pain. " '[There] is no use pretending,' " he tells his wife. " 'We have been abandoned here' " (p. 37).

Padre José is the only other priest remaining in Tabasco besides the whisky priest. But Padre José has been officially permitted to stay on because he has capitulated to the governor's decree that only married priests be allowed to live in Tabasco without being subject to arrest and virtually certain execution. Life would be far easier for Padre José if he could somehow forget the vows he had made in becoming a priest years ago. However, he knows that he will never be merely a husband and ordinary citizen like other men: he is still a priest, with the capacity to administer the sacraments even though he is in a state of mortal sin. Despite the fact that he has become a subject of public mockery, there are still people who require a priest to perform the traditional sacerdotal duties. Several times in the novel Padre José is entreated to render these services, but he is beyond any such appeals due to his distrust of others. He is cut off from his fellow townspeople in Villahermosa by his fear that he will be betrayed to the police, arrested, and shot. He cannot respond at all to the pain and suffering of others, for he is too weighed down by his own worries. Unable, therefore, to fulfill his priestly role, Padre José is imprisoned in a barren world where "life went on and on" and where there was "never anything to do at all —no daily Office, no Masses, no confessions, and it was no good praying any longer at all . . . nothing to do at all but sit and eat—eat far too much: [his wife] fed him and fattened him and preserved him like a prize boar" (pp. 39-40). If Mr. Tench is locked into a futile battle against dissolution, Padre José's primary wish—given the daily fear, distrust, and guilt he suffers beneath his bodily corpulence—is to *accelerate* the flow of time and bring closer the moment when he will be free of his earthly prison and may entrust himself to God's mercy. His longing to escape the bounds of a world of time and pain is suggested in the following passage in which Padre José is gazing up at the wheeling constellations: "The glittering worlds lay there in space like a promise—the world was not the universe. Somewhere Christ might not have died. He could not believe that to a watcher there *this* world could shine with such brilliance: it would roll heavily in space under its fog like a burning and abandoned ship. The whole globe was blanketed with his own sin" (p. 38).

The means of evading the harsh realities of existence in Tabasco are more tangible for Captain and Mrs. Fellows, a middle-aged couple who run a banana station near the Grijalva River. Captain Fellows is a determinedly jolly man. Like Mr. Tench he has an unretentive memory. For example, he forgets the day designated for packing and sending his bananas down the river to be sold, and his teenage daughter must oversee the task in his absence. Living in a jungle is an exciting adventure for Fellows—"doing a man's job, the heart of the wild: he felt no responsibility for anyone. In only one other country had he felt more happy, and that was in wartime France, in the ravaged landscape of trenches" (p. 41). Obviously his powers of idealization are considerable. Whenever painful reality threatens to encroach on his magic kingdom Captain Fellows wards off the demon with a cheerful scrap of improvised song. Thus, boating home up the river he serenades the alligators, " 'I don't like your snouts, O trouts. I don't like your snouts . . .' " (p. 41). If there is one painful act that even Captain Fellows is unable to romanticize it is his marriage. Mrs. Fellows, whose character anticipates that of Louise Scobie in *The Heart of the Matter,* is wed to nothing so much as to her suffering. Seemingly always lying in bed, her forehead swathed with handkerchiefs soaked in eau de cologne, Mrs. Fellows is horrified of death, particularly of death in a strange land. "Terror," Greene writes, "was always just behind her shoulder: she was wasted by the effort of not turning round" (p. 43). Rather than cope with this ultimate fear she translates it into forms (the heat, headache, fever) easier for her to bear, and twice the fun besides. She and Captain Fellows cooperate in each other's games of evasion whenever possible. They scrupulously avoid discussion of "taboo" subjects such as home, aging, loneliness, and of course death. Lying together in bed, struggling to maintain the illusion, the

> usually happy and the always unhappy one watched the night thicken from the bed with distrust. *They were companions cut off from all the world:* there was no meaning anywhere *outside* their own hearts: they were carried like children in a coach through the huge spaces without any knowledge of their destination. He began to hum with desperate cheerfulness. . . . (p. 52, my emphasis)

This passage, which employs an interesting combination of junction- and barrier-type frontier imagery, offers a paradoxical insight into the Fellowses' life: isolation is at the same time the cause and the result of their suffering.

One might well say that, at thirteen, their daughter Coral is still too young to have experienced pain of real significance. She had given up her religious faith at ten, but this could not have been a loss to cause much suffering at that

age. Coral is not yet aware of the threat of the unknown, represented by such realities as betrayal or aging or death. "Life
hadn't got at her yet: she had a false air of impregnability"
(p. 44). Because of the immaturity and inertia of her parents,
Coral is forced to assume certain adult responsibilities; it is
she, for example, who decides to give sanctuary to the hunted
priest, and she alone who stands up to the inquisitive lieutenant of police. But beneath the surface there is already an etiology for pain, even though Coral is still not conscious of its
presence. "Coral. . .had an answer to everything. She never
spoke without deliberation: she was prepared—but sometimes the answers she had prepared seemed. . .of a wildness.
. . . [ellipsis in original] They were based on the only life she
could remember—this. The swamps and the vultures and no
children anywhere, except a few in the village, with bellies
swollen by worms, who ate dirt from the bank, inhumanly"
(p. 45). In effect, Coral has had no childhood, as this
memory-formula suggests. Therefore her store of memories
for the future is impoverished. For Coral, "the future, full of
compromises, anxieties, and shame, *lay outside: the gate was
closed* which would one day *let it in.* But at any moment now
a word, a gesture, the most trivial act might be her sesame—
to what?" (p. 48, my emphasis). If Mr. Tench's adult life as a
dentist in the seedy little port was "fated" by a tooth-cast
found in an English waste-paper basket, what kind of future
could be expected for Coral, whose "sesame" will occur in the
atmosphere of tropical Tabasco?

So far as her future in this world is concerned, the question
is never to be answered, for by the end of the novel her life is
taken in an apparently gratuitous act of violence (which is
never made fully clear). But her brief contact with the whisky
priest, Greene more than hints, has turned her mind back to
God in time. Except for her appearance in the priest's dream
near the end, we see Coral for the last time in the novel on the
morning when the future strikes, as she edges through that
open gate into a genuine, if abbreviated, maturity. Doing her
father's work in the barn she comes upon a row of little
crosses which the priest had drawn in chalk to relieve his fear

while hiding there. At about the same time that she observes the crosses, Coral experiences her first menstrual pains. It seems to Coral that "a horrible novelty *enclosed* her whole morning: it was as if today everything was memorable" (p. 73, my emphasis). "Enclosed" I take to mean cut off from her "childhood" before this day. The "sesame" to the future, as the priest's dream suggests, has occurred. The anonymous police lieutenant's childhood had also been blighted by misery, but in his case the source of misery was extreme material poverty. He is a fiercely dedicated individual, a utopian socialist determined to see that his suffering is compensated by purging the state of those who have, in his view, contributed to its social inequities. Even foreign programs broadcast on local radio seem to him a sign of danger: "...this was his own land, and he would have *walled it in* with steel if he could, until he had eradicated from it everything which reminded him of how it had once appeared to a miserable child. He wanted to destroy everything: to be alone without any memories at all. Life began five years ago" (p. 33, my emphasis). The lieutenant is no "bystander." It is true that painful memories are a threat to his peace of mind, as they are for Mr. Tench, Padre José, and the father in the pious family. But the lieutenant is not content passively to bear the burden of the past or to dull the pain by convenient forgetfulness. Instead he conducts a personal war on those memories.

> The lieutenant walked home through the shuttered town. All his life had lain here: the Syndicate of Workers and Peasants had once been a [Catholic] school. He had helped to wipe out that unhappy memory. The whole town was changed.... The new children would have new memories: nothing would ever be as it was. There was something of a priest in his intent observant walk— a theologican going back over the errors of the past to destroy them again. (p. 32)

This last sentence points to one of the novel's central ironies: the priest-hunter has much in common with his quarry. However antithetical their ideologies, both their lives have been shaped by a religious sense.[9] We can see the underlying similarity perhaps most clearly in the genuine sympathy felt by both men for the pain of people other than themselves —a quality which sets them apart from the "bystanders." Walking through the plaza in Villahermosa, the lieutenant observes a group of children playing the roles of their heroes, Francisco Madero, Pancho Villa, and Emiliano Zapata, out to kill Yankees. Moved by the sight, he reflects that "it was for these [children] he was fighting. He would eliminate from their childhood everything which had made him miserable, all that was poor, superstitious, and corrupt." And what does the lieutenant have to offer them in the place of these remembered hardships associated (in his mind) with Christianity? The passage continues:

> They deserved nothing less than the truth—a vacant universe and a cooling world, the right to be happy in any way they chose. He was quite prepared to make a massacre for their sakes—first the Church and then the foreigner and then the politician—even his own [police] chief would one day have to go. He wanted to begin the world again with them, in a desert. (p. 77)

The lieutenant is clearly a kind of visionary, and a rather formidable one. His ideal, described in a passage closely related to the one above, is based on a "complete certainty in the existence of a dying, cooling world, of human beings who had evolved from animals for no purpose at all" (p. 33). As it is depicted in *The Power and the Glory*, the carious ambience of Tabasco seems dangerously close to the lieutenant's utopia.

However, though the lieutenant is a skillful and determined *guerrero* in the battle against sentience, his cause—at least as far as his *own* wounds from childhood are concerned —is doomed. His obsession with hunting down the last active priest in Tabasco provides him with a temporary distraction, but the pain is still demonstrably present beneath the starched and creased khaki drill, the polished brass, the well-oiled and loaded revolver at his hip. The pain darts to the surface when he is not prepared for it, as in this memory-formula where the lieutenant scrutinizes an old newspaper photograph of the priest in better days.

"They all look alike to me," the lieutenant said. Something you could almost have called horror moved him when he looked at the white muslin dresses [in the photograph of a first-communion celebration]—he remembered the smell of incense in the churches of his boyhood, the candles and the laciness and the self-esteem, the immense demands made from the altar steps by men who didn't know the meaning of sacrifice. The old peasants knelt there before the holy images with their arms held out in the attitude of the cross: tired by the long day's labour in the plantations, they squeezed out a further mortification. And the priest came round with the collecting-bag taking their centavos, abusing them for their small comforting sins, and sacrificing nothing at all in return. . . . (p. 30)

Small wonder that all priests look alike to the lieutenant, for his hurt and anger are so palpably *alive* within him that he is blind to the reality of any individual who might violate the pattern locked into his mind. Focusing his rage onto the blurred photograph—the plump and complacent clerical pose bearing in actuality little resemblance to the ragged fugitive of these days—the lieutenant can say, with real conviction, " 'We've shot him half a dozen times' " (p. 29). Given the lieutenant's obsession, his failure to recognize the whisky priest the first two times they actually meet is entirely fitting, is in fact all but inevitable.

### III

Greene's protagonist departs in most respects not only from the lieutenant's mental image of him, but also from the expectations of what might be called conventional Catholics regarding the behavior of the clergy. He is a drunkard, he has fathered a child, he often behaves like a hopeless coward. In his isolation, his guilt, his fear of pain and his longing to escape reality, the priest seems initially to have far more in common with the "bystanders" than with the heroic martyr in the book read by the pious and "abandoned" family in Villahermosa. But despite his shortcomings and the perilous circumstances of his existence in Tabasco, the priest continues "to pass life on."[10]

One attribute which distinguishes the priest from so many of the characters discussed thus far is his attitude toward memory. " 'I try to remember how happy I was once,' " he tells Coral (p. 54). In very broad terms, there are two distinct phases of his past to which his mind returns in moments of reverie. The first is the "old days," the period ending some eight years back, when the persecution began to affect his way of life. The photograph in the police station was taken during those years, when he wore his clerical costume freely, held daily mass, and observed the rules of the Church on such matters as fasting, abstinence, and confession. He had been a man of ambition in those days, presiding with authority over meetings of the Children of Mary and all the parish guilds, haggling without qualms over the price "per head" which local peasants should pay for marriages and baptisms, hoping someday to be promoted to the post of bishop in the state capital. The priest cherishes his memories of these times and looks back on them nostalgically as a period of comparative innocence.

But all of this changed when the state's anticlerical campaign got under way. Most priests abandoned Tabasco; those who stayed were imprisoned, and some were killed. The whisky priest for a time postponed any decision about whether he should flee. He simply drifted from village to village, depending on the generosity and care of the people to protect him. In return he would say mass and hear confessions—in a barn or hut safe from the police. During the first

year of his wandering he began to go to pieces. He neglected
his duties and drank heavily to mitigate his fear and loneliness. In a moment of drunken despair he sired a child by a
woman named Maria whom he scarcely knew. The last seven
years had been a period of steady degeneration and increasing peril. And yet he had remained in Tabasco, until he
finally became the last active priest in the state. Many times
he had attempted to escape, but somehow each time something came up (such as the child's appeal for help for his sick
mother in the first chapter) to prevent his flight to safety
across the border. By the time the story opens the priest is
utterly weary of being hunted. There are moments when he
longs to be caught so that his ordeal can come to an end.

These two phases of his past exist in the priest's mind as
opposed memory-formulas, one linked to innocence and joy,
the other to corruption and despair. The experiences of that
first year—especially the violation of his celibacy—operate
as the boundary between the two major phases. In the first
half of the novel the memory-formula detailing the priest's
degeneration dominates his mind, though when he visits the
village where Maria and their little girl live (Chapter One of
Book II), the transitional period is emphasized to such an
extent that it almost seems a distinct time-frame in its own
right. The priest's attire during his flight from the police early
in the novel is emblematic of the two major phases of his
career as a cleric:

> He wore what used to be town shoes, black and pointed:
> only the uppers were left, so that he walked to all intents
> barefoot.... He wore a shirt and a pair of black town
> trousers and he carried his attaché case.... [He] carried
> about with him still the scars of time—the damaged
> shoes implied a different past, the lines on his face sug-
> gested hopes and fears of the future. (p. 57)

As he heads "home" to the village of Maria and little Brigida in Book II, the priest reflects that

the years behind him were littered with . . . surrenders—
feast-days and fast-days and days of abstinence had been
the first to go: then he had ceased to trouble more than
occasionally about his breviary—and finally he had left
it behind altogether at [Frontera]. . . . Then the altar
stone went—too dangerous to carry with him. . . . [He]
was probably liable to suspension, but penalties of the
ecclesiastical kind began to seem unreal in a state where
the only penalty was the civil one of death. The routine
of his life like a dam was cracked and forgetfulness came
dribbling in, wiping out this and that. . . . He was a bad
priest, he knew it . . . but every failure dropped out of
sight and out of mind: somewhere they accumulated in
secret—the rubble of his failures. One day they would
choke up, he supposed, altogether the source of grace.
Until then he carried on. . . . (pp. 82-83)

Each of these "surrenders" is painful to the priest, but under
the circumstances he is willing to sacrifice a few fingers to
save an arm. Whereas Mr. Tench clutters his mind with trivial details to blot out the memory of his primary failures, the
priest—though he actually has not "forgotten" the sacrifice of
ecclesiastical paraphernalia associated with the "old days"—
always places highest priority on retaining his hold on the
essentials of his faith: "The simple ideas of hell and heaven
moved in his brain: life without books, without contact with
educated men, had peeled away from his memory everything
but the simplest outline of the mystery" (p. 89).

Approaching "home," the village where he first took the
plunge into corruption, the priest experiences a few rare
moments of exhilaration. He is secure in the knowledge that
people here will not betray him, and, although it has been six
years since his last visit, he allows himself to indulge in the
hope that he will even be welcomed. What he has forgotten,
for the moment, is that during those six years matters have
changed a great deal. When he enters the village, "like a beggar" in his ragged costume, he is received coolly. (He does
not yet know that the police have begun taking hostages in

all the villages he visits, killing those who refuse to give information concerning his whereabouts.) The priest "couldn't
help remembering the last time . . . the excitement, the gourds
of spirit brought out of holes in the ground . . . [ellipses in ori-
ginal] his guilt had still been fresh, yet how he had been welcomed" (p. 85). Finally the adults of the village, at Maria's
suggestion, approach and kiss his hand formally. The young
children, his Brigida among them, are bid to do the same, but
the priest perceives that they are "too young to remember the
old days when the priests dressed in black and wore Roman
collars and had soft superior patronizing hands . . ." (p. 86).
In his view they are like Coral Fellows: their memories are
impoverished, and their future thereby imperiled. After a few
minutes alone with Maria, the priest realizes that even she
has failed to retain the "scars of time"—the sense of guilt, in
this case—which he has carried with him since their fateful
encounter seven years back.

> He was astonished and a bit relieved by her resilience:
> once for five minutes seven years ago they had been
> lovers—if you could give that name to a relationship in
> which she had never used his baptismal name: to her it
> was just an incident, a scratch which heals completely in
> the healthy flesh: she was even proud of having been the
> priest's woman. He alone carried a wound, as if a whole
> world had ended. (pp. 93-94)

An important scene involving the priest and his daughter
occurs the next day, after the police have searched the village
and questioned all the inhabitants. The priest has been fortunate to avoid recognition but now he is urged to go away,
for he is a danger to the people who harbor him. Before leaving he stops to retrieve his attaché case (one of the few remaining relics of the "old days") at the rubbish dump, where
Maria had hidden it from the police; and it is in this setting,
with the reek of dissolution everywhere, that he sees Brigida
for the last time. Brigida is shockingly mature for her age.
Like Coral she has had no true childhood, and because she is

without both effective parental guidance and religious train-
ing—lacking at once a father and a Father—there seems to be
no way she can avoid a future of corruption and misery. The
priest "saw her fixed in her life like a fly in amber—Maria's
hand raised to strike: Pedro [a boyfriend] talking prematurely in the dusk: and the police beating the forest—violence
everywhere" (p. 111). From this point on, whenever the
priest thinks of Brigida he remembers this scene by the rubbish heap where he feels for the first time both a father's love
for his daughter and the intense pain stemming from his helplessness in preventing her corruption: "The world was in her
heart already, like the small spot of decay in a fruit" (p. 110).

After he leaves the village, the priest's hopes for places of
refuge are greatly diminished. One by one all his former sanc-
tuaries are sealed off from him due to the extreme tactics now
employed by the police. Thus the process by which the priest
is forced to "surrender" his ties to the past is accelerated,
making his suffering from isolation even more intense than it
had been before. The final hope for protection is destroyed
when the priest realizes that the mestizo who pretends to be
his guide and companion of the road intends to betray him
when they arrive in Carmen, the village where the priest
grew up. Here Greene accentuates the priest's sense of abandonment and despair by using a familiar version of the
border figure: ". . .it was more than the half-caste he was
leaving behind on the forest track: the mule stood sideways
like a barrier, nodding a stupid head, between him and the
place where he had been born. He felt like a man without a
passport who is turned away from every harbour" (p. 138).

By this time, his usefulness in Tabasco seemingly nullified,
the priest has begun seriously to consider the possibility of
escaping over the mountains into the relatively safe state of
Chiapas. Several people have suggested that he make the trip
across the border to (San Crostóbal de) Las Casas, where (as
one woman tells him) the churches are still open, mass is held
almost daily in private houses, with the priests "'all dressed
up like in the old days'" (p. 106). The image which this creates in the whisky priest's mind—inevitably linked with the

memory of his former "innocence" as a cleric—represents a powerful temptation. "He thought: If I go, I shall meet other priests: I shall go to confession: I shall feel contrition and be forgiven: eternal life will begin for me all over again" (p. 88). His quitting of Tabasco would mean not only his own salvation, but also the cessation of the systematic murder of villagers who refuse to give the police information about him.

> If he left them, they would be safe: and they would be free from his example: he was the only priest the children could remember. It was from him they would take their ideas of the faith. But it was from him too they took God —in their mouths. When he was gone it would be as if God in all this space between the sea and the mountains ceased to exist. Wasn't it his duty to stay, even if they despised him, even if they were murdered for his sake, even if they were corrupted by his example? He was shaken with the enormity of the problem: he lay with his hands over his eyes: nowhere, in all the wide flat marshy land, was there a single person he could consult. (p. 89)

The intricacies of the questions raised by both alternatives are too overwhelming for him to make a genuine decision either way, but he is not prepared yet to make the final "surrender." So he continues, with no foreseeable goal, to wander the "labyrinthine ways" of Tabasco.

To justify his presence in the dangerous state he needs wine for the mass. But in order to obtain wine without endangering the lives of friends in the villages, he must enter the very lair of his antagonist—Villahermosa, Garrido's capital. If escape to Las Casas represents the prospect of eternal life for the priest, Villahermosa offers him an altogether different condition: "The beetles were flocking out and covering the pavements: they popped under the feet like puff-balls, and a sour green smell came up from the river. The white bust of a general glimmered in a tiny public garden, all hot paving and dust, and an electric dynamo throbbed on the ground-floor of the only hotel" (p. 143).

Not long after his arrival in the capital the priest is arrested (his real identity again going unrecognized) for possession of contraband alcohol and is cast into the dark and fetid communal cell, ostensibly the innermost circle of the infernal realm. "This place," writes Greene, "was very like the world: overcrowded with lust and crime and unhappy love: it stank to heaven" (p. 169). Terrified at first, the priest gradually discovers that "after all it was possible to find peace there" (p. 169). This change in attitude is in fact quite consistent with his character. For as the night passes the inmates open up their lives to one another by sharing memories, and the priest empathizes with the abject suffering of these people. The night in prison offers him the first feeling of *home* that he has been allowed in years. So moved is he by the sense of kinship he feels, surrounded by God's plenty—murderers, thieves, prostitutes, beggars, an old woman arrested for having holy books in her home—that he abandons all defenses; he reveals his identity and even discloses the fact that a reward is offered for his capture. The other prisoners, though stunned by the rashness of this confession, respond in kind to the priest's overt demonstration of trust and compassion. When several of them denounce the police and their "blood money," the priest is "touched by an extraordinary affection. He was just one criminal among a herd of criminals . . . [ellipsis in original] he had a sense of companionship which he had never received in the old days when pious people came kissing his black cotton glove" (pp. 173-174).

Now this is an extremely important insight on the priest's part, but he is not yet ready to accept its full implications.[11] He is still too blinded by his idealized memories of the "old days" and his supposed innocence back then to act on this intimation of the truth. Therefore, instead of electing at this point to continue his service among the "herd of criminals" who have penetrated his long-standing isolation, he awaits a sign from God to show him what to do. When the police lieutenant fails to recognize him the next day and sets him free, charitably giving him five pesos (the price of a mass) into the bargain, the priest is certain that God is permitting him, at last, to escape across the border to that holy city, Las Casas.

However, before he is granted the merest glimpse of his nirvana, the priest must pass through a tortuous wilderness, which Greene describes as "a region of abandonment...a kind of limbo" (p. 199). On his way north to the mountains, he stops at the Fellowses' banana station and finds it inexplicably empty, deserted. Later, seeking shelter from a sudden storm in a rat-infested hut, he encounters a frightened Indian woman, all alone except for her dead infant who was apparently shot by James Calver, the fugitive American gangster whom the priest had been hearing about during his wanderings the last few weeks. When the rain subsides he sets off toward the mountains with the woman following in silence (she can speak only a few words of Spanish). After the recent experience of human fellowship in the prison, this return to virtual loneliness is all the more painful for the priest. Although he is fatigued and feels the approach of fever, he may not rest, for the rainy season has just begun and the steep mountain paths will soon be impassable. Time becomes elastic and his mind shuttles between the last eight years of flight and fear on the one hand, and on the other the peace and innocence associated with both the "old days" and his imminent future across the mountains. Suddenly, "for no apparent reason," he remembers

> a day of rain at the American seminary [which he had attended as a young man], the glass windows of the library steamed over with the central heating, the tall shelves of sedate books, and a young man—a stranger from Tucson—drawing his initials on the pane with his finger—*that* was peace. *He looked* at it *from the outside:* he couldn't believe that he would ever again *get in.* He had made *his own world,* and *this* was it—the empty broken huts, the storm going by, and [the] fear.... (pp. 200-201, my emphasis)

These two "worlds" are increasingly juxtaposed in his thoughts as he approaches a place in the mountainous terrain which he supposes is the boundary between the two states. He can do no more than suppose, and wonder whether he

will ever reach the *end* of fear, for "when there are no visible
boundaries between one state and another—no passport
examination or customs house—danger just seems to go on"
(p. 208). For this crucial border region Greene has constructed a particular landscape whose rugged features and
outsize dimensions perfectly objectify the frustrations and
paradoxes inherent in the psychic frontier zone through
which the whisky priest must pass in order to arrive at his
destination.[12] The priest has reached the edge of the plateau
which he and the Indian woman have been climbing for the
last day and a half. Beyond the edge the path drops off pre-
cipitously into a deep *barranca,* from the bottom of which it
then climbs the equally severe incline of the opposite bank.
To the observer gazing across the "border" from atop the
near side, the rocky ridge opposite looms directly ahead no
more than a few hundred yards away. But to arrive at the
other side by following the narrow and meandrous path—
and there is no other means of access—will entail several
hours of laborious walking. Thus for the already travel-
weary priest the passage to the end of eight years' horror is
laid out in a manner calculated to protract all the tensions
involved in this final "surrender" of his past in the rank,
entropic world of Tabasco: sanctuary and eternal life seem at
once proximate and remote, palpable and unreal.

To mark the division even further, on the near edge of the
*barranca,* where the priest now stands, Greene has stationed
a grove of crude Indian crosses like those which served as an
important symbol of the perseverence of the Christian faith
in its "purer," more primitive form in *Another Mexico.* The
sight of the strange crosses leaning at odd angles against the
darkening sky is no less impressive to the priest than it was to
Greene:

> . . . they were the first Christian symbols he had seen for
> more than five years publicly exposed—if you could call
> this empty plateau in the mountains a public place. No
> priest could have been concerned in the strange rough

group; it . . . had nothing in common with the tidy vestments of the Mass and the elaborately worked out symbols of the liturgy. It was like a short cut to the dark and magical heart of the faith—to the night when the graves opened and the dead walked. (p. 208)

Beneath the tallest cross the woman lays her dead child, genuflects in the peculiar Indian manner and deposits a small lump of sugar as a kind of token or offering in case a miracle should occur and the child's life be restored. The priest reflects, "here was faith—faith in the spittle that healed the blind man and the voice that raised the dead" (p. 209). Though deeply moved by her manifest devotion, the priest cannot stay here any longer—night approaches, along with more rain clouds—and, the woman showing no inclination to follow, he begins his descent alone. But after a while he begins to feel troubled about having abandoned the woman, so he climbs back up to the ridge, only to find her vanished. Hoping to ease his fever and gain strength for the journey ahead of him, the priest guiltily eats the sugar she had left behind and, with increasing apprehension, turns back a second time to descend into the pit.

What Greene is suggesting in this little geographical drama, as in the prison episode, is the density of the illusion which clouds the priest's vision. The scene is almost top-heavy with danger signs warning the priest to turn back, as the Indian woman had. The most important of all these omens are the crosses themselves—planted firmly on *this* side of the frontier, where their significance lies in direct relation to the putatively infernal, "abandoned" state of Tabasco. One is reminded of Greene's own departure from the Chiapan mountains, when the curious disappearance of a band of Indians who had been praying by the roadside seemed "like the boundary of a faith" which Greene was leaving behind in returning to tourist Mexico. But the whisky priest is still lured—quite understandably, of course, after what he has been through in the last eight years—by the seductive innocence of Las Casas.

Considering Greene's own disappointing and frustrating experiences in that "very Catholic town," one wonders what might have transpired were the priest to have walked straight on into Las Casas after finally arriving at the opposite rim of the *barranca*. For this to occur, Greene would have had to shuffle his geography even more than he has done already, because the town lies some eighty miles beyond the border at the point where the priest crosses—and he is in no condition to make such a journey by this time. In any event, the priest's progress toward Las Casas is necessarily interrupted when he reaches the first village on the Chiapan side and collapses next to a whitewashed building which he assumes is a barracks. It is a church.

During his recuperation the priest is the guest of Mr. Lehr, a German-American mining engineer, and Miss Lehr, his sister. If the Lehrs lived in Tabasco they would no doubt be part of the group of "bystanders." Inhabiting a less severe region, however, they manage to survive with all their illusions intact, their prosperity operating as a kind of buffer between themselves and any significant degree of pain. "Mr. Lehr and his sister had combined to drive out savagery by simply ignoring anything that conflicted with an ordinary German-American homestead" (p. 220). Thus they treat the priest with profuse hospitality, as they would any guest, but they show not the least curiosity about his harrowing experiences across the border. Themselves vigorous Lutherans (with a Gideon Bible in the guest room), they reveal the shallowness of their sympathy for the priest's recent suffering by directing tactless and wholly inappropriate criticisms of Catholicism to him: "'Too much luxury . . . while the people starve,'" charges Mr. Lehr; and, he goes on, "'It seems to me you people make a lot of fuss about inessentials,'" such as fasting and eating fish on Fridays (p. 219). The priest remembers such relatively trivial details only as "something in his childhood" (p. 219), yet the world to which he is now returning could be described in similar terms.

Despite the ossified attitudes of his hosts, the time spent at the Lehrs' comes as a welcome relief to the priest. He bathes daily in the "safe" water of the little stream by their home, reads New York newspapers that are only three weeks old, borrows a decent suit of clothes from Mr. Lehr, walks the streets again as a cleric, openly purchases alcohol, and—after squabbling with the faithful over the "price per head"—conducts masses, baptisms, and confessions by the score. Initially the priest relishes this resumption of his old role: "He felt respect all the way up the street: men took off their hats as he passed: it was as if he had got back to the days before the persecution. He could feel the old life hardening round him like a habit, a stony case which held his head high and dictated the way he walked, and even formed his words" (p. 226). Such a passage, with its revealing figure of the "stony case," shows the continuing influence of the memory-formula from the "old days." Brought to the surface and given new support by this apparent return to "innocence," the formula's power is sufficient to make the priest feel already "as if the last [eight] years had been a dream and he had never really been away from the guilds, the Children of Mary, and the daily Mass" (p. 225).

But this resumption of complacent piety cannot last, or rather it cannot continue to exist unopposed. The memories of the more recent past, though latent for a brief period, are not so easily cast off by one who still bears the "scars of time." The pleasure afforded the priest by his being once again free to enjoy a bottle of brandy, for example, is clouded over by his recollection of the last time he drank brandy, the night of his arrest and subsequent imprisonment in Villahermosa; and this memory triggers still others: "The memory was like a hand, pulling away the [stony] case, exposing him. . . . He turned the glass in his hand, and all the other glasses turned too: he remembered the dentist talking of his children, and Maria unearthing the bottle of spirits she had kept for him—the whisky priest" (p. 227). As when he took the lump of sugar left with the dead child by the Indian woman, each self-indulgence of the priest adds to the burden left on his conscience by the memory of what *he* has "abandoned" back in Tabasco. Bathing at the Lehrs', he feels

an enormous luxury lying there in the little cold stream
while the sun flattened.... [ellipsis in original] He
thought of the prison cell with the old man and the pious
woman, the half-caste lying across the hut door, the
dead child and the [Fellowses'] abandoned station. He
thought with shame of his daughter left to her knowledge and her ignorance by the rubbish-dump. He had no
right to such luxury. (p. 221)

It is not simply unpleasant memories which turn his mind
back to Tabasco, however. Glimpses of human courage and
fundamental perseverance under great hardship—glimpses
only valued partially at the time of occurrence because of the
priest's obsession with the flight to freedom—now come back
to him with an enormous force of reality far exceeding that of
the world to which he has escaped. In the middle of a timid
confession by a pious old woman the priest suddenly recalls,
"with an odd...homesickness," his companions in the prison, and all "the suffering and the endurance which went on
everywhere the other side of the mountains" (p. 232). Despite
the Church's teaching that one's first duty is to save one's
own soul, the conflict between the two worlds has clearly
shifted in favor of Tabasco, for the priest has finally begun to
realize that his true spiritual "home" is back across the mountains, that the old notion about his innocence was a fabrica-
tion shaped by his nostalgia for the times when his selfish
ambitions went unchallenged, that freedom and redemption
within the context of a "holy city" such as Las Casas have lost
their vital significance for him.[13] To be free and spiritually
pure in Las Casas is tantamount to an egoistic withdrawal
not unlike that of Padre José. Because this ultimate "surrender" is the most painful he has ever been faced with, and
because he is half in love with deathful ease, the whisky
priest continues the argument within himself. The outcome,
however, is already determined: "In three days, he told himself, I shall be in Las Casas: I shall have confessed and been
absolved—and the thought of the child on the rubbish-heap
came automatically back to him with *painful love*. What was

the good of confession when you loved the result of your crime?" (pp. 237-238, my emphasis).

The importance of the words "painful love" in this passage can hardly be overestimated. What the priest has discovered is that in human life, love—whether it be love of one's child or love of one's fellow man or love of God—is inextricably bound to pain and loss. This is, after all, one of the major implications of the story of the Incarnation and the Crucifixion. Thus the confluence of a man's most private and often selfish memories and fantasies becomes in the end an extension of his religious sense, a means of full recognition of his true role as a servant of God. All that is needed to transform the priest's reflections into action is a sign, some unmistakable indication that God's will coincides with his own burgeoning thoughts.

When, on the morning of the intended departure for Las Casas, his old betrayer turns up, the priest regards the man's sudden reappearance as being "like the small pain that reminds a man of his sickness..." (p. 238). In the mestizo's appeal that he return over the mountains in order to administer the last rites to Calver, the dying American gangster, the priest detects a trap. He is certain, regardless of the half-caste's protestations and all the evidence supporting the veracity of his "mission of mercy," that the police will be waiting for them. Entirely aware of the consequences of again traversing the border—as he was not during his previous crossing—the priest cannot resist the call to return to the state where dissolution itself is infused and transformed by the divine presence.[14] The priest's decision has already been made, but Greene stages the scene in a manner which again holds the moment so that its significance may be fully appreciated. "*Behind* [the mestizo], *across* the yard and *through* the open door, the priest could see Miss Lehr putting up his sandwiches.... She was wrapping [them] carefully in grease-proof paper, and her sedate movements had a curious effect of unreality. It was the half-caste who was real" (p. 238, my emphasis). The priest's mule is still pointed toward Las Casas, but the emphatically spatial terms through which Greene conveys the essential *distance* between the "sedate" preparations of Miss Lehr and the priest's disparate perspective establish beyond doubt the real goal of the imminent journey. The priest's transformed outlook is further indicated by the fact that he now associates the world of safety and innocence exclusively with Miss Lehr and her antiseptic unreality. Even as he starts off in the direction of Las Casa, he has already "forgotten Miss Lehr completely: the other world had stretched a hand across the border, and he was again in the atmosphere of flight" (p. 240). But he has not yet actually turned back, except in thought:

> ...there was no question at all that he was needed. A man [Calver] with all that on his soul... [ellipsis in original] The oddest thing of all was that he felt quite cheerful: he had never really believed in this peace. He had dreamed of it so often on the other side that now it meant no more to him than a dream. He began to whistle a tune—something he had heard somewhere once. "I found a rose in my field": it was time he woke up. (pp. 242-243)[15]

Finally, after the implications of this climactic frontier experience have been thoroughly impressed on both the character and the reader, the priest wheels the mule around and heads back, with "painful love," for the infernal paradise, Tabasco. As the two men leave the Chiapan village together they pass by the whitewashed church building which the priest had not recognized on the day of his arrival, and "that too belonged to a dream. Life didn't contain churches" (p. 244).

IV

Book III concludes with the brief encounter between the priest and James Calver, the latter's refusal to be shriven of sin before his death, the arrest of the priest and his removal to the prison in Villahermosa, where he sorts out his memories for the last time on the night before his execution. With the troubling recollection of Brigida by the garbage dump particularly heavy on his heart, the whisky priest goes to his death convinced that his mission on earth has been a failure. He has not saved a single soul—not even, he believes, his own; he must go to God empty-handed; soon "he wouldn't even be a memory" (p. 284). The remainder of the novel, as if to test the validity of the priest's last thoughts about himself, explores the direct and indirect effects of the priest's life on some of the characters he has encountered during his wanderings through Tabasco.

The consummation of the manhunt does not afford the police lieutenant the sense of victory that he had anticipated. Rather, he feels depressed, "as though now that the last priest was under lock and key there was nothing left to think about. The spring of action seemed to be broken. He looked back on the weeks of hunting as a happy time which was now over for ever. He felt without a purpose, as if life had drained out of the world" (p. 279). With no foreseeable campaign into which he can channel his fanaticism, the lieutenant is once again exposed to the pain of wounds festering deep within his mind, the inextricable memory of his blighted past. Yet in his final conversations with his prisoner, he has reluctantly come to recognize the priest not only as an individual who fails to conform to his mental image of priests as exploiters, but as "[not] a bad fellow" (p. 271). There is reason enough to suppose that, lacking both a functional "spring of action" and a sufficiently loathesome enemy, the lieutenant's utopian vision may give way to a more creative expression of his underlying religious sense.

The future of Captain and Mrs. Fellows, who are staying for the time being in the sweltering hotel in Villahermosa, seems devoid of even the most tentative prospect for hope. Their pathetic attempts to maintain the old defenses against fear and pain are doomed to defeat by the most severe

encroachment ever made by reality: the death of Coral. They
have agreed that any discussion of this loss is permanently
"taboo." Since a return to the banana station is out of the
question, their blueprint for escape calls for a trip back to England (their secular counterpart of the priest's Las Casas),
perhaps to settle and start a new life. This plan seems almost
to satisfy Mrs. Fellows, who has always longed to leave the
tropics anyhow. But such a conspicuous retreat brings no
relief at all to Captain Fellows. He does not want to forsake
his "man's job of work" in the picturesque jungle, and so the
idea of returning to England holds no appeal for his fantasy
life. Thus bereft of romantic adventure, he is vulnerable as
never before to painful memories. Regardless of the agreement with his wife, Captain Fellows cannot get Coral out of
his mind. He remembers in particular how she seemed to be
so strangely affected by something said to her by the fugitive
priest whom she had hidden from the police. However, Captain Fellows is not mentally equipped to wrestle with such
enigmas. He is too dependent upon the adolescent, mutually
palliative partnership with his wife to have the strength to
force the moment to its crisis: "They had both been deserted.
They had to stick together" (p. 290).

The morning on which the whisky priest is shot finds Mr.
Tench in Villahermosa, where he has been transported to
treat the police chief's nagging toothache. As he works on the
carious mouth of the *jefe,* Mr. Tench's mind drifts from subject to subject—the obscure pain in his stomach, a recent
letter from his wife informing him of her intention to obtain a
divorce, his plans to leave Mexico as soon as the peso stabi-
lizes—not dwelling long enough on any one of these for it to
take hold and necessitate genuine thought. But his customary
defensive maneuvers are suddenly interrupted when, through
the window of the chief's office, he sees the police dragging a
little man out into the yard to be shot. The dentist recognizes
the victim, and, caught off his guard, he watches the killing
in horror. "But I know him," reflects Mr. Tench. "Good God,
one ought to do something. This was like seeing a neighbour

shot." The rifles' thunderous reverberations "shook Mr. Tench: they seemed to vibrate inside his own guts: he felt rather sick..." (p. 294). The shock effects a direct exposure of the source of the dentist's own pain, the paucity and evanescence of his human relationships. The police have reduced their prisoner to a "routine heap" beside the wall of the Tabascan jail—"something unimportant which had to be cleared away." To Mr. Tench, however, the brief meeting with the living priest weeks earlier had not been so unimportant, as the elements retained in this memory-formula demonstrate: "He remembered the little man rising bitterly and hopelessly from his chair that blinding afternoon to follow the child out of town; he remembered a green watering-can, the photo of the children, that case he was making out of sand for a split palate" (pp. 294-295).

His mind thus stirred and his memory enriched by the inclusion of meaningful detail, the dentist renews his determination to extricate himself from Tabasco. Considering his propensity for forgetting his own resolutions, one may doubt that Mr. Tench's plans will be carried out. But there can be no question that he has been significantly influenced by his two associations with the priest: "an appalling sense of loneliness came over Mr. Tench, doubling him with indigestion. The little fellow had spoken English and knew about his children. He felt deserted" (p. 295). However absurdly he labels the sensation, Mr. Tench's numbed sensibility has been cauterized. He has felt another man's pain as his own.

The appearance of another anonymous and harried priest in the novel's final scene, a "tall pale thin man with a rather sour mouth, who carried a small suitcase" and wore pointed city shoes (pp. 300-301), suggests that the "scars of time" borne by the whisky priest are not yet healed and that Tabasco is not yet "abandoned." But the fetid atmosphere of Tabasco only exposes in elemental terms what is disguised elsewhere, for pain and loss are, in Greene's view, fundamental realities of human life everywhere. Yet in the end the terror of life may be accommodated and even affirmed, as

the novels of Greene's Catholic period (1938-61) attest. The
following description applies to Greene's religious vision as
well as to that of the whisky priest: ". . .at the centre of his
own faith there always stood the convincing mystery—that
we were made in God's image—God was the parent, but He
was also the policeman, the criminal, the priest, the maniac,
and the judge" (p. 136). Greene's admittedly melodramatic
interpretation of this doctrine provides him with a singular
angle of vision from which to explore his "region of extremes"
and find the presence of grace in the unlikeliest of places. For
if dissolution and misery and "abandonment" seem endemic
in Greene's Tabasco, there are also the Indian crosses within
its boundaries to remind us that suffering is not solely the
burden of mankind. "It was for this world," muses the
whisky priest, "that Christ had died: the more evil you saw
and heard about you, the greater glory lay around the death;
it was too easy to die for what was good or beautiful, for
home or children or a civilization—it needed a God to die for
the half-hearted and the corrupt" (p. 131). And Tabasco,
reeking with the stench of corruption of all kinds, like the
world, "stinks to heaven." Greene's version of the infernal
paradise myth is the least equivocal of the four under consideration. In his Catholic novels painful love is the fundamental link between God and man, and between man and
man. To the extent that his characters are able to face and
accept the burden of painful love, they may discover even
within a dying, cooling world the human counterpart of that
"greater glory."

# VIII

# *The* Barranca *of History: Mexico as Nexus of Doom in* Under the Volcano

There is a wisdom that is woe; but there is a woe that is
madness. And [yet] there is a Catskill eagle in some
souls that can alike dive down into the blackest gorges,
and sour out of them again and become invisible in the
sunny spaces. And even if he for ever flies within the
gorge, that gorge is in the mountains; so that even in his
lowest swoop the mountain eagle is still higher than
other birds upon the plan, even though they soar.

—*Moby-Dick*

I

The consideration of setting in imaginative writing involves
an inescapable paradox. On the one hand the writer is at
pains to create an environment in time and space which will
provide the fictional action with a necessary dimensionality
and which will convince the reader that he is confronting a
world that is, in some sense, real and meaningful. Yet at the
same time, even if there is an overt identification of the setting with an actual place such as London or Hannibal or Tabasco, the writer will probably not wish to depend so heavily
or exclusively on a literal verisimilitude that the reader expects to find—at the "correct" address—a municipal garden
with all the streaks of the tulips therein numbered accurately.

237

Instead the writer generally seeks a means by which he may exercise his prerogative to heighten reality where necessary in order to accommodate his imaginative vision while also satisfying in some manner the reader's instinctive desire for an intelligible orientation to the fictive world. Thus we find William Faulkner creating his own mythical kingdom complete with map and dates and social groupings; or D. H. Lawrence pitting the prosaic activities of the Mexico City drawing-room society against the ceremonials of the visionary company of Quetzalcoatl; or Graham Greene reconstructing the terrain and the boundaries of his "godless state" in southern Mexico, and synecdochizing the quality of life there by frequent references to various kinds of scavengers.

The paradoxical elements of place in fiction may be seen in perhaps their most extreme form in Malcolm Lowry's *Under the Volcano* (1947). In the justly celebrated letter to his English publisher Jonathan Cape, Lowry described his choice of setting for the novel as follows.

> The scene is Mexico, the meeting place, according to some, of mankind itself, pyre of Bierce and springboard of Hart Crane, the age-old arena of racial and political conflicts of every nature, and where a colorful native people of genius have a religion that we can roughly describe as one of death, so that it is a good place, at least as good as Lancashire, or Yorkshire, to set our drama of a man's struggle between the powers of darkness and light. Its geographical remoteness from us, as well as the closeness of its problems to our own, will assist the tragedy each in its own way. We can see it as the world itself, or the Garden of Eden, or both at once. Or we can see it as a kind of timeless symbol of the world on which we can place the Garden of Eden, the Tower of Babel and indeed anything else we please. It is paradisal: it is unquestionably infernal. It is, in fact, Mexico. . . .[1]

Lowry's Mexico, then, is intended to be both the Mexico of history, where one can still find cantinas and cockroaches

and the religion of death, and a land that lends itself with
relative ease to the symbol-making eye of the imaginative
observer. In choosing to view Mexico as both paradisal and
infernal, Lowry lays claim to the same mythopoetical construct as Lawrence and Greene had before him. And his read-
iness to emphasize "unquestionably" the primacy of the infernal divulges which side of the duality has the greater hold on
his imagination.

Critics have been sharply divided, however, over the
degree of Lowry's success in *Under the Volcano* in rendering
a locale that "is, in fact, Mexico." George Woodcock has
asserted that the novel is "influenced and even dominated by
the peculiar nature of Mexican existence." But the novelist
William Gass goes to the opposite extreme in his observation
that Lowry is "constructing a place, not describing one; he is
making a Mexico for the mind where, strictly speaking, there
are no menacing volcanoes, only menacing phrases...."[2]
Lowry's biographer Douglas Day lends support to Gass's
views when he contends that the Mexican setting of *Under
the Volcano* is only an "accident of geography," that Lowry's
fictional world is dominated by a landscape which is strictly
within. Day believes that "like most visionary artists" Lowry

> was acutely egocentric: his gaze was almost always in-
> ward, so much so that he was very nearly blind to the
> world outside—except in so far as it reflected his own
> thoughts and feelings. From time to time he would try
> mightily to focus on something outside himself—the
> world situation, friends, wives, the sound of a voice, the
> color of a sky—and hope that alcohol would help him
> get through such adventures. But, of course, it only
> helped him back inside himself, where an elusive inner
> Malcolm Lowry alternately laughed at and sorrowed
> with his brilliant, incompetent outer self. Such a man
> could write only about himself, which is precisely what
> Lowry did. It would be a cliché to say that he wrote
> "thinly veiled autobiographies"; but it would be the
> truth.[3]

Certainly there is much validity in Day's observations. Lowry was obviously a solipsistic writer given, with increasing frequency in later years, to observing himself in the act of observing himself. However, so far as *Under the Volcano* is concerned, it is a serious misjudgment to dismiss the choice of the Mexican setting as a mere accident of geography. For one thing, the visionary in Lowry found in the landscape and culture of Mexico a willing accomplice for his imaginative designs—something which he did not find in Canada, his other major fictional setting.[4] As the Mexican novelist Carlos Fuentes has pointed out, "the physical nature of Mexico—a cruel, devouring, sunbaked landscape—is filled with portents of magical distraction. Every force of nature seems to have a mythical equivalent in Mexico. No nation is quite so totemic...."[5] Furthermore, the euhemeristic myth of Mexico's past fostered by the Revolution—with its emphasis on the integrity of indigenous cultures, the deracination of those cultures by the conquering Europeans, and the re-conquest of the homeland by modern Revolutionists—inspired Lowry to scrutinize Mexican history in search of events, figures, and patterns which would enrich his own "drama of a man's struggle between the powers of darkness and light."

That Lowry sought out those aspects of the Mexican scene which, as Day says, "reflected his own thoughts and feelings," there can be little doubt. For that matter, the same thing could be said of Lawrence, Huxley and Greene. None of the Mexican novels by these four English writers is really *about* Mexico, in the way that B. Traven's "jungle novels" clearly are. Rather, all four treat the ways in which their protagonists undergo a violent experience of self-revelation in a land which dramatizes and embodies their deepest anxieties and hopes in stark and elemental terms. In Mexico one encounters great extremes of various kinds existing side by side, openly, even blatantly. As Terence Wright has said, "Colourful, grotesque, savage, Mexico is a land outside the normal world, a land in which life is 'tightened up a screw,' a land in which anything can happen."[6] In the case of *Under the Vol-*

*cano* the particular role played by the Mexican setting is both large and varied, and it is well worth close attention.

Lowry's novel takes place for the most part in a town called Quauhnahuac (according to Lowry a Nahuatl word meaning "where eagle stops," from which the Spanish name Cuernavaca derives), located in the mountains about fifty miles south of Mexico City.[7] In the extended description which opens the *Volcano* Lowry tells us that Quauhnahuac is a resort town of faded grandeur, with eighteen churches, fifty-seven cantinas, 400 swimming pools and many splendid hotels. Despite such accoutrements which have attracted a considerable population of foreigners, the town maintains beneath its surface something of the dark and threatening force of indigenous Mexico, a force which, as the following passage suggests, is inimical to modern civilization: "The walls of the town, which is built on a hill, are high, the streets and lanes tortuous and broken, the roads winding. A fine American-style highway leads in from the north but is lost in its narrow streets and comes out a goat track."[8] In general, one might say that Lowry's Mexico has a similar blighting effect upon the four principal characters who incessantly wander its broken and winding paths.

Indeed, before the end of the novel two of these four people meet violent deaths, so it is not without significance that the action occurs on that peculiar Mexican holiday known as the Day of the Dead. More accurately, the story encompasses one full year beginning and ending on the Day of the Dead. Chapter I is set on November 2, 1939, exactly twelve months *after* the events recounted in the other eleven chapters have occurred. The Day of the Dead is the Mexican version of All Soul's Day. During this fiesta in Mexico one is likely to encounter such sights as Indian women in shawls peddling *flores para los muertos,* ragged children playing gaily with paper skeletons suspended on a string and gorging themselves on little pieces of bread or candy shaped into human skulls, ironic verses called *calaveras* (literally, skulls) printed in the newspapers "eulogizing" living persons as though they

were dead, processions of mourners making their way to
local cemeteries to honor their departed friends and relatives
—and, if one is fortunate enough to be included in a native
family's festivities, one may find that the favorite meal of
deceased loved ones has been prepared and an extra place set
at the table. As this description suggests, for Mexicans the
fiesta of *los muertos* is an occasion for both sadness and
gaiety. Perhaps it is this combination, along with the maca-
bre trappings it has inspired, which frequently bewilders and
intimidates so many foreign visitors who behold the spectacle.

The fiesta has its origins in the more harrowing death-
rituals of the pre-Cortesian inhabitants of Mexico. While it is
doubtful that many modern Mexicans bother to deliberate
upon the more serious implications of their festival, the un-
abashed manner and the great popularity of the celebration
do suggest that something of the ancient attitude toward
death—that is, that death is a natural and positive part of the
life process and is therefore to be neither ignored nor dreaded
as the end of being—remains in the collective Mexican
psyche. In his chapter on the Day of the Dead in *The Labyrinth of Solitude,* the poet Octavio Paz offers a provocative
interpretation of the Mexican attitude toward death in relation to that quality of the national personality which Paz
feels constricts daily life: solitude, masked by stoicism and
*machismo.* In the century of "health, hygiene and contracep-
tives, miracle drugs and synthetic foods," the Mexican still
maintains an intimate relation to death. He "jokes about it,
caresses it, sleeps with it, celebrates it; it is one of his favorite
toys and his most steadfast love. True, there is perhaps as
much fear in his attitude as in that of others, but at least
death is not hidden away: he looks at it face to face, with
impatience, disdain or irony. . . ." Collectively, the Mexicans
"are seduced by death. The fascination it exerts over us is the
result, perhaps, of our hermit-like solitude and the fury with
which we break out of it. The pressure of our vitality, which
can only express itself in forms that betray it, explains the
deadly nature, aggressive or suicidal, of our explosions. . . ."⁹

In his only explicit commentary on these matters, Lowry's interpretation, if somewhat more affirmative, has much in common with that of Octavio Paz. Musing on the Zapotecan ruins at Monte Albán, Lowry writes:

> The sense of this past, of sorrow, of death: these are factors intrinsic in Mexico. Yet the [modern] Mexicans are the gayest of people, who turn every possible occasion, including the Day of the Dead, into a fiesta. The Mexicans laugh at death; that does not mean they don't take it seriously. It is perhaps only by the possession of a tragic sense of life such as theirs that joy and mirth find their place: it is an attitude that testifies to the dignity of man. Death . . . is tragic and comic at once.[10]

This ambivalent attitude informs Lowry's treatment of the theme of death in *Under the Volcano*, though the tragic element is clearly dominant. The novel carries an enormous load of death and dying—and even, as we shall see, love of death. The first words in the novel spoken by the protagonist, Geoffrey Firmin, are these: " 'A corpse will be transported by express!' " (p. 43). In fact, these five iambs become a major refrain in the book. Not quite so poetic, almost the last thing Geoffrey says at the end is " 'Christ . . . this is a dingy way to die' " (p. 373). In between these two lines there are (to mention but a few examples) a child's funeral, a hallucination of a man lying dead in a garden, references to the death and damnation of Marlowe's Doctor Faustus and to the House of Usher, a cantina called La Sepultura, scorpions who sting themselves to death, vultures "who wait only for the ratification of death," a dead dog lying at the bottom of a *barranca*, a wounded Indian found dying by the roadside, frequent allusions to the doomed Loyalist cause in Spain ("they are losing the battle of Ebro") and visions of the worse holocaust to come. The second of November is indeed a day of the dead in Quauhnahuac—a day which fairly crepitates with dying itself in 1938 and again with the painful memory of the dead a year later. "It should not be forgotten," Lowry wrote to Jonathan Cape, "that on that day in Mexico the dead are supposed to commune with the living" (*Letters,* pp. 69-70). As George Woodcock has aptly observed, the "exaggerated Websterian violence in real life—which actually existed in Mexico until comparatively recently—provides the setting and the symbolism through which Lowry's characters and their disaster are raised out of the personal frame of their author's life and into an autonomous world where their adventures, sordid and pathetic in themselves, are realized on the level of genuine tragedy."[11]

There is more to Lowry's Mexico, however, than death and tragedy alone. True, these are the primary strains, but the pattern as a whole is considerably more complicated. Chapter I, in which Lowry attempts above all to establish the emblematic terrain of his apocalyptic drama, contains some magnificent and suggestive descriptions of the mountainous landscape around Quauhnahuac—descriptions which, due as much to the suppleness of the style as to the kinesis perceived in the landscape, cannot rightly be called set-pieces.

> How continually, how startlingly, the landscape changed! Now the fields were full of stones: there was a row of dead trees. An abandoned plough, silhouetted against the sky, raised its arms to heaven in mute supplication; another planet, [Jacques Laruelle] reflected again, a strange planet where, if you looked a little further, beyond the Tres Marías, you would find every sort of landscape at once, the Cotswolds, Windermere, New Hampshire, the meadows of the Eure-et-Loire, even the grey dunes of Cheshire, even the Sahara, a planet upon which, in the twinkling of an eye, you could change climates, and, if you cared to think so, in the crossing of a highway, three civilizations; but beautiful, there was no denying its beauty, fatal or cleansing as it happened to be, the beauty of the Earthly Paradise itself. (pp. 9-10)

With its snow-capped twin volcanoes, its lush gardens, and its thick and sprawling forests, the Mexican landscape beguiles with beauty. It seems indeed to be paradisal. But for this very reason, in *Under the Volcano,* the landscape ultimately emerges as a conspirator in Geoffrey Firmin's damnation. For the twisting path which carries one amidst all the apparently Edenic splendor invariably brings one to the brink of that ominous feature of the Mexican terrain which has been there all along at one's feet, waiting:

> [Laruelle] passed the model farm on his right, the buildings, the fields, the hills shadowy now in the swiftly gathering gloom. The Ferris wheel came into view again . . . then the trees rose up over it. The road, which was terrible and full of potholes, went steeply downhill here; he was approaching the little bridge over the barranca, the deep ravine. Halfway across the bridge he stopped . . . and leaned over the parapet, looking down. It was too dark to see the bottom, but: here was finality indeed, and cleavage! Quauhnahuac was like the times in this respect, wherever you turned the abyss was waiting for you round the corner. Dormitory for vultures and city Moloch! (p. 15)

The pattern suggested by the two passages above—the redemptive ideal dissolving into infernal reality, the lost paradise, the reversal of beatific longing or expectation—is central to the novel. Douglas Day has offered a very useful commentary on this pattern in terms of what he calls the *chthonic* or earthbound level of meaning, "composed of natural elements either on or beneath the earth." Day points out that though Lowry's characters frequently dream of climbing the volcanic "magic mountains," they are sooner or later confronted with what lies *under* the volcano: the reeking, cloacal abyss. There is much talk of seeking water, the sea, fresh streams, a clear lake, but "the only water of significance in the novel is conspicuous by its absence: the cleansing, revivifying fountain [of life]. . . . Instead of water, we have alcohol. . . ."[12] The many gardens which exist in the novel are mostly untended, ruined, overgrown. The forest which surrounds Quauhnahuac and the village of Parián where the last two chapters take place is equated with Dante's dark wood, and the winding path running through it leads only to colossal danger. Thus the various clusters of *chthonic* images gradually mesh into a web of doom which entraps the characters, not despite but precisely because they aspire to impossible transcendent ideals. The imagery, says Day, is

> archetypally demonic in nature: that is, it employs the traditional affirmative apocalyptic images of the Mount of Perfection, the fertile valley, the cleansing stream or fountain, and the blossoming garden, but employs them in an inverted, ironic form. What had indicated fruition, now indicates sterility; what had represented cleansing, now represents corruption, and what had symbolized the soul's striving upward toward salvation, now symbolizes the descent into damnation. It is of a world turned upside down that Lowry writes.[13]

Carlos Fuentes' remarks (quoted earlier) about the equivalence of landscape and myth in Mexico come to mind. It is difficult to think of another setting that could have suited Lowry's purposes in *Under the Volcano* as perfectly as did Mexico.

II

Chapter I finds Jacques Laruelle, a middle-aged Frenchman and semi-retired film director, walking around the town of Quauhnahuac for the last time. He intends to return to France the following day after a four-year exile in Mexico. During his walk Laruelle's thoughts turn again and again to his late friend the Consul, Geoffrey Firmin, who was killed on the Day of the Dead just a year ago. Yvonne Firmin, the Consul's estranged wife and once the lover of Laruelle himself, had died that same day, trampled to death in the forest during a rainstorm by a runaway horse. The Consul's half-brother Hugh (who had also had a brief love affair with Geoffrey's wife, though Laruelle does not know this) had been in Quauhnahuac a year ago also, but after the deaths of his half-brother and Yvonne he had left Mexico on a futile mission to aid the Loyalist cause in Spain. As M. Laruelle proceeds from the faded Hotel Casino de la Selva to the railroad station, to the Borda Gardens of Maximilian and Carlotta, to the bridge over the fetid *barranca,* and out of the rain into the cantina adjoining a dingy cinema where the film *Las Manos de Orlac* with Peter Lorre is being shown tonight just as it was a year earlier—during all of these farewell visits to the landmarks of Quauhnahuac, Laruelle broods on the past. He thinks of his boyhood friendship with Geoffrey as well as of the tragic events of a year ago. And then, when Laruelle discovers an old letter written (but never mailed) by the Consul to his wife shortly after she had left him, we are introduced to still another phase in the protagonist's past. In the first chapter, then, Lowry not only establishes the terrain but also conveys, without resorting to straight exposition, a considerable amount of information about the tangled relations of the four principals. The overall emphasis rests, as Lowry wrote to Cape, on man's "ceaseless struggling toward the light under the weight of the past" (*Letters,* p. 66). The chapter closes with the "luminous wheel" (the Ferris wheel, Fortuna, time) revolving backwards until, as Chapter II begins, we are back to the Day of the Dead, 1938, and "'A corpse will be transported by express!'"

Before leaving Chapter I, however, we should note that the "weight of the past" theme involves more than the personal backgrounds of the four main characters. Also presented for the first time is the weight of the larger historical past, what Lowry calls "the slow melancholy tragic rhythm of Mexico itself" (*Letters,* p. 58). One of the places at which M. Laruelle stops during his farewell stroll through Quauhnahuac is the once-magnificent residence of the Emperor Maximilian and his wife Carlotta. Two aspects of the scene are worthy of notice. First, there is Lowry's description of the Borda Gardens themselves, a description which introduces the central image of the ruined garden.

> The broken pink pillars, in the half-light, might have been waiting to fall down on [Laruelle]: the pool, covered with green scum, its steps torn away and hanging by one rotting clamp, to close over his head. The shattered, evil-smelling chapel, overgrown with weeds, the crumbling walls, splashed with urine, on which scorpions lurked—wrecked entablature, sad archivolt, slippery stones covered with excreta—this place, where love had once brooded, seemed part of a nightmare. And Laruelle was tired of nightmares. France, even in Austrian guise, should not transfer itself to Mexico, he thought. (p. 14)

Among the many courtly talents which the Hapsburg prince Maximilian had brought with him to Mexico in 1864 was a taste for graceful architectural design (he had renovated the old viceregal palace at Chapultepec Park as well as the residence in Cuernavaca) and a passion for studying Mexico's botanical specimens. Carlotta also was dedicated to horticultural improvements in the capital. But these were hardly qualities to prepare them to bring order to a land seething with political turmoil and violent clashes between liberal and conservative factions. Resented by a majority of Mexicans as a foreign imperialist intruder whose only power depended upon the presence of the army which Napoleon III had landed in Mexico, Maximilian was captured and executed in 1867 by the forces of the Indian liberal president, Benito Juárez. Ironically, Maximilian himself had been something of a liberal, sincerely dedicated to the progressive reform as well as the stabilization of Mexico. In any event, all his well-intended European idealism—like his palace and his gardens—were fouled upon and shattered during the more substantial "nightmare" of Mexican existence.

Of equal importance to Lowry's use of this historical allu-

***************************************

# DO ALL ROADS LEAD TO GOD?

***************************************

NO, THEY DO NOT! Eastern religions and many
of the liberal religions of the West teach
that it doesn't matter which religion that
you believe in or which god or God you worship because all of us will wind up in the
same place anyway after we die.  In other
words, all men will eventually be saved. This
belief is known as UNIVERSALISM and is false!

JESUS CHRIST SAYS THAT THEY DON'T: Jesus said
emphatically: "I am the way, the truth, and
the life: no man cometh unto the Father, but
by me" (John 14:6); and: "Whosoever shall
confess me before men, him shall the Son of
man confess before the angels of God: but he
that denieth me before men shall be denied
before the angels of God" (Luke 12:8-9).

CHRIST'S APOSTLES SAY THEY DON'T: "Whosoever
denieth the Son, the same hath not the Father:
(but) he that acknowledgeth the Son hath the
Father also" (I John 2:23); "Neither is there
salvation in any other (than Jesus Christ):
for there is none other name under heaven
given among men, whereby we must be saved"
(Acts 4:12).

THE DEVIL SAYS THEY DO: The Devil and his demons know that if a man thinks that he will
be saved regardless of what he believes about
God, that man will see no need to heed Jesus
Christ's words to repent of his sins and accept Jesus Christ as his only personal Savior.  They know that without Jesus Christ, no
person can go to heaven and will spend an
eternity of suffering with them in hell.

***************************************

sion is the love of Maximilian and Carlotta, a love similarly
doomed to destruction by their unfortunate experience in
Mexico. Their love had seemed somehow in the beginning to
be embodied by the awesomely beautiful land which they
were sent to rule together. Lowry writes, "...how they must
have loved this land, these two lonely empurpled exiles,
human beings finally, lovers out of their element—their
Eden, without either knowing quite why, beginning to turn
under their noses into a prison and smell like a brewery, their
only majesty at last that of tragedy" (p. 14). Carlotta was to
go mad during a futile mission to France, where she tried desperately to convince Napoleon III not to abandon Maximilian
by pulling the French troops out of Mexico. She broke down
completely during a subsequent appeal for help from the
Pope, and was never to see her husband again.

But for a while, when they were together in Mexico, the
dream must have seemed to the royal couple a genuine blos-
soming of hope, perhaps even better (so great was their ignorance of the situation in Mexico upon their arrival) than they
had hoped for. That fragile dream did not of course survive
on the volcanic earth of Mexico even as long as the abbreviated three-year reign. But for Jacques Laruelle, standing by
their decayed palace three-quarters of a century later on the
Day of the Dead, their ghosts seem still to inhabit the Earthly
Paradise. He hears one of the ghosts speaking: "'It is our destiny to come here, Carlotta. Look at this rolling glorious
country, its hills, its valleys, its volcanoes beautiful beyond
belief. And to think that it is ours!'" Soon, however, the
ghosts' voices become shrill; they begin to quarrel bitterly.
"'No, you loved yourself, you loved your misery more than
I. You did this [i.e., brought us to Mexico] deliberately....'
'I?' 'You always had people to look after you, to love you....
You listened to everyone save me, who really loved you.'
'No, you're the only person I've ever loved.' 'Ever? You loved
only yourself....' And suddenly they were weeping together, passionately, as they stood" (pp. 14-15). The "ghosts"
are of course no longer Maximilian and Carlotta—or rather

no longer *only* the imperial couple—but Geoffrey and
Yvonne as well. Both couples suffered disillusionment and
separation resulting from their stays in Mexico, the breach
between them correlative to that between the mythical lovers
Popocatepetl and Ixtaccihuatl, the immutable twin volcanoes. The scene is typical of the way Lowry uses historical
allusion to embellish the story proper by relating it to larger,
recurrent patterns of human experience. The patterns are unified by their presence within the Mexican context.

Another historical analogue is introduced briefly in the
first chapter, one which grows in significance as the novel
progresses: that of the conquistador and his victim. As M.
Laruelle sits in the cantina Cervecería XX, he notices an illustrated calendar on the wall depicting the first meeting of Cortés and the Aztec emperor, Moctezuma: *"El último Empera-
dor Azteca,* it said below, *Moctezuma y Hernán Cortés rep-
resentativo de la raza hispana, quedan frente a frente: dos
razas y dos civilizaciones que habían llegado a un alto grado
de perfeccion se mezclan para integrar el núcleo de nuestra
nacionalidad actual"* (p. 27).* A relatively innocuous bit of
nationalistic bravado in itself, this picture, along with its
rather banal caption, becomes in the larger context of what
may be called the Conquest motif running throughout the
*Volcano* an ironic portent of considerable magnitude. Inferential evidence from the novel suggests that Lowry shared the
view that the Mexican Indian was never successfully assimi-
lated into Hispanic culture but was exploited, first by the
Spanish conquistadors, then for three centuries by the white
colonialists, finally—and most importantly in relation to
subsequent events in Lowry's narrative—by modern Mexico's right-wing elements. (Lowry does not seem to share the
distrust of leftist Revolutionists and their programs to mod-
ernize and "uplift" the impoverished Indian so strongly exhibited by Lawrence, Greene, and Evelyn Waugh. Though less

---

*"The last Aztec emperor . . . Moctezuma [,] and Hernán Cortés [,] repre-
sentative of the Hispanic race, stand face to face: two races and two civilizations which had arrived at a high degree of perfection mingled to form
the nucleus of our present nationality" (my translation).

doctrinaire, his position seems closer to that of Ralph Bates—
see Appendix.) We shall return to these matters later, but for
the moment it is sufficient to recognize that Lowry is once
again positing an historical analogue to the situation in which
the Consul will find himself (or *did* find himself in 1938).
However, the roles of Cortés and Moctezuma are in some respects the inverse of those played by Maximilian and Benito
Juárez: here the European is the ruthless aggressor and the
indigene the vanquished party. The two historical allusions
come together briefly at the end of Chapter I when Laruelle
sets fire to Geoffrey's agonized letter begging Yvonne to come
back to him, itself an echo of Maximilian and Carlotta's separation and anguish. Laruelle sees in the sudden illumination a
group of figures gathered around the bar. In an image which
anticipates similar ones to follow, Lowry describes these
huddled figures, including little children and peasant farmers
in loose white clothes and "several women in mourning from
the cemeteries and dark-faced men in dark suits," as they
appear to the European Laruelle: "[They seemed] frozen, a
mural: they had all stopped talking and were gazing round at
him curiously . . ." (p. 42). The immobility and the apparently
innocent curiosity of the dark-skinned people here will later
modulate into positive malevolence and the threat of revenge
against the white "exploiter." Lowry was clearly correct when
he told Cape that the opening chapter is "the foundation of
the book" (*Letters*, p. 58). The landscape, the time-frame
doubly emphasizing the fiesta of *los muertos*, the significant
recurrence of both the unseasonable rain and the showing of
the horror film *Orlac*, the historical analogues, and the luminous wheel revolving backwards—cumulatively such elements impress upon the reader the all-embracing power of
cyclicity which so dominates the novel.[14]


## III


The chief events of the next few chapters set in Quauhnahuac
may be briefly summarized. At seven o'clock on the morning

of November 2, 1938, thirty-year-old Yvonne Firmin arrives at the door of the Bella Vista bar. She has returned after an absence of almost a year without informing her husband Geoffrey, who sits drunk at the bar within after a night of debauchery. Their reunion is restrained, the tension beneath the surface glossed over by small talk and, on Geoffrey's part, repartee. As they walk out of the bar together and up the street to the home they once shared, Yvonne notices that several ragged men wearing dark glasses seem to be following them. Passing by the strange house in which she had once conducted her liaison with Geoffrey's oldest and closest friend Jacques Laruelle, Yvonne pointedly avoids looking at the line scrawled on one of its towers: *"no se puede vivir sin amar,"* one cannot live without loving.

Once back "home" the Consul (actually an ex-consul as he has recently resigned his post after the oil crisis in March) has a few more drinks and their conversation becomes heated. He ducks outside again in search of another cantina and falls down in the street, blacking out briefly. After a bracing nip offered by a friendly English tourist Geoffrey returns to the house where he rejoins Yvonne in her bedroom. Growing more tender toward each other as they reminisce about the first happy days of their marriage, they begin to make love. All the while Geoffrey imagines himself in a cantina as the sun rises. He proves to be impotent, rushes out to the patio where he pulls fiercely at another bottle (to which he declares his love), hallucinates of a man lying dead in the yard by his pool, collapses into a patio chair and passes out.

A while later Hugh Firmin, the Consul's thirty-year-old half-brother, appears at the house, having just returned from Mexico City where he had gone to cover a story for the London *Daily Globe*. In the pocket of Geoffrey's coat, which Hugh had borrowed, is a carbon of this story concerning an antisemitic campaign underway in Mexico, a campaign actively supported by a German legation.[15] Hugh is stunned to see Yvonne back in Geoffrey's home. As they greet one another it soon becomes apparent that Hugh is still guiltily in

love with Yvonne, though he does not speak to her directly
of his feelings. They go for a walk through the town (Geoffrey being still asleep) and decide to go on a horseback ride
together. The atmosphere of this episode of the ride (in Chapter IV)
is largely idyllic. Behind the two riders trot a pair of foals and
a woolly white dog. The mountain landscape is pristine, the
air delightfully crisp in the bright sunshine of late morning.
Still, here and there are signs of Mexico's other, darker side.
They pass by the prison watchtower and Hugh imagines
them being spied upon: "The world was always within the
binoculars of the police" (p. 106). As they ride on, up shaded
lanes and through clumps of trees and hedges, Hugh begins
to muse about his great cause, the war in Spain; and about a
man he had met in Spain, a Mexican named Juan Cerillo.
Cerillo, who now works in Oaxaca as a rider for the *Ejidal*
credit bank, had become a kind of heroic ideal to Hugh, a
man of action, a man genuinely dedicated to assisting his fellows in need. From Juan Cerillo, Hugh had learned something of the tragic history of Mexico. The nineteenth-century
reformer Benito Juárez, muses Hugh,

> had lived and died. Yet was [Mexico] a country with free
> speech, and the guarantee of life, liberty, and the pursuit
> of happiness? A country . . . [where] the land was owned
> by its people free to express their native genius? A coun-
> try of model farms: of hope?—It was a country of slav-
> ery [Cerillo had told him], where human beings were
> sold like cattle, and its native peoples, the Yaquis, the
> Papagos, the Tomasachics, exterminated through depor-
> tation, or reduced to worse than peonage, their lands in
> thrall or the hands of foreigners. . . . All this spelt Por-
> firio Díaz: rurales everywhere, jefes políticos, and mur-
> der, the extirpation of liberal political institutions, the
> army an engine of massacre, an instrument of exile. Juan
> knew this, having suffered it; and more. For later in the
> revolution, his mother was murdered. And later still
> Juan himself killed his father, who had fought with

Huerta, but turned traitor. . . . For man, Juan seemed to
be telling him, even as Mexico, must ceaselessly struggle
upward. What was life but a warfare and a stranger's
sojourn? Revolution rages too in the tierra caliente of
each human soul. No peace but that must pay full toll to
hell. . . . (p. 108)

Hugh's interpretation of these matters—attributed here
equally to Juan Cerillo—is of course not to be mistaken for
that of Malcolm Lowry. We have already seen that in *Under
the Volcano* Lowry has a way of turning the tables on his
characters' longings for the ideal, their dreams of ascending
magic mountains that do not exist save in the mind. But this
passage does suggest, at the very least, that Lowry was both
aware of the protracted anguish of the dispossessed *campe-
sinos* of Mexico and sympathetic with their lot. Moreover,
these musings may be seen as a further extension of the Conquest motif. The similarity between the two periods of upheaval is not, strictly speaking, precise—the role of the
aggressor, for example, has shifted somewhat to include the
dictator Díaz who had some Indian blood himself and, in the
beginning, was at least nominally a liberal. But the parallel
nevertheless serves metaphorically to suggest a recurrence of
exploitation, betrayal, and violent revenge. The correspondence between this cyclical pattern of Mexican history, with
its pervasive political and racial conflict, and human experience in general is made explicit in this instance.

Due in part, perhaps, to these unsettling thoughts, Hugh
suggests to Yvonne, while they ride slowly side by side, that
she might be wise to take Geoffrey and leave Mexico altogether. As they discuss this idea with growing excitement and
hope, Lowry introduces the motif of escape to a "northern
paradise," which appears from here on whenever Yvonne has
a chance to reflect on her future with Geoffrey. (One is reminded of the whiskey priest's dream of escape to the unsul-
lied paradise across the border in *The Power and the Glory.*
Yvonne's Canadian Eden proves to be no less illustory than

that of the "holy city," Las Casas.) Before such soothing thoughts can be savored fully, however, the two riders approach "the Malebolge...the serpentine barranca.... [And] then, all at once, they were in the ruin"—the residence and grounds of the Borda Gardens (p. 123). Immediately Yvonne becomes depressed, distant; for it was here, a few years earlier, that she and Geoffrey had run across Jacques Laruelle for the first time in Mexico, a meeting which precipitated the conflicts that finally ruptured her marriage. Here she stands again, in this place "where love once brooded," in the company of yet another man with whom she had betrayed Geoffrey, and not just any man, but his half-brother. Thus the ruins necessarily affect Yvonne in a personal way, recalling her own woeful past; while to Hugh (who is unaware of Yvonne's affair with Laruelle) the place offers merely an opportunity to discuss the moral dilemmas of liberalism. "'Maximilian and Carlotta, eh?'" he says. "'Should Juarez have had the man shot or not?'" To which Yvonne answers, significantly, "'It's an awfully tragic story'" (pp. 123-124). This exchange foreshadows—in terms of both the Conquest motif and the human level of the story proper—the ending of the novel.

While Hugh and Yvonne are off riding, Geoffrey wakes from a dream in which he had been hiking with someone into a northern region where looming ahead was the great Himavat, the totemic mountain of Hindu mythology. The dream is related to Geoffrey's father, who had disappeared when Geoffrey was a child in Kashmir—had simply wandered off one day into the Himalayas, perhaps in search of Himavat. Once he is more or less awake, Geoffrey staggers out into the garden where he has hidden a bottle of tequila. (Just as Geoffrey's dream seems to be an ironic echo of the Emmaus passage in Part V of *The Waste Land*, so his lurching progress through the ruined garden in search of the hidden bottle may be read as a parody of the Grail quest—though for Geoffrey alcohol is not far short of the Grail as a sacramental symbol.) Passing by a snake and one of the pariah dogs which seem to follow him everywhere, he approaches the adjoining public garden and encounters for the first time the sign which warns citizens, in effect, to keep off the grass. *"Le gusta este jardin? Que es suyo? Evite que sus hijos lo destruyan!"* he reads in impossible Spanish and then arrives at an even more impossible translation: "You like this garden? Why is it yours? We evict those who destroy!" (p. 128). These words, the Consul thinks to himself, amount to a dreadful warning, "perhaps a final judgment on one" (p. 128). Walking on through the public garden, he begins to feel drawn to the Farolito cantina in the village of Parián, and while he ponders this most perilous and (for him) attractive of places he nearly falls into the insidious *barranca* which winds through the garden. "Ah the frightful cleft, the eternal horror of opposites! . . . One was, come to that, always stumbling upon the damned thing, this immense intricate donga cutting right through the town, right, indeed, through the country . . ." (p. 130).[16]

The Consul is tempted to climb down into the ravine "to visit the cloacal Prometheus who doubtless inhabited it" (p. 131), but instead he engages Mr. Quincey, his dour American neighbor out tending *his* garden, in an amusing conversation about the Garden of Eden and the expulsion. He speculates that Adam may not have been "evicted" from the garden at all, that his punishment (and again the parallel with Greene's whiskey priest in the "Godless state" is manifest) may have consisted in his having to remain there, "alone, of course— suffering, unseen, cut off from God" (p. 133). The notion of the isolated man, at once a fugitive and a quester, condemned to inhabit a paradise bereft of its creator, turns the Consul's mind to one of his favorite exemplars. Speaking half to Quincey and half to Quincey's grey cat, he offers a brief, semi-coherent account of the career of an eccentric English pioneer, William Blackstone. In the early seventeenth century Blackstone

"arrived in what is now, I believe—no matter—some-where in Massachusetts. And lived there quietly among

the Indians. After a while the Puritans settled on the
other side of the river. They invited him over; they said
it was healthier on that side, you see. Ah, these people
[the Puritans], these fellows with ideas," he told the cat,
"old William didn't like them—no he didn't—so he went
back to live among the Indians, so he did. But the Puritans found him out, Quincey, trust them. Then he disappeared altogether—God knows where . . . [ellipsis in
original] *Now*, little cat," the Consul tapped his chest
indicatively . . . "the Indians are in here." (p. 135)

Mr. Quincey sees this apparently irrelevant digression as
merely another fantasy inspired by the D.T.'s—which, in
part, it is. But the story of William Blackstone has great personal significance for the Consul. Earlier he had told Yvonne
that he hoped someday to be buried next to Blackstone; then,
trying to explain why he had remained in Mexico after re-
signing his post as British consul, he told her " 'I'm thinking
of becoming a Mexican subject, of going to live among the
Indians, like William Blackstone" (p. 82). The Blackstone
story, like that of Geoffrey's father, who also "disappeared
altogether" from civilization, bears a certain relation to the
experiences "among the Indians" of both Cortés and Maximilian. Here, however, the Consul identifies with Blackstone
rather than with Cortés or Maximilian, for he sees himself as
a kind of visionary on a quest for secret knowledge associated with the primitive peoples, and not as a champion of
empire. Nevertheless it is possible for a benevolent foreigner
such as Blackstone or the Consul himself to be misinterpreted
by the natives as an exploiter—as Maximilian was by the
liberal Juarists, for example. These constantly changing faces
of conquistador and vanquished, exploiter and victim, are
bound up inextricably in the perennial configuration of conquest.[17] The resultant confusion of roles will prove to be
important later on.

After Hugh and Yvonne return to the house the threesome
decide to take an excursion that afternoon to the village of
Tomalín to attend an event known as a bullthrowing. On

their way to the bus terminal they are intercepted by Laruelle, who like Hugh is surprised and delighted to see Yvonne
back in Quauhnahuac, and who insists that they stop by his
house for a visit until their departure time. They enter the
bizarre house, the Consul determinedly not looking up at the
inscription on the tower (*no se puede vivir sin amar*), and
climb up to the roof, which commands a fine view of the
countryside. Taking Geoffrey aside, Yvonne begs him to give
her another chance, to call off this absurd outing and to be
alone with her for a while. But their very presence in the
house where Yvonne had betrayed him with Laruelle pricks
the Consul's jealousy and makes submission to her plea
impossible. Instead he wants only to be let alone, to be able
to go to the Farolito in Parián, the "lighthouse that invites the
storm, and lights it." Once there, he knows, "life reached bottom. But [there] also great wheeling thoughts hovered in the
brain" (p. 200). Forced to choose between loving Yvonne and
loving the spectacle of his own deterioration, he elects the
latter.

Back outside, they wander through the fairgrounds to
observe the fiesta in progress. As they approach the palace of
Cortés, Geoffrey notes a familiar man wearing dark glasses
who appears to be following him. The palace contains a
group of frescoes painted by the radical artist Diego Rivera,
depicting the horrors of the Conquest and two local heroes of
counter-conquest, Morelos and Zapata. (In fact, the murals
are replete with Mexican iconography which Lowry adopts
for his own purposes throughout the novel: bearded conquistadors on horseback brandishing swords, the white-linen-
clad Zapata with a machete and his legendary white horse,
the stealthy crossing of a *barranca*, Malinche and Cortés, a
white *hacendado* reclining in a hammock and being served a
beverage by an Indian servant, a coffer being filled with gold
coins, the defoliation of the native landscape and the sale of
fruits and melons in a marketplace, dead and dying Indians
lying prostrate amidst the headlong chaos and confusion of
conquest.) Standing at a distance from the frescoes, M. Laru-

elle suggests, one gets an impression which escapes the tourists who observe them at too close a range. " 'The slow darkening of the murals as you look from right to left,' " he says to the Consul. " 'It seems somehow to symbolise the gradual imposition of the Spaniards' conquering will upon the Indians.' " But the Consul, whose remarks here demonstrate again both the cyclicity and the shifting relationships involved in the Conquest motif, disagrees with the Frenchman. " 'If you stood at a greater distance still it might seem to symbolise for you the gradual imposition of the Americans' conquering friendship from left to right upon the Mexicans . . .' " (p. 212). The more Geoffrey stares at the murals, however, the less is he able to assume this detached, ironic perspective. Indeed, as he looks at the frescoes, the dark-skinned figures seem to come alive, to direct their menacing glare at none other than himself.

> The part of the murals he was gazing at portrayed, he knew, the Tlahuicans who had died for this valley in which he lived. The artist had represented them in their battle dress, wearing the masks and skins of wolves and tigers. As he looked it was as though these figures were gathering silently together. Now they had become one figure, one immense, malevolent creature staring back at him. Suddenly this creature appeared to start forward, then make a violent motion. It might have been, indeed unmistakenly it was, telling him to go away. (p. 212)

This warning the Consul is unwilling—and essentially unable —to heed until it is too late.

Not all Indians threaten the Consul however. As he and Laruelle walk on, passing by the *Banco de Crédito y Ejidal,* they encounter a man on horseback, "a fine-featured Indian of the poorer class, dressed in soiled white loose clothes. The man was singing gaily to himself. But he nodded to them courteously. . . . He seemed about to speak, reining in his little horse—on either side of which chinked two saddle-bags, and upon whose rump was branded the number seven . . ."

(pp. 212-213).[18] The Indian does not speak to them, but as he
rides away, singing and waving his hand, the Consul feels "a
pang. Ah, to have a horse, and gallop away, singing, away
to someone you loved perhaps, into the heart of all the sim-
plicity and peace in the world; was not that like the opportunity afforded man by life itself? Of course not. Still, just for a
moment, it had seemed that it was" (p. 213). Such feelings—
were they made known, and in the Consul's case they are not
—are easily misunderstood by a people accustomed to centuries of servitude and despoliation at the hands of European
adventurers. But the reader, permitted many such glimpses
of the Consul's secret longings, may make the connection
between these affirmative impulses and the story of William
Blackstone. Only for the Consul, as he had said to Quincey's
cat in the garden, pointing to his chest, "'the Indians are in
here.'" He now confides to Laruelle that he resents those who
interfere with his life by trying to get him to stop drinking
and to leave Mexico for some northern paradise. Despite all
their good intentions, Hugh and Yvonne and Laruelle are, he
says, interfering in his struggle against death, his great "'battle for the survival of the human consciousness'" (p. 217).

    After a frightening ride on a loop-the-loop contraption
called (after the play by Cocteau) La Máquina Infernal, Geoffrey joins Hugh and Yvonne on the bus headed "downhill" to
Tomalín and the bullthrowing. As the bus pulls out of town
they pass by more posters advertising the showing of *Las
Manos de Orlac*, posters depicting "a murderer's hands, laced
with blood" (p. 231); and by another sign in a municipal garden, this time read and translated correctly: "Le gusta este
jardín, que es suyo? Evite que sus hijos lo destruyan! Do you
like this garden, the notice said, that is yours? See to it that
your children do not destroy it!" (p. 232). Crossing a bridge
over the *barranca* ("its steep banks...thick with refuse...a
dead dog right at the bottom" [p. 233]), they stop briefly at a
tavern to pick up a passenger. The Consul tells Hugh that this
cantina is a gathering spot for fascist elements, and that the
new passenger is himself a Spanish fascist. This man he

describes as a *pelado* or "peeled one," one of those who " 'did not have to be rich to prey on the really poor' " (p. 235). This is one of several instances in the *Volcano* where Lowry taps a subject of unusually great importance within the Mexican context—greater in that context, in fact, than outside it. Generically the *pelado* (literally, "plucked," "bare," "penniless"—there is no suitable equivalent in English) is a widely recognized social type in Mexico. The Mexican social philosopher Samuel Ramos describes the *pelado* as "a form of human rubbish from the great city. He is less than a proletarian in the economic hierarchy, and a primitive man in the intellectual one. Life from every quarter has been hostile to him and his reaction has been black resentment. He is an explosive being with whom relationship is dangerous, for the slightest friction causes him to blow up." Ramos goes on to point out that the *pelado*, suffering from a deep sense of inferiority, masks his anxiety behind an illusion of his own virility, often asserted in violent and crude verbal explosions.[19] (The Consul's tormentors at the end fit this description quite well.) Interestingly, Lowry, like Samuel Ramos, recognizes the origins of the type in the Conquest. "A Spaniard, say, could interpret [the word *pelado*] as Indian, the Indian he despised, used, made drunk. The Indian, however, might mean Spaniard by it. . . . It was perhaps one of those words that had actually been distilled out of conquest, suggesting, as it did, on the one hand thief, on the other exploiter. Interchangeable ever were the terms of abuse with which the aggressor discredits those about to be ravaged!" (*Volcano*, p. 235). As for the *pelado* on the bus, his hands are "huge, capable and rapacious. Hands of the conquistador . . ." (p. 234). And in them he holds half a melon—conceivably, the bounty of Mexico.

Next there occurs (in Chapter VIII) the incident by the roadside, the seminal scene with which Lowry began the first versions of *Under the Volcano* in 1936. Here the Conquest motif is so explicit and so central a part of the main narrative action that it emerges as a theme in its own right. The bus

pulls to a stop when a man is seen lying along the edge of the
road, apparently wounded. Hugh, the Consul, the driver,
and the *pelado* all go out to investigate. The wounded man is
an Indian—the same man whom the Consul had encountered
in Quauhnahuac in Chapter VII and whom Hugh and
Yvonne had seen earlier during their ride. The man is bloodied and dying, his horse with the number seven branded on
its rump cropping grass nearby, the saddlebags missing.
Hugh begins to assist the Indian but is told that to interfere in
any way would be to risk arrest as an accessory after the fact.
As there are no telephones nearby and no ambulances, and as
the regular police are on strike, there is nothing to be done
but wait—and talk, as the Indian dies with each breath,
about the horror of it all. Meanwhile the *pelado*, after
inspecting the man himself, returns to the bus. In a last blind
gesture or appeal for help the Indian raises his hand and calls
to Hugh: "'Compañero.'"

Three "smiling vigilantes" appear and, threatening the
quixotic Hugh in particular, urge them to move on. Back in
the bus on the way to Tomalín, the Consul notices that the
*pelado's* "smeared conquistador's hands, that had clutched
the melon, now clutched a sad bloodstained pile of silver
pesos and centavos," loose change stolen from the body of
the dying Indian (p. 250). The *pelado*, far from being
remorseful for this predatory act, pays his fare with the
bloodied money. In a comment which has a tremendous reso-
nance, Lowry writes that the *pelado's* theft was "open and
above board, for all the world to know about. It was a recognized thing, like Abyssinia" (p. 252). —Abyssinia, not only
the all but defenseless nation ravaged by Mussolini as the
world watched and did virtually nothing, but also the land of
the abyss, the Inferno under the volcano where the intractable condition of existence is "the eternal horror of opposites."

Once the bullthrowing in Tomalín is over with, the threesome repair to the Salón Ofelia, where they intend to eat
supper after Hugh and Yvonne take a swim in a nearby

stream. As Geoffrey watches the other two enjoying themselves, his jealousy, which has been building throughout the day, begins to get the better of him. He resorts to the ultimate drink, mescal—ruinous companion of his deepest despair and wildest visions. Now Geoffrey has consumed up to this point (Chapter X) an incredible amount of alcohol of many kinds, straight whiskey, mixed cocktails, tequila, *habanero*, wine, beer, even a swig of bay rum hair tonic. But somehow he has been able, when necessary, miraculously to pull himself together and even to evince a remarkable lucidity. To drink mescal, however, is another matter. As he had told Laruelle earlier, " 'if I ever start to drink mescal again, I'm afraid, yes, that would be the end' " (p. 216). From the moment he begins to consume, and to be consumed by, mescal, the novel goes into the "high delirious gear" of the Consul's fatal plunge into elaborate conspiratorial fantasies, apocalyptic nightmare, and oblivion. The writing becomes quite complex, nowhere more so than in Chapter X, where historical analogues play a particularly important role.

IV

Set entirely in the cafe called Salón Ofelia—a name suggestive of, among other things, love's betrayal—Chapter X is literally concerned with the Consul's determination to go to the Farolito in Parián. Parián itself is an apocryphal state located in the northeastern corner of the actual state of Morelos. It is clearly very close to Popocatepetl and Ixtaccihuatl, on the other side of which lies the state of Tlaxcala. Significantly, Lowry's Parián was originally settled by "a scattering of . . . traitorous Tlaxcalans," and is at present the headquarters of the pro-fascist irregular police and the *sinarquistas* (p. 285). Thus Parián is a very dangerous spot to visit. But Parián, or more accurately the Farolito in Parián, is also a site of magical attraction to Geoffrey, a site for which—or so at least he tells himself—his soul yearns. The prospect of being there "filled him with an almost healing love and . . . the greatest longing he had ever known. The Farolito! It was a strange place, a place really of the late night and early dawn . . ." (p. 200). In Chapter X the Consul, sipping mescal, begins to equate the Farolito with eternity and his desire to go there with a quest for the transcendent. Though these illusions are never entirely dismissed, before the chapter is over both the Consul and the reader are, through a series of interrelated references to history and myth (the two being scarcely separable here), made to see the real import of flight to Parián.

"What is man," muses the Consul half way into his second mescal, "but a little soul holding up a corpse? The soul! Ah, and did she not too have her savage and traitorous Tlaxcalans, her Cortez and her noches tristes, and, sitting within her innermost citadel in chains . . . her pale Moctezuma?" (pp. 287-288). These lines might almost serve as a gloss on the metaphorical scheme of Chapter X. The Consul's sickness— diagnosed by his Mexican friend Dr. Vigil as " 'not only in body but in that part used to be call: soul' " (p. 144)—is the world's sickness, as manifested by her endless internecine conflicts. Praying to the Virgin of Solitaries for deliverance from his agony, the Consul begins by asking that Yvonne be allowed to realize her dream of a new life with him and concludes by urging that the world be destroyed. The chapter follows roughly the same course.

When supper is served the threesome by the proprietor, a Tlaxcalan named Cervantes, peace seems for a while restored. They make bawdy jokes about items on the menu, husband and wife exchange looks of longing, the Consul reminisces nostalgically on their meeting and betrothal in Granada three years earlier, Hugh begins to review the day's events starting with the horseback idyll of that morning. —Suddenly the Consul finds himself not at the table with the others at all, but seated on a grey stone toilet in a little room that seems at once like a monastic cell and a tomb. "And this, this grey final Consulate," he thinks, " . . . was doubtless a purely Tlaxcaltecan fantasy, Cervantes' own work, built to remind him of some cold mountain village in a mist. . . . Why was he here? Why was he always more or less, here? . . .Perhaps there was no time . . .in this stone retreat. Perhaps this was the eternity that he'd been making so much fuss about" (p. 294). (This is possibly a parodic allusion to the celestial and infernal thrones appearing in *Doctor Faustus,* Act V.) But the world of time is not so easily escaped. The Consul is brought back to mundane reality by the sound of Hugh's voice nearby, telling Yvonne that the man found dying by the roadside was the same man they had seen on their morning ride outside the cantina La Sepultura. Next the Consul discovers that beside him on the floor rests a lemonade bottle half full of mescal and that in his hand there is a travel folder describing the wonders of Tlaxcala. Still situated in the "Cave of the Winds, seat of all great decisions, little Cythère of childhood, eternal library, [and] sanctuary" (p. 293), he reads

SEAT OF THE HISTORY OF THE CONQUEST

VISIT TLAXCALA!

This pun on the word *seat* is not merely playful, for was not Moctezuma *"sitting* within [the] innermost citadel in chains" while a captive of the Spaniards in Tenochtitlán? and was not Cortés himself later *seated* on a stone beneath a cypress tree in Tacuba lamenting *la noche triste?* The "seat of history," as rendered in *Under the Volcano,* is an inglorious spot, scarcely a "sanctuary" at all. Yet, as the Consul muses, "where else could man absorb and divest himself of so much at the same time?" (p. 294).

The Tlaxcalans, a nation of fierce mountain Indians, were the bitterest enemies of the Aztecs until the arrival of the Spaniards. Though the Aztec empire by the turn of the sixteenth century was supreme in central Mexico, the Aztecs were never able effectively to subdue the Tlaxcalans. The Aztecs were relative newcomers to the area who ascended to

dominance by ruthless means and ruled their vanquished
enemies tyrannically: the Aztecs, that is to say, were themselves conquistadors. When the Spaniards appeared in 1519
they found, much to their delight, that many of the Indian
peoples of Mexico were chafing under Aztec oppression and
almost eager to form alliances with the powerful strangers in
order to insure an end to the dominion of the Aztecs. The
most important of these alliances—indeed one of the most
crucial factors of the entire Conquest—was the bond between
the Spaniards and the Tlaxcalans. This alliance was not
established without much bloodshed and anguish on both
sides, for the Tlaxcalans were above all a people with a proud
tradition of independence and a spirit of tribal patriotism
which made any reliance upon outsiders repugnant to them.
The pact with the Spaniards would almost certainly never
have been made had not the latter defeated the Tlaxcalans
decisively in a series of major battles.[20] The courage and discipline which the Tlaxcalans exhibited in these encounters
convinced Cortés of the advantage to be gained by enlisting
their aid against the more powerful Aztecs of neighboring
Tenochtitlán. Thus, rather than ravaging Tlaxcala and de-
stroying its idols as he had done after earlier victories over
other Indian peoples, Cortés followed a policy of restraint in
return for an agreement with the Tlaxcalans that they would
tender the Spaniards whatever support, in terms of man-
power and provisions, they could in the ensuing conflict
against the Aztecs. Despite the considerable evidence indicat-
ing that the Tlaxcalans agreed to the alliance because to do so
was politically and militarily expedient at that time, in the
euhemeristic myth the Tlaxcalans are seen as the betrayers of
their Indian brothers and lackeys to the foreign imperialists.
Lowry seems to have shared this latter view to some extent,
referring to the ancestors of the proprietor Cervantes as the
"savage and traitorous Tlaxcalans" who had "succeeded in
making Mexico great even in her betrayal..." (pp. 287,
285).[21]

The so-called betrayal of the Tlaxcalans is worked into the

larger pattern of human treachery and exploitation in the *Volcano*, as the Consul reads sections from the travel folder while Hugh and Yvonne continue their discussion of the incident by the roadside. Hugh believes that the fact that the *pelado* was a Spaniard is important. Before he can explain his idea to Yvonne, the Consul chimes in (though no one seems to hear him speaking from his "stone retreat"): " 'So that the man beside the road may be an Indian, of course.... And why an Indian? So that the incident may have some social significance to [Hugh], so that it should appear a kind of latter-day repercussion of the Conquest, if you please, so that that may in turn seem a repercussion of—' " (p. 296). Arousing no response from the others, Geoffrey goes back to reading the travel folder. The capital of the state, Tlaxcala City, he reads, is "said to be like Granada... *said to be like Granada, said to be like Granada, Granada...*" (p. 297). Granada registers forcefully in Geoffrey's mind because this was where he had first met Yvonne; they had become engaged while walking through the gardens of the Alhambra.[22] He continues reading the folder's garbled description of the "Seat of the History of the Conquest."

> Within the city limits of Tlaxcala is one of the oldest churches of the New World. This place was the residence of the first Apostolical See, named "Carolence" in honor of the Spanish King Carlos V...on the year 1526. In said Convent, according to tradition, were baptised the four [Indian] Senators of the Tlaxcaltecan Republic... being their God-Fathers the conqueror Hernán Cortés and several of his Captains.... In the chapel of the right side there is still the famous pulpit from where was preached in the New World, for first time, the Gospel. (p. 298)

In a manner reminiscent of T. S. Eliot's use of literary allusion in *The Waste Land*, Lowry juxtaposes the relative beauty and grandeur of the Indian peoples with their progressive decline since the Conquest. Contrasting the stark dignity of pre-Cortesian shrines and palaces with the "overloading style" of the colonial churches, the folder tells of young Xicoténcatl, the warrior prince, appealing to the rain-god Tlaloc for deliverance and haranguing his Tlaxcalan soldiers, "telling them to fight the conquerors to the limit, dying if necessary" (p. 301). The degeneration is most evident in the case of the emperor Moctezuma, once the most powerful man in all of Mexico. Now he is no more than a garish emblem stamped onto bottles of beer. To all of this Hugh, still expounding his pseudo-Marxian theory to interpret the incident by the roadside for Yvonne, provides a commentary more apt than he realizes: "'. . . first, Spaniard exploits Indian, then, when he had children, he exploited the halfbreed, then the pure-blooded Mexican Spaniard, the criollo, then the mestizo exploits everybody, foreigners, Indians, and all. Then the Germans and Americans exploited him: now the final chapter, the exploitation of everybody by everybody else—'" (pp. 299-300).

The Consul rejoins Hugh and Yvonne at the table. Looking at Yvonne, he thinks once again of Granada.

> But this time there was, as it were, a mist between them, and through the mist the Consul seemed to see not Granada but Tlaxcala. It was a white beautiful cathedral city *toward which the Consul's soul yearned* and which indeed in many respects was like Granada; only it appeared to him . . . perfectly empty. That was the queerest thing about it, and at the same time the most beautiful; there was nobody there, no one . . . to interfere with the business of drinking, not even Yvonne. . . . (p. 302, my emphasis)

As this passage strongly implies, Tlaxcala has become one in Geoffrey's mind with Parián: the two places both, in part, represent the solitary alcoholic bliss for which his "soul" yearns, and for which he invents paradisal fantasies. Presently he suggests that they should this very night catch the express for Tlaxcala, but the other two receive this wild idea

coldly. They seem, in fact, to be quite upset, probably because Geoffrey is obviously far gone on mescal. Geoffrey
becomes more and more angry, and begins to argue heatedly
with Hugh about politics and the dangers of "interfering" in
other people's lives—whether they be an Indian dying by the
road, or the Loyalists in Spain, or himself in the labyrinth of
alcoholism. Referring no doubt to his earlier vision of the
"seat of history," he tells Hugh to look

> back a thousand years. What is the use of interfering
> with [history's] worthless stupid course? Like a bar-
> ranca, a ravine, choked up with refuse, that winds
> through the ages, and peters out in a—What in God's
> name has all the heroic resistance put up by poor de-
> fenceless peoples . . . to do with the survival of the human
> spirit? Nothing whatsoever. . . . Countries, civilisations,
> empires, great hordes, perish for no reason at all, and
> their soul and meaning with them. . . . (p. 310)

One of the major purposes behind Lowry's use of historical
materials in Chapter X is to demonstrate the wide-ranging
implications of these views expressed by the Consul, to suggest the disastrous consequences of such views in human
terms. Writing to Cape about the importance of the material
in the travel folder, Lowry professed his belief that "there are
strange evocations and explosions here. . . . [The] whole
Tlaxcala business *does* have an underlying deep seriousness.
Tlaxcala . . . just like Parián, is death: . . . the Tlaxcalans were
Mexico's traitors—here the Consul is giving way to the forces
within him that are betraying himself" (*Letters,* p. 82). In
another letter he indicated that at this juncture the Consul
has "turned into a man that is all destruction—in fact he has
almost ceased to be a man altogether, and his human feelings
merely make matters more agonizing for him, but don't alter
things in the least; he is thus in hell" (*Letters,* p. 200).
Ranting about the destructive effects of "interference"
which have strewn the *barranca* of history with the refuse of
individual lives and fallen civilizations, Geoffrey eagerly

embraces a form of destruction that may be even worse: self-destruction, not only from alcoholism but also from the rejection of all commitment to anyone outside himself. His pain is perhaps even worse than that of Cortés during *la noche triste,* for Geoffrey has half-knowingly constructed his own hell.[23] Moreover, even if he calls it the "paradise of his despair," it is indeed hell and he must suffer its agonies to the fullest. Openly accusing Hugh and Yvonne of "'paddling palms and playing bubbies and titties all day under cover of saving me'" (p. 313), Geoffrey tells them that although he has been tempted by Yvonne's offer of a new life together in some "non-alcoholic Paradise," he has made up his mind that this is not what he wants after all. On the contrary, he insists, heading toward the door, "'I choose—Tlax . . . Tlax—Tlax'"; and then, "'I choose— . . . Hell,' he finished absurdly. 'Because . . . I like it,' he called to them, through the open window, from outside. . . . 'I love hell. I can't wait to get back there. In fact I'm running, I'm almost back there already'" (p. 314).

## V

In terms of actual narrative time, the last two chapters occur more or less simultaneously. As Geoffrey makes his way to his dubious paradise under the volcano, Hugh and Yvonne, after a brief delay, begin to search for him through the Dantesque dark wood. Lowry's notion that their search recalls the rites of the Eleusinian mysteries does not prevent it from seeming improbably circuitous and almost leisurely. Taking the longer path to Parián because of the two cantinas that might have persuaded the Consul to choose that route, Hugh and Yvonne encounter a series of ominous portents: vultures circling in the sky as the sun sets and storm clouds gather, the stench of decay from the ubiquitous *barranca,* the eerie chants of torch-bearing mourners descending from the cemetery in their ritual procession for *los muertos.* The couple take pause at the first cantina, El Petate, where Hugh goes in to inquire about the Consul. Waiting outside, Yvonne feels a strange dread and starts back alone into the darkening forest, where she stumbles upon a wooden cage containing an eagle "shivering in the damp and dark of its prison" (p. 319). On impulse she opens the cage and releases the bird which, relishing its freedom, soars off into the "deep dark blue pure sky" (p. 320). This gesture, though it is without conscious motive on Yvonne's part, is in the context of the Conquest motif suggestive of a liberation of ancient Mexico (the eagle being emblematic of the founding of Tenochtitlán) from its centuries of oppression at the hands of first the Aztec tyrants, and then of the displacing European civilization and its modern counterpart. It should be remembered that Lowry's translation of Quauhnahuac is "where the eagle stops." The caged eagle is like the Consul's Adam condemned to remain in a Godless garden. The soaring bird, a traditional emblem of the soul's liberation from the body, is analogous to Yvonne's dream of the northern paradise, and in the larger human context to a vision of history in which there are no *barrancas*—a romantic vision the appeal of which Lowry acknowledges but which he, like Greene, ultimately rejects as jejune and unreal. In both *The Power and the Glory* and *Under the Volcano* submission to the ambivalent extremes of Mexican existence, terrifying though it may be, amounts to an affirmation of the interdependence of spiritual aspiration and the fact of human limitations which bind man to his mortal condition. If he is to be compared with a bird, man most resembles the earthbound eagle with the serpent in its beak (Lawrence's symbol as well as Mexico's), or, at best, Melville's Catskill eagle which forever flies within the mountain gorge.

Yvonne, not yet freed from her own prison of suffering, feels only a sense of "utter heartbreak and loss" (p. 320) as the eagle disappears from sight. She has not long to wait, however. Hugh rejoins her, fortified by a few drinks. After stopping briefly at a second cantina, where Yvonne tries mescal " 'to find out what Geoffrey sees in it' " (p. 326), and where Hugh purchases a used guitar, they re-enter the forest, walking now in some haste. Hugh, quite drunk by now, falls behind, content to sing songs about the noble deeds of the Spanish Loyalists. Hearing gunshots ahead, Yvonne senses that Geoffrey is in danger and begins to run through the downpour. Suddenly she is confronted on the narrow path by a panic-stricken runaway horse with the number seven branded on its rump. Yvonne stumbles and is trampled by the beast. The moments of her dying are protracted by Lowry as he describes her final sensations:

> sinking, sinking, someone was calling her name far away and she remembered, they were in a dark wood, she heard the wind and the rain rushing through the forest and saw the tremours of lightning shuddering through the heavens and the horse—great God, the horse—and would this scene repeat itself endlessly and forever?—the horse, rearing, poised over her, petrified in midair, a statue, somebody was sitting on the statue, it was Yvonne Griffaton, no, it was the statue of Huerta, the drunkard, the murderer, *it was the Consul.* . . . (pp. 335-336, my emphasis)

In defense of this scene Lowry reminded Cape that during the Conquest the Indians, who had never before seen horses and who assumed that horse and rider were a single creature, regarded the strange beast as a supernatural being (*Letters*, p. 84). Such superstitions, aside from the logistic and other advantages gained by the use of both horses and gunpowder, played a major role in the Indians' downfall. It is of utmost significance that Geoffrey is, however innocent of the intention, responsible for releasing this horse which kills his wife. (This is of course the same horse whose rider was killed by the roadside in Chapter VIII.) Geoffrey's well-intended gesture in effect cancels out Yvonne's act of freeing the caged eagle and portends a renewal of the cycle of the Conquest. It is thus a poetically fitting consequence of his retreat to the Farolito/Tlaxcala. Again the Consul—along with Victoriano

Huerta, a reactionary general who betrayed the ideals of the Maderist Revolution of 1910 and probably had a hand in the murder of its central figure—is equated with the conquistador, here envisioned riding the beast of the apocalypse. Hugh, a would-be modern Orpheus (to whom martyrdom is "bad form"), pathetically strums his idealistic songs about the brotherhood of man on his guitar—while Yvonne dies, feeling herself "gathered upwards and borne towards the stars...flying softly and steadily towards Orion, the Pleiades..." (p. 336). Only in death is she thus allowed realization of a paradise liberated from "the eternal horror of opposites."

About an hour before these last events transpire, the Consul finds himself in his "Tlaxcala," the Farolito cantina in Parián, sipping mescal. "He was safe here; this was the place he loved—sanctuary, the paradise of his despair" (p. 338). He has come to the Farolito to drink in peace. But peace, alas, is not to be found here on this Day of the Dead. Chapter XII amounts to an extended accusation of all the Consul's sins, past and present, sins of both commission and omission for which he is determined to abjure responsibility till the very end. Though at first the bar is deserted except for the Consul, he hears the distant wail of voices, his own among them, reciting the fateful declension of his life: "'Borracho, Borrachón, Borraaaacho!'" (p. 337). One of the voices seems to be that of Yvonne pleading with him, but he deliberately blots out all thoughts of her with two swift mescals. Looking out the window he notes, with a certain inner satisfaction despite his apprehension, the almost sheer drop to the bottom of the prehensile abyss, nearby as always, with Popocatepetl towering overhead. As the latest draughts of mescal begin to take effect he has a brief vision which terrifies him: "...some unusual animals resembling geese, but large as camels, and skinless men, without heads, upon stilts, whose animated entrails jerked along the ground, were issuing out of the forest path the way he had come. He shut his eyes from this and when he opened them someone who looked like a policeman was leading a horse up the path, that was all. He laughed, despite the policeman, then stopped" (p. 341-342). In capsule form, this is the pattern of the Consul's behavior in the Farolito— intimations of imminent danger, desperate self-assurance that there is nothing to fear, the realization that catastrophe is unavoidable, the waiting.

Back in the bar Geoffrey is given a packet of letters he had left here some time ago, letters from Yvonne written after their separation confessing her longing to return to him if he would only ask her. We know, of course, from Geoffrey's unposted letter read a year later by Laruelle how he had wanted her back, but he had never actually asked her to return. And now here she is in Quauhnahuac anyhow, come back as they had both wanted, and what had resulted? Yvonne, reproaching Geoffrey without intending to, urging her sober northern paradise on him, has spent most of the day with Hugh, a former lover. And Geoffrey, miserably wanting Yvonne and at the same time not wanting her, has in effect consented to her dalliance by his inertia of will. He has, moreover, rejected her in favor of the Farolito, where he now sits, mescal-soaked, brooding guiltily over his inexplicable failure to love. The ironies become compounded in the ensuing encounter with the Indian girl María, a young prostitute. Geoffrey, unable to love earlier when the option to make a new start with Yvonne was still (relatively) open, performs his only natural act, the act of procreation, *after* having committed himself to the doom awaiting him at the Farolito. In part it is his awareness of this incongruity which makes the tryst with María so pleasureless for Geoffrey: "God is it possible to suffer more than this, out of this suffering something must be born, and what would be born was his own death" (p. 349). The scene dramatizes overtly the betrayal of his love for Yvonne which was implicit in his withdrawal to the Farolito in the first place.

On another level, the scene marks the Consul's decisive involvement in the pattern of the Conquest. The historical parallel here is inexact, to be sure, largely due to Geoffrey's apparent passivity. Nevertheless it is possible to discern in this coupling of the European Geoffrey Firmin and the Indian girl María an analogue of the union between Cortés and Marina, the Nahua princess. Marina, or Malinche as she is more widely known, was a beautiful young Indian girl "given" to the Spaniards as a prize of war by a conquered Tabascan chief. After she learned to speak Spanish she became invaluable to Cortés as a translator because of her knowledge of both the Mayan and Nahuatl languages. "She learned [Spanish] the more readily," writes Prescott, "as it was to her the language of love."[24] At first the mistress of a Spaniard named Puertocarreo, Malinche soon so attracted Cortés himself by her charms that he took her for his own mistress and sired a son by her. Once the victory over the Aztecs was achieved, however, and Cortés was joined in Mexico by his Spanish wife, Malinche was married off to still another of the conquistadors, one Juan Jaramillo. Octavio Paz treats Malinche as the archetypal *chingada*, or violated one, a symbol of the passive, masochistic traits that express the "female" side of the Mexican character since the Conquest.

> If the *Chingada* is a representation of the violated Mother [writes Paz], it is appropriate to associate her with the Conquest, which was also a violation, not only in the historical sense but also in the very flesh of Indian women. The symbol of this violation is doña Malinche, the mistress of Cortés. It is true that she gave herself voluntarily to the conquistador, but he forgot her as soon as her usefulness was over. Doña Marina [her Christian name] becomes a figure representing the Indian women who were fascinated, violated or seduced by the Spaniards.[25]

Like the Tlaxcalans, Malinche is popularly regarded by modern Mexicans as a traitor to her race.

María in the novel is more aggressive than her prototype. Indeed her proposition to Geoffrey, "Quiere María?", means "does María want?" rather than "do you want María?" (*quiere Vd. a María?*). Her role as aggressor is further indicated when she repeats her phrase in the bedroom, this time not as a question but as a declaration: "María wants." Geoffrey, for his part, despite his preoccupation with Yvonne (of whom María reminds him) and his fear of contracting venereal disease, makes not the slightest show of resistance. The ambiguity involved in the phrasing of María's statements, in the literal situation, and in the nature of the archetypal relationship between Cortés and Malinche suggests a reversal of the roles of *chingada* and conquistador, anticipating the book's final scene. Again Lowry appropriates Mexican materials—here the very core of the national myth as promulgated by Revolutionary ideologues—and adapts them to his own ends. For whatever the implications of the tryst with regard to the native myth, Lowry lays primary emphasis here on the Consul's attribution of treachery to himself rather than to any connivance on the part of María/Marina. And this emphasis is as it should be, for morally speaking the impulse to conquer and possess, however remote, is ultimately a self-betrayal, as the Consul finds out to his cost: "it was...calamity he now, with María, penetrated, the only thing alive in him now this burning boiling crucified evil organ..." (p. 349). The "violation" of María—presented rather as a violation of Yvonne—is what seals the Consul's doom. "'Now you've done it,'" his Faustian "familiars" hiss in his ear as he leaves María, "'now you've really done it, Geoffrey Firmin! Even we can help you no longer...'" (pp. 351-352).

Back in the main bar, he looks through the window and notes that the horse tethered outside seems familiar. When he goes to investigate, his suspicions are confirmed by the number seven branded on the rump of the animal. Geoffrey, recalling the incident by the roadside, feels sure that somehow those "Union Militar [fascist] fellows were at the bottom... of the whole business" (p. 354). Directly, a policeman approaches and begins to question him suspiciously. Nothing the Consul can say seems to mitigate the man's malevolence toward him. The policeman shoves the Consul roughly back inside the Farolito where, joined by other hostile officials, he continues the interrogation. Things become worse when Diosdado, the barman, reveals that the Consul had drawn a map of Spain and spoken passionately of Granada. They accuse him of deliberately avoiding payment for the drinks and the girl and of trying to steal the horse. "'You Bolsheviki prick? You member of the Brigade Internationale and stir up trouble?'" one of them asks. Geoffrey's intimation that he has been followed and spied on throughout the day seems to be confirmed when he is informed, "'We have been looking for you'" (p. 357).

To all their questions concerning his identity and his political beliefs, the Consul replies, only half in jest, that he is William Blackstone: for "had he not and with a vengeance come to live among the Indians?" (p. 358). Of all the figures who threaten him, the most menacing is the Jefe de Jardineros, perhaps the man responsible for all the signs in the public gardens. This official, clean-cut and dressed in tweeds, reminds Geoffrey of himself years ago when he was a Vice-Consul in Granada. It is as if he is being accused of some obscure but serious crime by his former self.[26] The bar is by now quite full, especially since the mourners have returned to town from the cemetery. The interrogation proceeds intermittently, as more mescal is quaffed and the Consul is surrounded by a gallery of grotesques who look on passively during his ordeal. There are two individuals, however, who exhibit some concern for his well-being. A toothless man playing the fiddle nearby warns him that his antagonists are "Brutos" not to be tampered with. He invites the Consul to escape to his own home. An old Tarascan woman then tells the Consul that this is a bad place for a foreigner to be. "'Muy malo,'" she says. "'These man no friend of Mexican people.... They no policía. They diablos. Murderers.... Vámonos'" (pp. 367-368). But the Consul steadfastly refuses to leave.

When the questioning resumes the Chief of Municipality searches his pockets and finds Hugh's dispatch concerning the antisemitic campaign backed by a German legation. Since the Consul has no passport with him, he cannot prove to them that he is not Hugh Firmin (whose signature is affixed to the dispatch), and they are not impressed by his protestations that he is only William Blackstone the English explorer, or that he is not a spy but a writer. Pointing at the dispatch one of them informs him, significantly using the German word, " 'It say you are *Juden*' " (p. 369, my emphasis). " 'You say you are a wrider,' " continues the Chief of Rostrums; " 'You no are a wrider. . . . You are . . . de espider [a Lowry coinage meaning spy], and we shoota de espiders in *Méjico*' " (p. 371, my emphasis). The "we" in question here clearly do not come from Mexico, as the Castilian spelling indicates. The international machinery of conquest is finally closing in on the hapless Consul.

With a mescal-inspired fortitude, Geoffrey is able to tolerate all of this absurd bullying, until one of the "Chiefs" confiscates the letters from Yvonne. Unwilling to accept her love when it was offered him, he is roused to a kind of heroic defiance by this defilement now that it is too late. The Consul's quixotic behavior here only calls our attention again to the fundamental dislocation or blockage of his natural affections. To highlight the Consul's sudden self-righteous rage, Lowry uses an image that closely resembles the celebrated screeching cockatoo which appears for a split second in a somewhat similar scene in *Citizen Kane*.

> Suddenly the Consul thought he saw an enormous rooster flapping before him, clawing and crowing. He raised his hands and it merded on his face. He struck the . . . Jefe de Jardineros straight between the eyes. "Give me those letters back!" he heard himself shouting at the Chief of Rostrums. . . . "You poxboxes. You coxcoxes. You killed that Indian. . . . You're all in it." (pp. 371-372)

As the clock strikes seven and the cock flaps again before his eyes, the Consul grabs a machete from a nearby table and threatens his accusers with it. His litany of counter-accusations becomes increasingly incoherent: " 'Only the poor, only through God, only the people you wipe your feet on, the poor in spirit...if you'd only stop interfering, stop walking in your sleep, stop sleeping with my wife, only the beggars and the accursed.' The machete fell with a rattle. The Consul felt himself stumbling.... 'You stole that horse,' he repeated" (p. 372).

A remark made by Lowry to Cape concerning all of Chapter XII seems especially apropos at this point. "[In] terms of human agony," he wrote, "...it can widen, I think, one's knowledge of hell. In fact the feeling you are supposed to get from this chapter is an almost Biblical one. Hasn't the guy had enough suffering? Surely we've reached the end now. But no. Apparently it's only just starting" (*Letters*, p. 84). The Consul's agony *must* be exacerbated and distended so that the truth about himself can finally penetrate his superabundance of defensive fantasies that allow him to continue justifying his human failings even as he delivers himself up for judgment. Despite all that he has suffered the Consul has not yet effectively been brought face to face with the reality of his life. By accusing the preposterous "Chiefs" of killing the Indian and stealing the horse and sleeping with Yvonne, he is obviously displacing and projecting his own oversize sense of guilt. Even his otherwise admirable desire to do something beneficent is tainted, partially, by the delusion of his own goodness. Thus, as he staggers out into the road to free the tethered horse—ironically, his only genuinely unselfish action in the novel—he is still caught up in the nexus of destruction, the ultimate *noche triste* in fact.

Reaching for the horse's bridle, he hears the final warning. " 'I blow you wide open from your knees up, you Jew chingao...you cabrón,' " says the Chief of Rostrums drawing out his pistol, " 'you pelado' " (p. 373).* But neither these revealing epithets nor the threat of death can deter him now.

---

*\*Cabrón* means cuckold. *Chingao* is a slang corruption of *chingado,* violated one. See Octavio Paz's comments on this term above.

The horse, unfettered, is spooked by a flash of lightning and bolts off into the woods for its appointed encounter with Yvonne. The Chief, good as his word, fires three spaced, deliberate shots into the Consul. Only as he lies dying does Geoffrey see who he really is and what he has become. "No one would help him even if they could," he reflects. "Now he was the one dying by the wayside where no good Samaritan would halt" (p. 375). Only the old fiddler is willing to call him comrade in the end, and this in hushed tones. *Pelado, compañero, chingao*—these are chief among the last words he hears directed at himself. Accepting them all, he discovers at last that he is bound to all humanity. An unwitting conquistador for the most part, he is also one of the exploited, violated as much by the tyranny of self as by the dehumanizing schemes of the fascists. But most fitting of all, finally, is the intermediate term, *compañero.* His own last utterance, addressed alike to his murderers and the bystanders, is this: "'No se puede vivir sin amar,'" words which, Lowry writes, "would explain everything" (p. 375). Unfortunately the moment of self-recognition, as in all tragedy, has come too late to alter his destiny. In his dying vision he sees himself climbing toward the snowy summit of Popocatepetl, only to realize that instead he is hurtling straight downwards:

> . . .the world itself was bursting, bursting into black spouts of villages catapulted into space, with himself falling through it all, through the inconceivable pandemonium of a million tanks, through the blazing of ten million burning bodies, falling, into a forest, falling—
> (p. 375)

himself now part of the putrescence gathering to a greatness in the cloacal *barranca,* beneath the perennial "seat" of Conquest. We evict, warns the terrible sign in the garden, those who destroy.

# IX

# *Under* Under the Volcano:
# *The Mexican Voyages*
# *of Malcolm Lowry*

O the mind, mind has mountains; cliffs of fall
Frightful, sheer, no-man-fathomed. Hold them cheap
May who ne'er hung there.

—Gerard Manley Hopkins

I

Malcolm Lowry first set foot in Mexico, by his own account,
on the Day of the Dead, 1936. Later he was to recall his entry
at Acapulco, the "going ashore, in a boat, the madman foam-
ing at the mouth, correcting his watch; the mile-high bodiless
vultures in the thunder."[1] Lowry's contact with Mexico before long assumed the phantasmagorical character suggested
by these portents. Using a most appropriate phrase, Lowry
once described himself as one "afflicted with Mexico." In an
article written late in his truncated career, he attempted to
account for this affliction as follows:

We may smile reading the travel advertisement: "Magic
Mexico, where the past mingles with the present, and the
days go by in a timeless golden haze."
And yet, there *is* a magic about Mexico, the days do
go by in a timeless haze, its romance and mystery are not

281

overstated. But what is the secret of the attraction, one might say the almost teleological psychic attraction, of Mexico? Why do so many people go there, and, having gone, long to return?[2]

The answers to these questions, like so many things pertaining to Lowry's life and personality, are elusive. One might begin with the very fact of secrecy which he sees in Mexico's allure. It would not be far from the truth to say that Lowry shared the passion for secret knowledge professed by the Consul in *Under the Volcano*. "The person who falls in love with Mexico," Lowry writes, "falls in love with a colorful and proud and present entity, it is true, but he is also involved, in the deepest sense, with a mystery." More to the point, however, is this comment concerning the *human* mystery which is somehow epitomized for him by the vicissitudes of Mexican existence: "Some people undoubtedly feel drawn to Mexico as to the hidden life of man himself; they wonder if they might not even discover themselves there."[3]

Mystery and secrecy—though not necessarily in the sense of arcana—loom as major obstacles in any examination of Lowry's own experiences in Mexico. Compared with the other English writers we are considering who visited the country, Lowry's exposure to Mexico was rather extensive. Altogether he spent about twenty-five months there on his two sojourns, more than two and a half times as long as his closest competitor in this regard, D. H. Lawrence. Though he spent over half of his time in Cuernavaca, Lowry also paid fairly substantial visits to Acapulco (about four months total) and Oaxaca (just under two months); and he stopped frequently in Mexico City, where he stayed for a total of almost four months. On his second trip to Mexico he also visited such places as Puebla, Taxco, Tlaxcala, and Zamboala. Yet despite the range of his travels, the length of his visits, and the obvious importance of the country to his work, our knowledge of Lowry's experience—particularly during the crucial first trip—is fragmentary at best.

A couple of reasons for this unfortunate situation may be cited. First, Lowry was concerned almost exclusively with using Mexico as a setting for his fiction. In addition to the *Volcano*, his two unfinished novels, *Dark As the Grave Wherein My Friend Is Laid* and *La Mordida*, have Mexican settings. All three works, and especially the latter two, draw heavily for material upon his travel experiences. But writing travel books as such apparently did not interest Lowry. Nor do his letters offer much assistance to the present inquiry, since very few of the 1936-38 period have survived.[4] (Fortunately there is a handful of valuable letters from the second trip, in 1945-46.) Thus our account of the two visits necessarily consists of a patchwork of comments by friends who were with Lowry at one time or another in Mexico, the extant letters, and inferences drawn from the semi-autobiographical materials in his fiction.

Lowry arrived at Acapulco in November of 1936 in the company of his first wife, Jan Gabrial Lowry. The couple had come from Hollywood, where Lowry was unable to find work at the film studios. In Mexico they hoped to be able to subsist on the monthly stipend sent them by Lowry's father, a wealthy Liverpool industrialist. The marriage was a most unhappy one. By the time of the Mexican trip there had already been several long separations. Despite their genuine affection for each other, Jan was already more than wary of her husband's drinking and of their poverty. For his part, Lowry suffered immensely from Jan's frequent infidelities. Mexico was to be their last chance for a life together. They remained in Acapulco for perhaps a few weeks, "only long enough for Lowry to discover mescal, tequila, pulque, and Mexico's splendid dark beer" (Day, p. 215). Then they rode the bus inland to Mexico City, where they stayed possibly about two weeks. Before Christmas they had settled in Cuernavaca, where Lowry was to spend the next year. At some point during these early weeks of the trip there occurred an incident involving a man dying by the roadside as others looked on helplessly—an incident which so intrigued Lowry by its manifold implications that he soon wrote a short story about it called "Under the Volcano." This seventeen-page story is the germ of the novel which Lowry would spend the better part of the next eight years writing and rewriting.[5]

Day feels that Lowry and Jan "were probably drawn to Cuernavaca by nothing more romantic than the fact that there was a large foreign colony there, with many literary types in it" (p. 216). Before long, however, Lowry discovered that the physical surroundings in this area were particularly well suited as a locale for the story he was writing. The Lowrys were renting a three-bedroom house on Calle de Humboldt, with a veranda commanding an impressive vista of the twin volcanoes. Along with a swimming pool and an overgrown garden, prominent features of their grounds were a serpentine *barranca* and a sewage ditch of a lesser size if not lesser danger to the unsuspecting pedestrian. Considering also the proximity of the "dark wood" outside the town, and of both the Borda Gardens and the palace of Cortés within it, one can scarcely question Day's contention that "if Lowry had been looking for Baudelaire's forest of symbols, with its myriads of correspondences, he could never have found a more appropriate spot than Cuernavaca" (p. 216). By May of 1937 Lowry had expanded the story into a complete first draft of roughly 40,000 words.[6]

Between mid-May and July 7, Lowry was paid a visit by his old friend and mentor, Conrad Aiken, who had come to Mexico seeking a divorce from his second wife and marriage to his third. Since Aiken's visit played an important role in subsequent developments during Lowry's first Mexican sojourn and also in the evolution of *Under the Volcano*, it is necessary to understand something of the nature of the relationship between the two writers.[7] After reading Aiken's novel *Blue Voyage* at the age of nineteen in 1928, Lowry was so overwhelmed by the sense of having found a literary and spiritual guiding light that he contacted Aiken about the possibility of establishing a kind of private tutorial. Much to Lowry's delight, Aiken agreed. From the beginning they got on famously, spending long hours during Lowry's vacations from Cambridge talking, rough-housing, drinking, and going over the manuscript of Lowry's apprentice-novel about the sea, *Ultramarine* (1933). In his autobiographical "essay" *Ushant*, Aiken writes that their dialogues "sometimes achieved a quite astonishing pitch of divination—and a kind of cooperative, and hallucinatory, alcoholic brilliance of statement unique in his [Aiken's] experience, the two minds and psyches complementing...each other in a moving braid of analysis..." (*Ushant*, p. 239). Aiken soon assumed the role of a substitute father for Lowry. Yet, as one might expect, there was a strong undercurrent of competitiveness between the two. Lowry, always hypersensitive concerning the subject of plagiarism, was guiltily aware that Aiken's influence was a yoke that he would eventually have to put off. It was not long until, only partly in jest, he "avowed his intention of absorbing all he jolly well could of [Aiken], in that curious and ambivalent relationship of theirs, as of father and son, on the one hand, and teacher and disciple on the other, absorbing him even to the point of annihilation..." (*Ushant*, p. 294). They would spar verbally with each other for hours on the question of the "creative *moritura*" in Aiken, and its desirability from Lowry's point of view.

The hostility between the two writers surfaced for the first time during their stay together in Granada in the summer of 1933, when Lowry had first met and fallen in love with Jan Gabrial. The two writers had not seen each other for any length of time since then, until Aiken arrived in Cuernavaca with his friend Ed Burra, a painter, and Mary Hoover, Aiken's wife-to-be. Aiken's affectionate description of their reunion is tinged with pathos. Aiken recalls

> the slightly absurd, but always altogether delightful, figure, advancing towards them with that stick of his— the tall sapling which he carried, because, he said, it helped him with his lumbago—advancing towards the camión, which had brought them over the mountains from Mexico City, his trousers knotted round the waist with a necktie, and looking as if they might fall off any minute; and grinning at them shyly, and affectionately,

and a little drunkenly.... A carelessly powerful and in-
gratiating figure, to which the curiously short arms,
which he habitually thrust a little before him, lent an
appealing appearance of helplessness. (*Ushant*, p. 348)

It did not take long before Aiken realized the extent of Lowry's misery in "that so tragic little house, with its discomforts
...and the dreadful stench from the little sewage canal which
ran directly beneath their bedroom windows" (p. 350). In the
throes of alcoholic and marital despair Lowry was suffering a
daily death, grappling with his "unappeasable vision" and
helplessly enduring "the perpetual clack of [Jan's] merciless
high heels, the pitiless and faithless heels, along that tiled
veranda, and over into his heart...while the thunderheads
punctually amassed themselves over the volcano for the tremendous assault of lightning and downpour at evening" (pp.
348-349). Jan, never one to be discreet in these extramarital
ventures, made a great show of going off for a week to Veracruz with another man. Lowry's already tenuous condition
degenerated rapidly, until he was "almost unable, in his despair, to work"—astounding that he could work at all in such
circumstances. Then, with Jan still gone, he

began a series of alcoholic fugues from which they were
often afraid he might never return. He would vanish for
a night: he would vanish for two. His appearance became more and more disheveled, and if he kept his sense
of humor, and his wonderful visionary gift of gab, nevertheless it was with an increasing irritability, on the one
hand, and an increasing indulgence in that fantastic mysticism of his, on the other...as in the years before, but
now with an almost insane obsessedness.... (p. 350)

As the weeks passed, the strain on the friendship between
Lowry and Aiken grew steadily worse. Their bibulous mid-
night conversations grew even more heated than usual. The
subject was often politics. Lowry, who "had drifted pretty
far, politically, towards something like communism," at-
tacked Aiken's abstract conservatism, and Aiken retaliated in

kind. There were "some pretty acrimonious scenes while they sat in candlelight, the thunderstorm intermittently dousing the electric lights, and drank the impossible tequila or the still more impossible *habanero*..." (p. 351).[8] The situation was not improved when one night in early July Lowry, staggering home in a rainstorm, stumbled and fell headlong into the sewage canal. Aiken, responding to his cries for help, had to retrieve Lowry from the reeking ditch and then cleanse him of the filth, dry him off, and put him to bed.

But the real crisis of Aiken's stay in Cuernavaca occurred a few days later during a very nearly violent clash in a cafe. The discussion began typically enough with the two men trading witticisms regarding the symbolic destruction of the father by his son. Soon, they both realized, it had developed into what Aiken calls the "final disposition of the extraordinary psychological situation between them..." (p. 352). Recalling aloud their previous conflict in Granada when the tantalizing Jan had made her first appearance, Lowry charges Aiken with plotting to "share" Jan with him, if only vicariously. To this accusation Aiken agrees: "'...to hand her on to you, I could thus keep her—at least, at one remove, and with your imagination to magnify it for me. Very simple. And twofold in function, too—for this might stop your drinking. Pull you together'" (p. 353). Such an admission, Lowry feels, amounts to clear evidence of Aiken's "first death" at Lowry's hands, "a kind of voluntary suicide." After a few more drinks—punctuated by toasts to "death and betrayal"—Aiken counters by suggesting that Jan's flagrant unfaithfulness demonstrates the evanescence of Lowry's supposed "victory" over himself. At this Lowry becomes furious, says he hates Aiken and could kill him right here and now, and not just symbolically. But the moment passes, and Lowry contents himself with an assertion of his psychic and artistic dominance: "'...listen to me,'" he declares calmly,

"it's your own voice now speaking—so how can you resume? You no longer know your own boundaries. You are a nation invaded. And as I'm younger, and as I'm

stronger, in appetite, in will, in recklessness, in sense of
direction, it will be no use your trying to compete with
me, you will only appear to be echoing *me*, imitating
*me*, parodying *me*—you will no longer have a personality of your own."

"If I ever had one [replies Aiken]. Here's to death and
betrayal." (p. 356)[9]

The conflict ended on amiable terms, at least on the surface.
A few days later Aiken was married, with Lowry and Jan in
attendance, and the friends parted company in peace. But the
very fact that both were gifted and ambitious writers, as Conrad Knickerbocker observed, had finally "made it impossible
for them to go on" after this climactic confrontation. "Com-
petition for the right phrase, the right insight, froze and mag-
nified unnaturally every human gesture. The writer in both
overburdened their relationship with the sheer weight of
words and analysis, speculation and introspection.... Exhausted, they disengaged."[10] Indeed, though they continued
to correspond, they were to see each other in person only
once more, and that sad occasion did not occur until seventeen years later at a literary gathering in New York.

Left alone together, Jan and Lowry attempted to reconcile
during the remainder of July and August. She stayed with
him, while he went on the wagon and exercised daily. This
fragile truce was shattered by the precipitate and unan-
nounced visit of another pair of old friends, Arthur and Ara
Calder-Marshall. The latter, seeing Lowry in comparatively
good condition and unaware of the recent debacle, suggested
a round of drinks. For Lowry the "round" lasted several days
on end, during which time he drank almost without sleep.
After a brief recuperation he began drinking again. About a
month later Jan, tired of pursuing her husband through the
cantinas of Cuernavaca, left "for a holiday with the French
Consul who lived down the road."[11] The Calder-Marshalls
cared for the desolate Lowry for a few weeks until, by the
third week of October, they lost all patience with him and
left town themselves.

Precisely how the solitary Lowry spent the next six weeks we do not know, but it cannot have been a happy period for him. Jan returned to Cuernavaca during the first week of December, not to stay but to gather her belongings before leaving Lowry for good. Together they bused up to Mexico City, where he made a last desperate attempt to convince her to give him another chance. Apparently she offered to remain only if he would give up drinking completely and at once. He refused.[12] Jan departed for California, leaving Lowry alone at their hotel in the capital.

"Now began a real *noche oscura* for Lowry," writes Day (p. 234). Shortly before Christmas of 1937—just over a year after his initial entry into Mexico with Jan—Lowry bused down to Oaxaca, his "City of Dreadful Night." He checked into the Hotel Francia, where D. H. Lawrence had stayed briefly in 1924, and turned to the city's celebrated mescal to drown his grief. Day has provided a vivid description of Oaxaca as it may have seemed to Lowry floundering in his abyss.

> Oaxaca, to the average tourist, is one of Mexico's bright spots. . . . But to Lowry it was a nightmare: he listened to a pair of fawns being slaughtered for his hotel's dining room; two enormous turtles, upended, bled to death on the pavement outside the hotel; a vulture perched on his washbasin. With these hallucinations (if they *were* hallucinations) came the old paranoia. He was being lured into drinking, then derided for being drunk. He was being spied upon by men in dark sun-glasses. (p. 234)

Oaxaca: there is "no sadder word," says Geoffrey Firmin— a word that is "like a breaking heart, a sudden peal of stifled bells in a gale, the last syllables of one dying of thirst in the desert."[13] And at the very center of that nightmarish region, for Malcolm Lowry no less than for Geoffrey Firmin, lies the Farolito. This locus of self-betrayal and doom, which Lowry transplants to his mythical state of Parián in the novel, was in fact a garish cantina located in Oaxaca (though there is also a Farolito in Cuernavaca, still extant, which may have contributed to the cantina in the novel). The Farolito, or little lighthouse, "the lighthouse that invites the storm, and lights it," was

> a strange place, a place really of the late night and early dawn, which as a rule . . . did not open till four o'clock in the morning. . . . At first it had appeared to him tiny. Only after he had grown to know it well had he discovered how far back it ran, that it was really composed of numerous little rooms, each smaller and darker than the last, opening one into another, the last and darkest of all being no larger than a cell. These rooms struck him as spots where diabolical plots must be hatched, atrocious murders planned; here . . . life reached bottom. But here also great wheeling thoughts hovered in the brain. (*Volcano*, p. 200)

This place, about which we know nothing beyond Lowry's evocative descriptions, left an impression upon him so profound that it became the single most compelling force—the magnetic center controlling all else—not only in his novel but also in Lowry's "afflictive" fascination for Mexico. As we shall see later on, not even the interposition of ten years spent in relative peace on the beach in British Columbia, nor a second marriage that was basically a happy one, could fully neutralize the dread hold it had upon his imagination.

Lowry's fear of persecution must have seemed confirmed by the treatment he received in Oaxaca. Sometime before Christmas he was thrown into jail, surely the last place a foreigner could wish to find himself in Mexico. Lowry, notoriously prone to embellish the details of his own legend, liked to attribute his incarceration to his having expressed liberal political views in a cantina. His fullest account appears in a letter to James Stern:

> I was thrown, for a time, in Mexico, as a spy, into durance vile, by some fascistas in Oaxaca (by mistake; they were after another man. How it arose was: he was a

friend of mine, very sober and a communist, and they could not believe, because he was sober, that he was an agitator and therefore thought he must be me, who was not sober, but, nevertheless, not an agitator, not a communist). I subsequently found it difficult to explain why I had absolutely had to be drawing a map of the Sierra Madre in tequila on the bar counter (sole reason was, I liked the shape of them). . . . On Christmas Day they let out all the prisoners except me. Myself, I had the Oaxaquenian third degree for turkey. Hissed they (as *Time* would say), "You say you a wrider but we read all your wridings and dey don't make sense. You no wrider, you an espider and we shoota de espiders in Mejico." But it was an improving experience. . . . They tried to castrate me too, one fine night, unsuccessfully, I regret (sometimes) to report. It ended up with a sort of Toulouse-Lautrec scene, myself, gaolers and all, simply walking, roaring with mescal, out into the night. They are looking for me yet.[14]

Day finds no evidence supporting Lowry's claim that he was imprisoned in the place of another man, though the idea does appear in his fiction. "The probability," writes Day, "is that Lowry came to the attention of the police through his conspicuous and continuous drunkenness, and that, after some difficulties over his passport (or lack of it) he was put in jail . . ." (p. 238). He spent perhaps eleven days in prison in Oaxaca, and his letters of this period are replete with complaints about how he was followed and harassed after being released. It was, as he wrote to John Davenport, "the perfect Kafka situation" (*Letters*, p. 11).

The more one scrutinizes the available information about Lowry's relatively brief but eventful stay in Oaxaca, the more one is convinced that the nature of his experiences there contributed enormously to the general tone which would eventually dominate *Under the Volcano*. If Cuernavaca provided Lowry with the basic situation and the talismanic landscape for his novel, Oaxaca (or his experience of it) provided him with the necessary conspiratorial atmosphere and with the self-destructive allure epitomized by the Farolito, "the place he loved—sanctuary, the paradise of his despair" (*Volcano*, p. 338). Furthermore, away from the buffering effects of a resort town and his English-speaking friends, Lowry was for the first time in a position to learn something about provincial Mexico. In this he was aided by a man named Juan Fernando Márquez, a Zapotecan about whom not a great deal is known. With Juan Fernando, Lowry established "one of the major friendships of his life. . . . This obscure figure . . . came to represent for Lowry his ideal of manhood: a true (as opposed to a literary) hero" (Day, p. 240). Thus Lowry was the only one of the writers examined in this study who formed a close friendship with a native during his stay in Mexico. This fact in itself—even apart from the "ideal of manhood" which Juan Fernando represented for Lowry— merits some consideration.

When he knew Lowry in Oaxaca, Juan Fernando was twenty-four years old. Unusually tall (six feet three inches) for an Indian, he was a descendant of Zapotecan kings, but also had some Spanish blood. Though he was educated as a chemist at the University of Mexico, he was committed to a life of service. Juan Fernando was employed as a rider by the *Banco Ejidal*, delivering money from the central bank to the smaller branches in the surrounding Indian villages to help with the collectivist agrarian reforms which President Cárdenas had instituted. Though the work was dangerous and poorly paid, Juan Fernando "gloried in the job: for its rigors, and for the ways in which it allowed him to help his people" (Day, p. 242). Apparently Lowry met Juan Fernando in a Oaxacan cantina, over mescal. According to Margerie Lowry, Malcolm "made many trips with [Juan Fernando] into the surrounding mountains" on the latter's deliveries of Ejidal money.[15] In addition to all the other qualities which Lowry found so inspiring in his new friend, the Englishman was deeply influenced by the man's explanation of the Zapotecan concept of time. This concept, which also embraces such related subjects as history and death, is described by Lowry in his "Garden of Etla" essay. Lowry had remarked to Juan Fernando that perhaps the reason that the Zapotecan ruins at Mitla and Monte Albán were relatively unknown to tourists was that the state of Oaxaca was too closely identified with its more recent past. "Had not, in the City of Oaxaca, Guerrero died, and for that matter, Porfirio Díaz been born? And were not both Juárez and...Cárdenas, Oaxaquenians, and besides, Zapotecans? And were not those people of his race two of the most formidable names in modern history?"[16] To all such queries Fernando can only smile. Lowry writes:

> His judgments were not mine. The very word formidable was not one he cared to use in that relation. Time nearly [sic, merely?] repeated itself; history likewise. To a Zapotecan modesty was an all-important quality.... Why boast about that which has been done before?
> ...Man he likened to the Valley of Etla. Perhaps I would understand this better if he said the Garden of Eden. Every man was, in a sense, his own Garden of Eden. To this extent others could be seen as spiritual modifications of oneself....
> ...[You] found yourself either within this symbolic garden or, mysteriously...you were made aware that you had been evicted from it.... [One] of the surest ways to become evicted was by boastfulness, though this had a deeper meaning than was contained in the mere word.... [The] moment you attributed any formidable value to yourself...you went out.
> Then, one of the most certain ways never to return was by excessive remorse, or sorrow for what you had lost. This to a Zapotecan...was another form of boasting: the assumption of the uniqueness of your misery.
> ... Fernando had strayed from the point: but somehow he had objected to the word formidable—[17]

These thoughts are admittedly a little obscure, as presented. But the reader of *Under the Volcano* will recognize in them

such notions as historical recurrence, the contemporaneity of
the past, the figure of the garden and the expulsion or eviction from it, the symbolic correspondence between various
human souls, and the paramount evil of egoism whether it be
manifested in *hubris* or self-pity. Even if we allow for a certain amount of distortion due to Lowry's personal interpretation of his friend's ideas, there can be no question that Lowry's thought—and particularly his understanding of reality
within the context of Mexico—was affected by his acquaintance with Juan Fernando. It was a debt that he would not
soon forget.

The exact date of Lowry's departure from Oaxaca is not
known, but Day cites evidence suggesting that he may have
left sometime in February of 1938. Political tensions in the
country were becoming acute about then; the oil crisis was
just a month off. As Day points out, it was "not a good time
to be an Englishman in Mexico . . ." (p. 245).¹⁸ Lowry was in
Mexico City until sometime in April, but we do not know
anything about his activities during these two months. During April he traveled over the mountains to Acapulco, his
port of entry, where he had been advised (incorrectly) to go
in order to secure an extension of his visa. Again, rather little
is known about Lowry's visit to Acapulco, which lasted
roughly two and a half months. He later told his wife Margerie that he had tried unsuccessfully to commit suicide by
drowning. Also during this time he made the acquaintance of
a man named Bousfield, an American tourist whom he identified, for some reason, with absolute human evil. "We know
about the shadowy Bousfield only that he and Lowry got into
several scrapes for which Lowry was truly ashamed, and
which he—normally the most open and indiscreet of men—
would never discuss with anyone" (Day, p. 246). Informed
finally by the office of *Migración* in Acapulco that he would
have to go back to Mexico City to renew his visa, Lowry returned to the capital in late June, accompanied by an agent
from *Migración* and the mysterious Bousfield. After some
confusion he was given a six-month extension. But by this

time agents sent by his father had contacted him, provided him with a lawyer, and arranged for all his debts to be paid. This accomplished, they put him on the train heading north. Thus, due to his father's intervention, Lowry abruptly departed from Mexico at Nogales in July 1938.[19]

"In Mexico," writes Douglas Day, "Lowry had lost his wife, gone further into alcoholism, come close to madness, been mocked, threatened, and...imprisoned. His disastrous twenty-month's stay ended with his being put on a train as if he were a delinquent adolescent who had misbehaved in school and was being sent home in disgrace" (p. 247). Nevertheless, Lowry's "affliction" for Mexico was to continue for over a decade. It was to find expression in the novel on which he labored for so long—probably the greatest work of fiction laid in Mexico written by a foreigner. This "affliction" was also to bring him back to the country on the eve of that novel's acceptance by the publishers, back to the fetid *barranca*, the ruined gardens, the religion of death, the Farolito, and the Oaxaquenian friend, Juan Fernando Márquez. As Conrad Knickerbocker has said so eloquently, "Mexico was fever, crisis, the dark night of the soul. Although the extremities were always to remain relative in [Lowry's] life, never again was he to pass through a valley as shadowed as the one that lay under the volcano."[20] —Not, at any rate, until he returned, half-terrified, to the same dark region, as if to pay tribute to the nightmare he hoped had finally run its course.

## II

Between August 1940 and November 1945 Lowry lived with his second wife Margerie in a shack they had built on the beach at Dollarton, British Columbia. This period, on the whole the happiest and the most productive of his entire career, was devoted to writing the successive drafts (four in all) of *Under the Volcano* and to finding a publisher for the work. A number of important changes were made as Lowry rewrote the book, chapter by chapter. He polished his use of colloquial Spanish and worked in a multitude of references to Mexican history and to contemporary events in Europe. The pivotal scene involving an Indian dying by the roadside was extensively elaborated until all its nuances were brought out. The sign in the garden, *"Le gusta este jardin que es suyo? Evite que sus hijos no lo destruyan!"*, was incorporated and gradually developed until it became emblematic of one of the novel's major themes. The motif of escape to a "northern paradise" was introduced, obviously the result of good times passed at Dollarton. Similarly, the character of Yvonne, based from the outset on Jan Gabrial, became increasingly sympathetic as Lowry grafted on certain of the more benevolent attributes of Margerie Lowry. Most important of all were the changes in the relationships of the central characters. In the earlier drafts Yvonne and Hugh had been lovers, while the Consul was her alcoholic father, separated from his wife Priscilla. In the final version Hugh and Geoffrey were made half-brothers, and Yvonne became the Consul's estranged wife as well as the former mistress of Hugh. "The point to be stressed," writes Richard Costa, "is that while Lowry was undergoing Moloch in Mexico . . . he was also *living* the early plot of *Under the Volcano*."[21] In other words the early versions depended all too closely upon the actual conflicts between Lowry and Conrad Aiken (represented by Hugh and the Consul, respectively), and between Lowry and Jan. Only through the exhaustive process of revision in the bracing atmosphere of Dollarton did Lowry transcend the muddle of real events and discover more illuminating possibilities through the exercise of his imagination. His alteration of the character relationships away from the biographical situation of 1936-38 amounts to what Costa terms the "victory of art over life."[22]

Just to prove how complete the victory was, Lowry decided in November of 1945 to return with Margerie to the scene of his old despair. Actually, the reasons he gave at the time of the trip were rather less histrionic than this. He

wanted to check on his usage of Mexican idioms, to look up
Juan Fernando Márquez (with whom he had lost contact in
recent years), and to show Margerie the country she had
come to know indirectly through his novel. The experiences
they shared during the greater part of this pilgrimage, which
lasted just over five months, are presented in Lowry's posthumously published and unfinished novel, *Dark As the
Grave Wherein My Friend Is Laid* (1968). As a novel, *Dark
As the Grave* is not a success. It is full of inconsistencies and
irrelevancies; its characters are, with the exception of the protagonist, totally vague, transparent, underdeveloped; its climax is unconvincing; it reads, in several long stretches, like a
shamelessly self-indulgent gloss on his earlier Mexican novel
—Lowry even referred to the book as "a sort of *Under Under
the Volcano*" (*Letters*, p. 267). In short, to use Costa's phrase,
*Dark As the Grave* is not a showpiece of the victory of art
over life. Lowry was unable before his death to complete the
elaborate incremental process which would have rendered it
a satisfying work of fiction. The editors, by poring over the
stacks of manuscript and notes and selecting certain versions
over others, have pieced together a work which strictly
speaking represents their own idea of the book rather than
what Lowry may have finally produced.[23] Only when all the
manuscript materials written by Lowry for *Dark As the
Grave* are published (if indeed they are ever published) can
the work be judged with any assurance as a novel, or rather a
novel-in-progress. Until such time it is perhaps best approached as a travel book.

Ordinarily one would hesitate to equate a fictional character with his author, even when a close relationship between
them is perceptible and can be demonstrated by biographical
data. In the case of *Dark As the Grave*, however, where the
process of imaginative elaboration of autobiographical narrative is incomplete, such an equation is possible. Primrose
Wilderness, the heroine, so far as she can be said to resemble
any human being, is clearly modeled on Margerie Lowry. An
even stronger argument can be made for equating her hus-

band Sigbjørn with his creator. As George Woodcock has observed, "Sigbjørn Wilderness *is* Lowry in a far deeper and more literal way than most characters can be described as *being* the novelists who create them...."[24] Indeed, in his preface to the book, Douglas Day states that the notebooks from which the published version of *Dark As the Grave* was pieced together so approximated an author's journal before being translated into fiction that "from time to time we had to cross out 'Malcolm said' and replace this with 'Sigbjørn said'; and there were many other names that had to be changed as well."[25] Bearing in mind that even an incomplete and partially-fictionalized book may contain *some* imaginary elements, the account which follows will use either the real or the fictional names depending upon which seem more appropriate in a given situation. When discussing scenes or passages from *Dark As the Grave* itself, it will be convenient to employ the names which appear in the book.

On November 28, 1945 the Lowrys flew from Vancouver to Los Angeles, where they spent two weeks visiting Margerie's family, and thence to Mexico City, arriving on December 11. During the flight Lowry was beset by numerous anxieties. To begin with, he was awaiting word from his publishers in England and America as to whether the final version of *Under the Volcano* would be accepted. His agent in New York, Harold Matson, had received the book with some misgivings, and Lowry was afraid that it would once again be rejected as an earlier draft had been, no less than thirteen times, in 1941. After so many years of exacting labor, the prospect of still more rewriting was most difficult for him to face. But there were more immediate "daemons" playing on his nerves during the long flight south. A fire had destroyed the Lowrys' shack eighteen months earlier and several manuscripts had been lost. In his grief Lowry had begun to drink again, a development which put considerable strain on his marriage. Among other things this trip was intended to serve as a kind of honeymoon during which he and Margerie might both enjoy themselves and renew the bond between them. But since their destination was Mexico, his old *tierra caliente* of the soul's anguish, where mescal could be had for less than a peso, the proposed honeymoon was anything but assured of being a success. Then there was his inordinate fear of passing through Customs—of "officials, border guards, Cónsuls, policemen, soldiers, figures of authority"—his horror of being turned back at the border (*Dark As the Grave*, p. 14). Yet despite all his forebodings about returning to the scene of his former misery, the scene also of the novel in which he had attempted to transcend that misery, Sigbjørn/Lowry is somehow reassured that rebirth rather than regression awaits him in the shadowy land across the border. Sigbjørn

> had suddenly a glimpse of a flowing like an eternal river; he seemed to see how life flowed into art: how art gives life a form and meaning and flows on into life, yet life has not stood still; that was what was always forgotten: how life transformed by art sought further meaning through art transformed by life; and now it was as if this flowing, this river, changed, without appearing to change, became a flowing of consciousness, of mind, so that it seemed that for them too, Primrose and he, just beyond that barrier, lay some meaning, or the key to a mystery that would give some meaning to their ways on earth: it was as if he stood on the brink of an illumination, on the near side of something tremendous, which was to be explained beyond, in that midnight darkness, but which his consciousness streamed into...and this flowing current appeared to him now in the guise of something irreversible.... (pp. 43-44)[26]

From the outset *Dark As the Grave* assumes the nature of this irreversible flow, in its prose style, in the meandrous reflections of its protagonist, in the constant circular movement of its two central figures. Over a third of the book takes place in transit between one place and another; typically, the focus of attention is the protagonist's overwrought anticipation of arriving at some spot ahead which is linked to his miserable past behind. Even in those chapters that are set in one locale such as Mexico City or Oaxaca, Sigbjørn and Primrose occupy themselves by walking about incessantly. One reason for this is that a major function of the trip was to exorcise the painful memories associated with all these places in Mexico. The Lowrys had determined, perhaps naively, that "they would make a pilgrimage to every hotel, every cantina he had known in the Thirties; and, by seeing them now as it were in the light of relative happiness and sanity, prove that they were not such nightmarish places as they had once seemed" (Day, p. 311).

Lowry was no more enamored of Mexico City than were the other English writers who visited it.

> Ah well, Mexico City, whose rush hour it was, seemed much the same [as in 1938], smells, noise, open cutouts, with which went the same invitation to get out of it as soon as possible: pulquerías, exactly as he had visualized them; the same peons; women with rebozos; cantinas; humped churches; so far at least there seemed little difference, save that there were more beer shops than formerly, and this inordinate number of ill-advised signs ordering one to drink ice-cold Coca-Cola. (pp. 72-73)

Walking the streets of the capital during their first night there, Sigbjørn—using the figure so prominent in the allusive subtext of the *Volcano*—thinks of himself, by virtue of his Mexican novel, as the conquistador of this land.

> In one way he was just walking happily down the street with Primrose . . . and looking forward to the future, to an enchanting holiday with her, and above all the opportunity of showing her Mexico. . . . In another he was treading, walking, much more seriously over a sort of spiritual battlefield, in which Sigbjørn, Cortez-like, was the conqueror, the horrors of experience here that had been so far transcended by the completion of his book and his presence in Mexico at all being the defeated

enemy. In yet another there was the sense that he had perhaps used treacherous forces to bring about his conquest . . . and by walking straight into the past like this, it was asking for them [i.e., the conquered] to have their revenge. On this level . . . the more he traveled upon it in his mind, the less like any kind of conquest was it, did it seem. Indeed it felt here more like a defeat, a monstrous defeat, a noche triste in fact. . . . (pp. 79-80)

This last premonition proves to be correct as, on an impulse, they check into the Hotel Coronada—where Lowry had gone with Jan in December 1937 in his futile attempt to convince his first wife not to leave him for good. Staying at this hotel, far from demonstrating his victory over the past, only convinces him that the past is still alive and waiting to take its revenge on him. "It was," writes Lowry, "as if the ghost of a man who had hanged himself had returned to the scene of his suicide, not out of morbid curiosity, but out of sheer nostalgia to drink the drinks again that had nerved him to do it, and wonder perhaps that he had ever had the courage" (p. 77). Sigbjørn tries to make Primrose aware of his troubled thoughts, but she is too caught up in her own excitement at being in a strange new place to give him any solace. When he confesses that he is more afraid of Oaxaca than anywhere else in the world, unless it is Cuernavaca, she immediately and gaily proposes that they go right away to Oaxaca, to Cuernavaca. Proclaiming already that she loves Mexico, she tells him that she wants " 'to drink what you drank and do everything that you did' " (p. 80). Before the night is over Sigbjørn begins to realize the folly of their well-intended notions of exorcising the old ghosts. It was

during the night, their first night in Mexico, that there had begun slowly to be borne in upon him the real positive psychic, if obscure, danger in which he stood and to which he had deliberately, and even delightedly, brought . . . them: . . . with [Primrose] it was a matter, in her concern for him, of laying ghosts. But with him it was rather

different.... [For] one thing by far the most potent
ghost he had to encounter was himself, and he had very
considerable doubts as to whether it wanted to be laid at
all. (p. 93)

Such disquieting doubts were to recur throughout the trip,
and more than once Lowry suggested to Margerie that perhaps catching the next plane headed north might be as good a
way as any to dispel the hold of the past. But she insisted that
they remain: "They had to see Cuernavaca and its *barrancas;*
they had to visit Oaxaca, to see the Farolito. And, of course,
there was Lowry's good angel, Juan Fernando Márquez...
and they could not very well leave Mexico before they had
seen him" (Day, p. 312).

They remained a week in Mexico City, and it was during
this time that something new and rather important began to
emerge in Lowry's view of Mexico. In fact, this development,
had Lowry lived long enough to bring out its entire significance convincingly in *Dark As the Grave,* might have made
the book a true companion piece to the *Volcano,* the two
works together representing a fully balanced picture of Mexico as both infernal and paradisal. Wilderness/Lowry began
to realize the new perspective during an incident at the Shrine
of Guadalupe. Sigbjørn and Primrose had gone there to
observe the annual festivities in honor of the Indian Virgin.
The scene outside the Basilica had been a pleasant one, as
they watched it from the safe distance of a *cerveceria* across
the street from the Shrine. Then there occurred a distasteful
episode which almost ruined the whole outing. Watching the
crowd milling outside, they looked on in horror as a drunk
carrying a stick suddenly and unaccountably began to beat a
blind woman who happened to be walking by, carrying a
dead dog. The people in the shop moved forward en masse to
watch this brutal scene, and Primrose's drink was upset. Sigbjørn went to pay the bill, but before he knew what was happening the drunk with the stick was inside the shop, threatening *him,* calling him an American imperialist. Sigbjørn's

protestations were cut short by the news that the police had been summoned. As he and Primrose made a quick exit, Sig-bjørn thought once again of the tangible dangers awaiting the unsuspecting foreigner in Mexico. Outside, the chaotic scene around the Shrine seemed at first to exemplify his thoughts. But in the midst of it all suddenly there was a sense of mys-terious yet unmistakable beatitude, persevering in spite of the raucous din.

> The tumultous scene about the basilica was very curi-ous: the merry-go-rounds and obscene or gruesome side-shows . . . with the shouts of "Step up ladies and gentle-men and see the amazing spectacle of the head that has his body devoured by rats," the wild pagan dances . . . and the feeling of definite *pilgrimage* toward the basilica . . . the sense of sacred miracle preserved in the midst of all this chaos, the contrast of the bishop speaking, or rather mutely opening and closing his mouth . . . and yet pronouncing in the midst of all this his benediction . . . on all present, even Sigbjørn and Primrose, as the yelling jukeboxes shrieked and whinnied in English louder and louder, "I'm dreaming of a white Christmas"—all this had an absurdity and horror, would have been justified as an experience simply by its overwhelming effect of absurdity and ugliness, but for the equally overwhelm-ing sense of something sublime everywhere present, of faith. (p. 101)

This scene, taken in its entirety from the drunk with the stick to the priest's eloquently mute benediction, approximates the intended progress of Wilderness/Lowry toward the eventual realization of a spiritual and psychic rebirth occurring pre-cisely *within* this land haunted by the specter of himself. The fact that the revelation occurs before the Shrine of Guada-lupe, through four centuries (and countless political vicissi-tudes) the most revered symbol in all Mexico, demonstrates again Lowry's knack of keying his personal myth to impor-tant elements of the native myth.

Welcome as it is, this first intimation of potential redemption is a fleeting one, and Sigbjørn's progress toward it is slow and tortuous. "No peace but that must pay full toll to hell," Lowry had written in *Under the Volcano* (p. 108). On December 18 the Lowrys, seated inconspicuously in the back as usual, rode the bus down the mountains to Cuernavaca. Lowry had not determined where they would stay in the town or how long they would remain there. His only plan regarding their arrival was to find a drink as soon as possible. As they approached Cuernavaca he began to compare it with the Quauhnahuac of his novel and was surprised to note so many differences until he remembered that *his* town was embellished by memories of "Oaxaca and sus anexas" (*Dark As the Grave*, p. 105). Stopping in a familiar cantina they were surprised and delighted to discover that there was an apartment available in the Quinta Dolores, a strange mosque-like building with great towers and chevron-shaped windows, the very place in which Lowry had housed his character Jacques Laruelle in the *Volcano*. During their first days in town Lowry, thinking of himself as Margerie's "guide, her Virgil, through these intricate regions of ancient fire and purge and transcendent beauty" (*Dark As the Grave*, p. 72), took her on a personal tour of the landmarks of his novel— the palace of Cortés with its disquieting murals depicting the Conquest, the Borda Gardens of the doomed lovers Maximilian and Carlotta, and of course the dread *barranca*. But after the initial excitement had worn off, Lowry began to have some misgivings about being back in Cuernavaca, for "it seemed to him that he was in grave danger of being taken over by his own fiction, of becoming a character in his own novel. The idea was fascinating, but terrifying" (Day, pp. 313-314). Again we have the conquistador gazing back on the spiritual battlefield and wondering if he is not after all the victim of his own schemes.

The Lowrys remained four weeks in Cuernavaca. The first two were uneventful as Lowry, becoming increasingly pre-occupied over the expected letter from the publishers concerning the fate of his novel, found himself less and less interested in his immediate surroundings. He began to depend on his wife to observe things in the town and describe them for him. Thus, in *Dark As the Grave*, as Primrose exults over the marketplace, the street singers, the great volcanoes, Sigbjørn is so bound up in his anxieties that he fails even to see such things. Why bother to look at them, he thinks, when everything in the end winds up cast into the *barranca* anyway? "... Sigbjørn found himself sinking more and more into fear, into a barranca, his own, a barranca of fear of he knew not what! Ah, the strangeness of Mexico, and this fear that possesses one like a paralysis..." (p. 164). On December 31 the anticipated letter arrived from Jonathan Cape, the English publisher. This letter, which included a reader's report with lengthy and obtuse objections to the novel, indicated an interest in publishing *Volcano*, but extensive changes were suggested. Although he was hurt and disappointed by this news, Lowry decided to meet the challenge by writing, with Margerie's help, an extensive defense of his book as it stood, including a chapter-by-chapter commentary. This remarkable document took the next two weeks to write. During its composition Lowry was frequently depressed—such exegesis cannot have been a pleasant task—and his drinking increased proportionately. On January 9, after an unsuccessful attempt to break the tedious routine with an excursion culminated in a bad quarrel and an evening of serious mescal-drinking, Lowry sliced open his left wrist with a razor. Apparently the attempted suicide was half-hearted. In any event, Margerie soon discovered him and called a doctor. After a few days' rest Lowry finished the letter to Cape and mailed it off on January 15.

If Lowry was too preoccupied, in one way or another, to pay much attention to Cuernavaca during the four weeks spent there, Oaxaca, site of both his worst misery and his profoundest contact with Mexico, was already on his mind. On New Year's Eve day, before receiving the letter from the publisher, the Wildernesses had made an excursion to the

village of Yautepec, about twenty miles southeast of Cuernavaca. Arriving there around noon, they decided to take advantage of the view to be had from the top of a large hill on
the outskirts of the village. From the top of the hill they could
see the whole valley surrounding them, and more.

> They laughed and then stopped. For beyond the vol-
> canoes far, far beyond the horizon, impossibly far away,
> almost like the White Sea and Arabia, almost like a
> dream, beyond the farthest mountains, as might have
> appeared the Promised Land to the Children of Israel . . .
> it had seemed to Sigbjørn, pointing, that there, dimly
> and for the first time, was a shadowy hint of Oaxaca.
> (p. 172)

Seen (or imagined) thus at high noon during a pleasant jaunt,
Oaxaca might seem a Promised Land, but the longer the idea
of actually going there remained in Sigbjørn's thoughts the
more the place took on the aspect of abyssal darkness. "No
darkness has the same quality of hopelessness as the darkness
in Mexico," Sigbjørn reflects at one point (p. 181). And for
Sigbjørn/Lowry Oaxaca was the heart—"The word was like
a breaking heart," the Consul had said—of that Mexican
darkness. Back in Cuernavaca two weeks later, after the
hedging letter from the publishers and the mescal and the suicide attempt, Sigbjørn climbs up to the roof of Quinta Dolores to take in the prospect of nocturnal Mexico:

> . . . here in the moonlight he looked out over Cuerna-
> vaca. . . . He looked north, south, east, west, even to the
> pyramid Teopanzolco. He thought of Christmas, New
> Year's Eve again, and what had been the New Year . . .
> and even of the Easter they had planned to spend here,
> all the festivals of hope. Then his fear, his sense of per-
> secution suddenly came back in full force, and as if in
> response to this he found that he was looking straight
> toward the light on the skeletonic prison watchtower.
> . . . [He thought of] the prison in Oaxaca, and that
> Christmas morning. . . . [North], south, east, and west,

he looked back over the rolling barren hills and tragic clefts, and broken roads, and cactus plains, and false volcanoes of his own life, and saw little light...save that afforded by madness: yet this was a fertile valley. Was he really looking over toward Oaxaca, were those dark plains Oaxaca?—Oaxaca, where was really Parián —and terror struck him again—his image for death.... [He] had never had the feeling so strongly that he was standing *within* his book.... (pp. 158-159)

Here Oaxaca is imagined not as a potential Promised Land to which Sigbjørn and Primrose may be led on their salvific pilgrimage, but as the wilderness itself—or rather Wilderness himself. It is part of the world he has created, his infernal Parián under the volcano, with its prison and its Farolito. And the worst of it is that he is already there, already standing *within* his "image for death."

Considering all of this, it would seem that the decision to board the bus and actually go to Oaxaca is, if not a surrender to anticlimax, then certainly a surrender to a death-wish, an extension of the earlier suicide attempt. It would seem so were it not for the fact that Oaxaca was also the home of Juan Fernando Márquez, Lowry's "good angel." Oaxaca, the locus of nightmare and misery, is at the same time the place in which Lowry had formed his great friendship with Juan Fernando. And for Sigbjørn/Lowry, Juan Fernando is the embodiment of "the lifeward principle" (p. 192), the "symbol of all Mexico" (p. 92). He is "the only saving grace of Mexico," and he "belong[s] to Oaxaca" (p. 83). Oaxaca, then, is both the Promised Land and the cactus plains of the wilderness, just as Sigbjørn/Lowry is both conquistador and victim. *Dark As the Grave* is the record of a pilgrimage that is essentially a quest for both death and the transcendent ideal. It is the allure of these dualities which accounts for the fact that for Lowry—as for D. H. Lawrence, who both feared and venerated the Indians—Oaxaca was the crux of the entire Mexican experience.

The Lowrys arrived in Oaxaca on January 18, 1946. They

checked into the Hotel Francia, where Lowry had stayed in
the bad old days after Jan's departure in 1937-38. Walking
around the town Lowry was struck by how different everything seemed from the City of Dreadful Night he had carried
in his mind through the years: "...there was the curious
sense of it being no longer Oaxaca" (p. 214). Another surprise befell him that first night during supper at the hotel.
Whom should he see sitting across the room but Bousfield,
the mysterious "dark angel" of his Acapulco days. Ashamed
of running across this reminder of his miserable past and
more than a little afraid that a reunion with Bousfield might
prove to be a temptation to resume his former ways, Lowry
dodged the man as long as he could. Two days later, however, Bousfield called on Lowry in the latter's hotel room.
The visit was brief and rather disappointingly dull. Now a
prosperous businessman and owner of a silver mine, Bousfield seemed anything but a dangerous man.

Lowry was beginning to doubt the accuracy of his former
impressions of Oaxaca. The place was neither as fearful nor
as beautiful as he had remembered it. If Bousfield had turned
out to be an ordinary mortal, might not Juan Fernando also
prove a disappointment? And the Farolito, would it now be
graced with a neon sign ordering one to drink ice-cold Coca-
Cola? Such thoughts provided new grounds for his fear of
confronting the "ghosts" of his past. After all, in order for
Sigbjørn/Lowry to be able to write the book he had been
contemplating, a novel called *Dark As the Grave Wherein
My Friend Is Laid*, for which he had already begun making
notes, he required—or so he had thought—some kind of
locale which would lend itself, at least in his mind's eye, to a
kind of marriage of heaven and hell. An outing to Monte
Albán postponed for another day the task of looking up Juan
Fernando. Despite their being a monument to Juan Fernando's Zapotecan heritage, Lowry did not find the ruins
very engaging. Back in Oaxaca itself the Lowrys discovered
in the course of a stroll through the city that the old Salón
Ofélia run by a man named Cervantes, the restaurant-bar in

which the Consul had taken his first mescal of the day in Chapter X of the *Volcano*, had become a drugstore. Then farther on they found that the *Banco Ejidal* where Juan Fernando had actually lived had been moved to another part of town, the old building left vacant. Half disappointed and half relieved, Lowry could not bring himself as yet to seek out the new location. Finally, on January 20, the Lowrys determined that, having come all this way in large part to see Juan Fernando again, they must find him no matter what. Once at the new *Banco Ejidal* they inquired about their friend, and, after some initial confusion, learned that he was dead. In horror they listened to the story of how Juan Fernando, suffering from mescal-induced delirium, had been shot six years earlier in a cantina in Villahermosa, Tabasco. (It is curious that in writing about these matters in *Dark As the Grave*, a book containing elsewhere so much commentary on the earlier Mexican novel, Lowry did not make more of the striking and rather disturbing similarity between Juan Fernando's death and the Consul's.) Leaving the bank in tears, the Lowrys proceeded to the Templo del Carmen (Alturo) where they said a prayer for the dead friend. The next day they journeyed to the ruins at Mitla but were still too depressed to take much interest in these Zapotecan burial grounds.

Waking early the next morning back in town, Lowry went alone from the hotel to pay tribute to the last of his Oaxacan specters, the Farolito. It was his final chance to discover whether the self-destructive lure of his past here still had any of the old power over him.

Why did such a grim inexplicable ecstasy attach his mind to these early morning debauches of his, [Sigbjørn] wondered. Was it because it was partly associated in his mind, not with evil but with consciousness? It was consciousness born of and intensified by sorrow and despair but it was still consciousness. . . . [Perhaps] he had not entirely wasted his time at the Farolito. Perhaps he had grown in some inexplicable manner there. Or perhaps what he had experienced was tantamount to some kind

of illumination, perhaps it was some sort of mystical experience that suffering had caused him to undergo. . . .
The Farolito was somehow associated with freedom.
. . . Could that have been called happiness? If not, why
did he look back upon it with such an inexplicable yearning? For . . . Fernando was not the only or even the
strongest tie to the Farolito. It was himself, his lonely
dying youth. (*Dark As the Grave*, pp. 251-252)

These interesting speculations—all but the last—would never
be confirmed with any final assurance, for what Lowry found
when he arrived at the Farolito was that it too had been
moved to a new location. He started to look for the new spot
but soon gave it up. The Lowrys left Oaxaca that same morning, after a stay of just four days. Douglas Day sums up the
significance of Lowry's second visit to Oaxaca as follows:
"Temporarily, at any rate, it seemed that the hoped-for exorcism of old ghosts had begun at last to work. Juan Fernando
. . . was dead, which was too bad; but they had seen the Hotel
Francia and the Farolito, and had learned (slightly to Lowry's
disappointment) that no particular horror inhered in them:
they were, simply, places" (Day, p. 354). Though Day errs
on one specific point—the Lowrys had *not* really seen the
Farolito—his conclusion, from a strictly biographical standpoint, is probably correct. During the long years of his work
on the *Volcano*, Lowry no doubt identified Oaxaca with his
Parián, a mental construct complete with its own Farolito.
Both Juan Fernando and his home town had become major
elements in Lowry's personal myth, which had so expanded
through the years that his return to the *real* Oaxaca was
bound to disappoint. And despite the relief Lowry must have
felt at the apparently successful "exorcism" of his old terrors,
one suspects that he was fundamentally downcast at the irrevocable loss of his "dying youth." The sense of anticlimax
certainly hovers over the final pages of *Dark As the Grave*.
Lowry, as if aware of this, resorts to extreme measures to
prevent its sabotaging the book. The interesting thing is that
even though he worked on *Dark As the Grave* in the years

after his second Mexican trip—after, that is, the discovery that Oaxaca did not live up to his expectations—he wrote the chapters leading up to his arrival there from his old "daemonic" point of view. Thus, having postulated the quintessential importance of Oaxaca and all it involved for him, he could not very well shift ground and admit that it was simply another place. Lowry's dilemma, as well as his means of resolving it in his writing, again recalls Lawrence's difficulty in reconciling the Indians of his "American vision" shaped before his visits to Mexico with those he came into contact with in Oaxaca.

If the Oaxaca of 1946 did not turn out to be the Parián of the Day of the Dead, 1938, it must be something else, something similarly correlative to the spiritual condition of Sigbjørn Wilderness: it must still *mean*. To say merely that Juan Fernando is dead and the old *Banco Ejidal* closed down will not do. These abrupt nullifications of the past which had had such significance for the protagonist cannot go unanswered. So, in the last chapter, Sigbjørn approaches the building where the old bank had been located, and where he and Juan Fernando had once commiserated with each other over a bottle of mescal. Sigbjørn finds the building unlocked and looks inside: "The whole place was in glorious bloom, packed along its entire length and breadth with blossoms and riots of roses. . . . [The *Banco Ejidal*] had become a garden. 'Remember Parsifal,' Sigbjørn told himself" (p. 245). As the Wildernesses leave Oaxaca, sitting for once in the front of the bus, "something seemed to have changed in Sigbjørn, he felt glad to be alive, he was enjoying the trip . . ." (p. 254). Then, looking out at the valley of Etla, the seat of the Zapotecan kings who were Fernando's ancestors, Sigbjørn realizes that the *Banco Ejidal* has indeed become a garden.

Etla again and the mountains, mountains, mountains of mysterious Oaxaca. Sigbjørn remembered eight years before the dreadful poverty of the villages, the pitiful few fields of corn and the sense of so much of the land

that could be used to bring fruitfulness to the people
lying idle simply for want of a little help. This time he
was conscious of a great change, directly the result of the
work of the Bank. Everywhere one saw rich green fields,
felt a sense of fruitfulness, and of the soil responding and
of men living as they ought to live, in the wind and sun
and close to the soil and loving the soil. Those farms
were lovingly tended too and cared for.... [The] fields
were terraced and contoured, the earth displaying the
feeling and genius of the people for their land—but they
never could have done it without the Banco's help....
   ...It was all so different from eight years ago....
Oaxaca had become the granary of nearly all of Mexico.
   ... (pp. 254-255)

The passage is doubly revealing. First, it amounts to the
fullest expression of Lowry's belief in not merely the historical necessity but also the practical efficacy of the Mexican
Revolution with regard to its important agrarian reforms.
Subsequent events during this Mexican visit would put a
damper on his belief in the right-mindedness of anyone connected with the government. He would even go so far, later
on, as to see the Revolution as fatuous, run by the devil, even
more corrupt than the *Porfiriato*. But on the local level at
least, as the above passage indicates, he saw that the Revolution's agrarian policies, administered by good men like Juan
Fernando, were producing dramatic results. The passage is
also interesting in its mythopoeic aspects, offering as it does
several hints as to what Lowry might have made of the Oaxacan experience had he been able to bring the book to completion. The elements are all here: Parsifal the quester, the physical and spiritual Waste Land or Wilderness, the descent into
darkness, the trials and temptations, the dead Fisher King
figure, the Chapel Perilous (a conflation of the old and new
Farolito and *Banco Ejidal*), the renewal of life. But if the
archetypal pattern, in rough form, is adumbrated in the conclusion of *Dark As the Grave*, the human embodiment of it,
as Lowry left him, is not quite up to the demands placed

upon him by the myth. The problem is that Sigbjørn's "rebirth" does not issue from a genuine resolution of his inner conflicts. Rather, he has merely inferred his rebirth from the external changes he has found in Oaxaca since his last visit. What would have happened had the Farolito been in its old spot, its doors open at four in the morning, with mescal to be had for less than a peso? Chances are that Sigbjørn would have had a few mescals and still have found—given the epic dimensions of his expectations—that the place, like the man Bousfield, had lost its "daemonic" influence over him. But he will never know for certain.

In *Under the Volcano* Geoffrey Firmin is finally stripped of all his escapist illusions and made to see the serious human failings of his existence. Sigbjørn, on the other hand, despite all his suffering, has not paid full toll to hell for the peace he believes he has found. Miscast as Parsifal, he was closest to realizing the truth about his life when he trod the spiritual battlefield as both conquistador and victim. Try as he might to will a cure into being, Lowry still carried the virus of his Mexican "affliction."

## III

> Mexico is the most Christ-awful place in the world in which to be in any form of distress, a sort of Moloch that feasts on suffering souls. . . . All in all a good place to stay out of. . . .
>
> —Letter to David Markson from Dollarton, postmarked May 20, 1954[27]

The Lowrys were back at the Quinta Dolores in Cuernavaca by January 23. With the letter to Cape out of the way and the Sirens' song of Oaxaca no longer beckoning, Lowry spent the next six weeks pleasantly enough, relaxing, swimming, and sun-bathing in the resort town. He and Margerie found time to make brief trips to Puebla and Tlaxcala. This period, writes Day, "seems in the main to have been one of the quietest of their lives" (p. 355). Even though Tlaxcala plays a rather important role in the key scene at the Salón Ofélia in Chapter X of *Under the Volcano,* Lowry does not appear to have felt any particular compulsion about the place. According to Margerie Lowry, "Nothing outstanding happened when we went to Tlaxcala. Malcolm had never been there before, [had] simply picked up somewhere the folder he quoted [in the *Volcano*]. It is a beautiful sleepy town in the mountains with a gentle river and cattle grazing on the banks and slopes."[28]

If there were still any ghosts to be laid the only place left to find them was Acapulco. By the beginning of March the Lowrys, becoming somewhat restless in their leisure, considered returning to British Columbia, but decided instead to devote a week to the last stop on their original itinerary. This move in itself suggests that Lowry was less than completely satisfied with the victory over fear he felt he had won at Oaxaca. In any event, they arrived in Acapulco on March 10 and checked into the Hotel Monterrey. Things began to go badly almost at once. As when they were first in Oaxaca, Lowry worried that the misdeeds of his 1938 visit would return to plague him and that at least part of him would welcome them back. He felt certain that he was being eyed suspiciously in the hotel by people who recognized him from the old days. To quiet his forebodings he and Margerie moved to another hotel closer to the beach. Unfortunately they were assigned here to room 13, and "the always superstitious Lowry was quite anxious throughout their third day in Acapulco, which was...March 13" (Day, p. 357). He cannot have derived much satisfaction when his fears proved to be correct the next day and disaster did strike in the form of two inquisitive officials from the Office of *Migración.*

The remainder of their time in Mexico was dominated by a frustrating and sometimes harrowing comedy of errors resulting from this conflict with officialdom. The experience was the chief subject of yet another unfinished Mexican novel, *La*

*Mordida*, which has not been published.[29] Lowry was informed that there was a file on him in the office which indicated that he had failed to pay a fifty-peso fine for overstaying his visa in 1938. He was thus in Mexico illegally at the moment. Lowry protested that he knew of no such fine and that his present visit to Mexico had been cleared by the Mexican Consulate in Los Angeles where he had obtained his visa in December. However, he had no proof of this, since, having anticipated only a short stay in Acapulco, the Lowrys had left their papers behind in Cuernavaca. The two officials were not convinced by his story and ordered the Lowrys to remain at their hotel until further notice.

The entire affair might well have been smoothed over at this point had it occurred to Lowry simply to pay the usual bribe, the *mordida* (literally, the "bite") by which one traditionally extricates oneself from such difficulties in Mexico. Fifty pesos, after all, was then only about ten dollars; this amount, plus perhaps a little additional payment for the two men's "trouble" in locating him, would probably have saved all concerned a great deal of confusion and distress. But Lowry was paralyzed by fear. His dread of figures of authority had returned with a vengeance. He could not think of anything to do for it but drink, which he proceeded to do despite Margerie's protestations. With Lowry unable to devise any plan of action, she was left to do all the negotiating with the officials. There ensued "one of the worst quarrels of their marriage" (Day, p. 359).

Six days of visits to the *Migración* office in town produced no results. When Lowry asked to see what was in his file, he was dutifully shown not only the documents pertaining to his unpaid fine but also copious evidence of his unruly behavior eight years earlier. He "had apparently been picked up time and again for drunkenness and misconduct. 'Borracho, borracho, borracho,' said the sub-chief, slapping the file. 'Here is your life'" (Day, p. 360). On March 20 Lowry was threatened with jail if the fine were not paid in the next three days. After more haggling, Margerie was allowed to go back alone to Cuernavaca and retrieve their papers and money. When she returned they paid the fine before the deadline and asked if they might now be permitted to leave. Their request was denied. Although the fine had been paid, the *Migración* office in Acapulco had to wait for further instructions from Mexico City concerning the "case." For the next ten days the Lowrys waited in their hotel without further word from the office.

On April 4, after twenty-six days in Acapulco, they were authorized to return to Cuernavaca. Two days after their arrival there Lowry received word from both his English and American publishers that *Under the Volcano* had been accepted for publication as it stood. This excellent news might have ended the second Mexican sojourn on a hopeful note but for the fact that the conflict with the federal bureaucracy was still not ended: it had simply shifted to Mexico City. The remainder of April was spent traveling back and forth between their apartment in Cuernavaca and the capital, where they were determined against all odds to clear up the misunderstanding. Lowry's description of these trips in his letter to Ronald Button gives some idea of what they had to endure.

It should be said that it is about fifty miles from Cuernavaca to Mexico City but this gives no idea of the character of the trip. Though it only takes two or two and a half hours it is necessary to climb to an altitude of over 10,000 feet and one frequently arrives deafened. The climate likewise is completely different: one leaves Cuernavaca in tropical heat and you are likely at this time of year to run into a snow storm in the mountains: beautiful in itself, such a journey, endlessly repeated under such conditions becomes a nightmare, especially since it is difficult to make reservations either by car or bus, both are prone to break down on the way, and from all this my wife's health especially began to suffer. Despite this we managed to keep every appointment during the following four weeks punctually, yet we never waited less than three hours [at the office] and usually four or five hours. We are far from wealthy people; had budgeted our vacation very carefully, and we were put to what was for us near fatal expense to make these frequent trips for ourselves and often an interpreter.... [We] calculated that we travelled well over a thousand miles during those four weeks simply between Cuernavaca and Mexico City and probably it was more like twelve hundred. (*Letters*, pp. 99-100)

It took two of these trips before they were even admitted to see the Chief of *Inspección*, one Señor Corunna. This official greeted them with the news that something else had been found against them. They had, he said, entered Mexico under false pretenses of being mere tourists when in fact they were both writers who were working while in the country. The penalty for this infraction was an additional fine of 500 pesos or else deportation. Lowry cannot have missed the irony of this latest turn of events. Back in 1938, while in the Oaxaca jail, he had been told by his captors that his alibi had not been believed: he was not a "wrider," as he had said, but an "espider," and "we shoota de espiders in Mejico." Now, a generous friend paid the 500 pesos for them, and they left for Cuernavaca with the Chief's assurance that all their papers would be returned and they would not be bothered further. Several days passed and the papers were not forthcoming. The trips back and forth over the mountains began again. The British Consulate for some reason refused to assist them. Meanwhile the Chief of *Inspección* "threw one obstacle after another at them: they could not leave [Mexico] until they had airline reservations. But they could not secure reservations until they had received their immigration papers—which they could not have until they had had photographs made" (Day, pp. 363, 365). Señor Corunna had taken to shouting hysterically at the Lowrys during their interviews, alternately insulting and threatening them. The ordeal began to take its toll on Lowry. His drinking, which had been heavy since

Acapulco, got no better; he frequently suffered from the
shakes; he began to depend on phenobarbital to control himself during the virulent sessions with Corunna and his menacing subordinates. Margerie, still resentful of her husband and
depressed by the entire situation, recorded her feelings of this
period in her journal:

> I am so tired, so tired, so tired, tired, tired, I don't care
> except for a dull anger that flames and rages now and
> then. . . . And hatred, and disgust that I'm dragged down
> myself with trying to drink with him and a hatred of bot-
> tles and exhaustion and a sense of my soul slipping away
> and my whole grip on life. I feel . . . a despair so utter . . .
> that all I want is death. Why don't I kill myself? Is it
> some vague lingering loyalty to [Malcolm] whom I must
> still love but now only hate and despise and fear?
> (Quoted in Day, p. 363).

The harassment continued through April. On May 2 the
Lowrys were sent to jail in Mexico City, there to remain until
the "Chiefs" decided what to do to them next. They were
treated with a surprising kindness and consideration at the
prison (where they spent several hours), except that someone
broke into their luggage and made off with a camera and
some of Margerie's clothes. Finally they were taken to the
railroad station and, in the company of an armed police inspector, put on a train headed north to the border. At Nuevo
Laredo they were ushered into another *Migración* office and
asked to sign a paper, a legal document they had difficulty
translating. Repeatedly they were assured that their own
papers were all in order and that they were definitely not
being deported. But Lowry had been by now so continually
lied to by the authorities that he lost all capacity to trust in
their word—"if all this," he writes, "why not *ley fuga*?" (*Letters*, p. 109). There was indeed cause for alarm, for when
they hesitated at first to sign the paper the inspector made
them aware (as if they had forgotten) that he was wearing a
gun and knew how to make good use of it. They had no

choice but to sign the paper. The next morning—it was May 4, 1946, seven weeks after they had first been descended upon by the two officials in Acapulco—the Lowrys were sent across the bridge into the United States, "legally" deported as undesirable aliens.

## IV

Banishment—this was the sentence pronounced again and again by the world upon Malcolm Lowry, who eventually faced the threat of eviction even from his "northern paradise" at Dollarton. His only recourse was the demonstrably unsatisfactory option of travel, that "migraine of alienation," as he once called it, [30] by means of which you go "from the society of people you are not quite sure like you, among people whom you know for certain despise you" (*Dark As the Grave*, p. 47). For obvious reasons Lowry never again returned to Mexico after the disastrous trip of 1945-46. But the country remained an important part of his mental landscape. Though he was to proclaim that an amicable truce had been reached between them in the final pages of *Dark As the Grave*, it is clear that Lowry never fully forgave Mexico for the pain inflicted on him there.

In the winter of 1947 the Lowrys made another voyage, this time to Europe via the Panama Canal. During the course of this trip, which is described in the novella "Through the Panama," Lowry indulged in some reflections which are suggestive of his ultimate stance regarding Mexico. The Lowry-persona, once again Sigbjørn Wilderness, is sailing with his wife Primrose aboard the S. S. *Diderot* down the west coast of the North American continent toward the Canal. One night in November they cross the border into the territorial waters of Mexico. Sigbjørn stands by the hour on deck gazing off at the dark coastline, with its "giant pinnacles, images of barrenness and desolation, on which the heart is thrown and impaled eternally...." [31] Sigbjørn, who is working on a novel based on the last trip to Mexico called *Dark As the Grave Wherein My Friend Is Laid*, takes down his thoughts in his journal throughout the voyage: "Indigo sea, black tortured shapes of mountains and sharp-pointed islands, a beautiful nightmare against a gold sky.... Try to sleep and cannot. Too close to Mexico?" ("Panama," p. 37).

As the *Diderot* passes by Acapulco, Sigbjørn recalls that this was the port of his original entry into Mexico in 1936. It is also the place where the protagonist of his novel "meets his nemesis," where " 'it' all began to happen" (p. 41). But more than this, Sigbjørn realizes that Acapulco emanates a meaning for himself, even now as he sails by it in safety. "A sense of exile oppresses me," he notes in his journal.

> A sense of something else, beyond injustice and misery, extramundane, oppresses, more than desolates, more than confounds me. To pass this place like this.... [All] this somber horror is lying calmly to port, slowly going astern, innocent as Southend-on-Sea.... I know what the feeling must resemble; exactly that of a ghost who revisits some place on earth to which it is irresistibly drawn. (pp. 41-42)

Yet, reasons Sigbjørn, how can he of all people be drawn to this of all places? Remembering the horror visited upon him by the government officials less than a year and a half ago, Sigbjørn drowns his inexplicable longing for Mexico in a scalding bath of scorn: "Country of the Absolute Devil.... How many Americans, Canadians, murdered there every year. Hushed up, without investigation, to save face. ... [The] Mexican government seems still controlled by Satan. ... All Mexicans know it, fear it, do nothing about it, finally, despite revolutions; at bottom it is more corrupt than in the days of Diaz" (pp. 42-43).

One could doubtless make a case for Sigbjørn's harsh judgment of the Mexican political machinery and those who exploit it. Also his personal rancor is quite understandable under the cirumstances. Nevertheless, Sigbjørn's inclination without reservation to attribute human error and wrong-doing, however dire their consequences, to a Satanic power controlling an entire country only obscures the real problem. After all, in his own case Sigbjorn, like the man who created him, had played no small part in the catastrophes which befell him during his two stays in Mexico. But to Sigbjørn *they* are wholly responsible for his sufferings as well as those of Primrose. "I'll get them for that," he vows, "if it is the last thing I do, on paper anyhow" (p. 43). And he tries to do precisely this, later on, recording his thoughts as the ship sails closer to the Canal: "A plague on all Central American republics with their corruption, their cuteness, their dictators, their mordidas, their tourists, their fatuous revolutions, their volcanoes, their history and their heat! The abomination of desolation, standing in the holy place" (p. 51). These are the words—almost endearing in their human grouchiness, their ingenuous equation of the trivial with the momentous—of a weary, ill-tempered tourist, not the cry of a soul in hell. It is as if the dimensions of the land which had aroused such a passionate and profound response in Lowry have suddenly been reduced, by the "I'll-get-them" motive, to something more manageable: hell reduces to heat, paradise to cuteness. Fortunately, at his best, in *Under the Volcano*, Lowry saw and wrote otherwise. Geoffrey Firmin did not for a moment doubt that he was living in hell, but he realized what Lowry seems finally to have forgotten: that hell "is not Mexico of course but in the heart" (*Volcano*, p. 36).

# Appendix
## The Fields of Paradise

Ralph Bates lived in Spain from 1923 to 1938. During that time he was affiliated with the Communist Party and involved himself in the problems of rural laborers. When the Civil War broke out he volunteered for service in the Loyalist Army and helped to organize the International Brigades. In the meantime he began his writing career, publishing several fictional works treating Spanish social problems, most notably *The Olive Field* (1936), and a biography of Schubert. In August 1937 he went to the United States on a fund-raising tour on behalf of the Loyalist cause, and it was in this capacity that he made his first visit to Mexico the following year. He remained there for about seven months and, when Franco's victory was imminent, returned to Mexico for another seven-month stay before relocating in New York, where he took a position as Adjunct Professor of Literature at New York University until his retirement in 1968. He now lives on Naxos in the Cyclades.

While in Mexico Bates stayed mostly in Mexico City and Villa Obregón, though he traveled extensively in the rural regions to the south of the capital. He seems in fact to have immersed himself in the country. In a series of magazine articles that he wrote about Mexico at the time, he makes reference to a personal meeting with President Cárdenas, whom he regards as "among the great figures of the age"; to having read not only "about all the books published on Mexico in the last few years" but also hundreds of letters sent to the

Cárdenas government by rural peasants; to having been invited to attend a session of the commissariat of an *ejido* in Puebla and a congress of peasants in Mexico City.[1] Though these articles touch on many political issues of the day, they return repeatedly to the impoverished, dispirited Indian as the focal point, and to the *ejido* system as the one hope for the future of Mexico. Indeed, Bates goes so far as to call the *ejido* "the sign of a new faith" that was gaining ascendancy over the embattled faith of the past, the faith represented by "the churchyard and the ruined presbytery."[2]

In "Conversations in Mexico," a personal essay that amounts to his only attempt at travel writing in a strict sense, Bates tells of an incident that took place during a hike into the mountains. Entering a forest glade he finds himself suddenly surrounded by sheep, the midday silence dispelled by a chorus of bleating. It is a fortuitous encounter (though not so fortuitous in the Mexican countryside) which seems to offer balm to the world-weary traveler, the refugee from communist betrayal and fascist reprisal.

> For some reason, to see flocks of sheep always creates in me a sense of innocence, of an age of innocence which I know well can never have existed. Perhaps because of long years of traveling along Sierra tracks, or because of innumerable conversations with shepherds, whose knowledge is traditional, such encounters at once create in me the sense of past time, the feuds of which have been forgotten though its poetry remains. It is an unfailing association, so that on this day, descending out of the pure sky and meeting the flock of sheep, I felt that I was in the Golden Land.[3]

The passage has already created in the reader an anticipation of a reversal: such paradisal innocence never existed. But before the return to reality actually transpires, Bates makes a telling allusion that indicates his rejection of another way of perceiving which, from his own point of view, would make a distinction between the real and the fanciful all but impossible: "Had I thought of writing about Mexico at that moment I believe I should have conceived some mystifying nonsense in the manner of Lawrence or Huxley."[4] By virtue of his long residence in provincial Spain and his fluency in the Spanish tongue, Bates was less susceptible than his countrymen to the Mexican mystique. This is made doubly clear later in the same passage, when the anticipated shattering of the illusion occurs. The shepherd of the flock turns out to be an Indian boy and (to Bates's disappointment) a beggar. As he looks down at the melancholy eyes and listens to the pathetic appeal for five centavos, Bates muses on the kind of "mystifying nonsense" that such a figure has inspired in other foreigners in Mexico:

> It is the remoteness or the intense sadness of the Indian face that has suggested to visitors that the race is mourning its overthrown splendors and its disgraced gods. The shepherd boy had such a face; violated innocence was in it, and this was to be heard in his voice also. . . . [However] it is not departed glories that the Indian mourns, but stolen lands. His submissiveness is the product of neglect, betrayal, and imposition. The remoteness of his gaze has no mystical origin: his will has been broken, and he has been robbed of his courage. There is the problem of Mexico; how to create in the Indian the desire for willful living.[5]

For Bates, the Indian—that crucial index to the foreign observer's sensibility—is not an inscrutable being who embodies the nightmare of violent revenge for ancient wrongs, but a contemporary social problem. Further: under the impetus of Cárdenas and the *ejido* program, "the problem is being solved, blunderingly and with appalling errors no doubt, but it is being solved."[6]

By the time he began work on *The Fields of Paradise*, Bates had already broken with the Communist Party, or at least with Stalinism. Though his loyalty was strained already by the sectarian in-fighting among Communist factions in Spain, he waited until the invasion of Finland by the Soviet Union in November 1939 to make public his complete disillusionment. "A specter is haunting the world," he wrote, "the specter of a revolution that is dead."[7] If the Russian Revolution was dead, however, the Mexican Revolution in the Cárdenas years showed signs of stirring to life. In a letter to me, written in June 1976, Bates says that his "total dissent from the official Stalinist view of revolution and long conversations with Mexican and Spanish 'peasantry' [were] what prompted me to write *The Fields*.... [The novel was] an effort to make distinctions between a natural personal rebellion and revolutions proceeding according to doctrines and creeds." Specifically, the novel must have been inspired by his experiences in the *ejidos*, by his belief that they were "the sign of a new faith."

*The Fields of Paradise* telescopes thirty years of the Mexican Revolution—from Díaz to Cárdenas—into a few months, and concentrates nationwide conflicts into those of a village called San Lorenzo. At the same time, since the historical Revolution is often referred to and "that man Cárdenas" is in power in the far-off capital, the novel in effect comments on the contemporary state of affairs in Mexico. Viewed in the latter sense, the situation in San Lorenzo at the outset of the novel scarcely speaks well for the accomplishments of the Revolution. Economically and spiritually the village is dependent upon the nearby sugar-cane hacienda owned by Epigmenio Rosas, who lives a day's ride away in the state capital. The hacienda is still run in the feudal manner, with the laborers bound by debt-peonage to the *patrón*. In the absence of don Epigmenio, the hacienda is looked after by his nephew Sulpicio Rosas, depicted as a coward, a braggart, a wastrel. Practically speaking, the man who controls San Lorenzo is the ruthless Braulio Acosta, who has ruled for years as judge, municipal president, and commander of the Agrarian Reserve Forces. His opposition has been effectually destroyed, either "in perilous ambush" (as the saying goes) or in extended prison terms. Ironically, Acosta had gained power

originally as a military leader in the Revolution. When the
move to unseat the Díaz dictatorship began, don Epigmenio
promised the villagers (mostly Indians) that he would give
them land—deceiving them, as one character puts it, "into
thinking they were serving the cause they were stupid enough
to believe was theirs"[8]—in order to get the people to fight
with rather than against him. He then made Acosta the commander of the local regiment, and Acosta "marched [the peo-
ple] all over the country . . . and they fought for him, and
when they came back Don Epigmenio gave a few useless
fields away and left others without any land at all" (p. 333).
In the end, most of the peasants went back to work on the
hacienda just as before the Revolution, thus acquiescing in
their servitude. Again, it is precisely this acquiescence, this
fatalistic lack of will, that defines the Indians' condition for
Bates:

> They had been deceived so many times; yes. When dur-
> ing the long years of Acosta's rule they had murmured
> among themselves, sullenly thinking of liberation, their
> courage had failed them. They had sat in the shadow of
> their huts, their own children before their eyes and had
> desisted. Care for their own children had kept them in
> submission. Plotting together in the sugar fields, among
> the tall canes, or merely glancing out of sullen eyes at
> other submissive eyes through the canes, they had
> thought of their families and had been cowed, cheated of
> their manhood by their paternity. (pp. 171-172)

Beneath the Indian submissiveness, as this passage suggests, smolders the "manly" passion for freedom, and the
first half of the novel is devoted to a peculiar turn of events
which ignites that passion into outright revolt. The chief
instigator of the conflagration is, all too appropriately, a fireworks vendor named Felipe Mantanzas. Felipe is not a native
of San Lorenzo but a solitary wanderer, a "man of the paths";
he is presented as a happy-go-lucky sort who is yet capable of
violence when treated unjustly. Thrown into prison as a

result of a couple of practical jokes at the expense of the rulers of the village, Felipe joins forces with a handful of dissident prisoners and becomes their leader. It is their jailbreak, while the rest of the village is attending the traditional Mass in honor of the year's harvest, that sets off the revolt. The peasant masses respond immediately by gathering in the plaza for a march on the tavern-fortress called "I Am Laughing," to which Acosta, Rosas and their supporters have retreated. When the siege stalls, the peasants—in a catharsis of frenzy—set fire to the tavern. The move succeeds, the oppressors are all killed or in flight; and before they realize what they have done, the peasants find themselves in complete control of San Lorenzo, at least for the moment. However, an equally momentous task remains ahead, as they soon discover—the task of consolidating their numbers (most of whom are illiterate and have no skills except those required of field laborers) into a functioning peacetime community. The last half of the novel is concerned with the difficult problems involved in planning for the future. The insurrection is not entirely successful until it has been legitimized by the federal government, which will decide whether the rebels have any legal claim to the hacienda, and whether an *ejido* may be established and financial credit granted.

*The Fields of Paradise* offers several specific parallels to the other English novels, in particular to *The Plumed Serpent* and *The Power and the Glory*. There is, to begin with, the romance between Felipe and Candelaria, the Indian girl whom he eventually weds. The kindling of their love—the figure is Bates's—is juxtaposed with the kindling of the rebellion in San Lorenzo, just as Lawrence juxtaposes the Kate-Cipriano affair with the uprising of the Quetzalcoatl cult. As in *The Power and the Glory*, the protagonist is a native Mexican; there is no English character to mediate between the Mexican scene and the reader. Also, like the whisky priest, Felipe is a man in flight, a fugitive from justice. (He had killed a cruel overseer in a moment of anger before the story proper begins.) The prison scene in *The Fields* is very reminiscent of that in Greene's novel. Both scenes amount to an immersion in collective human suffering, and the result in each case is a greater awareness on the protagonist's part of the essential bond between people entrapped in the world's prison-house.[9] Bates also uses spatial imagery involving a frontier and, though I find it far less vividly imagined than Greene's border between "Godless" Tabasco and "holy" Chiapas, the imagery functions in much the same way. In *The Fields*, San Lorenzo's immediate neighbor is the *ejidal* community of Santa Anita. The two villages are separated by a river (and in fact are in different states). Acosta, not wanting "his" peons to come under the influence of the more free and hopeful way of life in Santa Anita, has seen to it that there is no bridge connecting the two communities. To cross over, one must swim across the river, as Felipe does on several occasions.

As in all four of the major English novels set in Mexico, much of the plot in *The Fields of Paradise* turns on the question of whether the protagonist should remain in the place where violence threatens or whether he should escape to a place of safety and hope (or at least to a place imagined as such). Bates's treatment of this theme is rather less severe than that of his four countrymen. For one thing, once Rosas and Acosta and their supporters have been defeated, San Lorenzo's potential for further violence is much diminished. When Felipe considers leaving the village immediately after the revolt, he does so not because he is afraid of imminent violence but because he is not comfortable in the role of leadership which has fallen to him so precipitately during the crisis. After all, San Lorenzo is not his home, these are not his people, what more could he do there? Eventually, however, he realizes that his involvement in the villagers' cause has created a spirit of fundamental kinship that he has never before experienced, that a life of further wandering will never bring him any closer to "home" than he is now in San Lorenzo. Thus, after a brief withdrawal into the woods outside the village, he decides to return

out of instinctive loyalty to his prison companions, who
could not take to the paths.... To break out of prison
they had sworn companionship. Vengeance, hatred and
jealousy had been motives, as well as desire for liberty.
... And now, in order that they should escape retribu-
tion, San Lorenzo must survive. That was only just to
the villagers who had aided them. Bonds of companionship were not only expressed in words, but in deeds. The
promise given in the cell extended over the whole town.
(p. 281)

In short, despite the fact that Felipe's decision leaves untapped that enigmatic, horrible quality so deeply felt in the
corresponding scenes in the other novels, it is essentially the
same sort of decision; and like Kate, Anthony, the whisky
priest, and the Consul, Felipe accepts the consequences of his
decision. Furthermore, his acceptance of an identity within
the community does involve a kind of submission of self,
though admittedly by the end of the book that submission
seems comparatively painless. Where Kate finally gives in to
the land whose flowers are rooted in spilt blood, and both the
whisky priest and Firmin submit to the fetid *barranca*, Felipe
devotes himself to something much more benign: "It was the
fields, the barley fields and the green sugar crops that awakened his affection" (p. 283). Felipe dreams of one day trans-
forming San Lorenzo into what it had been before the Conquest: "a bower of greenery, of abundance, ...the Fields of
Paradise" (p. 264). Bates insists that the dream can be realized only gradually, by careful planning and with moderate
expectations in the early years. But once the *ejido* comes into
being—and there is every reason to believe that it will—the
prognosis for San Lorenzo is good, and Felipe can say to his
new bride, "'Come, let us set it all in order'" (p. 382). In
Bates the dualistic image is less equivocal than in the work of
his fellow English novelists. The myth has become politicized
and, as it were, domesticated. Mexico seems more nearly
paradisal than infernal.

# Notes

Chapter I: The Fascination of Mexico

1. Joseph Conrad, *Heart of Darkness* (1899); rpt. Norton Critical Edition, ed. Robert Kimbrough (New York: Norton, 1971), p. 8.

2. Janet Flanner, *Paris Was Yesterday, 1925-1939*, ed. Irving Drutman (New York: Viking, 1972), p. xxi.

3. Katherine Anne Porter, "The Mexican Trinity" (1921), rpt. in *The Collected Essays and Occasional Writings of Katherine Anne Porter* (New York: Delacorte, 1970), p. 399.

4. Porter, "St. Augustine and the Bullfight" (1955), rpt. in *The Collected Essays*, p. 94. For critical commentary on Miss Porter's Mexican experience and her use of it in her fiction, see George Hendrick, *Katherine Anne Porter* (New York: Twayne, 1965), pp. 28-51; William L. Nance, "Katherine Anne Porter and Mexico," *Southwest Review*, LV (1970), 143-153; and Colin Partridge, " 'My Familiar Country': An Image of Mexico in the Work of Katherine Anne Porter," *Studies in Short Fiction*, VII (Fall 1970), 597-614.

5. See Frank Tannenbaum, *Mexico: The Struggle for Peace and Bread* (New York: Knopf, 1950), p. 77.

6. See John Dos Passos, *The Best Times: An Informal Memoir* (New York: New American Library, 1966), pp. 171-172.

7. Katherine Anne Porter, "Why I Write About Mexico" (1923), rpt. in *The Collected Essays*, pp. 355-356.

8. Katherine Anne Porter, "Old Gods and New Messiahs," *New York Herald Tribune Books*, September 29, 1929, p. 2.

9. See Hank Lopez, "A Country and Some People I Love" (interview with Katherine Anne Porter), *Harper's*, September 1965, p. 62; Diego Rivera (interviewed by Miss Porter), "The Guild Spirit in Mexican Art," *Survey*, LII (April-September 1924), 174-178; and Rivera, "From a Painter's Notebook" (trans. Katherine Anne Porter), *Arts*, VII (January 1925), 21-23. Miss Porter's monograph concerning the exhibition is *Outline of Mexican Popular Arts and Crafts* (Los Angeles: Young and McAllister, 1922).

10. See Lopez, pp. 62, 65.

11. Katherine Anne Porter, "Rivera's Personal Revolution in Mexico," *New York Herald Tribune Books*, March 21, 1937, p. 7.

12. Robert E. Quirk, *Mexico*, Modern Nations in Historical Perspective (Englewood Cliffs, N.J.; Prentice-Hall, 1971), p. 103.

13. Katherine Anne Porter, "Hacienda," in *Flowering Judas and Other Stories*, rev. ed. (New York: Harcourt, Brace, 1935), pp. 284-285. Although Miss Porter's disenchantment with the Revolution is once again made explicit in the opening pages of *Ship of Fools* (Boston and Toronto: Little, Brown, 1962), it is worth noting that in interviews conducted in the mid-sixties she asserted her continued faith not only in the goals of the Revolution but in the success of the movement. See especially the interview with Hank Lopez (cited above).

14. B. Traven, *The General from the Jungle* (1939), trans. Desmond Vesey (New York: Hill and Wang, 1974), p. 60. Useful commentary on Traven's career and works include the following: H. R. Hays, "The Importance of B. Traven," *Chimera*, IV (Summer 1946), 44-54; Walter M. Langford, *The Mexican Novel Comes of Age* (South Bend, Indiana: Univ. of Notre Dame Press, 1971), pp. 51-70; Robert B. Olafson, "B. Traven's *Norteamericanos* in Mexico," *Markham Review*, IV (October 1973), 1-5; and Donald O. Chankin, *Anonymity and Death: The Fiction of B. Traven* (University Park, Pennsylvania: Pennsylvania State Univ. Press, 1975).

15. James Ruoff and Del Smith, "Katherine Anne Porter on *Ship of Fools*" (an interview), *College English*, XXIV (February 1963), 397.

16. Ibid.

17. Evelyn Waugh, *Robbery Under Law: The Mexican Object-Lesson* (1939; rpt. London: Catholic Book Club Edition, 1940), p. 272.

18. Carlos Fuentes, "Mexico's New Wave," *Venture*, III (December-January 1967), 128.

19. Ramón J. Sender, *Tales of Cibola*, trans. Florence Hall Sender, Elinor Randall, Morse Manley (New York: Las Americas, 1964), p. 326.

20. See Marie Seton, *Sergei M. Eisenstein* (New York: A. A. Wyn, 1952), pp. 205-213.

21. Antonin Artaud, "A Voyage to the Land of the Tarahumara" (1945; rpt. in *Oeuvres Completes d'Antonin Artaud*, Tome IX, Editions Gallimord, 1971), in *The Peyote Dance*, trans. Helen Weaver (New York: Farrar, Straus and Giroux, 1976), pp. 12, 15. See also Bettina L. Knapp, *Antonin Artaud: Man of Vision* (New York: David Lewis, 1969), pp. 102-165 passim; and J. G. Brotherston, "Revolution and the Ancient Literature of Mexico, For D. H. Lawrence and Antonin Artaud," *Twentieth Century Literature*, XVIII (July 1972), 181-189.

22. Quoted by Peter Lisca, "John Steinbeck: A Literary Biography," in *Steinbeck and His Critics: A Record of Twenty-Five Years*, ed. E. W. Tedlock, Jr., and C. V. Wicker (Albuquerque, New Mexico: Univ. of New Mexico Press, 1957), p. 9. See also Steinbeck and Edward F. Ricketts, *The Log from The Sea of Cortez* (1941; rev. New York: Viking, 1951), p. 75; and *Steinbeck: A Life in Letters*, ed. Elaine Steinbeck and Robert Wallsten

(New York: Viking, 1975), pp. 106-369 passim.

23. John Steinbeck, *The Pearl* (1945; rpt. New York: Viking, 1947), p. 21.

24. B. Traven, *The Night Visitor and Other Stories* (New York: Hill and Wang, 1966), p. 10.

25. Ibid., pp. 55-56.

26. B. Traven, *The Rebellion of the Hanged* (1936), trans. Esperanza López Mateos and Josef Wieder (New York: Knopf, 1952), p. 105.

27. Katherine Anne Porter, "The Mexican Trinity" (1921), rpt. in *The Collected Essays*, pp. 401-402.

28. Porter, *The Collected Essays*, pp. 397-398.

29. Ibid., p. 398.

30. Gustav Regler, *A Land Bewitched: Mexico in the Shadow of the Centuries*, trans. Constantine Fitzgibbon (London: Putnam, 1955), pp. 82-83. See also *The Owl of Minerva: The Autobiography of Gustav Regler*, trans. Norman Denny (New York: Farrar, Straus and Cudahy, 1959), pp. 355-375.

31. Regler, *A Land Bewitched*, p. 73.

32. Katherine Anne Porter, *Ship of Fools*, p. 11.

33. Artaud, *The Peyote Dance*, pp. 13, 15.

34. Regler, *A Land Bewitched*, p. 1.

35. Ibid., p. 88.

36. Graham Greene, *Another Mexico* (1939; rpt. New York: Viking, 1964), p. 178.

37. See Drewey Wayne Gunn, *American and British Writers in Mexico, 1556-1973* (Austin, Texas: Univ. of Texas Press, 1974); and Sheryl Sherman Pearson, "The Anglo-American Novel of the Mexican Revolution, 1910-1940: D. H. Lawrence, B. Traven, Graham Greene," unpub. dissertation (Univ. of Michigan, 1976). Gunn's book is a useful compilation of a vast body of information on the subject; he argues that "Mexico often had a striking effect" on its foreign visitors (of whom he mentions perhaps a hundred), "marking the beginning, the end, or a turning point of their careers" (p. ix). Pearson's study is concerned more directly with the interpretations of the Mexican Revolution in the fiction of Lawrence, Traven, and Greene, arguing that each was interested in particular aspects of the Revolution and undervalued or misunderstood other important aspects; that each created in his fiction a model of the "ideal revolution" which counters the Mexican experience; and that each novelist, as an outsider in Mexico, contributed new insights into the Revolution that make possible a comparison between their works and that native Mexican genre known as the novel of the Revolution. On the American writers and Mexico, see also Cecil Robinson, *With the Ears of Strangers: The Mexican in American Literature* (Tucson, Arizona: Univ. of Arizona Press, 1963).

38. George Woodcock, "Mexico and the English Novelist," *Western Review*, XXI (Autumn 1956), 22. Lowry is discussed all too briefly in this article. For fuller treatments by Woodcock of Lowry's use of Mexican materials, see "Malcolm Lowry's 'Under the Volcano'," *Modern Fiction*

*Studies,* IV (1958-59), 151-156; and "On the Day of the Dead," *Northern Review,* VI (1953-54), 15-21.

39. "Mexico and the English Novelist," pp. 22-23.

40. D. H. Lawrence, *The Plumed Serpent [Quetzalcoatl]* (1926; rpt. New York: Knopf, 1951), pp. 132-133.

41. Aldous Huxley, *Eyeless in Gaza* (New York: Harper, 1936), p. 401.

42. Malcolm Lowry, *Under the Volcano* (1947; rpt. Philadelphia and New York: Lippincott, 1965), p. 35.

43. Lawrence, p. 45.

44. Francis Fergusson, "D. H. Lawrence's Sensibility," in *Hound and Horn* (1933), rpt. in *Forms of Modern Fiction: Essays Collected in Honor of Joseph Warren Beach,* ed. William Van O'Connor (Bloomington, Indiana: Indiana Univ. Press, 1948; rev. 1959), p. 77. Fergusson is quoting two lines from T. S. Eliot's "Preludes."

45. In *Robbery Under Law,* Waugh observes that "the writer who has given most people their ideas about Mexico is D. H. Lawrence; and he hated it.... Every traveller to Mexico must read the *Plumed Serpent* [sic]; or at any rate the opening chapters. The early, satirical passages about Mexico City—the bull-fight, the tea party... 'all jade is bright green'...— are superb. Then his loneliness and his lack of humour and his restless, neurotic imagination combine to make one of the silliest stories in recent literature.... Nevertheless, for all its folly, the *Plumed Serpent* is a better guide to Mexico than [*Terry's Guide*]" (pp. 10-11). Later, in the midst of dire reflections about the Nazi influence in the Mexico of the 1930's, Waugh wonders: "Was the *Plumed Serpent* as fantastic as it appeared when we first read it?" (pp. 271-272). Graham Greene, in a letter to the author dated August 1, 1974, recalls that before he came to Mexico in 1938 he "had read *Mornings in Mexico,* but I never succeeded in reading more than a few pages of *The Plumed Serpent.* I don't think Lawrence had any influence on my views [of Mexico] as I very much reacted against him." In a letter to the author dated August 19, 1974, Margerie Lowry (Malcolm's widow), writing of the period after her husband's first trip to Mexico in 1936-38, says that both she and Lowry read *The Plumed Serpent* and *Mornings in Mexico.* Mrs. Lowry recalls that "we didn't like the former but very much liked the latter.... [Malcolm] admired Lawrence exceedingly, except for this one book." Lowry alludes to Lawrence's Mexican writings occasionally in *Dark As the Grave,* as Greene does at one point in *Another Mexico* (see p. 102). Huxley's reaction upon rereading *The Plumed Serpent* at the end of his own visit to Mexico is recorded at the end of *Beyond the Mexique Bay.* This important reassessment of Lawrence is discussed in my chapter on Huxley's travel book and the Huxley-Lawrence relationship. Ralph Bates, in a letter to me written in June 1976, states that he has "contempt" for *The Plumed Serpent* but enjoyed parts of *Mornings in Mexico.* "I do not regard Lawrence as well informed about Mexico.... He had written great novels [before] but I cannot admire the weakly conceived, rhetorical *Plumed S[erpent].*" For American reactions to Lawrence's Mexican writings, see Gunn, pp. 102, 123-124.

## Chapter II: The "Dark Blood" of America

1. D. H. Lawrence, *Studies in Classic American Literature* (1923; rpt. New York: Viking, 1964), p. 3.

2. See James C. Cowan, *D. H. Lawrence's American Journey: A Study in Literature and Myth* (Cleveland: Case Western Reserve Univ., 1970), p. 2. One is reminded of William Blake's mythic equation of America (albeit white America) with energy and of England under King George III with "Urizenic" bondage in his early prophetic works.

3. *The Letters of D. H. Lawrence*, ed. Aldous Huxley (New York: Viking, 1932), p. 262.

4. See Armin Arnold, *D. H. Lawrence and America* (London: Linden, 1958), pp. 23-35. Arnold refers to America as Lawrence's "place of refuge" during the war years.

5. D. H. Lawrence, *Phoenix: The Posthumous Papers of D. H. Lawrence*, ed. Edward D. McDonald (New York: Viking, 1936), p. 90. Hereafter cited in the text.

6. David Cavitch, *D. H. Lawrence and the New World* (New York: Oxford Univ. Press, 1969), p. 100.

7. Ibid., p. 103.

8. See Harry T. Moore, *Poste Restante: A Lawrence Travel Calendar* (Berkeley, California: Univ. of California Press, 1956), p. 68. Throughout this and the next chapter I have relied upon the dates and other information in this useful calendar. See especially pp. 68-83 on the American period.

9. Since this figure will be frequently discussed in subsequent chapters, it is necessary to point out here that Lawrence had made use of this "borderline" experience and of border imagery in novels written before his arrival in America. In *The Lost Girl* (1921; rpt. New York: Viking, 1968), Alvina Houghton, on her "journey across" the Italian countryside to Ciccio's mountain village, "felt she was quite, quite lost. She had gone out of the world, over the border, into some place of mystery" (p. 341). The protagonist of *Aaron's Rod* (1922; rpt. New York: Viking, 1961) is also traveling by train in Italy, just beyond the Alps: "[Aaron] was on the south side. On the other side of the time barrier. His old sleepy English nature was startled in its sleep. He felt like a man who knows it is time to wake up, and who doesn't want to wake up, to face the responsibility of another sort of day. To open his darkest eyes and wake up . . . and enter on the responsibility of a new self in himself" (p. 146). Soon, in the town of Novara, Aaron does "wake up," and he realizes that he has "crossed the dividing line, and [that] the values of life . . . [are now] dynamically different" (p. 148). In the "Nightmare" chapter of *Kangaroo* (1923; rpt. New York: Viking, 1960), R. L. Somers recalls the nights back on the Cornish moors, "so ancient and Druidical, suggesting blood-sacrifice. And as Somers sat there . . . he felt he was over the border, in another world. Over the border, in that twilight, awesome world of the previous Celts. The spirit of the ancient, pre-Christian world . . . he could feel it invade him in the savage dusk, making him savage too . . ." (p. 242). Lawrence's use of border imagery in these in-

stances is consistent, involving a journey to an unfamiliar region felt to be dark, alien, and not fully civilized, and a corresponding experience of psychological transport. Unlike the passage from "Indians and an Englishman," however, in each of the above examples the borderline perspective is relinquished and the mystery embraced.

10. It is unfortunately necessary, even at this late date, to emphasize the fact that Lawrence was not in any strict sense of the word a primitivist. Many readers, among them Aldous Huxley, have persisted in viewing Lawrence's interest in Indian religion as a call to "cluster at the drum." In *Beyond the Mexique Bay: A Traveller's Journal* (1934; rpt. London: Chatto and Windus, 1949), for reasons indicated in my Chapter IV, Lawrence is accused of urging us to "abandon the new privileges" of modern science in return for "the old treasure" of the primitive's intuitions and spontaneity (p. 314). Huxley, and many other readers after him, have imposed upon Lawrence a simplistic and literal-minded primitivism which does not encompass the insights presented in the passage quoted from "Indians and an Englishman." It must be admitted, however, that despite such cautions to his readers—and perhaps to himself as well—Lawrence is partially responsible, in works such as *The Plumed Serpent* and "The Woman Who Rode Away," for giving the impression that he favors a return to the primitive. Some of the reasons for this inconsistency in his Mexican fiction will be discussed presently.

11. *The Collected Letters of D. H. Lawrence*, ed. Harry T. Moore (New York: Viking, 1962), II, 715. Hereafter cited in the text as *Letters*. All of the quotations from Lawrence's letters are taken from this edition unless otherwise indicated.

12. See Harry T. Moore, *The Priest of Love: A Life of D. H. Lawrence* (New York: Farrar, Straus and Giroux, 1974), pp. 354-367.

13. Frank Waters, in "Quetzalcoatl Versus D. H. Lawrence's *Plumed Serpent*," *Western American Literature*, III (Summer 1968), 103-113, provides an account of the pre-Aztec origin of the god Quetzalcoatl, which Lawrence was inclined to overlook. The Aztecs were "warring tribes of crude Chichimecas or 'barbarians' who swept down into Mexico from the north about 1,000 [sic] A. D. and overthrew the cultured Toltecs.... The facade of the Aztec empire remained the Toltec culture, but the valid religion of Quetzalcoatl was distorted into a totalitarian cult of sun-worship with its wholesale human sacrifices.... It is the old, old story...of a transcendental religion distorted into a secular, materialistic ideology." Waters goes on to make the important point that the "Aztec vulgarization of Quetzalcoatl" rather than the more appealing Toltec original dominated Lawrence's understanding of the god and his use of him in his writing (p. 112).

14. Edward Nehls, ed., *D. H. Lawrence: A Composite Biography* (Madison, Wisconsin: Univ. of Wisconsin Press, 1958), II, 256.

15. D. H. Lawrence, *Phoenix II: Uncollected, Unpublished, and Other Prose Works*, eds. Warren Roberts and Harry T. Moore (New York: Viking, 1970). p. 252.

16. Graham Hough, *The Dark Sun: A Study of D. H. Lawrence* (London: Duckworth, 1956), p. 181. On the trip to Europe and Lawrence's conflicts with Murry, see Moore, *The Priest of Love*, pp. 377-382. See also Cavitch, pp. 145-148. Cavitch sees the European interlude as the crisis of Lawrence's adult life, when his already confused sexual identity became dangerously inverted.

17. D. H. Lawrence, *Mornings in Mexico and Etruscan Places* (London: Heinemann, 1956), p. 45. Hereafter cited in the text as *Mornings*.

18. See Hough, p. 181.

19. D. H. Lawrence, *St. Mawr and The Man Who Died* (1928; rpt. New York: Vintage, n.d.), pp. 158-159.

20. D. H. Lawrence, *The Plumed Serpent [Quetzalcoatl]* (1926; rpt. New York: Knopf, 1951), pp. 15, 71.

21. Witter Bynner, *Journey With Genius: Recollections and Reflections Concerning the D. H. Lawrences* (New York: John Day, 1951), p. 17. Hereafter cited in the text as Bynner. Later, under the spell of his fear of gangs of thieves in Chapala, Lawrence even speculated that " 'it was not a stray bullet that killed Ewart' " (p. 94). He suspected the insurgent Mexicans of seeking revenge against foreigners.

22. *The Quest for Rananim: D. H. Lawrence's Letters to S. S. Koteliansky, 1914 to 1930*, ed. George J. Zytaruk (Montreal: McGill—Queen's Univ. Press, 1970), p. 253.

23. Frieda Lawrence, *"Not I But the Wind..."* (New York: Viking, 1934), p. 140. This is one of several instances where Mrs. Lawrence places her emphasis, in her brief description of events during the first Mexican trip, rather differently than Bynner does. After taking one look at the Quetzalcoatl carvings, she tells us, she "ran after [the three men] for all I was worth. I got a glimpse of old Mexico then, the old sacrifices, hearts still quivering held up to the sun, for the sun to drink the blood. There it had all happened.... Fear of those people who don't mind killing and don't mind dying.... Dying and sacrifice and cruel gods seemed to reign in Mexico under its sunshine and splendour of flowers and lots of birds and fruit and white volcano peaks" (p. 140). The correspondence between Frieda's reactions here and some of those attributed to Kate Leslie in *The Plumed Serpent* is obvious.

24. On the misunderstanding between Lawrence and Vasconcelos—two of the great personalities of this century—see Bynner, pp. 26-28, 184-185; and Nehls, II, 227-231. For Vasconcelos' later response, see his review of Bynner's book, "Viajando con el genio," in *Novedades* (Mexico City), December 28, 1951, and January 4, 1952.

25. Nehls, II, 369.

26. Sheryl Sherman Pearson has shown in some detail those areas in which Lawrence's Mexican revolution in *The Plumed Serpent* corresponds with the historical Revolution (repatriation of the Indian, belief in the worth of indigenous arts and crafts, anti-clericalism, xenophobic tendencies, *mexicanismo*) and those areas in which they do not correspond (Lawrence's repudiation of *mestizaje*, his lack of sympathy for the Mexican

working class generally and the mestizo in particular, and his imposition of a hierarchical system on the Quetzalcoatl cult). I am in agreement with Dr. Pearson's view that Lawrence was particularly well disposed by his "paradigm of the New World" to appreciate certain of the Revolution's "extrapolitical overtones" (e.g., its fundamental myth of re-conquest and associated symbology), while at the same time his abstract vision blocked his sympathy for many of the Revolution's practical motives. See "The Anglo-American Novel of the Mexican Revolution, 1910-1940: D. H. Lawrence, B. Traven, Graham Greene," unpub. dissertation (University of Michigan, 1976), Chapter II. See also J. G. Brotherston, "Revolution and the Ancient Literature of Mexico, For D. H. Lawrence and Antonin Artaud," *Twentieth Century Literature*, XVIII (July 1972), 181-189; and Jeffrey Meyers, "*The Plumed Serpent* and the Mexican Revolution," *Journal of Modern Literature*, IV (September 1974), 55-72.

27. Again, it is instructive to contrast Bynner's description of events with those of Frieda Lawrence in her autobiography (see especially p. 139). Mrs. Lawrence stresses her own revulsion at the lice-picking of the servants and her own fear of bandits; she does not mention her husband's role in these incidents. Lawrence, of course, used the incident involving the nocturnal intruder in Chapter VIII of *The Plumed Serpent*.

28. L. D. Clark, *Dark Night of the Body: D. H. Lawrence's "The Plumed Serpent"* (Austin, Texas: Univ. of Texas Press, 1964), p. 100.

29. Edward Weston's piece on Lawrence (1930) is reprinted in Nehls, II, 370-372. Despite his mocking of Lawrence's "neurotic" fantasy, Weston goes on to say the following: "[But] then, —is there an Anglo-Saxon, even in normal health, who has not looked out on the passing Mexican landscape from his Pullman berth at night, without a feeling of awe? Something mysterious there, never to be fully understood by another race. Maybe the old gods *do* still rule!" (Nehls, II, 371).

30. Carleton Beals' remarks, originally published in 1938, are reprinted in Nehls, II, 227-229.

31. See Knud Merrild, *A Poet and Two Painters* (1939), reissued as *With D. H. Lawrence in New Mexico: A Memoir of D. H. Lawrence* (New York: Barnes and Noble, 1965), p. 338. Götzsche's account of this episode includes a reference to his own disgust at the cruelty of the bullfight. Lawrence's reaction is not mentioned.

32. Ibid., p. 343; see also p. 348. It is worth mentioning that in her autobiography Mrs. Lawrence recalled that she too had suffered from the separation: "It was winter and I wasn't a bit happy alone [in Hampstead]. . . . I felt lost without him" ("*Not I But the Wind . . .*," p. 141).

33. Merrild, p. 340.

34. *The Quest for Rananim*, p. 261.

35. Katherine Anne Porter, *The Collected Essays and Occasional Writings of Katherine Anne Porter* (New York: Delacorte, 1970), pp. 416-420.

36. Dorothy Brett, *Lawrence and Brett: A Friendship* (Philadelphia: Lippincott, 1933), pp. 166-168.

37. For information about Oaxaca during the Revolution, Lawrence's

experiences in and around the city, his friends there, and his writings of the time, I am indebted to Mr. Ross Parmenter, who graciously allowed me to read his unpublished manuscript, "Lawrence in Oaxaca."

38. Brett, p. 181.

39. See the description of Chapala in Clark, pp. 34-36, and also the photographs, plates IV-X.

40. Brett, p. 184.

41. Ibid., pp. 195, 169-170.

42. Ibid., p. 184.

43. Frank Waters describes a similar myth, the origin of which he traces back beyond the Aztecs to the Toltecs. The myth of successive Suns was "held by the later Aztecs and Mayas. It is still held today by the Navajos and by the Hopis in Arizona whose religious ceremonies, dances, songs, and myths are built on this five-world pattern . . ." (p. 111). This statement helps to lend some credence to Lawrence's monistic interpretation of the indigenous culture of the American continent.

44. Thomas R. Whitaker, "Lawrence's Western Path: 'Mornings in Mexico'," *Criticism,* III (1961), 221.

45. Ibid.

46. Ibid., p. 222.

47. Ibid., p. 224. Lawrence's attempt in these sketches at achieving the vitalist transcendence by "seeing both ways" is probably what Aldous Huxley had in mind when he formulated his doctrine of "balanced excesses" in *Do What You Will* (1929).

48. Ibid., p. 225. It is interesting that Lawrence is able to sympathize with the victimized Indian while at the same time repudiating the Revolution, which (in principle) fought to uphold the Indian's rights, along with those of the rest of the "mass of men."

49. Lawrence's letter to Eduardo Rendón, dated May 21, 1925, appears in Moore, *The Priest of Love,* p. 403.

50. See Mabel Dodge Luhan, *Lorenzo in Taos* (London: Secker, 1933), pp. 59-60, 69-73; and Frieda Lawrence, pp. 136-137.

51. See "Certain Americans and an Englishman" (1922), rpt. in *Phoenix II,* pp. 238-243.

52. Clark, p. 21.

53. E. W. Tedlock, Jr., *D. H. Lawrence, Artist and Rebel: A Study of Lawrence's Fiction* (Albuquerque, New Mexico: Univ. of New Mexico Press, 1963), p. 157.

54. Ibid., pp. 184-185.

55. Luhan, p. 230.

56. Waters, pp. 106, 108.

57. Lawrence Clark Powell, "Southwest Classics Reread: *The Plumed Serpent,* by D. H. Lawrence," *Westways,* LXIII (November 1971), 18-20, 46-49.

58. Hough, p. 140.

59. Ibid., p. 121.

60. *Kangaroo,* p. 356.

Chapter III: Lawrence's Mexican Nightmare

1. D. H. Lawrence, *Studies in Classic American Literature* (1923; rpt. New York: Viking, 1964), p. 171; and *The Plumed Serpent* [*Quetzalcoatl*] (1926; rpt. New York: Knopf, 1951), pp. 48-49, hereafter cited in the text.
2. Graham Hough, *The Dark Sun: A Study of D. H. Lawrence* (London: Duckworth, 1956), p. 124.
3. For a good analysis of Kate's vicissitudes in relation to Joseph Campbell's concept of the monomyth, see Jascha Kessler, "Descent into Darkness: The Myth of *The Plumed Serpent*," in *A D. H. Lawrence Miscellany*, ed. Harry T. Moore (Carbondale, Illinois: Southern Illinois Univ. Press, 1959), pp. 239-261.
4. L. D. Clark, *Dark Night of the Body: D. H. Lawrence's "The Plumed Serpent"* (Austin, Texas: Univ. of Texas Press, 1964), pp. 56, 59.
5. See Clark, pp. 52-55.
6. D. H. Lawrence, *Mornings in Mexico and Etruscan Places*, Phoenix Edition (London: Heinemann, 1956), p. 36.
7. Clark, pp. 65-66, 67.
8. Hough, pp. 132-133.
9. Ibid., pp. 129-130. Significantly, in the first draft of the novel, written at Chapala during the first Mexican trip, Kate does *not* participate in the Quetzalcoatl movement. In fact, at the juncture where Lawrence left off work on this version, Kate does not even remain in Mexico. L. D. Clark's description of the first draft (Clark, p. 101) indicates that Kate's only pledge to Ramón and Cipriano "consists of drinking with them a glass of wine whirled into a 'vortex,' and listening to Ramón's eight-page sermon on initiation in the 'Old Mysteries'.... But even this fails to make her respond further than to accept a token from Cipriano, an ancient ring with a snake on it.... We next find her packing to go to Europe, without having become a goddess or even a wife. At this point Lawrence stopped writing and both he and his heroine retreated, for the time being, from ...Mexico." In the published version of the novel, for reasons to be indicated later, Kate *had* to participate, even at the expense of her credibility as a character.
10. See J. G. Brotherston, "Revolution and the Ancient Literature of Mexico, For D. H. Lawrence and Antonin Artaud," *Twentieth Century Literature*, XVIII (July 1972), 183-187. On Malinche and the "*hijos de la chingada*," see Octavio Paz, *Labyrinth of Solitude: Life and Thought in Mexico*, trans. Lysander Kemp (New York: Grove Press, 1961), Chapter IV.
11. John B. Vickery, "'The Plumed Serpent' and the Eternal Paradox," *Criticism*, V (Spring 1963), 127.
12. In his essay "Reflections on the Death of a Porcupine" (1925), rpt. in *Phoenix II: Uncollected, Unpublished and Other Prose Works*, ed. Warren Roberts and Harry T. Moore (New York: Viking, 1970), pp. 460-474, Lawrence attempts to provide a rationale for the taking of life. Porcupines gnaw on the bark of pine trees and in time the pines will die. Though reluctant at first, Lawrence decides that "things like the porcupine, one must be able to shoot them, if they get in one's way" (p. 464). Man, as the highest

order of life thus far, must sustain and purify the overall life flow of which he is both subject and master. He must dominate the lower orders of life, or even destroy them when they challenge his position as master, or when they obstruct the flow of life. Lawrence's thought in this essay provides some clues as to what may have been his conscious rationalization for permitting Ramón to oversee the ritual executions in *The Plumed Serpent.*

13. Clark, p. 73.

14. Kenneth Rexroth, "Introducton," in *D. H. Lawrence: Selected Poems* (New York: Viking, 1959), pp. 20-21.

15. Katherine Anne Porter, "Quetzalcoatl" (1926), rpt. in *The Collected Essays and Occasional Writings of Katherine Anne Porter* (New York: Delacorte, 1970), p. 421.

16. Harry T. Moore, "*The Plumed Serpent:* Vision and Language," in *D. H. Lawrence: A Collection of Critical Essays,* ed. Mark Spilka (Englewood Cliffs, New Jersey: Prentice-Hall, 1963), pp. 71, 67.

17. Hough, p. 138. See also James C. Cowan, *D. H. Lawrence's American Journey: A Study in Literature and Myth* (Cleveland: Case Western Reserve Univ. Press, 1970), pp. 115-116, 120.

18. D. H. Lawrence, *Kangaroo* (1923; rpt. New York: Viking, 1960), p. 356. In his essay "Him With His Tail in His Mouth" (1925), rpt. in *Phoenix II,* written probably during the summer following the Oaxaca trip, Lawrence commented as follows: "We know, really, that we can't have life for the asking, nor find it by seeking, nor get it by striving. The river flows into us from behind and below. We must turn our backs to it, and go ahead. The faster we go ahead, the stronger the river rushes into us. The moment we turn round to embrace the river of life, it ebbs away, and we see nothing but a stony fiumara" (p. 429).

19. *The Collected Letters of D. H. Lawrence,* ed. Harry T. Moore (New York: Viking, 1962), II, 1045. Hereafter cited in the text.

20. See Harry T. Moore, *The Priest of Love: A Life of D. H. Lawrence* (New York: Farrar, Straus and Giroux, 1974), p. 401.

21. D. H. Lawrence, "Flying Fish," in *Phoenix: The Posthumous Papers of D. H. Lawrence,* ed. Edward D. McDonald (New York: Viking, 1936), p. 780. Hereafter cited in the text.

22. David Cavitch, *D. H. Lawrence and the New World* (New York: Oxford Univ. Press, 1969), pp. 189-190. See also Cowan, pp. 133-136. A similar instance of a writer turning, after the emotional rigors of a Mexican experience and the writing of a horrific novel inspired by that experience, to a tale of regeneration and hope, is Malcolm Lowry's "The Forest Path to the Spring," posthumously published in *Hear Us O Lord From Heaven Thy Dwelling Place* (1961).

23. See the passage about the river of life from "Him With His Tail in His Mouth," quoted in note 18 above.

### Chapter IV: Mexico as Scapegoat

1. Aldous Huxley, *Beyond the Mexique Bay: A Traveller's Journal,* Collected Edition (London: Chatto and Windus, 1949), pp. 1-2. Hereafter cited

in the text. Huxley's title alludes to the following lines from a poem by Andrew Marvell, "Bermudas":

Oh let our Voice his Praise exalt,
Till it arrive at Heavens Vault:
From thence (perhaps) rebounding, may
Eccho beyond the Mexique Bay.
Thus sung they, in the English boat,
An holy and a chearful Note.

2. Aldous Huxley, *Do What You Will*, Collected Edition (London: Chatto and Windus, 1949), p. 113.

3. Ibid., p. 114.

4. This seems to have been one of Huxley's pet ideas at the time. In a letter dated August 13, 1933, he writes that contemporary politics is "undoubtedly best studied in Central America." See *Letters of Aldous Huxley*, ed. Grover Smith (London: Chatto and Windus, 1969), p. 373. Hereafter cited in the text as *Letters*. Dr. James Miller, the anthropologist and Huxleyan sage in *Eyeless in Gaza* (New York: Harper, 1936), proclaims that "Savage societies are simply civilized societies on a small scale and with the lid off. We can learn to understand them fairly easily. And when we've learnt to understand savages, we've learnt, as we discover, to understand the civilized" (p. 443).

5. For contrast, see another letter to his father, dated April 29, 1933, in which Huxley makes one of his few remarks about Mexico in the *Letters:* "Mexico was unpleasant, but very curious" (p. 369).

6. George Woodcock, *Dawn and the Darkest Hour: A Study of Aldous Huxley* (New York: Viking, 1972), p. 186. To my knowledge Woodcock's is the best and most extensive treatment to date of *Mexique Bay*, a work which he justly sees as vital to a proper understanding of *Eyeless in Gaza*. See also Woodcock's important article, "Mexico and the English Novelist," *Western Review*, XXI (Autumn 1956), 21-27.

7. Aldous Huxley, *Point Counter Point* (New York: Harper, 1928), p. 380.

8. Woodcock, p. 187. In *Aldous Huxley: A Biography* (New York: Knopf, 1974), Sybille Bedford quotes Roy Fenton, a friend and host of the Huxleys on the trip, as stating that during their conversations at his coffee *finca* in Oaxaca, Huxley "'had very strong views...[of] the future, of what the world was going to come to...[sic] The advent of Hitler and the Nazis. And that was *there behind a lot of his thinking* [italics in original]. He came back and back to it. In the most extraordinary contexts. We were discussing Mexican mythology, and the Spanish Conquest—Aldous was trying to look at some analogy with the present time'" (p. 269).

9. See Aldous Huxley, "The Traveler's-Eye View," in his *Along the Road: Notes and Essays of a Tourist* (New York: Doran, 1925), pp. 33, 42.

10. Woodcock, pp. 188-189. Professor Woodcock, who has traveled in Mexico and written an account of his impressions, *To the City of the Dead*, goes on to say that if Huxley "had looked a little more deeply into the Mia-huatlan life, he would have found that its Indians were not in fact caught in

a circle of 'day-to-day animal living.' The Zapotecs, even today, have a high consciousness of their long tradition, a rich ceremonial life, and a piety which, though it may interpret the spiritual life differently from the way Huxley was on the point of adopting [i.e., that of a mystic], nevertheless raises their existence into something much higher and more meaningful than the merely animal" (p. 189).

11. See note 8 above. *Mexique Bay* was published just over a year before Huxley became actively involved in the pacifist movement in England.

12. Roy Fenton recalled that there was " 'a barbaric element in the Aztec thing which fascinated Aldous. This cruel queer cult . . . [sic] He was all the time trying to find a way of seeing WHY they had evolved this philosophy of having to appease the sun by slaughtering so many people; not out of vengeance, not in anger, but they felt they *must* appease the sun . . .' " (Bedford, p. 269). Again one is aware of Huxley following Lawrence's lead— but, as will be pointed out, to quite a different end.

13. Huxley does not mention the incident in *Mexique Bay*, but Sybille Bedford reports that he and Roy Fenton had an encounter with an armed, drunken Mexican in Ejutla which closely resembles the scene in Chapter Forty-One of *Eyeless in Gaza*. See Bedford, pp. 272-273, 319, 323.

14. *Along the Road*, p. 16. Considering his distinction between the true traveler and the tourist, Huxley's choice of a subtitle, *Notes and Essays of a Tourist*, is curious.

15. Ibid., p. 18.

16. Ibid., p. 42.

17. *Do What You Will*, p. 115.

18. Aldous Huxley, *Two or Three Graces* (1926), rpt., Collected Edition (London: Chatto and Windus, 1949), p. 103.

19. Aldous Huxley, *Jesting Pilate: The Diary of a Journey*, Collected Edition (London: Chatto and Windus, 1948), pp. 288-290.

20. Woodcock, p. 189.

21. The Lawrence-Huxley relationship has received considerable critical attention through the years. The discussion has been sharply divided between those who view Huxley as a devoted and unquestioning disciple of Lawrence until about 1934, and those who feel that the extent of the influence has been greatly exaggerated. Among the latter group are Woodcock (see pp. 130-133, 168) and Joseph Bentley, "Huxley's Ambivalent Response to the Ideas of D. H. Lawrence," *Twentieth Century Literature*, XIII (October 1967), 139-153. The other extreme is represented by Alexander Henderson, *Aldous Huxley* (New York: Russell and Russell, 1936; rpt. 1964), pp. 49-72; William York Tindall, *Forces in Modern British Literature, 1885-1956* (New York: Random House, 1956), pp. 172-173; and John Atkins, *Aldous Huxley: A Literary Study* (New York: Orion, rev. 1967), pp. 127-142. The most thorough and balanced treatment is Jerome Meckier's "The Lawrencian Interlude: The 'Latin Compromise' that Failed," in his *Aldous Huxley: Satire and Structure* (New York: Barnes and Noble, 1971), pp. 78-123. See also Henry Alexander, "Lawrence and Huxley," *Queens Quarterly*, XLI (January 1935), 96-108; Peter Quennell, "D. H. Lawrence and Aldous Huxley," in *The English Novelists*, ed. D. Verschoyle

(London: 1936), pp. 245-258; John H. Roberts, "Huxley and Lawrence," *Virginia Quarterly Review*, XIII (1937), 546-557; Norman Bartlett, "Aldous Huxley and D. H. Lawrence," *Australian Quarterly*, XXXVI (1964), 76-84; Pierre Vitoux, "Aldous Huxley and D. H. Lawrence: An Attempt at Intellectual Sympathy." *Modern Language Review*, LXIX (July 1974), 501-522; and Bedford, pp. 178-180, 191-194, 202-203, 209-228 passim.

22. See Aldous Huxley, "D. H. Lawrence," in his *The Olive Tree and Other Essays*, Collected Edition (London: Chatto and Windus, 1947), pp. 229-230. The essay was first published as the Introduction in *The Letters of D. H. Lawrence*, ed. Aldous Huxley (London: Heinemann, 1932).

23. Ibid., pp. 230-231. The emphasis is mine. The strong impact of Lawrence's personal vitality is recorded in Huxley's letters as early as December 1915, after their first meeting. Huxley wrote to his brother Julian of the plan to form the "eremitic colony," confiding that Lawrence impressed him as "a good man more than most," and again as "a great man" (*Letters*, p. 88). But in a letter to his father dated June 23, 1920, Huxley refers to Lawrence as "the slightly insane novelist" who seems to have lost, "along with his slight sexual mania, all his talent as a writer" (*Letters*, p. 187).

24. *Two or Three Graces*, pp. 119, 131.

25. Ibid., p. 180. Huxley himself once denied that Lawrence was the model for Kingham. In a letter written *circa* July 1930, he replies to a correspondent who questioned him on this matter: "Have I 'done' Lawrence? No. Kingham was concocted before I knew him—at least I'd only seen him once, during the War" (*Letters*, pp. 339-340). However, it must be remembered that this letter was written very shortly after Lawrence's death in March. Conceivably, Huxley was anxious to discourage any easy identification between the man for whom he still felt immense respect, affection, and sympathy, and the character of Kingham with his many shortcomings. George Woodcock has objected to what he regards as the facile assumption that Kingham is a fictional portrait of Lawrence. To Woodcock, the similarities between the two are superficial, while their differences are more substantial. Kingham seems to him more Dostoyevskian than Lawrencian. Woodcock also points to the fact that "Two or Three Graces" was written before the Florence reunion in late 1926 (see Woodcock, pp. 136-137). This last point is literally correct, but it does not follow that Huxley was incapable of caricaturing Lawrence before becoming his intimate. Huxley's earlier statements on Lawrence, discussed above, testify not only to the strong impression made upon him by Lawrence the man, but also, in the 1920 letter to his father (previously cited), to the fact that that impression did not preclude keen impatience with the writer.

26. Ibid., pp. 11-12.

27. Ibid., p. 129.

28. Woodcock, p. 132.

29. *The Olive Tree*, p. 231.

30. Huxley apparently undertook the task of writing *Do What You Will* at Lawrence's suggestion. In a letter to Huxley dated March 27, 1928, Lawrence commends Huxley's thinking about those who tried "to intellectualize

and so utterly falsify the phallic consciousness, which is the basic consciousness, and the thing *we* mean...by common sense.... But do do a book of the grand orthodox perverts. Back of all of them lies ineffable conceit." *The Collected Letters of D. H. Lawrence*, ed. Harry T. Moore (New York: Viking, 1962), II, 1049. The emphasis is mine.

31. *Do What You Will*, pp. 282-283. For Lawrence's approving comment on Huxley's book, see *The Collected Letters of D. H. Lawrence*, II, 1209.

32. Ibid., p. 308.

33. Ibid.

34. Meckier, p. 122.

35. Jerome Meckier sees Rampion as both "an idealized version of the Lawrence whom Huxley admired (but not necessarily the *real* Lawrence) and a satiric caricature embodying certain Lawrencian traits Huxley disliked" (p. 79). Meckier suggests that Huxley's ambivalent response was directed at "two D. H. Lawrences." Huxley deeply admired the Lawrence of 1916 who wanted to "go forward with Birkin and Ursula [of *Women in Love*] towards 'new life'...." But he rejected and subtly satirized the Lawrence of 1926 who was eager "to go back with Cipriano and Ramón Carrasco of *The Plumed Serpent* in search of 'that timeless, primeval passion of the prehistoric races.'" Meckier traces the impulse to satirize Lawrence/Rampion to "Huxley's feeling that Lawrence [was] no longer pursuing the themes Huxley previously regarded as their common concern..." (p. 81). It seems to me that while Meckier's argument has some validity—Huxley did prefer Lawrence's earlier writings, and he also became increasingly dubious of the viability of Lawrence's call to primitivism—nevertheless Meckier has assumed the existence of a conscious "rejection" of Lawrencian values that had not yet asserted itself at the time *Point Counter Point* was written. Also, the prevailing tone of all the scenes involving Rampion and those in which he is discussed by other characters is directly or indirectly deferential. Rampion is not a successfully drawn character—either as a portrait of Lawrence or as a personage in his own right. But it seems very unlikely that Huxley deliberately intended to satirize him. For other ironist interpretations, see Peter Firchow, *Aldous Huxley: Satirist and Novelist* (Minneapolis, Minnesota: Univ. of Minnesota, 1972), pp. 109-111; and Bentley, pp. 145-151.

36. *Point Counter Point*, pp. 402-403.

37. *The Collected Letters of D. H. Lawrence*, II, 1096.

38. *Point Counter Point*, pp. 316-317.

39. David J. Gordon, *D. H. Lawrence as a Literary Critic* (New Haven, Connecticut: Yale Univ. Press, 1966), p. 62. See Meckier, pp. 91-93.

40. Ibid., p. 92.

41. Aldous Huxley, *Brief Candles* (London: Chatto and Windus, 1930), pp. 240-241.

42. Ibid., p. 242.

43. Ibid., pp. 243-244.

44. *The Olive Tree*, p. 216.

45. *The Collected Letters of D. H. Lawrence*, II, 1096, 1105. Huxley did

not include this letter to Dorothy Brett, dated December 10, 1928, in his edition of Lawrence's letters. She had sent Huxley her Lawrence letters, but he wrote her back that he intended to cut out the "feeling-hurting passages." As he did with all of Lawrence's prolific correspondence with friends, Huxley selected only those which he considered the most interesting and informative without risk of damage to the feelings of living persons. See Huxley's *Letters*, pp. 346-347.

46. Aldous Huxley, *Brave New World and Brave New World Revisited* (New York: Harper, 1965), p. 150.

47. See "Aldous Huxley," in *Writers at Work: The 'Paris Review' Interviews*, Second Series (New York: Viking, 1963), p. 198. Huxley told the interviewers that he had relatively little trouble writing the descriptions in the English sections of *Brave New World*, but "I had to do an enormous amount of reading up on New Mexico, because I'd never been there. I read all sorts of Smithsonian reports on the place and then did the best I could to imagine it. I didn't actually go there until six years later, in 1937, when we visited Frieda Lawrence" (p. 198).

48. Aldous Huxley, "Foreword," *Brave New World*, p. xiv.

49. Ibid., p. xvi.

50. It is equally significant that Huxley himself spent only about a month in Mexico (as against Lawrence's ten months during three visits) and was never far—intellectually—from the lilies of the mind and spirit.

51. While Huxley's point here is basically valid, it is ironic that he had implicitly debunked the use of this method of reasoning, in a passage discussed earlier, by both the Indians clinging to their belief in magic and the modern Europeans re-enforcing their desire for "bigger and better armaments." See *Mexique Bay*, pp. 189-190.

52. *Point Counter Point*, pp. 166, 397.

53. Meckier, pp. 116, 123.

## Chapter V: Time and the Healing of Wounds

1. *Letters of Aldous Huxley*, ed. Grover Smith (London: Chatto and Windus, 1969), pp. 365-366. Hereafter cited in the text. It is possible that a novel Huxley had been thinking about as early as October 1930 was that which was later to become *Eyeless in Gaza*. He had written to his friend Robert Nichols that he was "pondering a kind of picaresque novel of the intellect and emotions—a mixture between *Gil Blas*, *Bouvard et Pécuchet* and *Le Rouge et le Noir*. I think it is quite impossible to do—but it will be fun to try and something may come out of the attempt—something none the worse perhaps for being quite different from what it was meant to be" (*Letters*, p. 343). If this projected novel, which is otherwise unidentifiable, was in fact *Eyeless in Gaza*, obviously some radical changes were effected during the lengthy process of composition and revision.

2. George Woodcock, *Dawn and the Darkest Hour: A Study of Aldous Huxley* (New York: Viking, 1972), p. 194. For additional information on

this period of crisis, see Sybille Bedford, *Aldous Huxley: A Biography* (New York: Knopf, 1974), pp. 287-314.

3. Ibid., p. 308. The degree of personal and artistic struggle involved in the writing of *Eyeless in Gaza* is further evidenced by Huxley's admission, after it was already in print, that he had "lost all sense" of what the book was like from an objective viewpoint. "I...[would] have liked, if it had been possible, to put it aside and look at it again after two or three years. Wolves at doors imposed immediate publication and I let it go, feeling uncomfortably in the dark about [the] thing" (*Letters*, p. 404).

4. There is a discrepancy in the references to Anthony's age in the novel. Chapter One, dated August 30, 1933, takes place on Anthony's forty-second birthday. But in Chapter Forty-Nine, set four and a half months later, Anthony tells Dr. Miller that he is forty-three.

5. Aldous Huxley, *Eyeless in Gaza* (New York: Harper, 1936), pp. 16-17. Hereafter cited in the text.

6. During the 1926-28 time sequence Anthony makes several approving references to Lawrence. For example, Lawrence is described as "one of the most powerful personality-smashers.... [There] are no 'characters' in his books" (*Gaza*, p. 110). This is of course roughly the same period when Huxley himself was most drawn to Lawrence the man and writer.

7. Woodcock (pp. 199-203) and Jerome Meckier, *Aldous Huxley: Satire and Structure* (New York: Barnes and Noble, 1971), pp. 147-148, present similar versions of this kind of plot reconstruction in their discussions of *Eyeless in Gaza*. While I have depended upon their chronological schemes to some extent, I have departed from their models by reducing the number of "time-frames" from six to five. As I see it, the period of 1933-35, which deals with Anthony's conversion, is the core of the novel and should not be treated as two separate sequences. The obvious reason for analyzing them separately, as Woodcock and Meckier have done, is the fact that Huxley does not relate them consecutively in the novel, but presents them both from the beginning as part of different phases in Anthony's development. That is, the chapters set in 1933, continuing through the Mexican trip (1, 3, 8, 12, 21, 26, 31, 37, 41, 47, 49, 51) exist side by side with the post-Mexico chapters set between February 1934 and February 1935 (2, 7, 13, 17, 23, 28, 32, 35, 38, 40, 42, 44, 46, 50, 53, 54). But as Meckier points out, Huxley's artistic strategy calls for a juxtaposition of two very different Anthony Beavises: the cynical, detached escapist and pedant of 1933, and the straightforward, sincere and committed mystic and pacifist of 1934-35. Putting the two Beavises side by side throughout the novel, Huxley forces us to ask how the radical change in personality and outlook could have occurred. The chief tasks of the book are to explain the relationship between the two Beavises, to disclose how they came to be, and finally to show that the two are actually one (along with all the earlier avatars). The point at which the two narrative threads are joined, and the vital link between the two Beavises, is the journey to Mexico.

8. See Woodcock, p. 200; and Derek S. Savage, "Aldous Huxley and the Dissociation of Personality," in his *The Withered Branch: Six Studies in*

*the Modern Novel* (London: Eyre and Spottiswoode, 1950), pp. 144-146, 152.

9. Meckier, p. 144.

10. Helen's subsequent description of this gruesome episode is worth remembering: " 'It almost fell on Anthony and me,' " she tells Mark Staithes between long draughts of wine. " 'On the roof of his house it was. And we had no clothes on. Like the Garden of Eden. And then, out of the blue, down came that dog—and exploded, I tell you, literally exploded.... Dog's blood from head to foot. We were drenched—but *drenched*' " (p. 232). As we shall see later, the sensations associated with "explosions" of one kind or another, usually accompanied by bloodshed, are important elements in Anthony's thought processes.

11. This paragraph gives expression to an important factor in Anthony's thinking about the nature of the force which governs time and fate. Huxley takes care here to link the lunatic in the mind who randomly deals out the "snapshots" of memory with the "imbecile recruit" who was the fortuitous agent of fate in the bombing accident. The same mechanistic teleological power, Thomas Hardy's "purblind Doomster," arranged for the calamitous descent of the dog in Chapter Twelve, as well as for several later occurrences of this sort.

12. It is most significant that Huxley shifts the rejection of Lawrence to before Anthony's trip to Mexico. This fact provides additional support for my contention that after years of reflection Huxley saw that the real import of his Mexican experience lay beyond his repudiation of the Lawrencian influence.

13. The Mexican place names in the novel are fictitious. However, by referring to the descriptions in *Beyond the Mexique Bay* we can determine that Anthony and Mark are following the route through southern Mexico (the state of Oaxaca) taken by the Huxleys on their Mexican journey of 1933. Puerto San Felipe is the coastal village of Puerto Angel. Tapatlán is Miahuatlán.

14. Bedford, p. 324. On the correspondence between Huxley and Anthony Beavis, see pp. 306-307.


Chapter VI: "Life on a Border"


1. Anthony Burgess, "The Greene and the Red: Politics in the Novels of Graham Greene," in his *Urgent Copy: Literary Studies* (New York: Norton, 1968), pp. 19, 15.

2. Graham Greene, *The Honorary Consul* (New York: Simon and Schuster, 1973), pp. 22, 197.

3. See Terry Eagleton, *Exiles and Émigrés: Studies in Modern Literature* (New York: Shocken, 1970), pp. 135-136. The excitement of being exposed to danger and corruption in unfamiliar surroundings has played an important role not only in Greene's choice of destinations for his travels and of fictional settings for his novels, but also in the kind of characters and plots

toward which he is inclined. In his autobiography, *A Sort of Life* (New York: Simon and Schuster, 1971), Greene describes himself as a manic-depressive type, and recounts the notorious episode in which he experimented with the suicidal game of Russian roulette in an attempt to overcome the depression and boredom from which he suffered following psychoanalysis at age sixteen. Though by the sixth try the thrill had worn off, his first brush with death succeeded in defeating his boredom for a time and allowed him to make the discovery that "it was possible to enjoy again the visible world by risking its total loss..." (p. 130). But the pattern remained a part of his adult life, "so that without experience of Africa I went on an absurd and reckless trek through Liberia; it was the fear of boredom which took me to Tabasco during the religious persecution, to a *léproserie* in the Congo, to the Kikuyu reserve during the Mau-Mau insurrection, to the emergency in Malaya and to the French war in Vietnam. There, in those last three regions of clandestine war, the fear of ambush served me just as effectively as the revolver from the corner cupboard in the lifelong war against boredom" (p. 133). In his excellent comparative study of Greene and Mauriac, Philip Stratford has pointed out the "pattern of alternance" central to Greene's life and works, alternance between boredom and excitement, peace and danger, life and death, the familiar and the unfamiliar. See his *Faith and Fiction: Creative Process in Greene and Mauriac* (Notre Dame, Indiana: Univ. of Notre Dame Press, 1964), pp. 53-59.

4. Graham Greene, *Journey Without Maps* (1936; rpt. New York: Viking, 1961), pp. 9-10, 11.

5. Ibid., p. 277.

6. For Greene, the child's awareness of "supernatural evil" is not a violation of his innocence; nor is the primitive view of supernatural power "evil" in the orthodox Christian sense. Instead, both are manifestations of extraordinary force and mystery which are left to be supernatural by sensibilities that have not yet developed an abstract understanding of good and evil. See Carolyn D. Scott, "The Witch in the Corner: Notes on Graham Greene's Mythology," in *Graham Greene: Some Critical Considerations*, ed. Robert O. Evans (Lexington, Kentucky: Univ. of Kentucky Press, 1963), pp. 232-235.

7. *Journey Without Maps*, p. 310.

8. Graham Greene, *Another Mexico* (1939; rpt. New York: Viking, 1964), p. 2. Hereafter cited in the text. The British edition is entitled *The Lawless Roads*.

9. *Journey Without Maps*, p. 159. See Gwenn R. Boardman, *Graham Greene: The Aesthetics of Exploration* (Gainesville, Florida: Univ. of Florida Press, 1971), pp. 1-2. This study traces Greene's use of "the central metaphor of the map" (p. 1) as an embodiment of his artistic quest throughout his writing. Boardman contends that each of Greene's journeys "exposed new levels of artistic consciousness and provided metaphors for [his] artistic development" (p. 3). She also points out the associations between Africa and Greene's childhood (p. 15), and between Mexico and his adolescence (p. 53).

10. Graham Greene, "Letter to a West German Friend," *New Statesman,* May 31, 1963; rpt. in *The Portable Graham Greene,* ed. Philip Stratford (New York: Viking, 1973), p. 599.

11. The excitement and expectation generated by looking across a border is the chief subject of "Across the Bridge" (1938), a story set at the Mexican border in Nuevo Laredo. Significantly, in this story Greene's narrator first mocks the idealization of the country "over there" which the border-magnetism can bring about, and then proceeds to sympathize with Calloway, the character who is victimized by the illusions thus induced. Greene sometimes plays on the different sensations evoked first by looking across a border (linked with the child's dreams of the future), then by actually traversing it, and finally by looking back across with nostalgia to the side left behind. He offers a thought in *Journey Without Maps* which pertains to these contrasting perspectives: "I find myself always torn between two beliefs: the belief that life should be better than it is and the belief that when it appears better it is really worse" (p. 13).

12. *A Sort of Life,* p. 74.

13. Ibid.

14. Stratford, p. 52. See also Ian Gregor, "The Greene Baize Door," *Blackfriars,* XXXVI (September 1955), 328-330. Gregor discusses the baize door as an "obsessive" symbol in Greene's fiction, and relates it to his use of border imagery to express his view of life "in vividly imagined spatial terms" (p. 330).

15. *A Sort of Life,* p. 74n.

16. Graham Greene, *This Gun for Hire* (1936), rpt. in *Three by Graham Greene* (New York: Viking, 1968), p. 145.

17. Graham Greene, *The Power and the Glory* (1940; rpt. New York: Viking, 1962), p. 135.

18. Ibid., p. 96.

19. Graham Greene, *The Shipwrecked* (1935; rpt. New York: Bantam Books, 1956), p. 127. The British title is *England Made Me.*

20. *The Honorary Consul,* p. 17. The emphasis is mine throughout.

21. The quoted phrase is part of a revealing passage in *Journey Without Maps* in which Greene describes the general confession preparatory to his formal conversion to Catholicism in 1926. His first confession, Greene recalls, was "like a life photographed as it came to mind, without any order, full of gaps, giving at best a general impression." Yet despite what was lost, the effort to retain with full intensity key moments from the past (not unlike Wordsworth's "spots of time") yielded new insights. "I couldn't help feeling," he continues, "that I had got somewhere new by way of memories I hadn't known I possessed. I had taken up the thread of life from very far back, from so far back as innocence" (p. 120). Greene's technique of selective memory, or what I am calling the memory formula, has precisely this quality of "a life photographed as it came to mind." The same figure is used, as we shall see in the next chapter, in connection with the character of the dentist in *The Power and the Glory.*

22. Graham Greene, "The Young Dickens," in *Collected Essays* (New York: Viking, 1969), p. 106.

23. R. W. B. Lewis, *The Picaresque Saint: Representative Figures in Contemporary Fiction* (New York: Lippincott, 1959), p. 220.

24. *The Portable Graham Greene*, p. 600.

25. In a very illuminating discussion of Greene's response to the politics of the Revolution, Sheryl Sherman Pearson points out three chief shortcomings in his understanding: (1) he does not give sufficient consideration to the legitimate historical basis of the Revolution's antipathy against the Church in Mexico; (2) he assumes misleadingly that anti-clericalism is equivalent to atheism, confusing the religious issue with an essentially political one; (3) he judges the Revolution as a whole on the basis of the Church-State conflict, thus obscuring or undervaluing other important issues. Dr. Pearson also argues convincingly that Greene's tendency to associate the ideology of the Revolution with those of totalitarian regimes in Europe before the Second World War militated against his receptiveness to the distinctively nativistic strain of the Mexican Revolution. See "The Anglo-American Novel of the Mexican Revolution, 1910-1940: D. H. Lawrence, B. Traven, Graham Greene," unpub. dissertation (Univ. of Michigan, 1976), Chapter IV.

26. We may recall that in "The Flying Fish" fragment (written in 1925) Lawrence had also used Veracruz as a symbolic frontier, a "true cross" between the dark and white consciousness, between Gethin Day's stay in Mexico and his return to England, and between his severe illness and his recovery.

27. See Henry Bamford Parks, *A History of Mexico*, Sentry Edition (Boston: Houghton Mifflin, rev. 1969), pp. 395, 400-401; and William Weber Johnson, *Heroic Mexico: The Violent Emergence of a Modern Nation* (Garden City, New York: Doubleday, 1968), pp. 414, 416-417.

28. In his "Introduction" to *The Power and the Glory* Greene remarks, "It was in Villahermosa that I came on traces of my principal character, though I did not recognize him at the time. Nothing was further from my thoughts than a novel. An inhabitant told me of the last priest in the state who had baptized his son, giving him a girl's name by accident, for he was so drunk he could hardly stand for the ceremony. Afterward he had disappeared into the mountains on the borders of Chiapas—perhaps he was killed by the Red Shirts, perhaps he had escaped to easier conditions" (pp. 2-3).

29. Greene is quoting from Ephesians 2:12. The "aboriginal calamity" is an allusion to a passage from Cardinal Newman's *Apologia Pro Vita Sua*. This passage, which is one of Greene's epigraphs to *Another Mexico*, ends as follows: "I can only answer, that either there is no Creator, or this living society of men is in a true sense discarded from His presence . . . *if* there be a God, *since* there is a God, the human race is implicated in some terrible aboriginal calamity."

30. Graham Greene, *The Heart of the Matter* (New York: Viking, 1948), p. 142.

31. In "The Lottery Ticket" (1938), a story set in Villahermosa, Greene makes hate one of his central themes. However, the protagonist's hate results from a betrayal caused by his own Liberal naiveté, which has been

exploited by the socialist governor to help in quashing his Catholic political opponent. Also, although the hate is triggered by circumstances in Tabasco, it proliferates to cover all human duplicity: "hate spread across Mr. Thriplow's Liberal consciousness, ignoring boundaries.... Individuals dropped and shrivelled in the enormous conflagration of his internecine war.... It seemed to Mr. Thriplow...that it was the whole condition of human life that he had begun to hate." See *Nineteen Stories* (London: Heinemann, 1947), p. 139. This story is not included in the American edition.

32. In a letter to the author, dated August 1, 1974, Greene indicates that on his only return visit to Mexico City—a brief stopover of a few days during one of his trips to Cuba in the early 1960's—he found the capital "as disagreeable a place as ever and very little changed. The few Mexicans I met on this visit...seemed to agree thoroughly with my books about their country!"

33. Evelyn Waugh, *Robbery Under Law: The Mexican Object-lesson* (1939; rpt. London: Catholic Book Club, 1940), pp. vii-viii. Hereafter cited in the text.

34. The emphasis supplied in all of these passages is mine. In fairness to Waugh, it must be pointed out that the overt political emphasis and the propagandistic methods used in *Robbery Under Law* are not typical of his work. After the book's publication Waugh apparently realized that his talents were not represented at their best in *Robbery*. When he reprinted selections from his travel writings in *When the Going Was Good* (1946) he wisely chose nothing from his book about Mexico.

35. Graham Greene, *The Confidential Agent* (1939), rpt. in *Three By Graham Greene*, p. 5. The emphasis is mine throughout.

36. Ibid., p. 51.

37. *The Power and the Glory*, p. 177.


Chapter VII: A Mexico of the Mind

1. Francis Thompson, "The Hound of Heaven" (1893), lines 1-4. The title of the original American edition of *The Power and the Glory* was *The Labyrinthine Ways*.

2. Richard Hoggart, "The Force of Caricature: Aspects of the Art of Graham Greene, With Particular Reference to *The Power and the Glory*," *Essays in Criticism*, III (October 1953), 447.

3. Graham Greene, *Another Mexico* (1939) rpt. New York: Viking, 1964), p. 64. This passage calls to mind some of Huxley's remarks on the Romantics in "Wordsworth in the Tropics" (1929), as well as the reflections on "untamed" nature in *Beyond the Mexique Bay* (1934). Huxley's general aversion to the undomesticated Mexican landscape seems, however, much more the product of the rational mind and its skeptical bent. Greene's sentiments appear to derive from more instinctive and temperamental sources.

4. See, for example, *The Comedians* (New York: Viking, 1966), p. 137. Here Greene speaks of the Haiti of "Papa Doc" Duvalier and the sinister

Tontons Macoute: "Haiti was not an exception in a sane world: it was a small slice of everyday taken at random."

5. See Karl Patten, "The Structure of *The Power and the Glory*," *Modern Fiction Studies*, III (Autumn 1957), 225-234. Patten identifies two interrelated structures in the novel, a temporal one (the central narrative of the hunt), and a spatial one (the series of symbolic encounters), which he calls a "radial pattern" (p. 225). See also R. W. B. Lewis' discussion of the priest's encounters in *The Picaresque Saint: Representative Figures in Contemporary Fiction* (New York: Lippincott, 1959), pp. 251-256.

6. Graham Greene, *The Power and the Glory* (1940; rpt. New York: Viking, 1962), p. 15. Hereafter cited in the text.

7. Aldous Huxley, *Eyeless in Gaza* (New York: Harper, 1936), p. 16. The chief difference between the two passages cited is that Greene is emphasizing the recurrence of "seedy" locales in Mr. Tench's past, while Huxley is more interested (at this point in the novel) in the random moments of time in Anthony Beavis' life which are frozen by the camera lens. Tench is conscious of a pattern, Beavis of the absence of a pattern. Huxley continues: "There was no chronology. The idiot remembered no distinction between before and after. . . . The thirty-five years of his conscious life made themselves immediately known to him as a chaos—a pack of snapshots in the hands of a lunatic" (pp. 16-17). As we have seen in Chapter V, Beavis eventually becomes aware of the continuity of experience and of his responsibility for his actions. In this he resembles Greene's Mr. Tench (to some extent) at the end of *The Power and the Glory*.

8. The last three paragraphs of Chapter One offer an excellent example of Greene's use of cinematic crosscutting or juxtaposition to establish a multiple perspective of his scene. A kind of graduated border image is employed here by Greene's moving the "camera eye" from Mr. Tench in his office, preparing himself impassively for "a little additional pain"; to the deck of the *General Obregon*, where a young girl sings a wistful song about a rose stained with "true love's blood," and where there is "an enormous sense of freedom and air" (p. 25); to the priest plodding off by mule into the darkness of the tropical forest, feeling acutely the pain of his lost freedom and his "abandonment." The three perspectives are linked spatially by the shoreline, while the three "cuts" are tied together by the overlapping sound of the boat's siren. See Dominick P. Consolo, "Graham Greene: Style and Stylistics in Five Novels," in *Graham Greene: Some Critical Considerations*, ed. Robert O. Evans (Lexington, Kentucky: Univ. of Kentucky Press, 1963), pp. 74-75.

9. On this point, see Marie-Beatrice Mesnét, *Graham Greene and the Heart of the Matter* (London: Cresset, 1954), pp. 25-26. Mesnét describes the lieutenant as "a Christian who has revolted but cannot return to a purely natural condition. . . . Even if he denies that there is a God . . . the very intensity of his hate can only be the effect of a belief still alive in spite of his own will. . . . A substitute God has to be found, when God is deserted." The utopian ideal provides this function for the lieutenant. Alan Grob likens the lieutenant's hunt to the journey of Saul of Tarsus along the road to Damascus. See " 'The Power and the Glory': Graham Greene's

Argument from Design," *Criticism*, II (Winter 1969), 24.

10. From Greene's Introduction to *The Power and the Glory*, p. 4.

11. For an excellent discussion of the priest's experience of communion at his new "home" in the prison, and of the way in which this scene foreshadows later developments once the priest enters Chiapas in Book III, see Peter J. Conn, "Act and Scene in *The Power and the Glory*," in *The Power and the Glory: Text and Criticism*, eds. R. W. B. Lewis and Peter J. Conn, Viking Critical Library (New York: Viking, 1970), pp. 327-330. Clearly a microcosm of Greene's fictional world, the prison episode has been praised by Lewis in *The Picaresque Saint* as "the most effective scene Greene has yet written" (p. 251), and more lavishly by Sean O'Faolain as "one of the finest scenes in all fiction." See *The Vanishing Hero: Studies in Novelists of the Twenties* (London: Eyre and Spottiswoode, 1956), p. 94.

12. Greene's geography in *The Power and the Glory* is noteworthy more for its dramatic immediacy than for its cartographical accuracy. Many times the whisky priest thinks of the possibility of escaping *north* across the mountains into Chiapas. In actuality, Chiapas borders on the south of Tabasco; to the north lies the Bay of Campeche, with the Gulf of Mexico beyond. But it is not unlikely that an inhabitant might associate the Chiapan border with the north, since it is on the main inland route toward Mexico City—which is itself "north" of Tabasco in one's mental geography, though it lies west-northwest on the map. A more important and suggestive geographical alteration in *The Power and the Glory* is Greene's use of the mountains as his "invisible boundary" between the two states. On the cartographer's map these mountains are located well *inside* the state of Chiapas. As we have seen in the discussion of *Another Mexico* in the last chapter, Greene tended to give priority to imaginative rather than "official" boundaries, even then. An apparent confusion about this matter has resulted in several errors in the map and caption describing the priest's journeys included in the Viking Critical Library Edition of the novel, edited by Lewis and Conn.

13. See Conn, pp. 327-328.

14. We may recall Greene's reflections at the Mexican border, in the Prologue to *Another Mexico*: "And so faith came to one—shapelessly, without dogma, a presence above a croquet lawn, something associated with violence, cruelty, evil across the way" (p. 3).

15. The priest had first heard the song about the rose in Chapter Four of Book I. After arriving at an anonymous village in the Tabascan forest, he heard a woman singing as he lay down to sleep in a hut. The two lines of the song that are audible (of which he recalls only a part of the first) are these: "'I went down to my field and there I found a rose. . . . I went down to my field and the rose was withered'" (p. 59). Greene's inclusion of the song at so strategic a juncture in the climactic scene rests on the assumption that the reader will not only remember the song but see its relevance to the priest's ruminations about waking from the dream of peace in the pasteboard paradise of Chiapas. I take the significance of the withered rose to be his triumphal acceptance of the world of time and suffering. In the opening chapter of *The Power and the Glory*, a girl aboard the departing *General*

*Obregon* sings a "melancholy, sentimental, and contented song about a rose which had been stained with true love's blood" (p. 25). Though not unrelated in meaning, this is probably not the same song heard by the priest in the village and remembered in the crucial border scene. In any event, the priest was too far inland to have heard the song "gently" sung by the girl on the boat. A. A. DeVitis, who contends that there is only one song heard by the priest on both occasions, suggests that Greene is alluding to Dante's multifoliate rose and to T. S. Eliot's rose image in "Ash Wednesday." See *Graham Greene* (New York: Twayne, 1964), pp. 94, 158, n. 7. The withered-rose figure also appears in *Another Mexico* (p. 252) and at the end of "The Lottery Ticket."

## Chapter VIII: The *Barranca* of History

1. Malcolm Lowry, *Selected Letters of Malcolm Lowry*, eds. Harvey Breit and Margerie Bonner Lowry (New York: Lippincott, 1965), p. 67. References to this collection will hereafter be cited in the text as *Letters*.

2. George Woodcock, "On the Day of the Dead," *Northern Review*, VI (1953-54), 15; William H. Gass, "In Terms of the Toenail: Fiction and the Figures of Life," *New American Review No. 10*, ed. Theodore Solotaroff (New York: New American Library, 1970), p. 53.

3. Douglas Day, Preface to Lowry's posthumously published *Dark As the Grave Wherein My Friend Is Laid*, eds. Douglas Day and Margerie Lowry (New York and Cleveland: World Publishing, 1968), p. xi.

4. See George Woodcock, "Under Seymour Mountain," *Canadian Literature*, VII (Spring 1961), 3-6. In presenting the case for Lowry as a Canadian writer, Woodcock contrasts the work set in Mexico with that set in British Columbia in a way which seems to me to suggest precisely what is lacking in the latter. "If Mexico stirred him through that combination of antagonism and attraction which so many Europeans feel there, Canada . . . stirred him through a sympathy that led towards total involvement. It is for this reason, perhaps, that in his Canadian stories the Websterian hell of *Under the Volcano* never comes into view. . . . No man goes down to destruction under Seymour Mountain, and along the beaches of Dollarton the phantoms with death's-head faces do not sing in the voices of demons as they did for Consul Firmin. On the contrary, here . . . there is a sense of redemption" (p. 4). I would concur with Harvey Breit, who writes in his Introduction to the *Selected Letters* (p. xiii), that though Lowry "knew Heaven, he knew Hell best. Though he knew hope, he knew despair better."

5. Carlos Fuentes, "Mexico's New Wave," *Venture*, III (December-January 1967), 128.

6. Terence Wright, " 'Under the Volcano': The Static Art of Malcolm Lowry," *Ariel*, I (October 1970), 76.

7. Douglas Day states that the real translation of Quauhnahuac is "Among the Trees." See *Malcolm Lowry: A Biography* (New York: Oxford Univ. Press, 1973), p. 215.

8. Malcolm Lowry, *Under the Volcano* (1947; rpt. Philadelphia and New York: Lippincott, 1965), p. 3. Hereafter cited in the text.

9. Octavio Paz, *The Labyrinth of Solitude: Life and Thought in Mexico*, trans. Lysander Kemp (New York: Grove Press, 1961), pp. 57-58.

10. Malcolm Lowry, "Garden of Etla," *United Nations World*, IV (June 1950), 45-46.

11. Woodcock, "On the Day of the Dead," p. 29.

12. Day, *Malcolm Lowry*, pp. 327-328.

13. Ibid., pp. 329-330.

14. These manifestations of multiple recurrence provide ample illustration of Lowry's professed belief in occult coincidences, or what he sometimes called the Law of Series. The pattern is of course further extended by the world situation at the time of the novel's action. Along with other factors to be explained subsequently, the specter of Germany in the thirties is represented throughout *Volcano* by the *Orlac* film, a Hollywood remake of a German horror movie starring Conrad Veidt. Ex-director Laruelle muses upon the days of the Weimar Republic, "when a defeated Germany was winning the respect of the cultured world by the pictures she was making" (p. 24). The blood-stained hands of the artist-turned-murderer in the film are clearly suggestive of the state of affairs in the Germany of 1938-39. "[What] a complicated endless tale it seemed to tell, of tyranny and sanctuary, that poster looming above him now, showing the murderer Orlac! An artist with a murderer's hands; that was the ticket, the hieroglyphic of the times. For really it was Germany itself that, in the gruesome degradation of a bad cartoon, stood over him" (p. 25). The world ascendency of Nazism, with its attendant racial pseudo-mythology, may be seen as roughly analogous to the Hispanic Conquest of the New World. Both of these are linked, however obscurely, to the Consul's continued presence in Mexico after the oil crisis of 1938, which resulted in a break of diplomatic ties between England and Mexico (then ruled by the Indian President, Lázaro Cárdenas). Finally, there is a dim suggestion that the Consul is further embroiled in the network of international conflict and inter-racial intrigue by an incident in his past. As the commander of an English warship (with the appropriately ironic name *Samaritan*) during the First World War, Geoffrey may or may not—we are never told for certain—have been responsible for the retaliatory murder of a group of German officers captured from a sinking submarine. In his letter to Cape, Lowry spoke of the novel's "severe classical pattern—you can even see the German submarine officers taking revenge on the Consul in the form of the *sinarquistas* and semi-fascist *brutos* at the end" (*Letters*, p. 88).

15. "On account of its internal instability and its proximity to the United States, Mexico attracted considerable attention from Nazi Germany, as a result of which there was a marked growth of reactionary and fascistic groups who were encouraged by German agents and assisted by German money. These forces received further stimulus from the victory of Franco in the Spanish civil war [sic]. Alone among all the governments of the Americas, the Cárdenas government was outspokenly pro-Loyalist, ship-

ping arms to the repubic until stopped by the 'non-intervention' program and giving welcome to a number of refugees at the end of the war. But Falangist propaganda had considerable influence in Mexico." Henry Bamford Parkes, *A History of Mexico* (Boston: Houghton Mifflin, rev. 1969), p. 409.

16. Lowry's use of the *barranca* here and elsewhere in *Under the Volcano* brings to mind the pivotal scenes involving another *barranca* in *The Power and the Glory*. As the passage quoted here indicates, Lowry's *barranca*, imaging as it does the notion of duality, bears some resemblance to Greene's use of the *barranca* as a border emblem suggestive of an inner division in his protagonist. However, Greene's *barranca* is something which the whisky priest must *traverse*, not once but twice. He must experience not only the descent into the abyss but also the tortuous climb out of it. In the *Volcano* there is really no question of the Consul's extricating himself from the abyss. For one thing, he *wants* to be there, and for another Lowry's abyss is in effect bottomless. As Geoffrey himself confesses in his unposted letter to Yvonne read by M. Laruelle in Chapter I, sometimes during his mescal-induced visions he can actually see the path leading out of hell, but he "may not take it" (p. 36).

17. It might be well at this point briefly to enumerate a few additional correspondences in the conquistador configuration. Always in some sense an authority figure, the conquistador may himself become the victim of a local power play. This happened even to Cortés, who had to contend with the possibly mutinous schemes of certain of his men as well as with betrayal at the hands of supposed allies among the Indians, and who was bypassed in the Spanish Crown's choice of the first Viceroy of New Spain. General domestic strife and overt marital discord were experienced by Cortés, Geoffrey's father, Geoffrey himself, and of course Maximilian. Cortés, Maximilian, and Geoffrey all had residences in Cuernavaca, with gardens which are (at the time of the novel's action) in a state of ruin. The same three men all had red beards. Each of them, at one time or another (Maximilian in his state portraits, the Consul at the end of Chapter XII), brandishes a sword. A minor and probably coincidental parallel between Geoffrey and Maximilian is the association between their supposed sexual impotence and venereal disease. One of Geoffrey's obsessive fears is that he has contracted syphilis. Maximilian's political enemies circulated rumors that his marriage was childless because the emperor had syphilis.

18. Dale Edmonds was the first critic to point out that this man, who along with his horse branded with the number seven will reappear in the crucial episode by the roadside in Chapter VIII, is, like Juan Cerrillo, a rider for the *Banco de Crédito y Ejidal*. The "chinking" saddlebags very likely contain money which he is to deliver to the impoverished villages in the mountains to the south of Quauhnahuac. The *ejido* is a communal property dating back for centuries in Mexican history. But the *Ejidal* bank was the creation of President Cárdenas, designed to subsidize the *ejido* communities. Edmonds demonstrates convincingly that the murder of this man and the theft of his saddlebags (in Chapter VIII) are probably the

work of the anti-Cárdenas, pro-fascist elements flourishing in Mexico in
the late 1930's. See "*Under the Volcano:* A Reading on the 'Immediate
Level,'" *Tulane Studies,* XVI (1968), pp. 86-88.
   19. See Samuel Ramos, *Profile of Man and Culture in Mexico,* trans.
Peter G. Earle (Austin, Texas: Univ. of Texas Press, 1962), pp. 57-63.
   20. See Charles Gibson, *Tlaxcala in the Sixteenth Century* (1952; rpt.
Stanford, California: Stanford Univ. Press, 1967), pp. 15-27. I am indebted
to my colleague, Professor Jack A. Haddick of the University of Houston
Victoria Campus, for bringing this useful work to my attention. Gibson
points out that even after the Spaniards had defeated the Tlaxcalans there
were some elements in Tlaxcalan society who favored a renewal of hostilities whenever the opportunity to do so with a favorable prospect for victory presented itself. The leader in this movement was a prominent military figure called Xicoténcatl. Interestingly enough, Lowry made use of
this name (with a slight misspelling) in Chapter V when the Consul greets
Quincey's cat with "'hello-pussy-my-little-Priapusspuss, my-little-Oedi-
pusspusspuss. . . . My little Xicotancatl'" (p. 134). It is also possible that
Lowry is alluding here to Xicoténcatl's father (who bore the same name), a
very old blind chief who was perhaps the strongest proponent of the bond
with the Spaniards. Father and son are referred to again in the Tlaxcalan
folder read by the Consul in Chapter X.
   21. Another reason for Lowry's interest in the Tlaxcalans was his belief
that (as part of their bargain with Cortés) they retained their pagan religion. He wrote to Cape that Tlaxcala "is probably the only capital in the
world where black magic is still a working proposition. . ." (*Letters,* p. 82).
See William H. Prescott, *History of the Conquest of Mexico* (1843; rpt.
New York: Everyman's Library, 1972), I, 293. I have relied upon Prescott
for much of the material on Cortés and the Conquest. In a letter to me
(dated September 2, 1974) Margerie Lowry confirms my suspicion that
Lowry had read Prescott's classic account to enhance his knowledge of and
his feeling for this period in Mexican history.
   22. The first man to make such a comparison between Tlaxcala and
Granada was Cortés himself. In a letter to the Spanish King he wrote that
Tlaxcala was "larger, stronger and more populous than the Moorish capital. . . and quite as well built" (as paraphrased by Prescott, I, 290). Since
Lowry on several occasions calls our attention to the correspondence between Granada and Tlaxcala, it is worth mentioning that the phenomenon
of conquest, with its attendant strife and betrayal, was a prominent feature
in the history of the Moorish province. In the 1480's and early 1490's the
power of the Moors was undermined by a bitter division in the ruling
family of Boabdil, a development which eventually allowed the Castilians
to drive the Moors from Granada. Almost eight centuries earlier, according to tradition, the Moors themselves had been aided in the overthrow of
the Visigoths by still another internal conflict in the ruling family. In 711,
the legend goes, Don Rodrigo (the last Visigoth ruler) was so aroused by
the sight of the beautiful Florinda la Cava bathing, that he proceeded to
rape her. In retaliation, her father Count Julian permitted the Moors to
attack the Iberian peninsula from Gibraltar, driving Rodrigo from power.

It is perhaps not merely coincidental that a version of this legend appears in a poem called "Profécia del Tajo" by Fray Luis de León, the same sixteenth-century Spanish poet whose line *"no se puede vivir sin amar"* adorns the tower of M. Laruelle's house in *Under the Volcano*. The latter line appears in a fanciful philosophical work concerning the various epithets for Christ (lily of the valley, prince of peace, and so on). See *De los nombres de Cristo* (1583-85), Vol. II (Madrid: Espasa-Calpe, 1943), p. 201. For bringing these parallels to my attention I am indebted to Samuel Johnson, professor of Spanish at the University of Houston Victoria Campus.

23. The reference to Cortés here is not gratuitous, for as should be apparent by this time, Lowry makes particularly extensive use of the Conquest story in Chapter X. In "choosing Tlaxcala" the Consul is recapitulating the decision of Cortés, after the devastating retreat from Tenochtitlán known as *la noche triste*, to seek sanctuary in Tlaxcala. Despite the aforementioned alliance with the Tlaxcalans, Cortés was by no means assured of being allowed peacefully to take refuge in that province. For one thing, the alliance had been made when the Spaniards were still seemingly unbeatable in battle, when they were so invincible that the Indians believed them to be sent by the gods, fulfilling the prophecy of Quetzalcoatl about the return of a bearded, white-skinned leader who would rule over Mexico. The defeated, downcast force which retreated to Tlaxcala would surely demolish that illusion. Also, along with hundreds of Spaniards who fell at Tenochtitlán were several thousand Tlaxcalan allies, a fact which could reasonably be expected to rouse the Tlaxcalans' wrath. In fact, Cortés' doubts proved to be ill-founded. Xicoténcatl the younger urged joining forces with the Aztecs to drive the weakened Spaniards out of Mexico, but he was overruled and the Spaniards were received warmly in Tlaxcala (see Prescott, II, 107-129). Geoffrey Firmin is not so fortunate in his reception at the Farolito in Parián.

24. Prescott, I, 185.

25. Paz, p. 86. Paz goes on to say of Malinche that she "embodies the open, the *chingado*, to our closed, stoic, impassive Indians.... This explains the success of the contemptuous adjective *malinchista*...[which is used] to denounce all those who have been corrupted by foreign influences. The *malinchistas* are those who want Mexico to open itself to the outside world: the true sons of La Malinche, who is the *Chingada* in person."

26. The reference to Granada, along with the Chief of Gardens' title (associated with the Alhambra), calls to mind once again the Moorish conquest, as well as the Spanish Civil War. Wherever he turns the Consul is, in one way or another, implicated in the atrocities of history. The *Samaritan* affair serves as a reminder of what may have been his personal contribution to the human refuse piled in the great *barranca* of time.

## Chapter IX: The Mexican Voyages of Lowry

1. Malcolm Lowry, "Through the Panama," *Hear Us O Lord From Heaven Thy Dwelling Place* (1961; rpt. New York: Capricorn Books,

1969), p. 42. These words appear in the traveler's journal kept by Sigbjørn Wilderness, the Lowry-persona in this posthumously published novella. In his biography of Lowry, Douglas Day concludes that Lowry probably entered Mexico on the *first* day of November 1936, but for obvious reasons preferred to think of his entry as coinciding with the Day of the Dead, which falls on the second. See *Malcolm Lowry: A Biography* (New York: Oxford Univ. Press, 1973), p. 214. Unless otherwise indicated, all of the data concerning Lowry's activities in Mexico are derived from this source, which will hereafter be cited in the text.

2. Malcolm Lowry, "Garden of Etla," *United Nations World*, IV (June 1950), 45.

3. Ibid., pp. 45, 46.

4. In a letter to me, dated August 19, 1974, Margerie Lowry, Malcolm's widow and the co-editor of his *Selected Letters*, writes regarding the letters of the 1936-38 period, "It's a [miracle] that there are any at all. I found copies of them in an old notebook that somehow still existed. There are no more [extant]."

5. The short story, later incorporated with numerous alterations into Chapter VIII of *Volcano*, was first published in *Prairie Schooner*, XXXVII (Winter 1963-64), 284-300.

6. That this draft, no longer extant, did exist, has been testified to by Conrad Aiken, Arthur Calder-Marshall, and others who actually saw it in Cuernavaca. See Day, p. 219.

7. For useful treatments of the Lowry-Aiken relationship, see V. L. O. Chittick, "*Ushant's* Malcolm Lowry," *Queen's Quarterly*, LXXI (Spring 1964), 67-75; Richard Hauer Costa, "Lowry/Aiken Symbiosis," *Nation*, CCIV (June 26, 1967), 823-826; and Day, pp. 220-224 passim. The most extensive and suggestive treatment, of course, is Aiken's own *Ushant: An Essay* (New York: Duell, Sloan and Pierce, 1952); see especially pp. 239-240, 291-297, 322-326, 348-361. *Ushant* will be cited hereafter in the text.

8. In an editorial letter to the *Times Literary Supplement*, February 16, 1967, p. 127, Aiken states that these arguments were the direct source of the clash between the Consul and his half-brother Hugh in Chapter X of *Under the Volcano*. Hugh defends the political ideals espoused by Lowry in 1937, while the Consul represents Aiken's more disinterested position.

9. The single most painful "invasion" made by Lowry into Aiken's literary domain was the expropriation of the story of William Blackstone, the eccentric English explorer of the seventeenth century. Aiken had for years been planning to use Blackstone as an exemplar of a kind of individualism he greatly admired. In the course of their conversations about writing, Lowry became so fascinated with Blackstone that "at once, and without so much as a by-your-leave, [he had] taken over the Blackstone idea as his own" (*Ushant*, p. 294). Blackstone does, of course, appear as a symbolic ideal upon which the Consul broods in *Volcano*. It is almost certain, however, that Lowry's particular use of the "Blackstone idea" was finally his own. Aiken eventually utilized Blackstone in his long poem about American individualism, *The Kid*. See Chittick, pp. 72-74.

10. Conrad Knickerbocker, "The Voyages of Malcolm Lowry," *Prairie*

*Schooner* XXXVII (Winter 1963-64), 308-309. Aiken wrote that every angle of their relationship "had been studied in mirrors, each of them with an eye to its use; each of them with an eye to making use of it first. And after all, in that so-long elaborated symbiosis, who was to say just what was whose, and just which properties, of perception or invention, belonged to either?" (*Ushant*, pp. 356-357).

11. Arthur Calder-Marshall, "Malcolm Lowry," unsigned essay, *Times Literary Supplement*, January 26, 1967, p. 58. See also Day, pp. 224-229. Day suggests that this French Consul bears some relation to the Frenchman Jacques Laruelle in the *Volcano*, with whom Consul Firmin's wife Yvonne has a brief affair.

12. Lowry's version of this scene appears in the reminiscences of Sigbjørn Wilderness in *Dark As the Grave Wherein My Friend Is Laid*, eds. Douglas Day and Margerie Lowry (New York and Cleveland: World Publishing, 1968), pp. 87-89. Hereafter cited in the text. Jan Gabrial wrote a short story called "Not With a Bang," *Story*, XXIX (September-October 1946), 55-61, which may represent her own version. If, as Day believes, the story *is* based on actual events, it would suggest that Lowry played a far more active part in the separation than his own version allows. On the basis of the story, Day maintains that Lowry actually drove Jan away, or else in effect ran from her, because he could not face up to his inability to love her in an adult manner. Jan realized that she could not handle him (no one really could), and so "got out in time, instead of being pulled into Lowry's self-constructed maelstrom with him" (Day, p. 233).

13. Malcolm Lowry, *Under the Volcano*, (1947; rpt. Philadelphia and New York: Lippincott, 1965), pp. 35, 48. Hereafter cited in the text.

14. Malcolm Lowry, *Selected Letters of Malcolm Lowry*, eds. Harvey Breit and Margerie Bonner Lowry (New York: Lippincott, 1965), p. 29. Hereafter cited in the text.

15. Letter to me, August 19, 1974. One of the villages visited was called Parián, the name which Lowry was to use for his apocryphal province in the *Volcano*. Day states (p. 243) that Juan Fernando was transferred to another branch of the *Ejidal* bank in Cuicuitlán and thus separated from Lowry *before* the end of 1937. If this date is accurate, it would mean that the actual contact between the two men lasted only about two weeks (though they continued to correspond)—during the same time that Lowry was supposed to have been in prison.

16. Lowry, "Garden of Etla," p. 46.

17. Ibid., pp. 46-47. There is a striking similarity between these concepts enumerated by Lowry and some of those discussed by Octavio Paz in *The Labyrinth of Solitude: Life and Thought in Mexico*, trans. Lysander Kemp (New York: Grove Press, 1961). See especially pages 54-56 for Paz's summation of the Mexican attitudes toward historical cyclicity, death and the impersonality—a term used also by Juan Fernando—of existence.

18. Day contends, unjustly in my opinion, that all the political turmoil in Mexico at this time "seems to have gone right over Lowry's head" (p. 245). Presumably this conclusion is based on the fact that Lowry's extant letters are concerned primarily with personal matters and make no refer-

ence to the major events of the time. It seems likely, however, that his association with Juan Fernando Márquez, whose job and political affiliation have already been mentioned, would have created a certain awareness of the general situation in Mexico. Certainly in *Under the Volcano* we can find evidence of a considerable grasp not only of contemporary political developments in Mexico, but also of their relation to the dominant patterns of Mexican history since the Conquest. Day's biography provides ample testimony to Lowry's astonishing ability somehow to absorb a great many things going on around him even when he was deepest in his cups.

19. Many of the details in this paragraph are taken from Lowry's letter to Ronald Button, a legal deposition dated June 15, 1946. See *Letters*, pp. 93-94.

20. Knickerbocker, p. 309.

21. Richard Hauer Costa, *Malcolm Lowry*, Twayne World Authors Series (New York: Twayne, 1972), p. 53. These details of Lowry's revisions of the *Volcano* are all derived from Costa's excellent comparative analysis of the different versions. See especially pp. 86-105 passim. See also Day, pp. 258-274 passim.

22. Ibid., p. 86. Both the general nature and the function of Lowry's post-Mexico alterations of the *Volcano* rather remind one of Aldous Huxley's displacement of the Lawrencian influence as a causative factor for his Mexican journey in *Eyeless in Gaza*. Huxley, it will be recalled, made his protagonist Anthony Beavis eschew Lawrence's vitalist doctrines *before* rather than during his trip to Mexico, in order to place greater emphasis on other developments which took place while Beavis was in the country.

23. Many of these same criticisms are made by George Woodcock, "Art as the Writer's Mirror: Literary Solipsism in 'Dark as the Grave,'" in his *Odysseus Ever Returning* (1969), rpt. in *Malcolm Lowry: The Man and His Work*, ed. George Woodcock (Vancouver, British Columbia: Univ. of British Columbia Press, 1971), pp. 67-68. See also Costa, p. 116. One of the very few critics to take *Dark As the Grave* seriously as a novel—and a successful one at that—is Matthew Corrigan, "Masks and the Man: The Writer as Actor," *Shenandoah*, XIX (Summer 1968), 89-93. Curiously, the same critic later wrote an unfavorable piece on the book, the article really amounting to an attack on the publishing industry's exploitation of unfinished works by deceased authors. See "Malcolm Lowry, New York Publishing, & the 'New Illiteracy,'" *Encounter*, XXXV (July 1970), 82-93.

24. Woodcock, "Art as the Writer's Mirror," p. 68.

25. Day, Preface, *Dark As the Grave*, p. xv.

26. *Dark As the Grave*, especially the first three chapters concerning the flight "down the map," is saturated with border imagery, the example quoted being the most memorable of these. For Lowry, the border is associated with the rejection of himself by some form of authority, along with a resultant sense of obscure guilt because of the rejection. For an account of the origin of this fear of being turned back at a border, see Day's biography, p. 254.

27. This letter, which does not appear in *Selected Letters*, was published in *Canadian Literature*, VIII (Spring 1961), 44.

28. Letter to me, dated August 19, 1974.

29. Day states that *La Mordida*, on which Lowry worked sporadically from 1947 to 1954, "consists of 352 typed pages, as well as hundreds of pages of earlier draft versions, and is on deposit in the Special Collections Division of the University of British Columbia Library" (p. 356, n. 11). In the letter to me cited above, Mrs. Lowry (who holds the copyright to the manuscript) indicates that she is undecided about whether to publish *La Mordida*. "It's in a very rough state and might have to be published as a journal. On the other hand this would be impractical as some of it is written in the third person so I don't know what to do about it. . . . All the important data [as] regards the actual happenings are in the letter to Ronald Button." This last is a legal deposition (previously cited) and may be considered an accurate reconstruction of the last seven weeks the Lowry's spent in Mexico. I have relied upon this letter, in addition of course to Day's biography, for my own account of this period.

30. Malcolm Lowry, "Present Estate of Pompei," *Hear Us O Lord From Heaven Thy Dwelling Place*, p. 177.

31. "Through the Panama," p. 35. Hereafter cited in the text.

## Appendix: The Fields of Paradise

1. See "The Future of Mexico," *New Republic*, October 19, 1938, pp. 296-299; "Close-Up of Mexico," *New Republic*, May 10, 1939, pp. 25-26; "Conversations in Mexico," *Virginia Quarterly Review*, XV (July 1939), 393-407; "Mexico's 1940," *New Republic*, August 9, 1939, pp. 10-12, August 16, 1939, pp. 41-43; "Mexico in Turmoil," *New Republic*, January 8, 1940, p. 59; and "Mexico: Another Spain," *New Republic*, September 14, 1940, pp. 210-213. A Mexican-set novella by Bates is "The Burning Corn," *Virginia Quarterly Review*, XV (October 1939), 561-622, rpt. in *The Undiscoverables and Other Stories* (New York: Random House, 1942), pp. 113-175.

2. "Conversations in Mexico," p. 400.

3. Ibid., pp. 393-394.

4. Ibid., p. 394.

5. Ibid., pp. 394-395.

6. Ibid., p. 395.

7. Ralph Bates, "Disaster in Finland," *New Republic*, December 13, 1939, p. 221. On Bates's involvement in the Spanish Civil War and his break with Stalinist communism, see Stanley Weintraub, *The Last Great Cause: The Intellectuals and the Spanish War* (New York: Weybright and Talley, 1968), pp. 236-237, 291-294, 329-330; and Katherine Bail Hoskins, *Today the Struggle: Literature and Politics in England During the Spanish Civil War* (Austin, Texas: Univ. of Texas Press, 1969), pp. 124-129.

8. Ralph Bates, *The Fields of Paradise* (New York: Dutton, 1940), p. 197. Hereafter cited in the text.

9. Bates in fact praised the prison scene in *The Power and the Glory* when he reviewed Greene's novel. See "Via Crucis," *New Republic*, April

22, 1940, p. 549. Since Bates had not yet completed *The Fields of Paradise* when he wrote this review, it is possible that—despite their different views about Mexico—Bates was influenced by Greene's treatment of the scene in the prison. An equally striking point of comparison between the two novels is their treatment of the conflict between the Revolution and the Catholic Church. In his review, Bates speaks approvingly of Greene's suspenseful rendering of the priest's flight and eventual capture by the police lieutenant, but he sees a serious flaw in the ideological conflict dramatized by that story. The priest's attitude toward poverty, for instance—his statement to the effect that it is better to allow the poor to die in filth and wake in heaven than to give them earthly power and wealth, which will militate against their dependence upon God's grace—amounts to a misrepresentation of the Catholic point of view, according to Bates. He also finds the police lieutenant an incredible antagonist who offers no serious challenge to the priest's views and who, in the end, adopts the priest's pietism without realizing it. In short, Bates feels that Greene fails to make a serious claim on the reader's thought because Greene is unable (or unwilling) to see the tactical advantages of a faith that could win the people's support precisely by advocating the attempt to clean up filth and alleviate poverty. Bates may well have had these points in mind as he wrote Chapters 19-21 of *The Fields of Paradise*. It is in these chapters that Felipe becomes involved in a series of heated disputes with Canon Mendoza, a reactionary prelate from the state capital. Bates's portrayal of Canon Mendoza is surprisingly sympathetic; Mendoza gradually softens his stance on the rebellion and tries to conceive of a metaphysical bridge across the "abysm between the Revolution and the Faith," a bridge designed not merely "to lead men from one side to the other . . . [but] into a new land where the apposition did not exist" (p. 343). The result, however, is unilluminating. Mendoza finally decides that while there is no logical bridge over the abysm, "the plain and simple man," not requiring logical consistency, could perhaps *pretend* that the abysm did not exist. While Bates's dialectic seems anything but an improvement upon Greene's, his very attempt at such improvement (as a professed nonbeliever) is remarkable.

# Bibliography

## A. Primary Sources

Bates, Ralph. "The Burning Corn." *Virginia Quarterly Review*, XV (July 1939), 393-407; rpt. *The Undiscoverables and Other Stories*. New York: Random House, 1942.

⸻. "Close-Up of Mexico." *New Republic*, May 10, 1939, pp. 25-26.

⸻. "Conversations in Mexico." *Virginia Quarterly Review*, XV (July 1939), 393-407.

⸻. *The Fields of Paradise*. New York: Dutton, 1940.

⸻. "The Future of Mexico." *New Republic*, October 19, 1938, pp. 296-299.

⸻. "Mexico: Another Spain." *New Republic*, September 14, 1940, pp. 210-213.

⸻. "Mexico in Turmoil." *New Republic*, January 8, 1940, p. 59.

⸻. "Mexico's 1940." *New Republic*, August 9, 1939, pp. 10-12, August 16, 1939, pp. 41-43.

⸻. "Via Crucis." *New Republic*, April 22, 1940, pp. 549-550.

Greene, Graham. *Another Mexico*. 1939; rpt. New York: Viking, 1964.

⸻. *Collected Essays*. New York: Viking, 1969.

⸻. *Collected Stories*. New York: Viking, 1973.

⸻. *The Comedians*. New York: Viking, 1966.

⸻. *The Heart of the Matter*. New York: Viking, 1948.

⸻. *The Honorary Consul*. New York: Simon and Schuster, 1973.

⸻. *Journey Without Maps*. 1936; rpt. New York: Viking, 1961.

⸻. *Nineteen Stories*. London: Heinemann, 1947.

⸻. *Our Man in Havana*. New York: Viking, 1958.

⸻. *The Portable Graham Greene*. Ed. Philip Stratford. New York: Viking, 1973.

⸻. *The Power and the Glory*. 1940; rpt. New York: Viking, 1962.

⸻. *A Sort of Life*. New York: Simon and Schuster, 1971.

⸻. *Three by Graham Greene*. New York: Viking, 1968.

⸻. *Travels With My Aunt*. New York: Viking, 1970.

Huxley, Aldous. *Along the Road: Notes and Essays of a Tourist*. New York: Doran, 1925.

——. *Beyond the Mexique Bay: A Traveller's Journal.* 1934; rpt. Collected Edition, London: Chatto and Windus, 1949.

——. *Brave New World and Brave New World Revisited.* New York: Harper, 1965.

——. *Brief Candles.* London: Chatto and Windus, 1930.

——. *Collected Essays.* New York: Harper, 1959.

——. *Do What You Will.* 1929; rpt. Collected Edition, London: Chatto and Windus, 1949.

——. *Eyeless in Gaza.* New York: Harper, 1936.

——. *Jesting Pilate: The Diary of a Journey.* 1926; rpt. London: Chatto and Windus, 1948.

——. *Letters of Aldous Huxley.* Ed. Grover Smith. London: Chatto and Windus, 1969.

——. *Point Counter Point.* New York: Harper, 1928.

——. *Two or Three Graces.* 1926; rpt. Collected Edition, London: Chatto and Windus, 1949.

Lawrence, D. H. *Aaron's Rod.* 1922; rpt. New York: Viking, 1961.

——. *The Collected Letters of D. H. Lawrence.* 2 vols. Ed. Harry T. Moore. New York: Viking, 1962.

——. *The Complete Short Stories of D. H. Lawrence.* 3 vols. New York: Viking, 1961.

——. *Kangaroo.* 1923; rpt. New York: Viking, 1960.

——. *The Letters of D. H. Lawrence.* Ed. Aldous Huxley. New York: Viking, 1932.

——. *The Lost Girl.* 1921; rpt. New York: Viking, 1968.

——. *Mornings in Mexico and Etruscan Places.* Phoenix Edition, London: Heinemann, 1956.

——. *Phoenix: The Posthumous Papers of D. H. Lawrence.* Ed. Edward D. McDonald. New York: Viking, 1936.

——. *Phoenix II: Uncollected, Unpublished, and Other Prose Works by D. H. Lawrence.* Ed. Warren Roberts and Harry T. Moore. New York: Viking, 1970.

——. *The Plumed Serpent [Quetzalcoatl].* 1926; rpt. New York: Knopf, 1951.

——. *St. Mawr and The Man Who Died.* Rpt. New York: Vintage Books, n.d.

——. *Studies in Classic American Literature.* 1923; rpt. New York: Viking, 1964.

Lowry, Malcolm. *Dark As the Grave Wherein My Friend Is Laid.* Ed. Douglas Day and Margerie Lowry. New York and Cleveland: World Publishing, 1968.

——. "Garden of Etla." *United Nations World,* IV (June 1950), 45-47.

——. *Hear Us O Lord From Heaven Thy Dwelling Place.* 1961; rpt. New York: Capricorn Books, 1969.

——. *Malcolm Lowry: Psalms and Songs.* Ed. Margerie Lowry. New York: New American Library, 1975.

——. *Selected Letters of Malcolm Lowry.* Ed. Harvey Breit and Margerie Bonner Lowry. New York: Lippincott, 1965.

————. *Selected Poems of Malcolm Lowry.* Ed. Earle Birney. San Francisco: City Lights Books, 1962.

————. *Under the Volcano.* 1947; rpt. Philadelphia and New York: Lippincott, 1965.

————. "Under the Volcano." *Prairie Schooner,* XXXVII (Winter 1963/ 64), 284-300.

Waugh, Evelyn. *Robbery Under Law: The Mexican Object-Lesson.* 1939; rpt. London: Catholic Book Club, 1940.


B. Secondary Sources


Aiken, Conrad. *The Collected Novels of Conrad Aiken.* New York: Holt, Rinehart and Winston, 1964.

————. *Ushant: An Essay.* New York: Duell, Sloan and Pierce, 1952.

Alexander, Henry. "Lawrence and Huxley." *Queen's Quarterly,* XLI (January 1935), 96-108.

Allott, Kenneth, and Miriam Farris. *The Art of Graham Greene.* New York: Russell and Russell, 1951.

Anon. "Aldous Huxley." *Writers at Work: The "Paris Review" Interviews,* Second Series. New York: Viking, 1968, pp. 193-214.

Anon. "The Greeneland Aboriginal." *New Statesman,* January 13, 1961, pp. 44-45.

Arnold, Armin. *D. H. Lawrence and America.* London: Linden, 1958.

————. *The Symbolic Meaning: The Uncollected Versions of "Studies in Classic American Literature."* London: Centaur Press, 1962.

Artaud, Antonin. *The Peyote Dance.* Trans. Helen Weaver. New York: Farrar, Straus and Giroux, 1976.

Atkins, John. *Aldous Huxley: A Literary Study.* 1965; rev. New York: Orion, 1967.

Aub, Max. *Transito.* Coll. in *Obras en un acto.* 2 vols. México: Imprente Universitaria, 1960.

————. *El zopilote y otros cuentos mexicanos.* Barcelona: Editora y Distribuidora Hispano Americana, 1964.

Bartlett, Norman. "Aldous Huxley and D. H. Lawrence." *Australian Quarterly,* XXXVI (1964), 76-84.

Bedford, Sybille. *Aldous Huxley: A Biography.* New York: Knopf, 1974.

Bentley, Joseph. "Huxley's Ambivalent Response to the Ideas of D. H. Lawrence." *Twentieth Century Literature,* XIII (October 1967), 139-153.

Birnbaum, Milton. *Aldous Huxley's Quest for Values.* Knoxville, Tennessee: Univ. of Tennessee Press, 1971.

Boardman, Gwenn R. *Graham Greene: The Aesthetics of Exploration.* Gainesville, Florida: Univ. of Florida Press, 1971.

Bowering, Peter. *Aldous Huxley: A Study of the Major Novels.* New York: Oxford Univ. Press, 1969.

Bradbrook, Muriel. *Malcolm Lowry: His Art and Early Life.* New York: Cambridge Univ. Press, 1974.

Bradbury Malcolm. "Malcolm Lowry as Modernist." *Possibilities: Essays on the State of the Novel.* London: Oxford Univ. Press, 1973, pp. 181-191.

Brander, Laurence. *Aldous Huxley: A Critical Study.* Lewisburg, Pennsylvania: Bucknell Univ. Press, 1970.

Brenner, Anita, and George R. Leighton. *The Wind That Swept Mexico: The History of the Mexican Revolution 1910-1942.* 1943; rpt. Austin, Texas: Univ. of Texas Press, 1971.

Brett, Dorothy. *Lawrence and Brett: A Friendship.* Philadelphia: Lippincott, 1933.

Brooke, Jocelyn. *Aldous Huxley.* Writers and Their Work. London: British Council Pamphlets, 1954.

Brotherston, J. G. "Revolution and the Ancient Literature of Mexico, For D. H. Lawrence and Antonin Artaud." *Twentieth Century Literature,* XVIII (July 1972), 181-189.

Burgess, Anthony. *Urgent Copy: Literary Studies.* New York: Norton, 1968.

Bynner, Witter. *Journey With Genius: Recollections and Reflections Concerning the D. H. Lawrences.* New York: John Day, 1951.

[Calder-Marshall, Arthur]. "Malcolm Lowry." *Times Literary Supplement,* January 26, 1967, pp. 57-59.

Cavitch, David. *D. H. Lawrence and the New World.* New York: Oxford Univ. Press, 1969.

Chankin, Donald O. *Anonymity and Death: The Fiction of B. Traven.* University Park, Pennsylvania: Pennsylvania State Univ. Press, 1975.

Chittick, V. L. O. "*Ushant*'s Malcolm Lowry." *Queen's Quarterly,* LXXI (Spring 1964), 64-75.

Clark, L. D. *Dark Night of the Body: D. H. Lawrence's "The Plumed Serpent."* Austin, Texas: Univ. of Texas Press, 1964.

Clark, Ronald W. *The Huxleys.* New York: McGraw-Hill, 1968.

Conrad, Joseph. *Nostromo, A Tale of the Seaboard.* 1904; rpt. New York: Holt, Rinehart and Winston, 1961.

Corrigan, Matthew. "Malcolm Lowry, New York Publishing, & the 'New Illiteracy.'" *Encounter,* XXXV (July 1970), 82-93.

————. "Masks and the Man: The Writer as Actor." *Shenandoah,* XIX (Summer 1968), 89-93.

Costa, Richard Hauer. "Lowry/Aiken Symbiosis." *Nation,* CCIV, June 26, 1967, pp. 823-826.

————. *Malcolm Lowry.* New York: Twayne, 1972.

Cowan, James C. *D. H. Lawrence's American Journey: A Study in Literature and Myth.* Cleveland: Case Western Reserve Univ. Press, 1970.

Cross, Richard K. "Malcolm Lowry and the Columbian Eden." *Contemporary Literature,* XIV (Winter 1973), 19-30.

Daleski, H. M. *The Forked Flame: A Study of D. H. Lawrence.* Evanston, Illinois: Northwestern Univ. Press, 1965.

Day, Douglas. *Malcolm Lowry: A Biography.* New York: Oxford Univ. Press, 1973.

————. "Of Tragic Joy." *Prairie Schooner,* XXXVII (Winter 1963/64), 354-362.

DeVitis, A. A. *Graham Greene*. New York: Twayne, 1964.

Dos Passos, John. *The Best Times: An Informal Memoir*. New York: New American Library, 1966.

Doyen, Victor. "Elements Towards a Spatial Reading of Malcolm Lowry's *Under the Volcano*." *English Studies*, L (February 1969), 65-74.

Duffy, Joseph M., Jr. "The Lost World of Graham Greene." *Thought*, XXXIII (Summer 1963), 229-247.

Dyson, A. E. "Aldous Huxley and the Two Nothings." *Critical Quarterly*, III (1961), 293-309.

Eagleton, Terry. *Exiles and Émigrés: Studies in Modern Literature*. New York: Shocken, 1970.

Edmonds, Dale. "*Under the Volcano*: A Reading on the 'Immediate Level.'" *Tulane Studies*, XVI (1968), 63-105.

Epstein, Perle S. *The Private Labyrinth of Malcolm Lowry: "Under the Volcano" and the Cabbala*. New York: Holt, Rinehart and Winston, 1969.

Evans, Robert O., ed. *Graham Greene: Some Critical Considerations*. Lexington, Kentucky: Univ. of Kentucky Press, 1963.

Fagen, Patricia W. *Exiles and Citizens: Spanish Republicans in Mexico*. Austin, Texas: Univ. of Texas Press, 1973.

Fergusson, Francis. "D. H. Lawrence's Sensibility." *Forms of Modern Fiction: Essays Collected in Honor of Joseph Warren Beach*. Ed. William Van O'Connor. 1948; rev. Bloomington, Indiana: Indiana Univ. Press, 1959, pp. 72-79.

Firchow, Peter. *Aldous Huxley: Satirist and Novelist*. Minneapolis, Minnesota: Univ. of Minnesota Press, 1972.

Freeman, Mary. *D. H. Lawrence: A Basic Study of His Ideas*. Gainesville, Florida: Univ. of Florida Press, 1955.

Fuentes, Carlos. "Mexico's New Wave." *Venture*, III (December-January 1967), 125-131.

Gabrial, Jan. "Not With a Bang." *Story*, XXIX (September-October 1946), 55-61.

Garcia, Reloy. "The Quest for Paradise in the Novels of D. H. Lawrence." *D. H. Lawrence Review*, III (1970), 93-112.

Gibson, Charles. *Tlaxcala in the Sixteenth Century*. 1952; rpt. Stanford, California: Stanford Univ. Press, 1967.

Glicksberg, Charles I. *Modern Literary Perspectivism*. Dallas, Texas: Southern Methodist Univ. Press, 1970.

Goodheart, Eugene. *The Utopian Vision of D. H. Lawrence*. Chicago: Univ. of Chicago Press, 1963.

Gordon, David J. *D. H. Lawrence as a Literary Critic*. New Haven, Connecticut: Yale Univ. Press, 1966.

Gregor, Ian. "The Greene Baize Door." *Blackfriars*, XXXVI (September 1955), 327-333.

Grob, Alan. "'The Power and the Glory': Graham Greene's Argument from Design." *Criticism*, II (Winter 1969), 1-30.

Gunn, Drewey Wayne. *American and British Writers in Mexico, 1556-1973*. Austin, Texas: Univ. of Texas Press, 1974.

Hall, James. *The Tragic Comedians: Seven Modern British Novelists.* Bloomington, Indiana: Indiana Univ. Press, 1963.

Harmer, Ruth Mulvey. "Greene World of Mexico: The Birth of a Novelist." *Renascence,* XV (Summer 1963), 171-182, 194.

Hays, H. R. "The Importance of B. Traven." *Chimera,* IV (Summer 1946), 44-54.

Heilman, Robert H. "The Possessed Artist and the Ailing Soul." *Canadian Literature,* VIII (Spring 1961), 7-16.

Henderson, Alexander. *Aldous Huxley.* 1936; rpt. New York: Russell and Russell, 1964.

Hendrick, George. *Katherine Anne Porter.* New York: Twayne, 1965.

Hoffman, Frederick J. "Aldous Huxley and the Novel of Ideas." *Forms of Modern Fiction: Essays Collected in Honor of Joseph Warren Beach.* Ed. William Van O'Connor. 1948; rev. Bloomington, Indiana: Indiana Univ. Press, 1959, pp. 189-200.

Hoggart, Richard. "The Force of Characature: Aspects of the Art of Graham Greene, With Particular Reference to *The Power and the Glory.*" *Essays in Criticism,* III (October 1953), 447-462.

Holmes, Charles. *Aldous Huxley and the Way to Reality.* Bloomington, Indiana: Indiana Univ. Press, 1970.

Hoskins, Katherine Bail. *Today the Struggle: Literature and Politics in England During the Spanish Civil War.* Austin, Texas: Univ. of Texas Press, 1969.

Hough, Graham. *The Dark Sun: A Study of D. H. Lawrence.* London: Duckworth, 1956.

Huxley, Julian, ed. *Aldous Huxley: A Memorial Volume.* London: Chatto and Windus, 1965.

Hynes, Samuel, ed. *Graham Greene: A Collection of Critical Essays.* Twentieth-Century Views. Englewood Cliffs, New Jersey: Prentice-Hall, 1973.

Kermode, Frank. *D. H. Lawrence.* Modern Masters. New York: Viking, 1973.

Knapp, Bettina L. *Antonin Artaud: Man of Vision.* New York: David Lewis, 1969.

Knickerbocker, Conrad. "The Voyages of Malcolm Lowry." *Prairie Schooner,* XXXVII (Winter 1963/64), 301-314.

Knipp, Thomas R. "Gide and Greene: Africa and the Literary Imagination." *Serif,* VI (June 1969), 3-14.

Kunkel, Francis L. *The Labyrinthine Ways of Graham Greene.* New York: Sheed and Ward, 1959.

Langford, Walter M. *The Mexican Novel Comes of Age.* Notre Dame, Indiana: Univ. of Notre Dame Press, 1971.

Lawrence, Frieda. *"Not I But the Wind..."* New York: Viking, 1934.

Leal, Antonio Castro. "El México de David Herbert Lawrence." *Cuadernos Americanos,* I (1942), 181-196.

Leech, Clifford. "The Shaping of Time: *Nostromo* and *Under the Volcano.*" *Imagined Worlds: Essays on Some English Novels and Novelists in Honour of John Butt.* Ed. Maynard Mack and Ian Gregor: London: Methuen, 1968, pp. 323-341.

Lewis, R. W. B. *The Picaresque Saint: Representative Figures in Contemporary Fiction.* New York: Lippincott, 1959.

———, and Peter J. Conn, eds. *The Power and the Glory: Text and Criticism.* New York: Viking, 1970.

Lisca, Peter. "John Steinbeck: A Literary Biography." *Steinbeck and His Critics: A Record of Twenty-Five Years.* Ed. E. W. Tedlock, Jr., and C. V. Wicker. Albuquerque, New Mexico: Univ. of New Mexico Press, 1957, pp. 3-22.

Lodge, David. *Graham Greene.* Columbia Essays on Modern Writers. New York: Columbia Univ. Press, 1966.

Lopez, Hank (interview with Katherine Anne Porter). "A Country and Some People I Love." *Harper's,* September 1965, pp. 58-68.

Luhan, Mabel Dodge. *Lorenzo in Taos.* London: Secker, 1933.

McDonald, James L. "Graham Greene: A Reconsideration." *Arizona Quarterly,* XXVII (Winter 1971), 197-210.

Markson, David. "Myth in *Under the Volcano.*" *Prairie Schooner,* XXXVII (Winter 1963/64), 339-346.

Martin, Dexter. "D. H. Lawrence and Pueblo Religion: An Inquiry into Accuracy." *Arizona Quarterly,* IX (1953), 219-234.

Meckier, Jerome. *Aldous Huxley: Satire and Structure.* New York: Barnes and Noble, 1971.

Merivale, Patricia. "D. H. Lawrence and the Modern Pan Myth." *Texas Studies in Literature and Language,* VI (Autumn 1964), 299-305.

Merrild, Knud. *With D. H. Lawrence in New Mexico: A Memoir of D. H. Lawrence.* 1939; rpt. New York: Barnes and Noble, 1965.

Mesnét, Marie-Beatrice. *Graham Greene and the Heart of the Matter.* London: Cresset Press, 1954.

Meyers, Jeffrey. "*The Plumed Serpent* and the Mexican Revolution." *Journal of Modern Literature,* IV (September 1974), 55-72.

Michener, Richard L. "Apocalyptic Mexico: *The Plumed Serpent* and *The Power and the Glory.*" *University Review,* XXXIV (June 1968), 313-316.

Moore, Harry T., ed. *A. D. H. Lawrence Miscellany.* Carbondale, Illinois: Southern Illinois Univ. Press, 1959.

———. *Poste Restante: A Lawrence Travel Calendar.* Berkeley and Los Angeles: Univ. of California Press, 1956.

———. *The Priest of Love: A Life of D. H. Lawrence.* New York: Farrar, Straus and Giroux, 1974.

Moynahan, Julian. *The Deed of Life: The Novels and Tales of D. H. Lawrence.* Princeton, New Jersey: Princeton Univ. Press, 1963.

Nance, William L. "Katherine Anne Porter and Mexico." *Southwest Review,* LV (1970), 143-153.

Nehls, Edward, ed. *D. H. Lawrence: A Composite Biography.* Vol. II. Madison, Wisconsin: Univ. of Wisconsin Press, 1958.

O'Faolain, Sean. *The Vanishing Hero: Studies in Novelists of the Twenties.* London: Eyre and Spottiswoode, 1956.

Olafson, Robert B. "B. Traven's *Norteamericanos* in Mexico." *Markham Review,* IV (October 1973), 1-5.

Parkes, Henry Bamford. *A History of Mexico.* 1938; rev. Boston: Houghton Mifflin, 1969.

Partridge, Colin. "'My Familiar Country': An Image of Mexico in the Work of Katherine Anne Porter." *Studies in Short Fiction*, VII (Fall 1970), 597-614.

Patten, Karl. "The Structure of *The Power and the Glory*." *Modern Fiction Studies*, III (Autumn 1957), 225-234.

Paz, Octavio. *The Labyrinth of Solitude: Life and Thought in Mexico*. Trans. Lysander Kemp. New York: Grove Press, 1961.

Pearson, Sheryl Sherman. "The Anglo-American Novel of the Mexican Revolution, 1910-1940: D. H. Lawrence, B. Traven, Graham Greene." Dissertation. Univ. of Michigan, 1976.

Porter, Katherine Anne. *The Collected Essays and Occasional Writings of Katherine Anne Porter*. New York: Delacorte, 1970.

――――. *Flowering Judas and Other Stories*. 2nd ed. New York: Harcourt, Brace, 1935.

――――. "Old Gods and New Messiahs." *New York Herald Tribune Books*, September 29, 1929, p. 2.

――――. *Outline of Mexican Popular Arts and Crafts*. Los Angeles: Young and McAllister, 1922.

――――. "Rivera's Personal Revolution in Mexico." *New York Herald Tribune Books*. March 21, 1937, p. 7.

――――. *Ship of Fools*. Boston and Toronto: Little, Brown, 1962.

Powell, Lawrence Clark. "Southwest Classics Reread: *The Plumed Serpent*, by D. H. Lawrence." *Westways*, LXIII (November 1971), 18-20, 46-49.

Prescott, William H. *History of the Conquest of Mexico*. 2 vols. 1843; rpt. New York: Everyman's Library, 1972.

Quennell, Peter. "D. H. Lawrence and Aldous Huxley." *The English Novelists*. Ed. D. Verschoyle. London, 1936.

Quirk, Robert E. *Mexico*. The Modern Nations in Historical Perspective Series. Englewood Cliffs, New Jersey: Prentice-Hall, 1971.

Ramos, Samuel. *Profile of Man and Culture in Mexico*. Trans. Peter G. Earle. Austin, Texas: Univ. of Texas Press, 1962.

Regler, Gustav. *A Land Bewitched: Mexico in the Shadow of the Centuries*. Trans. Constantine Fitzgibbon. London: Putnam, 1955.

――――. *The Owl of Minerva: The Autobiography of Gustav Regler*. Trans. Norman Denny. New York: Farrar, Straus and Cudahy, 1959.

Rivera, Diego. "From a Painter's Notebook" (trans. Katherine Anne Porter). *Arts*, VII (January 1925), 21-23.

――――. "The Guild Spirit in Mexican Art" (trans. Katherine Anne Porter). *Survey*, LII (April-September 1924), 174-178.

Roberts, John H. "Huxley and Lawrence." *Virginia Quarterly Review*, XIII (1937), 546-557.

Robinson, Cecil. *With the Ears of Strangers: The Mexican in American Literature*. Tucson, Arizona: Univ. of Arizona Press, 1963.

Rodriguez, Antonio. *A History of Mexican Mural Painting*. Trans. Marina Corby. New York: Putnam's, 1969.

Ruoff, James and Del Smith. "Katherine Anne Porter on *Ship of Fools*" (interview). *College English*, XXIV (February 1963), 396-397.

Sagar, Keith. *The Art of D. H. Lawrence*. Cambridge, England: Cambridge Univ. Press, 1966.

Savage, Derek S. "Aldous Huxley and the Dissociation of Personality." *The Withered Branch: Six Studies in the Modern Novel*. London: Eyre and Spottiswoode, 1950, pp. 129-155.

Sender, Ramón J. *Dark Wedding*. Trans. Eleanor Clark. Garden City, New York: Doubleday, Doran, 1943.

———. *Hernán Cortez*. Mexico City: Ediciones Quetzal, 1941.

———. *Mexicayotl*. Mexico City: Ediciones Quetzal, 1940.

———. *Tales of Cibola*. Trans. Florence Sender, Elinor Randall, Morse Manley. New York: Las Americas, 1964.

Seton, Marie. *Sergei M. Eisenstein*. New York: A. A. Wyn, 1952.

Simpson, Leslie Byrd. *Many Mexicos*. 1941; 3rd ed., rev. Berkeley and Los Angeles: Univ. of California Press, 1952.

Spilka, Mark, ed. *D. H. Lawrence: A Collection of Critical Essays*. Twentieth-Century Views Series. Englewood Cliffs, New Jersey: Prentice-Hall, 1963.

Steinbeck, John. *The Forgotten Village*. New York: Viking, 1941.

———. *The Log from The Sea of Cortez*. New York: Viking, 1951.

———. "The Miracle of Tepayac." *Collier's*, December 25, 1948, pp. 22-23.

———. *The Pearl*. New York: Viking, 1947.

———. *Viva Zapata! The Original Screenplay by John Steinbeck*. Ed. Robert E. Morsberger. New York: Viking, 1975.

Stratford, Philip. *Faith and Fiction: Creative Process in Greene and Mauriac*. Notre Dame, Indiana: Univ. of Notre Dame Press, 1964.

Swan, Michael. "D. H. Lawrence: Italy and Mexico." *A Small Part of Time: Essays on Literature, Art and Travel*. Chester Springs, Pennsylvania: Dufour, 1961.

Tannenbaum, Frank. *Mexico: The Struggle for Peace and Bread*. New York: Knopf, 1950.

Tedlock, E. W., Jr. *D. H. Lawrence, Artist and Rebel: A Study of Lawrence's Fiction*. Albuquerque, New Mexico: Univ. of New Mexico Press, 1963.

Tindall, William York. *D. H. Lawrence and Susan His Cow*. New York: Columbia Univ. Press, 1939.

———. *Forces in Modern British Fiction, 1885-1956*. New York: Vintage Books, 1956.

Traven, B. *The Bridge in the Jungle*. New York: Hill and Wang, 1967.

———. *The Carreta*. New York: Hill and Wang, 1970.

———. *The Cotton-Pickers*. New York: Hill and Wang, 1969.

———. *The General from the Jungle*. Trans. Desmond I. Vesey. New York: Hill and Wang, 1974.

———. *Government*. New York: Hill and Wang, 1971.

———. *The Kidnapped Saint & Other Stories*. Ed. Rosa Elena Luhan, Mina C. Klein, H. Arthur Klein. New York: Lawrence Hill, 1975.

———. *March to the Monteria*. New York: Hill and Wang, 1971.

———. *The Night Visitor and Other Stories*. New York: Hill and Wang, 1966.

———. *The Rebellion of the Hanged*. Trans. Esperanza López Mateos and Josef Wieder. New York: Knopf, 1952.

————. *The Treasure of the Sierra Madre.* New York: Hill and Wang, 1967.

————. *The White Rose.* London: Robert Hale, 1965.

Vickery, John B. " 'The Plumed Serpent' and the Eternal Paradox." *Criticism,* V (Spring 1963), 119-134.

Vitoux, Pierre. "Aldous Huxley and D. H. Lawrence: An Attempt at Intellectual Sympathy." *Modern Language Review,* LXIX (July 1974), 501-522.

Vivas, Eliseo. *D. H. Lawrence: The Failure and the Triumph of Art.* Bloomington, Indiana: Indiana Univ. Press, 1960.

Waters, Frank. "Quetzalcoatl Versus D. H. Lawrence's *Plumed Serpent.*" *Western American Literature,* III (Summer 1968), 103-113.

Weintraub, Stanley. *The Last Great Cause: The Intellectuals and the Spanish Civil War.* New York: Weybright and Talley, 1968.

Whitaker, Thomas R. "Lawrence's Western Path: 'Mornings in Mexico.'" *Criticism,* III (1961), 219-236.

Wilshire, A. D. "Conflict and Conciliation in Graham Greene." *Essays and Studies 1966.* The English Association. New York: Humanities Press, 1966, pp. 122-137.

Woodcock, George. *Dawn and the Darkest Hour: A Study of Aldous Huxley.* New York: Viking, 1972.

————, ed. *Malcolm Lowry: The Man and His Work.* Vancouver, British Columbia: Univ. of British Columbia Press, 1971.

————. "Malcolm Lowry's 'Under the Volcano.'" *Modern Fiction Studies,* IV (1958-59), 151-156.

————. "Mexico and the English Novelist." *Western Review,* XXI (Autumn 1956), 21-32.

————. "On the Day of the Dead." *Northern Review,* VI (1953-54), 15-21.

————. "Under Seymour Mountain." *Canadian Literature,* VII (Spring 1961), 3-6.

Woolmer, J. Howard, ed. *A Malcolm Lowry Catalogue.* New York: Woolmer, 1968.

Wright, Terence. " 'Under the Volcano': The Static Art of Malcolm Lowry." *Ariel,* I (October 1970), 67-76.

Zabel, Morton Dauwen. "The Best and the Worst." *Craft and Character.* New York: Viking, 1957; rpt. *Graham Greene: A Collection of Critical Essays* (ed. Samuel Hynes), Englewood Cliffs, New Jersey: Prentice-Hall, 1973, pp. 30-48.

————. "Graham Greene." *Forms of Modern Fiction: Essays Collected in Honor of Joseph Warren Beach.* 1948; rev. Bloomington, Indiana: Indiana Univ. Press, 1959, pp. 273-279.

Zytaruk, George J., ed. *The Quest for Rananim: D. H. Lawrence's Letters to S. S. Koteliansky, 1914 to 1930.* Montreal: McGill-Queen's Univ. Press, 1970.

# Index